DANGEROUS DECEITS

DANGEROUS DECEITS

FRANK WELSH

HarperCollins*Publishers*

HarperCollins*Publishers*
77–85 Fulham Palace Road,
Hammersmith, London w6 8jb

Published by HarperCollins*Publishers* 1999
Copyright © Frank Welsh 1999

9 8 7 6 5 4 3 2 1

The author asserts the moral right to be
identified as the author of this work

A catalogue record for this book is
available from the British Library

ISBN 0 00 257029 7 (hardback)
ISBN 0 00 257144 7 (trade paperback)

Set in PostScript Linotype Minion with Photina display
by Rowland Phototypesetting Ltd, Bury St Edmunds

Printed and bound in Great Britain by
Clays Ltd, St Ives plc

CONTENTS

INTRODUCTION   xi

Prologue

Scopetino Farm, San Donato, 11 October 1994   1
The prison gates close   5

1 *The Rise of the Afrikaner Volk*

Blood brothers   9
Jingling coin, not pious sentiment   21
Apartheid; the skunk among nations   26
Apartheid's assassins   35

2 *Caveat Investor*

A palpable exaltation   42
Formation of an entrepreneur   47
Partners   53
Enter Askin   65

3 *The Facts Emerge*

Lies, damn lies, and bankers' reports   75
Absa emerges   83
Absa flexes its corporate muscles   92
The Hoberman Commission   103

4 *Florence, October 1994*

Susie's fightback   113
Italian justice   130
Plundering the public purse   132

5 *Wondrous Deceitful*

Release?   140
Reflections   157

6 *Askin and Some Allies*

Home again   163
The alliance forms   180

7 *Safety at Sea*

A brotherly helping hand   189
The Governor as Father Christmas   204

8 *Some Truths Emerge*

Unprofessional and reckless management   217
Dr Stals' lecture   229
Why Tollgate was killed off   238

9 *Sinners and Bankers*

Hoberman delenda est   245
Askin sues   254

10 *Absa in the Ascendant?*

Absa go to market   261
Absa in court   272

11 *Nemesis Looms*

A complex charade   278
The Law's delays   284
Not just one, but several bombs are ticking   290

12 *The End Approaches*

Judge Heath takes up the case   303
Slavering over free cash   309

From the heart of the Beast   318
'My mind is made up. Don't confuse me
   with the facts'   320
One door closes   327

13 *Winners and Losers*

Endgame   340

CHRONOLOGY   347
APPENDICES   350
INDEX   367

The sacrifices of Masses, in the which it was commonly said, that the Priest did offer Christ for the quick and the dead, to have remission of pain or guilt, were blasphemous fables, and dangerous deceits.

Articles of Religion, 1562

INTRODUCTION

Five years after South Africa's first freely elected government took office in May 1994, much of the apartheid state's apparatus has been dismantled, the Truth and Reconciliation Commission has exposed some of the heinous crimes committed in apartheid's name (and some, albeit a smaller number, by apartheid's opponents), and investigating commissions have been appointed to expose corruption. A free press reports uncomfortable facts, and parliamentary opposition flourishes. Among men and women of goodwill the possibility of national unity seems, perhaps, achievable.

But threats continue to abound, and one of these is the continued existence of unreformed institutions surviving amid apartheid's disintegration. Afrikaner 'Christian Nationalist' governments enjoyed 46 years of uninterrupted power between 1948 and 1994, during which period the notorious policy of white supremacy and black humiliation was designed, implemented, and seen to fail. Even though the structures of apartheid have now been dismantled, nearly half a century of power was used to ensure that key positions were occupied by sympathisers. The South African judiciary, armed services, public broadcasting, foreign and civil services, and regulatory bodies were systematically filled with Afrikaners, with only a few token English-speakers. Such a concentration of power in the hands of a small minority (Afrikaners constitute perhaps one tenth of the population) is not to be quickly eradicated.

Uniting and reinforcing Afrikaner power, ever since its foundation in the 1920s, has been the Broederbond. This highly secret society – 'the Brotherhood' in English – numbered among its members all South Africa's prime ministers and presidents, from Dr Malan in 1948 to President de Klerk, most cabinet ministers and a high proportion of judges and senior civil servants. Few organs of state were not controlled by Brothers – and some so remain.

Among these redoubts is the South African Reserve Bank. Although by far the larger part of the country's business community is English-speaking, and English is the common language of commerce, the Reserve Bank remains a stronghold of Afrikaner hegemony. In the years when South Africa was the 'skunk among nations', pressured by international sanctions, the Reserve Bank constituted a key agent in bolstering the South African financial system. Until 1996 all its executives and directors were Afrikaner, appointed by apartheid governments, and its Governor an eminent Brother.

In recent years the Broederbond has moved with the times, and it has indeed been instrumental in leading the Afrikaner community to adjust to the very different circumstances of majority rule; but the Afrikaner banking Brothers have clung doggedly to their positions of very considerable power.

The South African Reserve Bank remains an internationally recognised central bank, taking its place among others in the weighty conferences of world finance, but the legacy of apartheid flourishes in less reputable circles. During President Botha's period of rule, state-sponsored murder and intimidation squads led by members of the police and defence forces committed thousands of acts of terrorism and murder. Under the guise of detective and security firms, some of the most notorious of these still exist, plying for trade, and finding it provided by Afrikaner bankers.

It was the misfortune of Julian Askin to become their victim.

As an optimistic investor at the hopeful time of Nelson Mandela's release in 1990, Askin was systematically deceived by officials at the Broederbond's Trust Bank into acquiring one of the country's best-known public companies, with over 20,000 employees. Within two years the bank had forced the company into liquidation.

There followed a systematic campaign of harrassment, much virulent press comment and the sequestration of Askin's assets, culminating in his violent arrest in 1994 by the Italian authorities and his subsequent imprisonment. Only after six months' legal action was this acknowledged by the Italian authorities to have been illegal, carried out at the prompting of the Afrikaner establishment and with the connivance of local officials in Florence.

Askin's release was effected largely by the courage of his wife, Susie, assisted by retired members of the British Secret Service, MI6. With their help, the Askins, once safely back in England, mounted an investigation of the events that had led up to Julian's imprisonment. In the course of this they uncovered the role of the South African Reserve Bank in secretly and illegally enabling the Trust Bank and its successor, the Amalgamated Banks of South Africa (Absa), to survive years of politically-motivated lending.

Since then Askin has attempted to clear his name by bringing Absa and its officials before an English court, an attempt which up to now has been successfully resisted by the bank. This resistance has not been confined to legal procedures. Serious threats against both Askins have been made by the 'guys at the Afrikaner bank'. The most prominent of these is a self-confessed murderer from the most notorious of the apartheid regime's terror squads.

For even longer – it is now over five years since a South African judge formulated the first accusations against him – the South African authorities have made no legal attempts to bring Askin to trial, although simple methods of doing so, including extradition from the UK, have been available. Equivocation and prevarication have been their only arguments.

No sustained attempt has therefore been made to put all the allegations made against Askin to the test, although the more prominent ones have been exposed. Against the solid facts of official deceit and Askin's persistence in trying to bring his case before a court, any other criticisms must remain of minor significance: only a trial will bring a definitive explanation – and Askin has spent millions of pounds in trying to bring one about.

It will be clear that while much of the evidence contained in this book comes from named witnesses or has already been published, some of the more sensitive items have been procured by the London-based intelligence-gathering firm CIEX, and with the co-operation of the international security community. Of necessity, some of these sources are disguised. When information has been volunteered, at considerable personal risk, from South African citizens, anonymity has been guaranteed.

This is, as yet, not a story with a tidy ending. The judicial commission established by President Mandela to enquire into the illegal activities of the Afrikaner bankers has not yet completed its report.

*   *   *

This book could not have been written without the unstinting co-operation of Julian Askin in making available a daunting collection of documents – and many of the livelier parts are taken directly from the recollections of Julian and Susie Askin. Many of the informants, in particular those in South Africa and Italy, must remain anonymous. To them I offer a joint tribute for their patience, and often for their courage. Many journalists have their work recorded in this book, some with admiration, and others with the opposite. I gratefully acknowledge the help of Jonathan Ball, who read a draft with great care, of Lisa Darnell, Michael Holmes, David Sherwin, Anthony Amhurst, Stephen Morris, Robert Lacey, Martin Welz, Johan Claasen and Storm Riley.

The books consulted include *The Infernal Tower*, by Bob Aldworth, Jeremy Gordin and Benjamin Trisk (Johannesburg, 1996), which admir-ably details some of Absa's misdemeanours, Dan O'Meara's invaluable *Volkscapitalisme* (Cambridge, 1983) and Tim Parks's *Italian Neighbours* (London, 1995). For the Broederbond see *The Broederbond*, I.Wilkins and H. Strydom (Johannesburg, 1978).

Frank Welsh
March 1999

Prologue

Scopetino Farm, San Donato, Italy:
Tuesday 11 October 1994, 7a.m.

The coarse name (scopetino may be translated as 'fucklette') of this Tuscan cottage belies its charm. A stone farmhouse, converted for renting out as a one-bedroomed principal apartment, with a couple of guest rooms, has a wide view over the rolling countryside, although it is only ten miles from Florence. A swimming pool, nearly as big as the house, is well tucked away, backed by vineyards and olive groves. At one end of the house is a little wine-processing unit with modern stainless steel vats, where Franco, who looks after the land, makes some very respectable wine from the grapes. His wife, Franca, sees to the laundry and cleaning. For some twelve months the cottage has been rented by an English couple, Julian and Susie Askin. Julian is 46, a rubicund, curly haired, amiable man, becoming a little portly as middle age looms. Susie is strikingly pretty, slight, and invariably elegant. Both are fully of energy and enterprise, bubbling with good humour. It would be easy to categorise them as typically upper-middle class English – moving between Annabel's and Ascot, shooting and fishing in season, slightly dotty about dogs – and to dismiss them as amusing lightweights. To do so, as did many who should have known better, could prove an expensive mistake. The Askins can display persistence, great initiative and tenacious courage, qualities which they were to find essential to their survival.

Julian was completing a three-year tax exile, prudently undertaken to shelter the very considerable profits of a previous City of London coup. Another quirk of English law had kept them abroad in that their two miniature long-haired dachshunds would have to face six months'

1

detention in quarantine. The dogs, Poppy and Daisy, ranked among the other great loves of Julian's life; he has no children of his own, but is devoted to Susie's daughter Charlotte, now studying at Newcastle University and who lost her own father at the age of six.

The daily routine at Scopetino has been for Julian and Susie to drive into Florence, park on the Lungarno, unpack two folding Italajet motorcycles, each sling a bag containing a dog round their necks and ride off to their destinations, dogs' ears streaming in the breeze. Susie has been learning Italian at the Dante Alighieri school, while Julian works in the British Institute library: each, of course, with a dog companion. They met for lunch, usually at Harry's Bar, where the dogs had their own corner, before driving back to the farm. This pleasant existence was interrupted by Daisy's untimely death on 21 March. She is buried in the straggly oakwoods at Scopetino, wrapped in one of Julian's sweaters, accompanied by her favourite toy, and commemorated by an epitaph written by Julian:

> 28.12.1987–21. 03. 1994
> A long-haired dachshund,
> pursuer of game
> She lies here with Renard
> A friend of that name
> A lover of oakwoods
> the marsh and the moor
> her short life ended here on a foreign shore.

Julian was working on a novel which was to be based upon his experiences in South Africa between 1990 and 1993. These had ended badly, and to Julian's mind entirely unjustly, with a lawsuit being brought against him in South Africa. He believed that he had been deliberately lured into investing many millions in South Africa by being given deliberately false information from a bank which now forms part of the largest bank in South Africa. Moreover, he was beginning to suspect that there was something suspicious about the liquidation of this investment, forced upon him by the same bank, which has led to the claim being made against him. Since the claim was backed by a sequestration order, which froze all his – very considerable – assets, Askin has very reluctantly just agreed to settle this. Although the payment demanded is only a fraction of the original sum, it is not the money involved as much as the sense of injustice that troubles Askin, aggravated by some snide and tendentious press comment. He is by any standards a rich man, a millionaire several times over, while Susie has her own fortune. Their London home in Chester Square, an expensive address, looks over to Lady Thatcher's splendid residence; their new Cape Town house, on Rhodes Drive, has been a famous centre of Cape society. Both are impressive residences, although the Askin's personal tastes – witness the folding motorcycles and their modest Italian cottage – are unpretentious. But Julian was indignant at his treatment by the South Africans, and had agreed to meet their much reduced demands in order to avoid the nuisance of protracted litigation and to unlock his frozen funds. The projected novel was however, soothing his feelings, and both he and Susie were looking forward to final visits from some of their English friends before handing the keys of Scopetino back to the owners and returning to London. The Askin's horizons seemed clear, and the forecast for settled weather.

Until 11 October 1994. Just before 7a.m., Poppy began barking furiously, refusing to be silenced by sleepy expostulations or kicks under the bedclothes from the Askins who were recovering from flu and had taken sedatives the night before. The only likely intruders were wild boar, old enemies of Franco's who not infrequently grubbed under the farm fence to raid the vegetable garden, but to give Poppy the chance of chasing whoever it might be, Julian fumbled his way to the front door. Then the nightmare began. Two men, unshaven, in leather jackets and jeans, smashed the door back, knocking Julian against the wall, and shoving a machine pistol into his neck. 'Are you Julian Askin? Who else is in the house?' Askin yelled back, 'Who the hell are you? What do you want?' and shouted a warning to Susie, telling her to put on a dressing gown. Although there was a telephone in the bedroom there was no time to call for help – the open bedroom door was only three steps from the front door, and one man was immediately inside, while the other kept Julian's head forced back against the wall, the pistol pressing into his neck. It has to be understood that the cottage is small. The hall leads directly into the only other rooms – the living room, bedroom and bathroom. Once you are through the front door the whole apartment lies open.

Ignoring Susie, the man in the bedroom rifled Julian's open briefcase, removing his passport, before ripping open Susie's handbag, throwing its contents one by one across the room. But he replaced her passport. Until then – and only minutes had passed the intrusion bore all the signs of an abduction. Poppy's continuous barking was already worrying Julian – would she get herself shot? Repeated questions as to what the men wanted went unanswered. Julian was convinced that the raiders were looking for guns or drugs, especially when they threw out the contents of a large bowl of lavender. Susie later said, 'They had no arrest warrant, no identification . . . and because we thought we were going to be kidnapped we didn't ask . . . didn't say, "we're British citizens, you can't take us like this." All you see is the guns – they were waving all over the place. We were kind of doing what we were told.' Abductions are frequent enough in Italy, usually of members of rich families for ransom, but it is not often that a foreigner is targeted. The fact that the attacker put back Susie's passport, although leaving everything else scattered, gave her a clue. 'Julian, it isn't what you think it is! I think your friends down South have been busy,' she called.

By that time a third man had shown up, more presentable, and less aggressive than the first two, brandishing no weapon, and speaking French, which Julian understood. 'Monsieur Askin, you must come with us to Florence.'

Prosperous middle-class English people live protected lives. The police, who can be unpleasant enough to those they disapprove of, still retain some deference towards the respectable citizen; and the respectable citizen still looks with confidence to the police for protection. Dirty armed men, bursting into a private house, without a warrant, physically assaulting the occupants, could only be criminals. This delusion, that the forces of law and the judicial system in Italy bore any resemblance to those of Britain, was to be painfully shattered.

Julian Askin reacted with traditional sang-froid: he was going nowhere until he had, unlike his captors, washed and shaved. This he proceeded to do, accompanied by one particularly thuggish man who held a gun to Askin's head the whole time. By this time he had accepted that the intrusion had something to do with the police, although no identification was produced in spite of repeated demands. After this concession he was grabbed and bundled into a waiting car. Susie was told they were going to the Florence Questura, the police headquarters, and that she might follow, if she could; directions were given by the amiable third man. In the meantime she was left, stunned, standing at the front door as her husband, a gun pushed into his ribs, was bundled into an unmarked car. It was difficult, almost impossible, to believe that this was in any way a proper official action, but before leaving, Julian, terrified of nothing more serious than being kept waiting in a queue while things were explained, armed himself with a book, pencil and notepad.

The police – for that is what in fact, however unlikely it seemed, the unsavoury men were – drove into Florence at high speed, one leaning out of the car window waving a paddle marked *Servizio di Stata*, to force reluctant traffic out of their way, hammering on the panels of cars which did not immediately move over.

The Florence Questura is a grubby, decaying building dating from the Fascist period. Once inside the urgency evaporated as the police relaxed over a coffee, while writing a fax to be sent to Pretoria, South Africa, announcing the successful arrest of the much-wanted master criminal, Julian Michael Cuming Askin, the South African 'Goldfinger'. This was the first indication that Askin received – still no warrant was produced – of an ostensible reason for his arrest. But it was at least clear that some part of the South African government system – 'those friends down South' – badly wanted to lay its hands on Askin. The facts that he had already agreed a settlement of the claims that had been made against him, that no other charges had been preferred, and that even if they had, no extradition treaty existed between South Africa and Italy were no deterrent to the vendetta that had now begun.

The prison gates close

Susie Askin arrived at the Questura at about 10.30 a.m. (accompanied, naturally, by dog Poppy). At that stage she was not unduly perturbed, believing that whatever misunderstanding had led to Julian's removal could be quickly sorted out; her main problem was finding a legal place to park. When she entered the Questura she found 'a totally smoke-filled room, with three people, fags hanging out of their mouths, tapping away at typewriters. As I walked in Julian said "I am afraid this is looking rather bad, very serious. I think they're going to take me to prison".' Looking back, the Askins were convinced that the police clerical activity was concerned with putting some paperwork in place to conceal the fact that the arrest had not been correctly authorised. Julian made repeated demands to see some sort of warrant, or any official paper, but was answered only with abuse. Susie's lessons at the Dante Aleghieri institute proved useful as she was required to tell Julian that he was being arrested 'because of the South Africans' and was to be immediately finger-printed, photographed and handcuffed before being taken to prison. An application for his extradition had been made and the South Africans wanted him there before Christmas.

It soon emerged that the communications between Florence and Pretoria were well maintained. Although the report of his arrest was ostensibly from one police force to another, full details were immediately transmitted both to the Italian and South African press, appearing in the same day's evening editions of the South African papers and as a leading item in the Italian local television news.

After being allowed a brief meeting at which it was agreed that an immediate approach to the British Consul in Florence must be made, the dangerous criminal was driven once more with maximum drama (at breakneck speed, sirens wailing, banging on the doors of any car that did not immediately get out of the way) to the Solliciano gaol. On the outskirts of town, adjoining the Pisa – Florence autostrada, this huge modern complex is surrounded by a high concrete wall, patrolled by guards armed with machine pistols. Askin was put in a filthy cell (he found the place reminiscent of Tom Wolfe's *Bonfire of the Vanities*) for some time before being taken out for questioning.

At this time he was still a complete innocent, having never seen anything of the law in action; even after having spent a year in Italy he was still unaware of how that country functions. The previous weekend he and Susie had been staying at the Villa d'Este on Lake Como, playing with speedboats, lunching on the lake and idling by the swimming pool – a far cry from Solliciano prison. When being asked what drugs he was taking his reply was, 'one Pharmaton and a thousand milligrams of vitamin C a day.' It took two episodes of interrogation by bellowing guards and two more periods of several hours' incarceration before the penny dropped: he was a rare bird in the Italian penal system, a convict without a drug habit.

After this inauspicious start, Askin was made to hand over his watch, cufflinks, cash, passport and signet ring. The guard not being convinced that Askin's collar stiffeners were as described, a prison officer who spoke some English was summoned to discuss these dangerous looking weapons. Askin was then made to strip, stand on a black plastic bin liner, turn his back to the guard and squat. While this was going on the guard pulled on a pair of plastic gloves. Askin anticipated a pair of plastic fingers up his fundamental orifice, as all movies of the genre usually suggest. Fortunately, the Buddha position enticed only a swift squint from the guard, no drugs having scattered on to the floor. He was then escorted through a few locked doors, picking up two sheets, a pillowcase, a thick blanket, a plate, a bowl, a beaker, a plastic knife and a metal fork and spoon. A few minutes later he was placed in a small cell on his own and the keys turned behind him. He was told he would be moved into the main prison within a few days.

He stayed in his filthy cell for three days, relieved at least to be alone. The unrelenting aggression of the guards and their complete lack of interest in his predicament presaged a little of what was to come. The food was inedible: a friendly trusty – a great contrast to the violent and abusive warders – warned him, correctly enough, that the water in the cell was undrinkable, and managed to obtain a few oranges for him. On these Askin subsisted for those first traumatic days. In the cell the bunk mattress was a thin strip of yellow foam, heavily gouged, full of cigarette burns and covered in matted black human hair. There was a single tap, a filthy unwashed lavatory with no seat, no towels or soap. The stench was of urine and cigarette smoke, stale bread and dried sweat. The noise at night was indescribable: a cacophony of human wretchedness. It would be a week before he had his first glass of water.

Askin had, fortunately, ignored the police and brought a book with him, the recently published *Wine Dark Sea* by Patrick O'Brian. It was an impeccable choice, since O'Brian's characteristic prose stands – and received – a number of successive readings. Building personal fortifications against as yet dimly perceived threats, he resolved to keep a diary and write to his wife each day: Susie was to be his lifeline to the outside world. Askin realised that if the South Africans were prepared to go to these lengths he must have ruffled some very powerful feathers in that country. If the South African police were successful in extraditing Askin it was certain that conditions would be no better, but given the South African system's notorious carelessness in allowing so many of their captives to jump from high windows and fall down staircases, highly likely that his period of incarceration would not be for long. But at this stage he relied upon being in Italy, a member of the European Union, a civilised democracy where manifest injustices would surely not be allowed.

Askin knew himself to be completely guiltless of any criminal activity. He was willing, even anxious, to defend himself against any charges which might be brought in a court free from improper influences. There was only too much evidence that a fair opportunity would never be allowed in South Africa, and he declined to return in order to make the attempt, but it had, probably naively, occurred to nobody that Italian justice could be bought.

To explain the nature, and the power, of the enemies made by Askin requires a chapter to itself.

CHAPTER ONE

The Rise of the Afrikaner Volk

Blood brothers

Late in the evening of 31 May 1902 the Boer Republics of the Orange Free State and the Transvaal finally surrendered to the British, bringing two and a half years of bitter warfare to an end. Surprisingly enough, considering the quantity of high explosives expended and the numbers employed – nearly half a million British and some ninety thousand Boers – the military casualties of the Anglo-Boer War had been light; only some seven thousand among the Boers and similar numbers of British were killed in the actual fighting. Disease accounted for many more – another sixteen thousand British dead – but the most serious losses were among the Boer civilians herded into refugee 'concentration' camps in the later stages of the conflict.

The causes of so grave a conflict – the most expensive effort made by Britain, and the only large-scale imperial war that she ever had to fight – have been much discussed. Tensions had existed for a generation between the Republic of South Africa, usually known as the Transvaal, ruled by old President Kruger and his faithful followers, the dour, unbending, sternly Calvinist Dutch-speaking farmers – Boers – and the British colonies of the Cape of Good Hope and Natal. A previous small and episodic fight in 1879 had resulted in a humiliating defeat for the British, but the resulting peace had established formal British hegemony in Southern Africa.

Shortly after the discovery of gold in huge quantities over a considerable extent of the Transvaal had transformed the situation as thousands of British, Australians, Cape Colonials, Americans and Jews – all English speaking – threatened to overturn the traditional Dutch supremacy. A

9

clumsy attempt at armed intervention – the Jameson Raid of 1895 – and much subsequent duplicity on the behalf of the British Conservative government of the time, had undermined Boer faith in British integrity. The other republic, the Orange Free State, previously neutral and tending to follow the Cape, threw its weight behind the Transvaal, by now set to become the centre of Southern African power as gold began to pour out in ever-increasing quantities.

The actual conflict was begun by the Boers as a pre-emptive strike which failed. Subsequent confrontation between large armed forces had occupied only the first nine months of the war, made famous by the sieges of Ladysmith, Mafeking (defended by Colonel Robert Baden-Powell), and Kimberley. After some humiliating reverses in which the Boer militia proved their superiority over well-trained British regulars, the British armies, reinforced by Canadian, Australian, New Zealand and Indian soldiers, had pushed the numerically inferior Boer forces out of their cities. President Kruger fled to Holland while the republican capitals, Pretoria and Bloemfontein and the new boom city of Johannesburg were occupied and placed under colonial government, with Lord Milner (whose intransigence had been largely responsible for causing the war in the first place) at its head. But the 'Commandos', perhaps the most effective fighting men in military history, refused to give up, and continued a guerrilla campaign for two more painful years. Ranging over an area the size of France, under such brilliant leaders as Christian de Wet, Jan Christiaan Smuts, Koos de la Rey and Louis Botha, units of mounted infantry a few hundred strong and without heavy weapons, eluded the British and inflicted a number of damaging defeats.

Lord Kitchener, the dour and unapproachable British commander, found the solution by restricting the Boer horsemen with hundreds of blockhouses. This limitation of the Commandos' freedom of movement was supplemented by a policy of devastation: burning crops, destroying farmsteads and stock, and gathering the rural population in refugee camps. Conditions in these camps – often known as concentration camps after the practice of the Spanish forces in the Cuban campaigns of 1895–8 – were sometimes horrible; rations were insufficient and disease was rife. Photographs of dead and dying children in the last stages of emaciation aroused indignation, internationally and within Britain itself. The energy of Emily Hobhouse and other protesters combined with the angry condemnation of the Liberal opposition in the British parliament to force improvements, but by then probably over 20,000 men, women and children had perished in the camps. From a total population of not much over 400,000 this was a dreadful proportion. There were few republican families who did not have relatives to mourn, and the scars were permanent.

Understandably enough, many Boers remained bitterly opposed to the resumption of British rule, even although this proved to be unprecedently generous. As soon as peace was restored considerable efforts and a good deal of money were expended in restoring the damaged economy. In an effort comparable to that made in Europe after the Second World War, political life was quickly re-established, free of any restraints, as the citizens of the former republics were given full political rights – more liberal, indeed, than those they had been granted under the previous republican governments. Within five years the Transvaalers were able to elect (somewhat to the annoyance and surprise of the British) a government with a majority of Afrikaners, as the Dutch-speakers were beginning to be known. By 1909 all South Africa, the two former Boer republics and the British colonies of the Cape of Good Hope and Natal had agreed to unite in the Union of South Africa. The agreement was confirmed by the British parliament and the new country joined the ranks of the independent British dominions alongside Canada, Australia and New Zealand.

The first election to the Union of South Africa's parliament resulted in an Afrikaner government headed by former generals Louis Botha, Jan Smuts, and J. M. B. Hertzog. Only a few years before all had been doing their best to kill British soldiers, but were now swearing allegiance to the King-Emperor. Brought about by a Liberal government, in which Winston Churchill, who had been captured by the Boers during the war, played a leading part, those concerned congratulated themselves on what seemed a prudent, wise and even magnanimous move. Only the non-white majority of South Africans were disillusioned. Hitherto they had enjoyed the right to vote on the same terms as other electors in the Cape Colony, the most populous province, and had trusted that this would be extended to the rest of the Union (in the former republics black political rights did not exist, and in Natal they had been severely restricted). Instead the whole issue was fudged, with the Cape electors retaining their franchise, but with only white South Africans being able to vote in the remainder of the country or be elected to parliament; it was the first of a series of encroachments on the political rights of the majority which culminated in the notorious policy of 'grand apartheid'. Black, Coloured and Indian leaders, seeing themselves deserted by their 'flabby friend', Britain, began to organise the defence of their own rights. They were fighting a losing battle, and each successive decade saw an erosion of these rights, but one of the defence organisations did manage to survive and develop a tradition of black leadership. This was the African National Congress whose leaders were missionary-educated, English-speaking journalists, solicitors, doctors and pastors, sober and decent Protestants in the British Victorian pattern, able to submerge previous internal black dissension and rivalries in a common cause.

The former provinces retained much of their previous individualism in the new South Africa. The Act of Union, in an effort to soothe provincial pride, had decreed that parliament should meet in Cape Town, while the seat of government would be the old capital of the Transvaal Republic, Pretoria, an inconvenient thousand miles away. The Orange Free State was gratified by having its capital, Bloemfontein, named as the seat of the Supreme Court. Both Pretoria and Bloemfontein remained essentially small towns with largely Afrikaner communities. These were restricted to the business of government, whereas Cape Town and Johannesburg developed as the English-speaking strongholds of commerce.

Among the Afrikaners Smuts and Botha, together with many others, were indeed deeply impressed by what they believed to be British generosity in the post-war settlement. When the 1914 war with Germany broke out they enthusiastically supported the British. First Botha and then Smuts took the field against the German armies in South-West and East Africa, at the head of forces composed jointly of British regulars and the burghers who twelve years before had ridden with them against the Empire's soldiers. An African contingent distinguished itself in Egypt and on the Western front and Smuts became a member of the supreme British command, sitting next to his old enemy Lord Milner in the War Cabinet. With the end of the war South Africa found herself numbered among the victorious powers: Smuts and Botha were active in the

Versailles negotiations and Smuts was responsible for much of the structure adopted by the new League of Nations.

Not all Afrikaners however followed the lead of Botha and Smuts. James Barry Munnik Hertzog, Judge and General of the Orange Free State, who had led his own Commando in the Anglo-Boer war, was less enthusiastic about the imperial connection. Lacking the industrial base and the great potential of the Witwatersrand gold mines that enabled the Transvaal to move quickly back to more than pre-war prosperity, the Orange Free State was entirely agricultural, and many farms had been devastated during the war, resulting in widespread poverty among the white rural population. Although Hertzog had joined Botha's cabinet, he proved an uncomfortable colleague, and walked out in November 1913 to form his own political group, the National Party. The new party was given powerful support when, at the outbreak of the First World War, many former Commandos, including the old heroes de Wet and de la Rey, and General Beyers, who had only months previously sworn loyalty to the government and Crown as commander-in-chief, sided with the Germans and joined in an armed rebellion against the Union government. They were hunted down by Afrikaners, defeated by Afrikaners, tried by Afrikaners and shot by Afrikaners. The division – the 'broedertwis' – between those Afrikaners who fought against the Germans in East Africa and on the Somme, and those who remained resentful of the British connection, became permanent.

After the ignominious collapse of the rebellion republican resistance to liberal Imperialism was diverted into social, political and economic forms. In the 1915 parliamentary election Hertzog's National Party gained 27 seats (including all but one of the Free State constituencies) at the expense of Botha's South Africa Party and the English-speaking Unionists, both ardent supporters of the Allied war effort. Further support was given to the Nationalists when the replacement of Dutch by Afrikaans as an official language became a bitterly argued controversy. Most educated Boers, such as President Steyn of the Orange Free State and Jan Hofmeyr, founder of the Afrikaner Bond in the 1880s, spoke and wrote correct Dutch. Many, in fact, thought and wrote in English, but to many republicans, especially the poorer classes, Dutch was nothing more than the language in which the Bible was written. Their usual medium, both in speech and unofficial writings, was the local patois,

Afrikaans. Evolved as a simple method of communication between Dutch-speakers, slaves and Hottentots in the eighteenth century, Afrikaans had been purposefully developed, again since the 1880s, as a formally structured language. Just as independence movements in Ireland reacted against English rule by encouraging the revival of the Irish language, so did South African republicans encourage the development of their own distinctive tongue. Inventing a new language was to prove a good deal more effective than re-establishing an old one.

By the 1920s Afrikaans grammar – wonderfully simple – had been formalised and an Afrikaans literature was burgeoning; in its short existence Afrikaans has produced a corpus of writings remarkable by any standards, even although many Afrikaners have preferred to write in English. Speaking Afrikaans became an absolute necessity for any self-respecting nationalist and a focus of Afrikaner pride. In 1927 Afrikaans replaced Dutch as an official language, but English continued to be essential in commerce and industry which remained almost entirely a British preserve.

As the First World War drew to an end and German defeat appeared inevitable, some young Afrikaners decided on a peaceful assertion of their people's rights, taking their struggle into the social arena. In their twenties, they had been too young to play an active part on the Anglo-Boer war. Although they called themselves 'Young Africa', echoing the 'Young Turks' of Mustapha Kemal, they had little in common with Kemal's arrogant army officers. It was a critical time of the war, as Ludendorff's spring offensive had brought the German armies within 40 miles of Paris, and a time when pro- and anti-British passions were at their height. Young Africa's first meeting was in the suburban house of a railway clerk, D. H. C. du Plessis, his colleagues on the first committee being similar serious middle-class youths. They had their photographs taken for the event, unsmiling, in reprehensible dinner jackets, Dominus William Nicol, then 31 years old and minister of Irene, a garden suburb of Pretoria, being the only member with a public profile. Henning Klopper, another railway clerk, was elected as chairman, with Ds. Nicol as vice chairman.

The meeting in du Plessis' house had been inspired by a near riot a few weeks previously. On 27 April a Johannesburg National Party gathering addressed by an enthusiastic teacher with the improbable name of

Ivanhoe Makepeace Lombard and by the rising star of the Nationalists, Dr Daniel Francois Malan, had been broken up by mob violence.

Apart from a strong sense of Afrikaner identity, a concomitant distaste for British Imperialism and liberalism and the aims of Young Africa, in the words of the movements historian, Professor A. N. Pelzer, 'people were allowed in who thought it was just another cultural society'. But Young Africa quickly developed into something very different and a good deal more sinister.

On 21 September 1920 the Afrikaner Broederbond was formed from Young Africa with Klopper as chairman and Dr Naudé, a representative of the older generation who fought in the Anglo-Boer war, and one of the irreconcilable six who voted against the peace in 1902, as vice chairman. Although the name recalled that of the earlier Afrikaner Bond founded by Jan Hofmeyr there was no other similarity. Hofmeyr's organisation had included such English-speaking liberal politicians as J. X. Merriman, Prime Minister of the Cape Colony, but the Broederbond was to be narrowly, rigidly Afrikaner with nothing at all liberal about it. Within a year of its foundation, on 26 August 1921, the Broederbond went underground, to become a secret society, with strict rules and elaborate rituals.

It was only the first of many changes of character, and methods that the Broederbond was to experience. At that time the society was very much based in the Transvaal towns; only ten years later was the first cell in the Cape Province established, where conditions were very different. Although the influence of the Broederbond became pervasive throughout Afrikaner society, it remained very much a Transvaal organisation opposed to capitalist business, with many northern Broeders suspiciously distrustful of their rich Cape colleagues. Afrikaner businessmen in the Cape Province had already established their own commercial empire – Nasionale Pers (National Press), Santam and Sanlam, respectively newspaper publishers, insurers, and financial companies of considerable importance. The National Party in the Cape was run by prosperous middle-class men, supporters of the old NGK, the state Church, and not the fundamentalist 'Doppers' represented by Naude and Nicol.

With the foundation of the Nasionale Pers in December 1914, stimulated by the failure of the Afrikaner rebellion, Nationalists acquired their own newspaper, *De Burger*. From the first issue the newspaper was edited by Dr Daniel Francois Malan, that portly cleric who had sat out the Boer War, much to the disgust of more active participants, 'drinking coffee in Keeromstraat'. *De Burger* quickly proved the potential economic power of the Afrikaner community by inspiring the collection of nearly a quarter of a million pounds to assist the imprisoned rebels in the 'Helpmekaar' movement. Nasionale Pers shareholders also financed in 1918 the Suid-Afrikaner Nasionale Trust Maatskappy, better known as Santam, principally in order to provide short-term credit to Afrikaner farmers, and its wholly-owned subsidiary Sanlam, a life assurance company intended to service the same market. Of these Sanlam went on to develop into the more important organisation, a successful challenger to their existing English counterpart, the South African Mutual Life Assurance Society, the 'Old Mutual'.

Apart from the Nasionale Pers, the new organisations were either co-operatives or mutual benefit societies. For many reasons, Afrikaners were suspicious of everything to do with capitalist finance, the low standards of education in the republican Transvaal and their attachment to the land being perhaps the most important by unfitting so many to take up work in industry. In the minds of the *takhaars*, the rural Boers of the Transvaal, memories of the 1895 Jameson Raid, financed by Cecil Rhodes, and the extinguishing of their little, comfortably corrupt republic by the hordes of prosperous *uitlanders* who had flocked to the Witwatersrand gold mines, lingered to add to the resentment. Some of the most prominent 'Randlords' were Jewish and anti-Semitism had become an accompaniment of nationalism; the bloated caricature figure of 'Hoggenheimer' became the embodiment of ruthless capitalism.

At the time that Young Africa developed into the Broederbond the National Party was enjoying a parliamentary success. The general election of March 1920 made it the largest bloc in the lower house, with 44 seats against the South Africa Party's 41. The balance of power was held by the Unionists, with 25, and the new Labour Party, with 21 seats. Louis Botha's death in 1919 had robbed his South Africa Party (SAP) of much Afrikaner support, leaving as it did the Anglophile Smuts as Prime Minister, backed by the great mining houses. In order to avoid a possible Nationalist–Labour majority the English Unionists, the old party of Cecil Rhodes and Dr Jameson and anathema to the Nationalists, were forced into the arms of Smuts' SAP. Thus reinforced the SAP won a solid majority in a 1921 election, when Nationalists and the Labour party together only mustered 54 seats against Smuts' 79.

Within two years the whole balance of power changed. Inspired by the same consciousness of being treated as inferiors that brought the Broederbond into being, the white industrial workers and miners, largely English-speaking, combined with the Afrikaners. A violent strike was suppressed by the Smuts government with brisk ruthlessness and two hundred died. The spectre of 'Hoggenheimer' allying capitalism with the unrepentant Imperialist Smuts was invoked, and a 1924 parliamentary election brought a coalition of Nationalists and Labour to power. For the first time the emergent Broederbond had direct access to the seat of government.

It took the Broederbond some time to get there as it remained centred in the Transvaal and composed largely of clerks, teachers and policemen. Hertzog's Nationalist Party was unsympathetic, believing that the 1926 Westminster Conference, which defined the concept of the British Commonwealth of independent nations, had accepted the principle of South African independence. In parliament the Broederbond's support was minimal until 1934, when the two old Boer war generals, Hertzog and Smuts, brought their parties together in a 'Fusion' government. Dr Malan and some other rigid Afrikaners broke away to form their own 'Purified Nationalist Party' and this gave the Broederbond its opportunity.

Hertzog, who was nothing if not open, found the Broederbond's secrecy repellent, and tore into their policies in a fierce speech in November 1935:

> When will that foolish, fatal idea cease with some people that they are the chosen of the gods to govern over all others? The English-speaking section has tried this with the Afrikaans-speaking section, but they did not succeed. The Afrikaans-speaking section has also tried it with the English-speaking section, but they also have failed. Neither the one nor the other will ever succeed in a policy of domination.
>
> I want to ask you whether our language and our freedom are of so little value and significance to us that we should

once again stake it in a gamble from pure racial animosity and fanaticism?

When I exclaimed, 'Very pretty, surely flattering to the soul of the Afrikaans-speaking Afrikaner such as you and I', I had unfortunately forgotten one thing – that it is clear from the provisions of prescriptions of the Broederbond as well as from the circular letter of the Executive Council, and of Professor van Rooy, that where they speak of the Afrikaner, or of Afrikanerdom, which must dominate in South Africa, you and I, who are not brothers, are not included. You and I will have to be satisfied that we shall never have the privilege to share in the Broederbond domination in South Africa. We are not Afrikaners.

But, what is more, not even all the brothers count as Afrikaners or are considered worthy of sharing in that superlative privilege of domination. According to the test laid down by the Executive Council and Professor van Rooy, for true Afrikanership nobody can have a claim to Afrikanership other than persons who have set themselves the ideal of Afrikanerising . . .

The Members of the Bond are not many – at the outside 2,000. But the power of the Bond does not lie in its membership, but in its secret organisation, which, for instance, is spread over the whole Free State like a network for the purpose of active propaganda. In this network, every vestige of information of any sort that may be useful to the National Party, true or untrue, is caught up and disseminated . . .'

Considering what was to be the state of things fifty years later, when the Broederbond's hand could be felt in every area of public life, and much also of private life, Hertzog was prophetic when he continued: 'What is there to prevent brothers seeking to promote one another's interests? . . . Has this not already happened without being discovered? . . . what protection have you and I and our children, who are not members of the Broederbond, against the misuse of influence by brothers whereby we are prevented from attaining what is legitimately and rightfully our due?'

Outside parliament the Brothers' influence had indeed, as Hertzog was well aware, been rapidly expanding. Their front organisation, the Federation of Afrikaans Cultural Associations (FAK) established in 1929, had encouraged the development of an Afrikaner identity. A parallel junior organisation, equally secret, the Ruiterwag (Ruiter = horseman: ruiterlik = frank, chivalrous: wag = guard), was formed. Literature, history, even music, had to have an Afrikaner flavour: if the traditions did not exist, they were invented.

Everything English was spurned. Parallel organisations were earnestly discovered. Scouts, Guides, Rotary, Chambers of Commerce, Students' Unions, even the Red Cross, were given Afrikaner equivalents. When some Afrikaners developed their own version of fascism, Louis Weichardt's Greyshirts formed in the image of Hitler's SA and Mussolini's fascists, and Hans van Rensburg's Stormjaers, a homespun imitation of Hitler's Stormtroopers, emerged.

At the same time the Broederbond was able to widen its representation away from its original lower-middle-class base as Afrikaners began to extend their commercial power. New enterprises were begun in sectors hitherto dominated by the English-speakers, of which the most important was banking. South African banking was at that time divided almost entirely between two London banks, Barclays and the Standard Bank of South Africa, their only competition being the much smaller Holland-based Nederlandsche Bank voor Zuid Afrika, a fraction of the size of either of the British banks (14 South African branches in contrast to Barclays' more than 400 in 1922). When Sanlam, the new Afrikaner insurance company, ran into trouble shortly after its foundation it had to rely upon the Standard Bank to save it from liquidation. The only Afrikaner financial institutions apart from Sanlam and Santam were tiny savings banks such as Spaar-en Voorskot Bank (Sasbank), set up with a capital of £300 by some schoolteachers.

When, in 1934, the first Afrikaner bank 'Volkskas' (People's Treasury) was founded by Broederbond capital and directed by Brothers, Pretoria was naturally chosen as its headquarters. The moving spirit behind Volkskas was J. J. Bosman, a clerk-bookkeeper very much from the same background as other Transvaaler Broeders, who with 54 members of the Bond put together £1,500 of capital to begin another small savings-and loan bank. Its first chairman was J. C. van Rooy, Broederbond chairman, who had in the same year stated 'the Afrikaner Broeder-bond must rule South Africa'.

At that time it did not look as though Volkskas could do much to help. Barclays alone employed a capital of some £14,000,000, and neither that bank nor Standard was willing to offer support; indeed they attempted to have Volkskas prosecuted under the Usury Act. But the Broeders rallied round. Led by Dr Albert Hertzog, the Prime Minister's son, a hardline nationalist opponent of his father's, a fund-raising delegation travelled the country and succeeded in effecting some improvement. Even so, in 1941, when Volkskas succeeded in obtaining a commercial banking licence, its paid-up capital was still only £37,000.

Events were, however, moving favourably for the development of Afrikaner capitalism. 1938 had seen the centenary celebrations of the 'Great Trek', that exodus of Dutch-speaking farmers who, outraged by British imperial insistence of the legal equality of all races, moved out of the British colonies to found a succession of small republics. After some quarrelling among themselves, these were later consolidated into the Orange Free State and the Transvaal. Trekking in their ox-drawn wagons, facing atrocious conditions and the hostility of the black nations they were displacing, the Great Trek had indeed been a remarkable feat and had been magnified by Afrikaner mythology into something a good deal more glamorous and distinguished than the inconvenient facts warranted. At its centenary, celebrated by eight ox-wagons moving slowly to Pretoria where the great Voortrekker monument was to be erected (neither Hertzog nor Smuts, tainted as they were by their co-operation with the English could attend the opening ceremony), Afrikaners benefited by an emotional resurgence. It came at an inconvenient time.

Within a year the Second World War had broken out and the South African parliament had to decide between neutrality and participation in the Allied cause. Nationalists, and indeed most Afrikaners, with little love for Britain and their often German forebears, plus their only moderate enthusiasm for democratic principles (none whatsoever for these when it came to non-whites) were solidly for neutrality. Smuts, however, employing his unequalled authority and status, persuaded parliament to declare war on Germany and enter the war. Many Afrikaners volunteered to join the Allied forces but a disgruntled majority dissented.

Jingling coin, not pious sentiment

The Broederbond were able to take advantage of events. Still dependent for most of their support on the lower-middle classes of the Transvaal, a reconciliation between them and the capitalists of the Cape became possible. Martinus Louw, the talented strategist of Sanlam's board, and himself a Broeder, (typically having begun his career as a schoolteacher) suggested the creation of a straightforwardly capitalist Afrikaner enterprise, one which would set aside the previous ideals of small co-operatives. A 'Volkscongres' met in 1940 to consider what could be done to counter the pervasive English influence on the economy, and to enable the Afrikaner, in Louw's words 'to realise *his* legitimate struggle to assert *himself* in the economic domain'. Although there was much rhetoric about the condition of the 'poor whites' and the need for socialism, especially from Albert Hertzog, the congress agreed to Louw's proposals. The Federale Volksbelegging (Federal People's Investments, FVB) that resulted was an unashamedly profit-making organisation, its first undertaking to produce dividends; shareholders were to be paid 'in jingling coin rather than pious sentiment'. But it took the weighty backing of Sanlam and the active participation of Broederbond workers to extract the investments from the conservative Afrikaner public.

Ideological purity was to be enforced by the Broederbond's public front organisation, the FAK, working through the new Economic Institute. In all matters of policy, the Institute was to be the final judge. It was a solidly Broederbond institution, the chairman being L. J. du Plessis, with Piet Meyer as secretary and Ivanhoe Lombard, the veteran agitator of 1918, as treasurer. With Institute backing but against considerable opposition (du Plessis was forced to resign his chairmanship) Volkskas was able to shed its co-operative status and to become a public limited company. As such it did not escape Broederbond domination; Dr A. J. Stals, who replaced du Plessis as chairman, was a prominent Broeder, as were all his successors and colleagues. Volskas remained, too, very much a Pretoria-based operation, with very few branches outside the Transvaal.

In Cape Town Sanlam, although equally susceptible to Broederbond influence, was pursuing a more adventurous policy. Attempting to

21

escape from the constraints of its constitution as a mutual benefit society in the same way that Volkskas had attempted to break from its co-operative constraints, Sanlam established a subsidiary, Bonuskor, in order to provide risk capital for investment, an activity which Volkskas was neither equipped nor inclined to undertake. A more immediately striking example of Cape initiative was the foundation of the new Voorbrand Tobacco Company. Again, a Broederbond controlled enterprise, its first directors were Dr Stals and Dr Nicolaas Diederichs, the Bond's chairman from 1938 to 1942, together with a young man who was to become very well known, the twenty-three-year-old Anton Rupert. In his long career Anton Rupert has moved to a considerably more liberal position, but in 1940, when Voorbrand was founded, he was an enthusiastic and extreme right-winger and Fascist sympathiser.

Until that time the Broederbond had been able to claim with some show of credibility that, in spite of Hertzog's opposition, it was primarily a cultural organisation, concerned above all with safeguarding traditional Afrikaner values. These were understood as being closely related to a fundamentalist Protestantism, which contrived to ignore most of the New Testament's more revolutionary assertions of the brotherhood of all men. Afrikaner theology understood that the blacks had been created to be the servants of white masters; about the Coloureds, the mixed-race people with a fair share of Dutch genes, opinions were allowed to differ.

With the rise of European Fascism a new role model became available. Even those Nationalists who had remained faithful to Prime Minister Hertzog and avoided joining Malan's discontented 'purified' followers were attracted to the rising dictators; Oswald Pirow, the talented Minister of Justice, who believed Portugal's Salazar had discovered the answer to South Africa's problems and Dr Hans van Rensburg, administrator of the Transvaal province, director of Santam, Sanlam and Volkskas, who had been an admirer of Hitler since 1932. In what must have been a comic episode the unathletic Dr Malan got himself on to a horse to make a suitable entrance into a Greyshirt rally.

Encouraged by the initial German successes in 1940 the Nationalists came together once more as Hertzog and Malan formed the Re-united Nationalist Party. Oswald Pirow organised the New Order as an openly Nazi party; Hans van Rensburg resigned his post to take over the Ossewa

Brandwag (Ox-wagon Guard, OB) which attracted over 200,000 members but did little more of importance than to distribute anti-democratic propaganda and organise extensive but inept sabotage. Afrikaner 'kultuur' began to look very much like Nazi 'kultur'.

Although the parliamentary Re-united Nationalists frowned upon the antics of the OB, whose programme included the abolition of such degenerate democratic bodies as elected assemblies, the Broederbond fought to retain a foot in both camps. Both L. J. du Plessis and Piet Meyer, members of the key Economic Institute board, were OB members, and lost their posts, but du Plessis became chairman of the Unity Commission established to bring together the quarrelling Afrikaner institutions. Smuts was once again, with his old friend Winston Churchill, in the centre of the Allied fight against the Axis powers, and as they had done thirty years before Afrikaners and English South Africans fought together in the Western desert and in Italy, perpetuating the division between them and the Nationalists.

Helped by the Allied victories from 1943 onwards, which forced the more Fascist Afrikaners to recalculate their political affiliations, the Nationalists succeeded in healing the most obvious divisions. Hertzog was forced into the wilderness, and with his departure an era ended. In Hertzog's time Nationalists were certainly no liberals, but they were democrats, willing to work within South Africa's parliamentary and legal systems. Their electorate was severely restricted – no Indian or Coloured women, (white women were enfranchised in 1930) no blacks at all after 1934 on the general electoral roll, but governments were appointed and fell according to the freely expressed wish of that limited electorate. It might be remembered that most Victorian British parliaments were elected by a small minority of the total adult population.

Future Nationalist leaders were to go much further than Malan in their willingness to push what democracy existed to the point of breakdown and to interfere brutally with judicial processes in order to achieve their ambitions, and the Broederbond was behind them all.

Dr Malan, who had managed to combine fidelity to parliamentary systems with his Greyshirt sympathies, became party leader and in the general election of 1948, and to general astonishment, Prime Minister. Old Jan Smuts, a world figure, whose first government post had been as Attorney-General in the Transvaal Republic half a century before, founder of holistic philosophy, Field Marshal, who had assisted in the establishment of both the League of Nations and the United Nations, was ignominiously defeated. The National Party had attained control of parliament, although with a minority of the votes cast; the era of apartheid was about to start. It took some time before the final links with Britain could be cut, but by 1961 South Africa was a republic, no longer a member of the British Commonwealth, with its own currency, the rand (R), replacing the pound sterling which had existed even in the old Transvaal republic.

An immediate effort was begun by the new administration to ensure that Afrikaners – and apart from a few token English-speakers Nationalist governments were solidly Afrikaner – would be able to hold on to power. Using dubiously constitutional methods Malan's government energetically filled the most senior posts in the civil service, armed services, judiciary and public industries with fellow-Afrikaners, often promoting poorly qualified individuals. It was the sort of clean sweep that was later seen in many new African countries. But one vital area remained under English control. Although it had emerged at the centre of political power – every Prime Minister or President for the next forty-six years, and almost all cabinet members and senior civil servants were to be Broederbond members – the Brotherhood had only limited influence in the business world. Afrikaners represented about 60 per cent of the white population, but in 1948 they held only 5 per cent of top management posts and 15 per cent of lower managerial and professional posts – and these were much greater proportions than ten years previously; at the outbreak of Second World War the figures were 3 per cent, 8 per cent and 9 per cent respectively. In particular banking, finance and the stock exchange remained obstinately English. Sanlam was ready and able to promote Afrikaner business, but could find few Afrikaner entrepreneurs, the exception that proved this particular rule being Anton Rupert.

With the help of the old Prime Minister's nephew, Dirk Hertzog – like Rupert a Fascist sympathiser – a new company was formed which acquired distilling and trading interests as well as the original Voorbrand tobaccco company. By June 1947 (by which date Mr Rupert's political views had most probably been modified), the Rembrandt Tobacco Company was established with an authorised capital of £200,000, and of course the directors, Stals, Dirk Hertzog and Rupert, with Ivanhoe Lombard as secretary, were all Broeders.

Anton Rupert must be one of the most outstanding businessmen of the post-war world; the company he founded, Rembrandt, is now a vast, greatly diversified enterprise with holdings in such well-known companies as Rothmans, with 67 per cent held by Rupert's interests and the Distillers Corporation. The controlling Swiss company Richemont, with annual profits of some £1,000 million owns such famous names as Baume and Mercier, Alfred Dunhill, Sulka, Mont Blanc and Purdey. The Ruperts – the business is now run by Anton's son, Johan – have substantial mining interests in Gencor, Billiton and Goldfields of South Africa, and in NetWork Holdings, the largest pay-TV operator in Europe.

Although his political views changed radically as he saw the potentially disastrous effects of the Nationalists' apartheid policies (by 1960 he was ostracised as a dangerous radical by the formidable Prime Minister, Dr Verwoerd) Rupert remained the leading figure of the Afrikaner business world, on the board of Sanlam, but anathema to the conservative Pretorian directors of Volkskas, who regarded all Cape Town finance as tainted with cosmopolitanism and allied with Hoggenheimer.

In 1950, when the second Economic Congress was held, Afrikaner financial control of the country's economy had advanced substantially, but was still a fraction of that of the competing, English-speaking sector. Only 5 per cent of the commercial banking sector (although nearly one third of the much smaller savings and trust banks), a mere 1 per cent of the building society movement, but a significant 11 per cent of the insurance market (mainly Sanlam) was in the ownership of those Afrikaners sympathetic to the Broederbond. The only other non-British bank of any size, the Nederlandsche Bank, swam against that current by changing its name in 1951 to the Netherlands Bank of South Africa (twenty years later the board compromised by changing once more to the inoffensive title 'Nedbank'). There was still much remaining for the Broederbond to do.

Apartheid; the skunk among nations

The first Nationalist governments of Dr Malan (1948–54) and Hans Strydom (1954–58) were primarily concerned with ensuring white Afrikaner supremacy – 'baaskap'. The policies commonly known as apartheid, glossed by their supporters as 'separate development', which made South Africa 'the skunk among nations' were only developed fully under the protracted guidance of Dr Hendrik Verwoerd, Minister of Native Affairs from 1950 and Prime Minister from 1958 to 1966.

It was sometimes claimed, and with apparent justice, that apartheid had its roots in British imperial practices of the previous century. During the nineteenth century London governments were convinced, for the most part rightly, that colonists could not be relied upon to behave properly towards the native peoples. Occasionally very tough attitudes had to be taken towards colonial malpractices: Governors were recalled and constitutions such as that of Natal suspended when it became too apparent that the black communities were being excessively persecuted. In order to protect the interests of these communities, some were hived off as protectorates under imperial administration. In that way the Basuto, Swazi and Tswana peoples were able to preserve their own societies and way of life and emerge in the twentieth century as independent states. Others were less fortunate. The Xhosa and Zulu were absorbed into the Union of South Africa where their privileges were considerably fewer than those which had earlier been accorded to the black communities living within British colonies. In early colonial Natal in the 1840s two million acres had been set aside for black settlement, which did not imply that the rest of the country was unavailable for black farming. Very large areas in addition were owned or leased to black farmers, but whites were completely excluded from areas that had been set aside for blacks. The intention of this was to safeguard – as the name of Protectorate implies – black interests.

The rationale behind apartheid, or separate development, was different, being to preserve white domination by a series of expedients, earnestly discussed over many years – and it should not be forgotten that the Afrikaners were very serious about finding some reasonable explanations for what appeared their unreasonable actions. Apartheid depended on a peculiar interpretation of human rights. It is true, as Afrikaners argued, that South Africa is in a very different position from most other African countries. Parts were settled by white immigrants spreading north and east from the Cape of Good Hope, others by black communities moving slowly south. The land originally was occupied by neither white nor black but by the indigenous Khoisan, the Hottentot and Bushmen peoples, brown-skinned and slightly-built. As blacks and whites moved into Khoisan territory the inhabitants were either driven out or absorbed into the new communities.

In the early years of the nineteenth century the generation of disruption known as the Mfecane, set in motion by the rise of the Zulu people, scattered black communities as far as a thousand miles from the epicentre and established new black states over a wide area of Southern Africa. This was the time when the Matebele founded the state ruled first by Mzilikazi and then by Lobengula, later dispossessed by Cecil Rhodes and when the great chief Moshoeshoe formed his Sotho people into a kingdom. Only after the Mfecane did the present groupings of communities in South Africa become more or less settled. Industrialisation brought other changes. The demand for labour in the gold mines of the Witwatersrand and later in the twentieth century during the rise of manufacturing industry, siphoned millions of blacks from their original habitations into the great conurbations. Xhosa, Pedi, Sotho, Tswana, Swazi, Mpondo and the descendants of many other once proudly distinct communities found themselves crowded together into the miserable 'townships' that clustered outside every city.

It was the endeavour of apartheid measures, initiated by Verwoerd and continued after his assassination by his successor, Balthazar Johannes Vorster, Prime Minister from 1966 to 1978, to force this fractured society back into what it saw as traditional modes; an impossible task. After two hundred years of disruption very few solid blocks of black land-ownership existed, the biggest of these being the Transkei district of the Eastern Cape, the home of the Xhosa, Thembu and Mpondo people. Other black 'homelands' – derisively known as Bantustans – that were identified by the Nationalist governments were little more than fictions. Some, like Bophutatswana, intended to be the homeland of those Tswana not resident in the old Bechuanaland protectorate which after 1960 became the independent republic of

Botswana, were scattered in 36 small parcels of land over hundreds of miles.

In spite of the often laughable nature of these 'states' Nationalist governments insisted that all South African blacks should be identified as citizens of one or another. By this device they could be denied any political rights in South Africa itself: if they were citizens of Bophutatswana they had political rights in that state just as the inhabitants of Botswana itself were able to control their own affairs. This was however a complete fiction; only in the Transkei and to a lesser degree the Ciskei was there any semblance of independent government and these governments were generally corrupt and ineffective.

Pushed into action by the new nations which had emerged after the Second World War the United Nations reluctantly took action against South Africa. The United States and Britain were generally slow in accepting the international indignation at South African policies but after the police massacres at Sharpeville and Soweto became common knowledge indignation was unstoppable. Pressure for change took the form of economic sanctions, primarily of the export of arms and oil to South Africa and the refusal of foreign consumers to buy South African products.

South African reaction to international attacks was vigorous. Helped by the fact that few of its critics were blameless and many had regimes considerably more reprehensible than South Africa's, together with covert arrangements with other governments (Israel was notably co-operative, but France and Italy were also willing to assist) Nationalist governments were able to defy external pressures. 'Sanctions busting' stimulated the growth of new state-owned industries. Armscor developed the production and sales abroad of a wide variety of advanced weaponry. South Africa tested its own atomic bomb and manufactured a small stockpile, while chemical and biological weapons reached at least the stage of advanced trials. Sasoil developed coal-based oil substitutes, but there were also many opportunities to divert cargoes of oil products from their ostensible destinations. A moral dimension was given to South African resistance by characterising all the newly independent African regimes as corrupt tools of Russian aggression – accusations credible enough to find sympathetic support in Britain and the United States. Internal opposition was sometimes violent, but disorganised and sporadic, and rarely damaged the increasingly severe police and army controls.

The late sixties and early seventies had seen something of a boom, the 'golden age' of apartheid when the economy grew at an average rate of between 6–8 per cent per annum. Foreign investment burgeoned, approaching a total of R7,000 million by 1974, attracted by returns in investment of, typically, 18 per cent. This sort of expansion produced in turn a rapid growth in service industries, investment banks, stock-brokers, business-schools and accountants. In all these developments Afrikaners were now taking their share. In 1938, only 5 per cent of financial institutions were in Afrikaner ownership; by 1975 this had risen to 25 per cent. In the same period Afrikaner investment had risen from 3 per cent of the manufacturing and building sectors to 15 per cent. Most of this growth had taken place in the 27 years of Nationalist government; at the start of the half-century of Nationalist adminis-trations in 1949, Afrikaners had owned only 6 per cent of both the both finance and manufacturing sectors.

Membership of the Broederbond followed the same pattern. In 1952 58 per cent of Broeders described themselves as educators: there were, it seems, no businessmen at all, or no one willing so to describe themselves. Twenty-five years later, only 21.6 per cent were educators, but 12.5 per cent were businessmen or bankers – and among these were all the executive directors of the South African Reserve Bank, in absolute con-trol of the country's economy.

It was South Africa's intervention in Namibia, Angola and Mozam-bique that eventually stretched the resources of the apartheid state to breaking point. June 1976 might be chosen as the point when things had obviously changed for the worse. In this month pictures of school children in Soweto being shot down by police flashed round the world. South African excuses were no longer acceptable. The new Carter administration in the US was not prepared to follow through Henry Kissinger's support of South Africa as a bulwark against communism. America and Britain both agreed with a mandatory United Nations arms embargo, and the inflow of foreign capital dried up, reversing into a net expatriation of capital. The real growth rate not only declined, but it began to reverse.

Businesses, both Afrikaner and English, that had previously

co-operated with the government, demanded changes, all in the direction of softening the hard lines of apartheid. Harry Oppenheimer, active member of the Progressive Party, joined with Anton Rupert, former Fascist and present Broeder to form the Urban Foundation. This well-intentioned body attempted to enlist the 'most responsible section of the urban black population' against 'the irresponsible economic and political ambitions of those blacks who are influenced against their own real interests from within and without our borders' – meaning, most obviously, the African National Congress. That organisation had survived many vicissitudes, and under the direction of Nobel Peace Prize winner Albert Lutuli, had achieved international recognition, which had not prevented Nelson Mandela, Lutuli's successor, being sentenced to life imprisonment. The ANC had held out against violent resistance for half a century, and eventually adopted the policy only with much hesitance; the people themselves, deprived of constitutional representation, crowded into miserable squatters' townships and harassed by oppressive legislation, brutally enforced, took to unorganised violence as the only possible form of resistance.

The very moderate aims of the Urban Foundation were enthusiastically supported by both English and Afrikaner business, with Oppenheimer's Anglo-American Corporation donating R11 million. All major banks and financial institutions made substantial contributions – except Volkskas. That bastion of conservatism and Broederbond control held aloof. Andries Wassenaar, director of Nasionale Pers, chairman of Sanlam, the largest Afrikaner institution, and a Broeder himself, published a book (*Assault on Private Enterprise*, Cape Town, 1977) critical of Vorster's policies and state interference, which also marked the divergence between Nationalist business ideas in the Cape and the financial heart of the apartheid regime, Pretoria. Dr F. Cronjé, chairman of Nedbank, took the lead in the discussions which led to the formation of the Progressive Federal Party, which became the official opposition after the 1977 elections. More than ever before Volkskas became the National Party's Counting House and the conduit for all those financial transactions that the apartheid governments wished to keep hidden from the public view.

The division between Cape Nationalists, always more receptive to the great world outside South Africa than the more primitive, self-centred

Afrikaners in the Transvaal, became marked in political as well as economic affairs. Dr Andries Treurnicht, Broederbond chairman, a clergyman reactionary even by Boer standards and a supporter of Albert Hertzog, had been directly responsible for the policy which had led to the Soweto deaths by insisting that black children should be taught in Afrikaans, the hated language of the oppressor, rather than in English. Soweto and its aftermath forced even Treurnicht to abandon so disastrous a policy. On the other, 'verligte' side of the Nationalist party, the Cape newspaper *Die Burger* wrote in November 1976 that apartheid had failed, and that the 'inexorable alternative' must be accepted; this was defined as granting 'co-equal citizenship' to 'people of different colour' in an entirely new constitution.

Vorster became less and less able to cope with the divisions within his party and Afrikaners looked to his likely successor, Dr Connie Mulder, Minister of Information and the Interior. Completely unscrupulous, but lacking the ability to make effective use of his lack of principle, Mulder worked closely with General Hendrik van der Bergh, whose internment during the second World War on account of his Nazi sympathies and his vigorous willingness to use similar methods – 'I have enough men to commit murder if I tell them: Kill! – I don't care who the prey is' – had earned him elevation to the head of the Bureau of State Security (BOSS).

Probably the most effective and unscrupulous intelligence service in the modern world, BOSS and van der Bergh worked closely with Mulder and the Secretary of Information Dr Eschel Rhoodie. A secret fund of R64 million was created to service Rhoodie's activities. In addition the much larger sums made available to BOSS were used, according to Rhoodie himself in:

> attempts to purchase leading South African, British, French and American newspapers; establishing and financing both an international news magazine – *To The Point* – and a pro-government English-language newspaper in South Africa – *The Citizen*; purchasing numerous newspapers and magazines all over the world; subsidising pro-South African programmes on international television networks; setting up a 'moderate' black newspaper in the Bophuthtswana bantustan;

funding the production of pro-South African movies with big-name stars; arranging Vorster's clandestine visits to the presidents of Senegal, Zaire and Ivory Coast and wangling a state visit by former Nazi, John Vorster, to Israel; providing money to the president of the Seychelles; trying to bribe Nigerian politicians to recognise the 1976 'independence' of the Transkei bantustan; financing a Norwegian parliamentary party; underwriting (successful) election campaigns against US congressmen and Senators hostile to South Africa; paying former US President Gerald Ford to address a Houston seminar on trade with South Africa; retaining Labour and Conservative Party members of the British parliament to work for South Africa behind the scenes: compensating members of the Japanese Diet for 'their cooperation ... in regard to labour unions'; retaining a US public relations firm and numerous lobbyists to promote SA interests; financing special supplements on SA in Western media; identifying and wooing future political leaders in various countries; setting up 'neutral' international front organisations to promote South Africa; subsidising several supposed academic research institutes; paying the expenses of, and providing luxury accommodation and other perks and services – including sexual – to prominent local and international figures who spoke out for South Africa; purchasing vast luxury property holdings throughout southern Africa, the US and Europe.

The deployment of such immense secret funds inevitably involved much deception and fraud as Rhoodie and his associates diverted huge sums – R13 million 'borrowed' by Louis Luyt, chairman of the South African Rugby Football Association in a single escapade. By the time the whole fabric of deception collapsed, the Information Scandal, also, predictably, known as Muldergate, in 1978, brought down Prime Minister Vorster as well as Mulder, Rhoodie and van der Bergh.

With the exception of such isolated figures as the Finance Minister, Professor Owen Horwood, a Natalian fellow-traveller, all concerned were Afrikaners. All departments of government and administration, police and the armed forces were now firmly under Afrikaner control.

Decent Afrikaner traditions, exemplified by old Prime Minister Hertzog, racially hegemonist and reactionary though they were, had been rooted in the acceptance of constitutional and legal restrictions; they were now supplanted by a corrupt, secretive and unprincipled establishment. And the uniting force behind this distasteful society was Hertzog's old foe, the Afrikaner Broederbond.

Vorster's successor, P. W. Botha, the 'Great Crocodile', assumed office as Prime Minister in 1978. Since he had previously been Minister of Defence, the most influential portfolio in the government, for twelve years, Botha came to office with a great deal of power, skilled in operating the non-constitutional mechanisms. He was a man of ferocious temper and great energy, dedicated to the preservation of white hegemony, and a dedicated Broeder. Botha however acknowledged that the received wisdom of apartheid would simply not do. Reform was an absolute necessity, but reform was to be a strictly controlled process that did not endanger white supremacy. 'Only a fool would keep travelling on the same road, even when it has been washed away, if there is a better road to reach his objective.'

Botha's better road was the doctrine of 'Total Strategy'; propounded by the French General André Beaufre as a solution to the French problems in Algeria. The fact that the policy had been a total failure in Algeria might have given pause, but Botha and his close associate, General Magnus Malan, successor as Defence Minister in 1980, were convinced. An intellectual rather than a fighting soldier, a committed Broeder, son of Nationalist MP Dr A. I. Malan, Speaker of the Assembly and chairman of Volkskas, General Malan provided the stick of unscrupulously applied unlimited force that was supposed to be matched by Botha's carrot of constitutional reforms.

These were radical, but ultimately ineffective. The government was reorganised as an executive presidency, the grosser forms of apartheid were removed, and a complex tripartite parliamentary system was devised to offer Indian and Coloured representation. Since this amounted to only the semblance of power, it was received with little enthusiasm and the black majority remained voteless and impotent.

Whatever changes in American foreign policy supervened – all administrations were conscious of the important black vote, strongly anti-South African (though usually profoundly ignorant of South African realities) – the hard-right Republican wing was strongly represented in business, and continued to be reliably supportive of apartheid governments*. Often working closely with the CIA, while under the rule of the notorious Bill Casey, the right-wingers tempered any anti-apartheid measures that might be forced on US governments. With the advent of the Reagan government official support became more open and some of the previously enacted legislation enforcing sanctions was cancelled. Bolstered by such allies, Botha and Malan at first exercised a near-absolute power, tempered only by parliamentary dissent to both right and left and a growing international pressure for economic sanctions in the United Nations. Unyielding repression and brisk intelligence work effectively emasculated any internal resistance that the ANC and the more militant Pan African Congress (PAC) were able to mount. Government repression was considerably assisted by secret co-operation with Chief Mangosuto Buthelezi's Zulu Inkatha movement, which was the grateful recipient of growing amounts of state funding.

The heart of the new Botha government, which relegated the cabinet to a secondary position, was the State Security Council, (SSC) which reported directly to the President. Quickly characterised as the 'SS Council', the new body included the Ministers of Defence, Foreign Affairs, and Law and Order, together with their senior permanent officials. Supported by an extensive secretariat, the SSC controlled twelve Joint Management Centres, chaired by army brigadiers, in an echo of Oliver Cromwell's attempt to govern England through eleven major-generals. Cromwell had a lively sense of the possible, and unlike the Afrikaners quickly abandoned his attempt at centralised rule, but Botha and Malan persisted with their National Security Management system, supported by all the resources of a modern nation state. South Africa became in most respects a military autocracy, bolstered by a parliamentary majority, with the active support of a considerable part of the financial industrial establishment (indeed with the state ownership of important industries) and the passive tolerance of the rest.

---

* The willingness of American right wingers to ignore international law has not waned. As late as 25 August 1998 one L. Paul Bremer, described as 'Reagan's ambassador at large for counterterrorism', advocated (in the *International Herald Tribune*) that the USA should encourage political assassinations, ignore the United Nations, and attack terrorist camps even in friendly countries.

Apartheid's assassins

Details of the more outrageous activities of the State Security Council (SSC) emerged only slowly, and are still emerging. The department mainly concerned with 'counter revolutionary strategy' was Stratcom, or 'Trewits', reporting directly to the SSC. Stratcom's 'Hard' section dealt with such straightforward issues as the direction of Captain Dirk Coetzee's notorious 'Vlakplaas' murder squad, sabotage and blackmail, many of whose activities were revealed in the 1995 trial of Coetzee's henchman, Colonel Eugene de Kock. The 'Soft' undertakings were more complex, including the guidance of front activities, which included the 'Confederation of Employers of South Africa' (COFESA) headed by Hein van der Walt and 'Businessmen for South Africa', intended to combat the more liberal, generally English-speaking business organisations. Sympathetic politicians abroad, who included in Britain numerous Conservative MPs and at least one Labour, were encouraged to spread anti-Mandela propaganda. Dozens of companies were established, usually controlled by military or police officers. Lamont Market Research, in Randberg, run by Major-General Gerhard Bruwer, was a front for the police 'dirty tricks' department whilst Global Capital Investments, established by the Pretoria lawyer and naval reserve Commander E. Pinz, was used to frame the SWAPO advocate Anton Lubowski, later murdered by the Stratcom 'hard section'. Although most of the assassinations were of black activists and their families, prominent white opponents of apartheid, such as Dr Rick Turner, Ruth First, David Webster and Jackie Quinn were all accounted for by the official security services, serving under commissioned officers of the police and army, and on the instructions of government ministers.

The connection between political murders and state funding was made explicit by one well-informed source. Dr Eschel Rhoodie, who had collaborated enthusiastically with Connie Mulder in the secret distribution of public money, was prepared to be forthcoming about the murder of Dr Robert and Mrs Smit and its possible link with the government's clandestine activities in an interview secretly recorded in October 1987 (published in *Noseweek* 31 July 1993) Rhoodie admitted:

Let's admit that Dr Smit did uncover some massive secret fund that was there illegally, or for no sound moral or political reason, and that he thereby threatened the secrecy of the funds and the position of the people administering, or maladministering that fund . . . Have you ever wondered why no Afrikaans newspaper has ever bothered to research and list all the secret funds which exist? . . . all the secret funds of Foreign Affairs, Information, the Security Police – all pale into insignificance when we talk of the Defence Special Procurement Fund.

Rhoodie speculated 'There were rumours, at first just rumours, that the fund, which ran into hundreds of millions every year and over the past fifteen years (up to 1987) probably totalled three billion rand, was not used for the purchase of weapons. For instance, it was used to give R75 million to the Department of Information for its secret operations.' Asked the question, 'Do you believe the Smits were murdered by some criminal, or assassinated because he stumbled on a great big dirty secret?' Rhoodie answered in one reluctant word: 'Assassinated'.

The responsibility for collecting and dispensing secret funds in the post-Muldergate period was entrusted to the Directorate of Covert Collections, (DCC) a unit of the South African Defence Force, headed by Brigadier (later promoted to General) J. J. (Tolikie) Botha. Colonel At Nel, Botha's lieutenant, was implicated in the most disreputable of DCC activities, that of Brigadier Dr Wouter Basson, head of the secret chemical and biological research programme.

As the end of Nationalist domination grew near, it was essential that some effort be made to sweep away the traces of these activities. An attempt was first made immediately after Mandela's release when on 5 March 1989 Judge Louis Harms began an extremely tentatively named Inquiry into Certain Alleged Murders. Incredibly, the Harms Commission came to the conclusion that 'no hit squad was established at Vlakplaas' although at least seventy murders and numerous operations of destruction, deception and arson, had been carried out from there.

This obviously nonsensical conclusion led to the establishment of a second enquiry by Judge Goldstone in October 1991, the Commission of Inquiry Regarding the Prevention of Public Violence and Intimidation. A raid by the Goldstone Commission on the DCC's office produced evidence alarming enough for Botha's successor President de Klerk to appoint a third enquiry in November 1992, this time led by the head of the Air Force, General Pierre Steyn. His report was never published, and for very good reasons, since it uncovered a list of crimes together with indications that many of the perpetrators were preparing to carry on their lucrative trades whatever political changes might be brought about.

Steyn reported that 'the availability of and easy access to secret funds coupled with the Total Onslaught syndrome has resulted in these activities becoming self-generating and self-perpetuating.' There were 'definite signs' of covert operations continuing, creating violence and intimidation, implicating the DCC, the Army staff, some army Reconnaissance units, and Wouter Basson's Seventh Medical Battalion. There was a need for immediate and encompassing action at all levels, including top officials, and dismissals of individuals involved in DCC front organisations. Among those to go were General Kat Liebenberg and C. P. van der Westhuizen. One other senior officer, Lt. Gen. Georg Meiring survived to become Defence Force chief only to be condemned in April 1998 by a judicial commission.

Steyn found that that the DCC had been involved in bribing politicians and carrying out *coups d'état* in the Bantustans, fanning unrest through murder, intimidation and arming political factions, escalating violence to thwart the government's efforts at reform, corruption in illegal arms deals, and 'involvement in planning assassination with great political implications'. Some uncomfortable allegations were made. The British Chemical and Biological Defence establishment was called in to corroborate the allegation that the ANC guerrillas had been using chemical weapons (in fact these had been 'planted' by the South African army). It was reported, with what accuracy it cannot be said (although the implication of Belgian ministers at the highest level in corrupt activities has since been clearly signalled) that the Chief of Staff of the Belgian Defence Force could make available $US10 million for DCC operations.

But at once the most sinister, and the most vigorous, of the secret operations were those of Wouter Basson. The son of an Afrikaner police colonel, Basson qualified in medicine before joining the army, where he was rapidly promoted to brigadier by the age of 30. Although he continued to practise, once acting as President Botha's private physician, Basson's main activity was in biological and chemical weapons research. The Seventh Medical Battalion became notorious for its application of such methods in South African border wars, especially in Angola, but the research was carried out in two facilities near Pretoria. Steyn commented that 'an elimination group, under Dr Brigadier Wouter Basson', comprising ex-members of a group previously run by Charl Naude, of the 'Spes Magte' (Special Forces), had been in charge of all the Defence Force assassination attempts; and Dr Basson shows no signs of going away.

An article in the London *Observer* of 7 June 1998 reported:

> The South African military scientist in charge of the former apartheid regime's top-secret chemical and biological warfare programme used a network of British business contacts to amass a personal fortune, the *Observer* can reveal.
>
> Brigadier Wouter Basson, a 47-year-old physicist, is now reviled in South Africa after details emerged of his role in the weapons programme.
>
> South African prosecutors have visited Britain to investigate his network of contacts. Last week a former major, in British intelligence admitted receiving payments of £2.5 million transferred into a bank account in his name, by a company Basson controlled.
>
> The international investigation is trying to trace £30 million which was to be spent in Europe under the guise of Project Coast – a top-secret scheme, led by Basson, to acquire materials to make chemical and biological weapons in the dying years of apartheid.
>
> Basson has been called to give evidence about the project this week at the Truth and Reconciliation Commission hearings in Cape Town. Scientists working under Basson developed special poisons to cause heart failure, cancer and sterility in the black population. One aim was to develop devices to kill opponents of apartheid without trace.
>
> These included poisoned T-shirts designed to kill student

activists and screwdrivers fitted with 'micro-needles' filled with deadly chemicals. Brutal experiments were carried out on live baboons and dogs. One of the most extraordinary plans was a scheme to develop a pill to turn whites into blacks, enabling the 'master race' to infiltrate the ranks of the enemy.

Basson faces criminal charges alleging that he siphoned millions of pounds from Project Coast into his personal accounts. Last summer prosecutors from South Africa's Office of Serious Economic Fraud interviewed a number of British executives about his activities in this country.

Basson ran a network of front companies based with their accounts in the UK, Luxembourg, Belgium, Switzerland and Croatia. These were set up to acquire chemical weapons technology.

Among his British contacts was Major Roger Buffham, a former bomb disposal expert who worked for military intelligence and is now head of security at the Jockey Club.

Basson ran the South African Army's Seventh Medical Battalion. But his role went far beyond medicine. He and his scientists worked on projects that are incredible to Western researchers. In one of the most bizarre schemes, three chimpanzees were used in experiments to make black women infertile.

The infertility programme was headed by Daan Goosen, 47, a respected vet and pathologist. Goosen was managing director of a South African Defence Force front company, Roodeplaats Research Laboratories. 'The chimps were a cover for developing an anti-fertility vaccine,' said Goosen, 'I was told the growing black population was the overwhelming threat to white South Africa. The anti-fertility project was approved by the South African Defence Force at the highest levels.'

Animal rights groups also claim that organophosphates were tested on live animals, often young baboons and dogs, so researchers could see how long it took them to die.

One of the most lethal devices said to have been developed

was a fence combining barbed wire and a deadly charge of electricity to enable police to erect mobile barricades around rioters.

After a series of security leaks in the early 1990s, the South African Defence Force's counter-intelligence service began investigating Basson. Project Coast was closed down at the end of 1992. Basson left the army months later.

Following the Truth Commission's hearings, Basson is expected to go before a criminal court to answer the fraud charges.

He is also accused of trying to sell 1,000 Ecstasy tablets to undercover police. It is alleged that government laboratories manufactured up to a ton of the drug at a secret laboratory near Pretoria.

The very great sums of money, lavishly dispensed, over many years, bought South Africa many loyal supporters in Europe, among all ranks of society. In Geneva, for example, the police ensured that copies of all faxes that might interest the South African intelligence services were routinely delivered to them. In London members of the Metropolitan Police, unable to rid themselves of the idea that other white policemen having to deal with recalcitrant blacks must be in the right, were in regular contact with the police representative, Brigadier Fourie, in the South African High Commission. And, naturally, excellent contacts had been built up with the various intelligence services in different countries. Throughout Europe a network of informers, collaborators, agents and sympathisers had been built up, well funded to a degree that made official intelligence services peevishly envious, and completely lacking inhibitions. Anything went in the service of such generous paymasters.

Friendly relations with European banks were earnestly cultivated by the Nationalist government, with particular energy in the sanctions-beating campaign. One example was the development of laser-boring techniques in South Africa, which enabled gun-barrels to be bored with exceptional accuracy, replacing the traditional method of horizontal-boring on a lathe (one company in Sheffield was, as late as 1980, still producing guns for the British Army on a machine first installed in 1869).

The South African process resulted in barrels of great strength which could take nuclear warheads. Through Bank Banesto in Madrid a deal was negotiated with the notorious arms dealer Carlos Cardoen in Chile to sell the manufacturing rights, which were then used in production of the G5 and G6 howitzers; payment was transmitted to South Africa through Bank Banesto. Factories in Italy produced ammunition and such useful items as cluster bombs for South Africa with full official approval. All, of course, in contravention of the internationally agreed sanctions. In Switzerland Fritz Leutwiler, previously chairman of the Bank for International Settlements, proved a staunch friend.

The illegality of so many of these activities had led to very large sums of money being squirrelled away, both personally and by institutions. Protecting these overseas assets was naturally a vital priority of the Afrikaner financial community and any threat to their safety provoked quick and violent reactions. When Julian Askin's suspicions that he had been cheated by the South African financial institutions were known to be leading him to investigate these activities and would possibly expose the continuing role of outwardly respectable bankers in maintaining the unprincipled systems of the apartheid era, he became a dangerous man.

Once secure in an Italian prison an accusation of fraud, however flimsy and unconvincing, would be enough to procure his extradition to South Africa, where he could be dealt with in the manner of which that country's security forces had become famous. So, at least, it was judged, and given the money so liberally dispensed in Italy, as in other countries, by successive South African governments, rightly judged. However weak the legal case might be, enough individuals had been suborned to override legalities: and there was particular urgency in this case. Much past scandal had already been uncovered but Askin might be able to prove how the financial conspiracy continued under the new multi-racial government that had come to power in 1994.

All these activities, clandestine and open, absorbed huge sums of public money which had to be disposed of and accounted for (in so far as any accounts were kept) away from scrutiny: and all this was funnelled through the Broederbond bank, Volkskas. And Volkskas was by 1992 the leading constituent of the new Afrikaner bank, Absa, with a former Armscor and Volkskas director, Dr Daniel Christiaan Cronjé, a Broeder in good standing, about to take control.

CHAPTER TWO

Caveat Investor

A palpable exaltation

In January 1989, when Julian Askin first thought seriously about a considerable investment in South Africa, that country did not present much attraction to potential investors. Conscription, necessary to assist in quelling urban violence and in the military adventures in Angola and Namibia, was deeply unpopular. The financial costs of armed intervention, and of the genuine, if belated attempts at reform, were crippling. As part of the 'Total Strategy' Botha's government planned to provide such services as the country could afford equally to everyone irrespective of race. Such tinkering with the infrastructure of apartheid cut little ice internationally. Responding to growing demands for economic sanctions international pressure increased as South Africa's few remaining friends were reluctantly obliged to take such action.

American and British investors had been pulling out with increasing frequency since 1984, when President Botha's promises of real reforms appeared to be postponed. One famous speech, in August 1985, announced with some hyperbole as the occasion when the President would formally declare his intention of 'Crossing the Rubicon', turned out to be nothing of the sort. It was followed immediately by the Chase Manhattan Bank's announcement of its refusal to renew a large loan. The South African government was obliged to reschedule – i.e. delay – repayments of its foreign borrowings. Economic growth, which had been positive, although erratic, promptly went into reverse. International banks began to desert the country. Barclays Bank, still the biggest international bank in South Africa, had already, obedient to Nationalist dictates that no major bank should be controlled from abroad, sold a majority interest to South African shareholders. In November 1986 Barclays London completed its disinvestment by selling off the remaining 40 per cent of its South African company, then restructured as the First National Bank of South Africa (FNB), owned 25 per cent by the Southern Life Association and 22.5 per cent by Anglo-American; in this way some of the original political liberalism and international sympathies of the original bank were maintained. A few months later FNB obliged Citicorp of America (First National City Bank of New York) by taking over its South African subsidiary. At about the same time the London Standard and Chartered Bank sold the remaining 39 per cent shareholding in their South African bank at a very considerable loss. The new Standard Bank was tightly controlled, with two assurance companies, Liberty Life holding 30 per cent and the Old Mutual 20 per cent, and Goldfields of South Africa and Rembrandt owning 10 per cent each.

Whilst other foreign bankers were quickly disinvesting after the Rubicon disappointment, the Swiss, always reliable allies of the rich, rushed to support their Afrikaner friends in government. Fritz Leutwiler, president of the Swiss National Bank and the Bank for International Settlements, hastened to Pretoria on hearing the news of South Africa's forced debt rescheduling. Quite specifically, loyal ally of apartheid that he was, Leutwiler did not suggest asking for any political change as a quid pro quo for his support.

In spite of a rise in the price of gold, still the most positive factor, the South African economy was held together only by the energetic negotiations of the Finance Minister, Barend du Plessis, which resulted in the agreed postponement of loans due for repayment in 1986–7, in the hope that economic growth might just, with a lot of luck, enable the money to be repaid in by the delayed date of 1990. In that year South Africa would have to find $US7,000 million, but hopes of doing so were disappointed. Once more the economy plummeted, the currency weakened further, and by the end of 1988 the country's foreign reserves had tumbled to a level lower even than that of the tiny former British protectorate of Botswana.

South African banks lurched from crisis to crisis; Nedbank, which alone among the indigenous banks had abandoned the secretive practice of keeping hidden reserves off its balance sheet, found itself in serious trouble immediately after President Botha's disappointing Rubicon speech. Succumbing to government pressure the bank had made imprudent loans to Triomf Fertilizers, a company controlled by the belligerent Afrikaner, Louis Luyt, whose R13 million 'borrowed' from Eschel Rhoodie had not been enough to keep the inaptly named Triomf afloat, although Luyt himself survived. With the connivance of the managing director of Nedbank, Rob Abrahamsen, Triomf's real position was concealed from Nedbank's board, and Luyt continued to borrow increasingly large sums. By the time Triumf collapsed, in 1986, Nedbank was probably owed R330 million: the shareholders' funds at that time were R534 million. Nedbank had compounded its bad judgement by overextending its foreign assets. In September 1985 the bank found itself unable to honour its commitments and had to close its New York office. Nedbank was soon bailed out by the giant insurance society, the Old Mutual, underwriting a R350 million share issue. This was, of course, publicly revealed but further assistance from the South African Reserve Bank was not. Luyt went on with a conspicuous public career, in the course of which he was able to borrow more money from Nedbank's rival, Volkskas, which was soon itself forced to look to the South African Reserve Bank for help. They did not look in vain, for the Reserve Bank was by then entirely under the sway of the Broederbond.

One of the protective devices put in place as part of the many efforts to defend the South African currency had been the creation of a two-tier exchange rate which, combined with strict currency controls, it was hoped might stem the flow of money abroad. The 'Financial Rand', intended to be both a form of currency control and an incentive to foreign investors, was made available at a discount to the normal 'Commercial Rand', which had to be used by South Africans for all international payments. South African residents wishing to invest abroad but denied access to the Financial Rand were therefore placed at a substantial disadvantage. In bad times the difference could be as much as 50 per cent, and the late 1980s were bad times indeed.

The effect of these restrictions was twofold. On the one hand foreign investors had the opportunity to make substantial profits. They could buy a gilt-edged South African government stock yielding say, 15 per cent, and receive, with the Rand discounted at 50 per cent, some 22.5 per cent on the investment, and if an investor was borrowing Swiss francs at 6 per cent the profits could be enormous. In this way South African borrowing abroad could be maintained, subject only to the usual exchange rate risks.

Conversely, South African residents had to obtain Reserve Bank permission to invest abroad, permission which was rarely given – unless, as it later became apparent, there were political reasons for so doing. The effective premium that had to be paid by South Africans led to the predictable outcome that such investors would do everything in their power to avoid paying so much over the odds. Currency control evasion became a national preoccupation, concealment was endemic; the best methods of investing abroad without informing the authorities were eagerly discussed in clubs, outside churches, and at every social occasion. Lawyers touted among their clients new and ingenious devices for avoiding the law without getting caught, and the less scrupulous simply ignored legal requirements. Legally and illegally, thousands of millions of rand left South Africa for safer foreign havens. Some offenders were charged, and severely punished. Henry Harper and Alan Young of the African Bank got fourteen years for exchange control contravention, but it is significant that these were English-speakers employed by a non-Afrikaner bank. Effectively, Broeders were exempt from exchange control.

In January 1989 the intransigent 'Great Crocodile', President Botha, had a stroke, and resigned his office as Prime Minister. Almost his last act before going was to sign an agreement ridding South Africa of its extremely costly – in both human and financial terms – involvement in Angola and Namibia, an agreement which did much to restore South Africa's international reputation. The establishment of Namibia, formerly South-West Africa, as an independent country had been a result of the end of the cold war, which had also enabled the USA and USSR to put a stop to their support of the opposing parties in Angola. When, in the autumn of 1989 the Berlin Wall was demolished, the events which led to German unification the following year and the dissolution of the USSR in 1991 were well under way. Soviet imperialism could no longer be regarded as a challenge to South Africa. The previous July, Botha had admitted to Hank Cohen, the American Assistant Secretary for African Affairs, what he would never have dared to say in public: 'Unless we bring in blacks as full partners, the country won't be fit for my grandchildren.'

The problem which successive apartheid governments had brought upon themselves was that they had imprisoned or banned every opposition leader and party with any real clout. Only the Zulu Chief Mangosuto Buthelezi, highly suspect in the eyes of most non-Zulus, had contrived to remain on reasonable terms with the authorities (partly by co-operating with the government's secret death squads). The only possible partner retaining international credibility with whom a solution could be negotiated was Nelson Mandela, still imprisoned after 26 years. But Mandela would consent to be freed only on his own terms, admitted as 'a full partner' and without renouncing the option of violent resistance. It took until February 1990 before this, the start of a new South Africa, was brought about.

Julian Askin remembers that moment:

> Susie and I were staying at Ston Easton Hotel near Bath in Somerset when we heard the news. We turned on the television, opened a bottle of champagne, and toasted the grand old man as he walked to freedom. Millions remember where they were when John F. Kennedy was murdered: I will retain an equal, undying memory of this moment. The crowds were massive, the expectation huge, heightened by the delay in his appearance. Eventually he emerged with Winnie and walked into a world whose collective fascination and joy was unlike anything I had known. It was mesmerising. The sense of elation was palpable: one of the most famous events of the twentieth century was being enacted before our eyes. We were excited and optimistic. I turned to Susie and said 'they can't stop him now. It's irreversible. It is this that now makes South Africa a place to invest.'

Whilst a wave of euphoria swept the rest of the world, reactions in South Africa were mixed. For thirty years Nationalist propaganda had portrayed Mandela's ANC as a tool of the communists; a speedy recantation was therefore needed. In truth the ANC's official views had never been more radical than a moderate Christian Socialism, somewhat to the right of the British Labour party of that era. Some of its most active members were indeed communists, including Joe Slovo, whose wife

Ruth First had been murdered by the South African security forces, and Chris Hani, later assassinated by a pair of right-wing extremists, but with the developing entente between the USA and USSR the debate was becoming academic. The PAC, more extreme and violent, with their cry of 'one settler, one bullet', were finding themselves marginalised, whilst at the other extreme the Zulu Inkatha were collaborating willingly with the Nationalists.

President F. W. de Klerk, who succeeded Botha, had at that time no intention of allowing direct majority rule, envisaging rather some form of entrenched protection for minorities as had been inserted into the constitution of Zimbabwe. Given the much larger minorities in South Africa, where over a quarter of the total population were white, Coloured, or Indian, such an aim did not seem unrealistic, and it took over four years and a great deal more bloodshed before it was abandoned. When that eventually occurred, in April 1994, and political power passed into the hands of a black majority, the levers of economic power remained still firmly in white hands. But in February 1990, although both white right-wingers and militant blacks harboured suspicions, optimism was widespread.

Formation of an entrepreneur

By 1989 Askin was already something of an old Africa hand. Born in 1948, his father, an Irish Guards officer, had left when Julian was only two years old. Attending King's School, Bruton, an ancient foundation (dating from 1519, before Henry VIII's dissolution of the monasteries, and therefore one of the last English medieval schools) in a beautiful small Somerset town, Askin did well both athletically and academically. He played at Junior Wimbledon in 1967, represented his school in rugby, hockey, athletics and boxing (he later fought under Amateur Boxing Association rules, and never lost a fight). On at least one occasion Askin proved his ability to look after himself. Simon Fuller, a younger contemporary remembers an incident when 'Jungle Jules' Askin stood up to the leader of a gang of violent youths and knocked him through the windows of the 'Blue Ball' in the High Street. Admitted to the

London School of Economics, one of the most distinguished parts of the University of London, Askin spent only a term at that notorious hotbed of radicalism. With student unrest about to culminate in the May 1968 disturbances in Paris, the LSE was even more left-wing than usual. It was not an environment in which young Askin felt comfortable. With his sporting and literary tastes he would have been more at home in an Oxbridge college. Business was, he considered, about creating wealth or, more vulgarly, making money, a sentiment with which John Maynard Keynes would doubtless have agreed. Very quickly, he saw the merits of striking off on his own.

In 1969 Askin moved to Johannesburg, working for the Schlesinger organisation, before returning to Britain. Rightly identifying the energy industries as offering unparalleled opportunities he worked for a company servicing North Sea Oil rigs before joining Graham Beck who was beginning to be identified as South Africa's leading participant in the coal industry. This job took Askin to the USA for the first time. But the pull of Africa was too strong to resist, and by the end of the seventies Askin had returned to Johannesburg, displaying a new talent as a journalist. *Finance Week*'s fortnightly column 'Only Askin' was a perceptively satirical commentary on South African finance and industry whose characters became famous. One of his victims was Laurie Goldberg – 'Tryon' – and Askin's caricatures were sufficiently accurate to drive Goldberg from the country. His first novel, *The Gold Connection*, published with the encouragement of Robin Moore, famous for his book and film *The French Connection*, employs the device of thinly disguised personalities vying with a number of aptly described real ones, (although Askin had to go in person to extract his royalties from a reluctant Moore). Appearing on TV, Askin became a well-known and, although not in certain quarters, popular figure.

It was at the house of one of Askin's friends, Jamie Inglis the head of the insurance company Liberty Life's investment division, that Askin met his future business partner, Hugo Biermann. Born into the Afrikaner purple, son of Admiral Biermann, head of the South African Defence Force, and godson of the Great Crocodile, P. W. Botha, Hugo was described as 'a perfect foil for the brilliant, volatile Askin'. The two young men were able to do very well procuring strategic supplies for South Africa during the United Nations embargo. This was arranged by their firm Intertechnic, the South African agent for the Swiss arms firm Oerlikon Buhrle (which, interestingly enough, had its offices in the South African Reserve Bank building). Biermann had shared student rooms at Stellenbosch University with Mervyn Key, who was to play a prominent role, and was part of his circle.

With the establishment of Thatcherism in Britain the opportunities in the London market attracted Askin and Biermann there, where Julian met Susie Wilson. Susie, the only daughter of a prosperous stockbroker and a staunchly Presbyterian Scotswoman, had developed clear ideas of what she wanted to do after leaving Croydon Girls' High School, which was to make a career in fashion. Following the advice of her realistic parents, she spent a year in Switzerland learning French, followed by three years with a couturier learning the whole trade, from measuring and cutting patterns to designing. An early marriage to a young merchant banker, Philip Robinson, soon collapsed and was followed by a more rewarding, and considerably more exciting marriage to Max Wilson, sixteen years her senior.

A South African entrepreneur, the restlessly active Wilson was one of those people who made and lost fortunes. Founder of the Overseas Visitors Club, which earned for Earls Court the sobriquet of Kangaroo Valley, and of an airline which became British Caledonian, Wilson converted the *Reina del Mar* into a cruise liner, and built a number of hotels, including one in the Bahamas. While life with Max Wilson was never dull, Susie had found time to build up a useful London property business together with her brother. When Max Wilson died suddenly in 1981 Susie was left with a young daughter, Charlotte, and a business in dire difficulties – Wilson had only emerged from bankruptcy the year previously. These she set about solving, demonstrating great courage and energy in an unfamiliar world: courage and energy were qualities that Susie Askin was to find invaluable in the coming years.

Askin and Biermann's first London venture, into insurance broking and investment management, having been reasonably successful a more profitable opportunity in London was sought. At this time, when instincts for discovering profitable opportunities had been sharpened by the tax reforms (which, for the first time in a generation, removed the restrictions on capital accumulation that had hampered British enterprise), many clever and acquisitive young men were busily trawling the Stock Exchange lists for potential acquisitions. Askin and Biermann began the exhausting business of commuting between Johannesburg and London in pursuit of such an opportunity.

The attraction of finding a company however small, unprofitable, and generally odd that was quoted on a stock exchange, was that it avoided a long wait to procure such a listing. An unquoted company had to produce solid evidence of year on year growth and fulfil many other official requirements before it could obtain such a quotation and thereby access to the public's finance. It was some time and only after many disappointments that Askin and Biermann hit on Thomson T. Line, a manufacturer of wooden caravans in the small Scottish town of Falkirk. On the face of things Thomson T. Line, then losing some £300,000 a year, and with virtually no prospects, was unpromising: but the company's shares were indeed quoted, although very little traded, on the London Stock Exchange. A relatively modest stake enabled the two to buy the company – Askin lending Biermann his share. As soon as it became known that a new management had taken over, and even more so after such a change had produced improved profits, the capital of a company like Thomson T. Line could be expected to shoot up in value. Askin and Biermann did not disappoint their supporters, who included some of the best names in the City of London.

Thomson T. Line shares rose satisfactorily enough, but the real coup came in 1986 when a takeover was agreed of more than £100 million with the Sangster family, owners of Vernon's Pools. The Sangsters retained a small stake in Thomson T. Line and Robert Sangster became a non-executive director. His young and unqualified son Guy was given a job, but Askin and Biermann retained the management of the joint enterprise. Their performance was everything that had been expected. Diversifying the industrial side of Thomson, profits rose to £1.9 million in 1987 and £5.4 million in 1988. After an abortive attempt to merge with a similarly successful company, Suter, Thomson T. Line found themselves in no position to resist a bid from the other large football pools and gaming firm, Ladbrokes.

They did, however, put up a brilliant defence, in the course of which the share value rose to 76 per cent above the prevailing immediate market value, the final sale price being a cash offer of £185.7 million. The Sangster family had made a great deal of money, as had the management and outside shareholders. Ladbrokes' triumph was short-lived, as the launch of the National Lottery in 1995 brought the previously lucrative football gambling industry crashing down and in 1996 Ladbrokes found it prudent to write off their whole interest in Vernon's Pools.

Now several million pounds the richer after the sale of Thomson T. Line, the Askins were planning a return to South Africa. Both Julian and Susie loved the magnificent scenery of the Cape Peninsula and the more relaxed society of the Western Cape, something of a backwater compared to Johannesburg and its intense pressures. They had already found what might well be the finest site near the city, a six-acre plot on Rhodes Drive, Constantia, with magnificent views to the Cape Flats and the Hottentot Hollands mountains, sheltered by the slopes of Table Mountain. Susie had decided to replace the existing house with a faithful replica of a Cape Dutch homestead, using traditional materials, original wherever possible, and work was already well underway on what was to become a centre of Cape Town social life, Steenhuis.

Askin had already identified one South African company as a likely candidate for acquisition. This was Tollgate, an old established firm recently re-organised by a couple of energetic entrepreneurs, Mervyn Key and Johan Claasen. One of the Johannesburg Stock Exchange's largest companies, Tollgate had a turnover of R1,000 million and employed over 20,000 people; it also possessed the essential advantage of a secondary quotation on the London Stock Exchange.

Julian Askin's previous success in the City of London had left him with the enthusiastic backing of some well-known British investors, delighted at the profits he had made for them. Any opportunities that Askin might present would be assured of at least close attention from these institutions. With their support Tollgate, deploying its advantage in having shares traded on the London Stock Exchange, could acquire earnings in sterling and other hard currencies, funded from London – and South African shareholders were avidly searching for opportunities to invest abroad.

Hampered by the exchange controls, the only legal way South Africans had been able to protect their stock market investments against the falling value of their own currency was to buy shares in those companies quoted on the Johannesburg Stock Exchange which had substantial foreign earnings. The shares of such companies, which included such important organisations as Anton Rupert's Rembrandt tobacco company and Liberty Life, together with the overwhelmingly powerful Anglo-American Corporation, commanded substantial premiums over those other shares which were backed only by South African rand earnings, premiums commonly of as much again as 50 per cent. Given their quotation on the London Stock Exchange and some British acquisitions, Tollgate shares could well provide such a premium, effectively handing over a similar profit to any investor.

The Johannesburg Stock Exchange is something of an oddity. It is internationally important, the eleventh largest in the world, ranking just after Hong Kong in terms of market capitalisation, and bigger than all other African exchanges put together. But its size is overwhelmingly due to the preponderance of a few very large institutions. The Oppenheimer family's Anglo-American Corporation alone accounts for more than 40 per cent of the total capital of quoted companies. Sanlam owns another 12 per cent, Anton Rupert's Rembrandt Group 10 per cent, with the Old Mutual, Liberty Group and Anglovaal bringing the total to over three quarters of the stock market in the control of six groups. Deceptively few publicly quoted companies remained as possible purchases, and Tollgate indeed then represented the only sizeable industrial company with the vital asset of a London quote.

Although such firms as Anglo-American doubtless maintained high standards of professionalism and probity, the conditions imposed by the Johannesburg Stock Exchange did not insist on such rigorous requirements, being in this and most other respects considerably laxer than those of London or New York. A peculiarity of the Johannesburg exchange was that pyramids of company holdings were widespread. It was common in this way for a bloc of share-holding in one public company to control another publicly quoted company, and so on, enabling a relatively small shareholding effectively to exercise influence over very considerable assets. The requirements to produce information for shareholders were, by comparison with those in the USA or Britain, minimal. Especially in such sensitive areas as director's emoluments, contracts, and shareholdings, South African companies' annual reports were silent. This was even more so with banks, where at that time very little indeed had to be reported to shareholders. Nor are South African accountancy firms, even those associated with such great international names as Coopers or Price Waterhouse, accustomed to so strict an adherence to the best professional practice. Conflicts of interest and downright malpractice were commonplace and eventually led to scathing judicial condemnations of the whole profession. While therefore Julian Askin could count himself fortunate in having identified so likely a target as Tollgate, warning signals of *caveat emptor* were certainly flashing. But there was little else to choose from, since so many publicly quoted companies had major institutional shareholders unlikely to be willing sellers.

Partners

At the beginning of 1990 Tollgate Holdings was controlled by another South African company, Duros, owning 68 per cent of the share capital. Duros itself was something of an oddity; as late as 1987 it was quoted on the Johannesburg stock exchange as a furniture maker, much declined from its previous eminence as a supplier to the British royal family. Its directors included one Lawrence Miller, senior partner of the solicitors Miller, Gruss, Katz and Traub, who was well known for his ingenuity in arranging offshore investments. According to one press report, Duros' shareholders were 'desperate to sell', and Miller introduced the purchasers. These were initially Christo Wiese, Gordon Verhoef, a friend of Miller's, and David McCay, shortly afterwards joined by Mervyn Key and Laurie Mackintosh. The intention was to transform the company into a financial services and investment company, which it did well enough to be congratulated by the London *Investors Chronicle* as 'singularly successful' as early as August 1988.

Key and Claasen formed an effective partnership; Key ebullient and plausible, floridly good-looking, an astute lawyer ready to sail very close to the wind indeed, Claasen withdrawn, controlled but equally ready to take risks. Both men, then in their late thirties, had been fellow students, with Wiese, at Stellenbosch University. English South Africans usually sought admission to such universities as Wits in Johannesburg or UCT in Cape Town, but Stellenbosch, an Afrikaans-language institution had become popular among some English-speakers ambitious to find a place in the Afrikaner business world, where a knowledge of the language had become a shibboleth. As an Afrikaner, Johan Claasen had a built-in advantage over the English-speaking Keys and had made his way rapidly through the management of the Broederbond-controlled bank, Volkskas, to become senior General Manager of the Volkskas Industrial Bank. Before joining Volkskas he had served with Sanlam Bank, part of the Cape Afrikaner Sanlam group: animosity persisted between Cape and Transvaal Afrikaners and the move to Volkskas was something of a cultural shift. But Claasen made a name for himself throughout the Afrikaner community by arranging a visit of the New Zealand All Blacks rugby team, financing the tour and making substantial loans to the Ellis Park Rugby Stadium. Leaving Volkskas early in 1986 Claasen had branched out on his own to buy a well-known but ailing hosiery manufacturing company, Arwa. It was an unusual adventure for a banking executive, but Claasen successfully transformed his company into what appeared to be a profitable organisation.

Arwa was a Volkskas customer with an overdraft of some R2 million. When Volkskas refused a request to increase this to R3 million, Claasen took the business to Trust Bank, another Sanlam subsidiary, who proved a good deal more generous. Within a year he was able to obtain a public quotation for Arwa shares, at which time Mervyn Key joined the board. Mervyn Key had been as successful as Claasen in another field, practising as a solicitor in Johannesburg so profitably as to be able to buy Rhebokskloof, one of the most famous Paarl vineyards where he lived in considerable style. Many of his commercial interests had a sporting flavour; as well as his participation in the Ellis Park affair he was involved with the Kyalami motor racing circuit, the site of the South African Grand Prix.

Of the other directors of Duros (Verhoef did not stay long) Christo Wiese was the best known, a future director of the South African Reserve Bank and Sanlam, chairman of both the Boland Bank and Pepkor, a retail group. Laurie Mackintosh, an accountant, had previously been with Arthur Andersen, the famous international firm, but had worked with Mervyn Key for more than twenty years. David McCay was, together with Johan Rupert, a founding director of the Rand Merchant Bank. Describing himself as a 'merchant banker', a conveniently loose term, McCay remained on the board only until November 1988, but continued as a close collaborator of Key and Mackintosh in the affairs of Kyalami. Martin Irish, a Johannesburg stockbroker, and a friend of Key's became a non-executive director of Duros.

Under its new ownership the old furniture company was then reconstructed as a holding company with merchant banking and insurance divisions, operating from Johannesburg, and an embryonic industrial holdings company. This latter was greatly increased as Claasen built up his shareholding in Duros using Arwa paper with McCay's investors contributing Drivetech, an automotive parts distributor which continued to enjoy a Stock Exchange listing. Some smaller unlisted companies were bought. The new board began to look for further acquisitions.

The first major opportunity to present itself, in February 1988, was Tollgate Holdings. This venerable enterprise had started life in 1861 as the Cape Town and Green Point Tramway company, taking in 1896 the bold step of introducing electric trams to replace its horses. In spite of its considerable asset base, the advantage of having had a quotation on the London Stock Exchange since 1948 and respectable earnings, Tollgate was not the most exciting of investments, and was commonly regarded as one of the Johannesburg Stock Exchange 'dogs'. A stake of 49.5 per cent, effectively a controlling interest, was not difficult to obtain. In December of the same year Claasen joined the Duros/Tollgate board as chairman, bringing with him a controlling shareholding in Arwa and Michael Lewis, chairman of Hosken Consolidated Investments. Hosken, an insurance group, was the second largest shareholder in both Arwa and Duros and managed the group's now considerable pension fund. By that time Duros, as well as a developing merchant banking arm, now had control of two major quoted companies, Tollgate and Arwa, plus the shares in Drivetech, with Claasen and Key holding a controlling interest in the whole group.

In order to arrive at this position both men had been obliged to borrow heavily, Key from the First National Bank, where he was on close terms with David Stewart, manager then of the Stock Exchange branch, subsequently of Commissioner Street, the two most important branches in the Johannesburg financial district. Stewart's customers also included Laurie Mackintosh, Michael Lewis and Martin Irish, which made possible some very convenient if somewhat peculiar transactions. Claasen, however, while making use of Stewart's services, continued on good terms with the ever-obliging Trust Bank.

A relative newcomer to South African banking, the Trust Bank of Africa had been established in 1954 as a more adventurous Afrikaner counterpart to the stolid and conservative Volkskas. The Trust Bank had its head office in anglophone Cape Town; between there and Pretoria, the seat of Afrikaner Nationalist government, there was a wide cultural gap. With a creative banker in the shape of Dr Jan Marais at its head the Trust Bank set itself to attract non-Afrikaner business with a 'very glittering "gilt-covered" approach conveying the message of an ultra-modern custom-fit financial approach' in which effort it was assisted by some expensive decor and many beautiful blondes in fashionable mini-skirts. It was at a time when the rapid rise of the Bank of America from an unimportant Italian bank in San Francisco to the biggest bank in the world was attracting many emulators, most of whom were to share in that bank's equally speedy decline.

In spite of its highly visible differences of practice and policy, the Trust Bank was, almost as much as Volkskas, a Broederbond-sponsored enterprise. Its initial sponsor, Federale Mynbou, had been established in 1953 as a merger of two Sanlam-controlled investments: Bonuskor, an industrial investment company, and Federale Volksbeleggings (FVB), the creation of the 1950 Afrikaner Volkscongres. Federale Mynbou's first chairman, Wentzel du Plessis, previously a senior civil servant, had been dismissed by Prime Minister Smuts because of his Broederbond membership. His successor, Dr W. B. Coetzer, together with most of Federale's board, were also Broeders.

As might have been expected Trust Bank's policies led to both rapid growth and its usual concomitant, serious trouble. By 1977 gross over-lending on property transactions had left the bank with virtually no net liquid assets. One such property adventure was to be the trigger for disaster. An English speculator, Bill Mitchell, had acquired some farm land near Hermanus, a popular seaside resort to the east of False Bay, which he had turned at a very considerable profit into plots for holiday cottages, just before the Administrator of Cape Province banned any such further developments which were rapidly ruining the coast-line.

Given the endemic corruption of the Afrikaner Nationalist administration it was not long before that problem was circumvented, and seven new developments were – in secret – approved by the Administrator. All were controlled by Mitchell. Trust Bank, stimulated by the fact that their general manager, Sonny Shar, and the financial director, George Home, had been allocated shares in Mitchell's business, offered to finance potential buyers. Branch managers were encouraged by the award of 'prizes' which included Mercedes cars and holidays in Hong Kong, to persuade their customers to take out loans. Totally unsuitable borrowers who would never have dreamt of owning a house at the seaside, or raising an overdraft, were led to believe that they could re-sell their plots at a huge profit.

This wildly optimistic prospect was sold, for hard cash, to Trust Bank: and it took very little time before the inevitable crash occurred, leaving Trust Bank with many millions of bad debts and a general manager having decided to leave permanently for the USA. Volkskas declined to bail out its deviant fellow-Afrikaners leaving that unpleasant task for the Cape Afrikaner institution Sanlam, to foot the bill. This it did with a bad grace, selling its holding in Volkskas and vowing to take revenge on Volkskas by supplanting them as Afrikanerdom's bank with their own 60 per cent owned subsidiary, the Bank Holding Corporation of South Africa, Bankorp. This was to be the holding company for three banking enterprises; Senbank, (Central Merchant Bank) acting as a merchant bank, Santam Bank, concentrating on consumer finance, and Trust Bank.

In charge of Sanlam at this critical period was the energetic Dr Fred du Plessis, described as 'dominant, ruthless, intolerant, irrationally brilliant', who wanted a conspicuously successful Afrikaner bank. Trust Bank, during the 1980s, was to be forced into rapid growth by any means, always a perilous strategy for a bank, and especially one whose managers had proved themselves corruptible and incompetent. A central part of this strategy was the acquisition of large, often controlling interests in quoted industrial and commercial companies. The fact that the bank was controlled by a mutual insurance company was an added danger. Policy holders' funds would have been more properly spread among low-risk investments, and by no means used to finance an expansionist policy with a potential to devour cash.

By the time Trust Bank began its co-operation with Tollgate, Sanlam had been obliged by Trust Bank's new dash for growth to invest close to R1,000 million in support of Bankorp's balance sheet, increasing its holding to 81 per cent. But by that time, on the face of things, all seemed to be going well; Bankorp's operating profit increased from R56 million to R 87 million and forecasted at least as good a profit for 1988. Trust Bank, which in the early eighties had had to suspend dividend payments, was now able to increase them.

In the earlier days of their relations both Tollgate and Trust Bank insisted on the intimacy of their working practices: it seemed an alternative to downright acquisition might lie in a 'partnership' between bank and customer. In an advertisement published by Trust Bank in March 1989, the General Manager of their Corporate Bank, Koos Morland, was quoted as saying, 'The Oxford Dictionary describes a partnership as those who share with one another in some activity, especially in a business where they share risks and profits. That's especially true of our relationship with Johan Claasen and Mervyn Key. They have no hidden agendas.' Claasen responded by saying, 'I expect a lot from my bank. The old methods and loyalties are a thing of the past.'

This intimacy was to prove essential to the rapid expansion that Claasen and Key intended. In February 1989 the residue of Arwa shares were acquired. The public transport business of Tollgate had been doubled by the acquisition of bus operators United Passenger Transport Investments. This, it was said, expanded the old Cape enterprise into the hinterland and brought with it the Greyhound fleet of buses providing regular services between the major South African cities (and by a brisk bit of financing, the greater part of the purchase price was recovered by a resale of an unwanted part of the business). In July of that year Tollgate claimed that another new venture, Entercor, had a turnover of R45 million. Itself a mini-conglomerate, Entercor comprised public relations and advertising agencies, a film producer, the South African Greyhound coaches, the Budget car rental franchise, a safari company, and, perhaps most interesting, a long lease of the Kyalami motor racing circuit through Motor Racing Enterprises (MRE).

Another major acquisition was 25 per cent of the share holding in Gants, an important food processor in the Cape, an industry which had suffered considerably under anti-apartheid sanctions, but which stood to regain its previous position as the world's largest exporter of tinned fruit once these were lifted – and this seemed to be clearly possible quite soon. By May 1989 this share-holding had been expanded to complete control of the company. Buying these companies increased pressure on Tollgate's cash-flow both in the costs of acquisition and in the very considerable collateral debt that was assumed. The Gants family, for example, owed R160 million to their bankers – chiefly Volkskas; Motorvia was borrowing R140 million from the Trust Bank and both these debts were transferred to Tollgate – in addition to the R60 million cash Tollgate had already paid to the vendors. And all this expenditure was before embarking upon the vital capital expenditure needed in many of the poorly equipped plants to say nothing of the 2,500 buses owned by Tramway Holdings requiring programmed replacement. By the end of 1989 Duros/Tollgate had liabilities to their bankers of nearly R400 million.

There was no industrial logic in putting such enterprises as Gants under the same management as the other components of the Tollgate group. Some clout could be given to that merger only by suggesting that since Gants Holdings also included an agricultural machinery distributor, this might be managed alongside the existing Tramways subsidiary of Drivetech (which supplied and manufactured automotive parts), Motech (builder of bus bodies for the Tramways company), and Multimech (servicing heavy commercial vehicles). It was feeble reasoning and Tollgate remained a hodge-podge of disconnected parts: the transport businesses were a logical unit but had no relevance to holdings in hosiery manufacture or food processing.

More significant seemed to be the personal advantages to some of the directors. Claasen (by disposing of Arwa) and David Gant, (whose remaining share holding – the family had sold just under half its 53 per cent of stock to Tollgate – was performing very sluggishly), had both been able to reduce their extensive bank borrowings by the cash proceeds of their sales. Very considerable advantages also accrued to the lending banks: Volkskas' executives were greatly relieved to have precarious individuals, with few remaining assets, replaced by public companies.

In March 1989, nine months into the company's financial year, due to end in June, the Tollgate board felt sufficiently sure of their prospects to arrange for the journal *Finance Week* to publish a 56-page supplement. Based upon unaudited figures to 31 December 1988 the tone was extremely optimistic. Earnings per share were forecast to rise from 20 cents to 50 cents for the current year, while Arwa profits before tax of R20 million were forecast. 'Don't attribute it to good fortune,' the leading article declared, 'as much as to clear design ... Duros has quickly grown into an oak tree of an industrial-financial conglomerate.' Johan Claasen was compared to Chrysler's Lee Iacocca for his 'rescue' of Arwa:

> ... turnarounds require an unlikely combination of skills. The cool-headed planning abilities of the professional man- ager have to be merged with an entrepreneur's enthusiasm and risk profile: determination, ruthlessness, compassion, charisma and a successful gambler's instinct for timing are all vital ingredients.
>
> Acquisitions, on the other hand, require a completely dif- ferent set of skills. What's needed here is the ability to analyse an industry, strategic vision, financial skills and a sensitivity to people's needs.
>
> It's a rare person who combines these talents, let alone can translate them into a model for the SA manufacturing industry. Yet this is precisely what Johan Claasen did.

In the same issue of *Finance Week* Dennis Shepherd, managing direc- tor of Arwa, was reported as 'confidently' predicting 'sustainable earn- ings growth' of 30 per cent on the current year. In reasonably sophisticated financial circles such forecasts are made with considerable care and taken seriously, but to have done so with Tollgate would have been an error. The – again unaudited – 12-month results to June 1989 showed a somewhat less exciting picture. Very high depreciation and interest had still resulted in a profit before tax of R27 million, in line with the first-half figures, but increases in extraordinary losses and outside shareholders' interests forced the retained profit down from R9.5 million for six months to R6.7 million for the year: yet earnings per share could be, and were, presented as 84 cents per share compared with 24.2 cents for the half-year (and, ominously, 31.7 cents for the previous, audited, full year). With current borrowing running at R175 million there was a total of R58 million of net current liabilities – and both the shareholdings of the directors and their borrowings were dangerously high.

Nor was all well within the management. Recognising that neither Mervyn Key nor Johan Claasen had the time or talents to instal proper management reporting procedures and procure financial discipline within so widely varied an enterprise, they had recruited a senior executive with the necessary qualifications, Hendrik Gerhardus Diedericks, generally known as Hennie.

Forty-seven years old in 1989, Diedericks was the exemplar of a self-made, respectable, upright, middle-class Afrikaner, an elder of the Dutch Reformed Church, a member in good standing of the Broederbond, married with three children. Joining Trust Bank straight from school at Nylstroom, a small town in the Northern Transvaal (named by Boer pioneers who believed they had discovered the River Nile) and working his way through college in his spare time, he moved rapidly upwards in Trust Bank, becoming head of the investment and savings division at the very early age of twenty-four. In 1978 Diedericks moved to Volkskas and again did well, working in the corporate finance division before becoming a senior general manager in 1984. At forty-two, he was an established figure in Afrikaner banking. It was then that he was invited to become a Broeder, which he regarded as a signal honour and accepted with alacrity.

Running the business of Volkskas in the stormy days that followed was a challenging task. He was working at Volkskas under a younger man, Dr Danie Cronjé, a more ambitious and aggressive character from a more privileged background, and with a considerably wider outside experience, Diedericks felt that he could do better in the more flexible world outside Afrikaner banking.

In August 1988 Diedericks was invited by Johan Claasen to become Managing Director (besturende direkteur) of Tollgate Holdings. Chairman Claasen retained full responsibility for Arwa, very much his own baby, while Mervyn Key managed the day to day affairs of Entercor and Laurie Mackintosh ran Motorvia.

Diedericks described himself as the paid official (betaalde amptenaar) on a five-year contract. With only a modest shareholding, he shared little of the controlling directors' ambition – or their willingness to take risks and to engage, as it turned out, in doubtfully legal activities. His job was to ensure that the machine ran smoothly and that effective management controls were put in place – not, given the character of the principal shareholders, an easy task. On the face of things Duros/ Tollgate offered exciting prospects. At the financial year end of June 1988 Duros owned 49.5 per cent of Tollgate, both businesses being separately listed on the Johannesburg Stock Exchange. Owning less than 50 per cent, Duros did not have to consolidate Tollgate in its own balance sheet, and was therefore able to omit that group's borrowings, which, since these stood at some R70 million, was a wel- come relief.

Diedericks' confidence in his new position was bolstered when he was made aware of the close relationship the company enjoyed with his former bank. When later he collated his recollections of the time in a careful affidavit, he recorded:

> Right from the outset it was made clear to me by both Trust Bank officials and by Claasen that they were in partnership with the Tollgate Group and that they had chosen Tollgate Holdings as a vehicle to position Trust Bank in the corporate market . . . This was confirmed to me by the managing direc- tor of Trust Bank, Mr Kobus Roets in discussions with me . . . These assurances as to partnership with the Trust Bank were confirmed on many occasions. In each and every takeover which had taken place Mr Claasen had negotiated the financing and obtained it without difficulty . . . There is no doubt at all that the relationship . . . was one of a very intimate financial partnership. Trust Bank were fully in the picture as to precisely what was happening in the Tollgate Group. Partly as a result of this close relationship, no security for the borrowings was either demanded by Trust Bank or offered by the Tollgate group. In my view any other bank would have insisted on full security.

It was indeed an unprecedented, and highly unprofessional state of affairs. Banks may well make foolish decisions, carried away by enthusiasm for some favourite entrepreneur and often fail to ensure that proper security is maintained, but at least they make the effort to convince themselves that such transactions are at arm's length. But Trust Bank, according to Diedericks, offered their loans at very low rates, and on the clear understanding that these would be repaid only by ultimate conversion into equity and long-term funding. And the sums involved were, by Trust Bank standards, immense. In 1989 the total advances of Trust Bank were just short of R12,000 million; their loans to Tollgate, described as 'a movable feast', could be as much as R600 million, or 5 per cent of the bank's total lending and a sum somewhat in excess of its capital (then R579 million) – and all without any real security. This was a quite extraordinarily lax performance, even by Trust Bank's previous perilous standards. Years later, Marinus Daling the chief executive of Sanlam, admitted that all Tollgate's problems stemmed from the too-rapid expansion of 1989–90 – an expansion expressly encouraged by Sanlam.

Such support was a powerful incentive to lavish spending by the Tollgate board, and the rapid expansion that took place in the financial year 1988–9 severely strained both the balance sheets and the management systems of the companies, which Diedericks was then attempting to install. Between June 1987 and June 1988, although Tollgate's income went up from R145 million to R205 million, the profit before tax actually declined slightly, and, ominously the long term loans, all from the company's bankers, rose from R3 million to R36 million. Creditors also took some of the pain by a substantial increase in net current liabilities. Furthermore, Diedericks discovered that there were a number of irregularities in many of the Duros/Tollgate accounts which the other directors could not explain. The auditors, the international firm of Price Waterhouse, shared Diedericks' concern and there was some doubt that they would be prepared to certify the accounts for the year due to end on June 1989. Under this pressure, the accounting period was prolonged for another six months to December 1989 and the accounts were certified without qualification.

Diedericks however remained convinced that the results even at the extended year-end were likely to be so poor that the directors would have to omit the payment of the usual dividend. This would indeed normally have been the prudent course of action, but would have had a drastic effect on the share price and the other directors with their large shareholdings would have found their banks, deprived of the security for their loans, clamouring for repayment. Claasen personally owed Trust Bank some R32 million, covered to a great extent by his shareholdings in Duros/Tollgate. Diedericks made the non-executive directors conscious of these facts. Michael Lewis remembered his meeting with a 'very determined' Diedericks, who 'spoke openly of a capital restructure', the need to find new avenues of finance, other bankers, and concluded 'We will have to pass the dividend, Michael. We need to conserve our resources and admit our situation.' Lewis telephoned the other non-executive director, Martin Irish, 'insisting on an immediate discussion' at which Diedericks reiterated his concern.

A week or two later a meeting was held at the Trust Bank's offices between Koos Morland and Gerbie Strydom of the Trust Bank and Diedericks, Irish and Lewis, at which Diedericks bluntly told the bankers that Tollgate was insolvent. Irish recalled that 'faces went white' and 'reaction was vivid'. The following day senior Tollgate executives joined a board meeting at which the Trust Bank officials were also present. This, it should be said, was in itself so unusual a step as to underline the very special relationship which existed between the board of Duros/ Tollgate and its bankers. Bank representatives may well be called into board meetings to consult on specific issues, but it was customary in Duros/Tollgate to have full joint meetings with Trust Bank representatives, which gives support to allegations that the bank officials were indeed acting as 'shadow directors'. The management reports stated that 'losses were mounting' and painted a 'very bleak' picture of an 'incredibly dismal' state of affairs. Both Irish and Lewis were appalled at such an 'astounding revelation' as no such situation had been previously reported to them. Unless the Trust Bank was willing to support Tollgate the continuance of the meeting would be 'a waste of time'. Both men had much to lose: Irish was the company's broker and Lewis chairman of investment companies with large shareholdings in Duros/Tollgate. They therefore demanded the bank's assurance of continued support be given to the company. Much to their surprise, and even more to their relief, the Trust Bank representatives were very relaxed. Morland assured them that there was no need to worry. 'The security we have today is exactly the same security we had yesterday. We are committed to supporting the Group.'

Although this was as firm a declaration of confidence as could be desired, it was apparent that new investment was urgently necessary. When Mervyn Key heard of Julian Askin's possible interest he asked a mutual friend, Alan Greenblo, editor of *Finance Week*, to effect an introduction.

Enter Askin

In October 1989, having acquired all Laurie Mackintosh's and most of Mervyn Key's shares, Claasen controlled over 70 per cent of Tollgate. At the first contact with Askin, Claasen was dismissive. Tollgate's expansion was in full flow and he wanted to remain in charge as an executive chairman. Diedericks took the view that the company was far too highly geared and another R100 million of equity capital – not more borrowing – was needed. Claasen, he said 'did not consider this suggestion particularly attractive but agreed to appoint Finansbank to provide an independent assessment and proposals concerning the capital reconstruction of the group'. Subsequently many discussions took place with Trust Bank on the possible conversion of some of their loans to equity, which came to nothing. Only as the shadows lengthened and the seriousness of the financial situation implacably presented by Diedericks became clear did Claasen resign himself to selling out.

If the same picture had been presented to Julian Askin, it is unlikely that he would have gone any further, but the pig he was being asked to buy was kept firmly in its poke. Mervyn Key was a convincing salesman, and Askin was ready to be convinced. Making a great deal of money, legally and as a result of one's own talents (assisted, naturally, by good luck), tends to induce feelings of unconquerable optimism. Askin was convinced that in South Africa he could reproduce the success he had experienced in London.

By the time Askin and Key got down to serious discussions in December 1989 the near-desperate situation in Duros/Tollgate had become apparent to the board. Irish and Lewis, as non-executive directors, were not involved with the initial negotiations and had expressed themselves satisfied by Trust Bank's assurance of support. Lewis, who as chairman of Hosken represented the second largest shareholder, gave Askin glowing reports of Duros' prospects, but the inconveniently honest Hennie Diedericks was bound to make all his reservations clear to any prospective investor. It was therefore essential to keep Askin away from any contact with him. The fairly specious excuse was given that any visits to the company's headquarters might provoke gossip which could influence the share price: would Mr Askin therefore please discuss any proposals only with the controlling shareholders? Their bankers, Trust Bank of Africa and Volkskas were well known to Askin; he had indeed been a customer of the Johannesburg Bree Street branch of Trust Bank for many years. Both banks agreed that they would be happy to make all the financial information available for Askin's investigations.

It looked a remarkable opportunity. British banks, indeed any respectable banks, are deeply reluctant to disclose their customers' affairs to an outsider, both to protect their customers' interests and – more importantly to the banks – to avoid any charge that, by giving inaccurate information, they might entice the enquirer into a false situation. Bankers' references, therefore, are famously non-committal. In contrast the South African banks went out of their way to reassure Askin of Duros/Tollgate's financial stability. The group, the banks claimed, although highly geared, was doing well; they had complete faith in the management, and would be fully prepared to continue, and even perhaps to increase, the facilities they had extended. After all, both Johan Claasen and Hennie Diedericks had been directors of the banks in question and ran the group in close collaboration with their former colleagues. Mervyn Key's position was clarified in a meeting with one Mr Postmus, head of the South African Reserve Bank's Exchange control department at which Key and two executives from Senbank, the merchant banking affiliate of Trust Bank, were present. Key was given a glowing recommendation by Mr Postmus, who provided Askin with suitably impressive information on the prospects of Tollgate. He also confirmed that Askin would be regarded as a bona fide foreign investor, a necessary qualification in view of the financial proposals which included support from the South African banks. Askin expressed some surprise that so much of Tollgate's debt was in the form of overdrafts without any fixed terms of repayment, but was assured (by Strydom and Morland) that the bank did not require any such agreements, the eventual intention being to convert at least part into some form of long-term investment.

With Askin being loaded with such encouraging and, as it turned out, misleading information he could not under any circumstances be allowed to meet Hennie Diedericks who knew the truth of the company's critical situation. Diedericks, it was clear, must speedily be disposed of, particularly since he was making himself more than usually difficult.

Gerbie Strydom of Trust Bank, who had been kept informed of the negotiations with Askin, was being pressed by Diedericks for a meeting in order to discuss a possible solution to Tollgate's financial dilemma. Faced with Strydom's procrastination Diedericks felt he had to go higher, and arranged a meeting with the bank's managing director Chris van Wyk. At the last moment, on 14 March when actually on his way to meet van Wyk, Diedricks was diverted to Key's farm at Rhebokskloof. There, for the first time, he was told of the agreement which had been negotiated. His affidavit states:

> It would now appear that the new incoming shareholder was deliberately prevented from speaking to me in order to prevent him from obtaining first-hand information about my experiences with the Tollgate Group . . . I had the impression at the time (now confirmed) that Messrs Claasen and Key and Trust Bank preferred me not to be involved, especially against the background of my outspoken points of view concerning the way the Tollgate Group should be managed, its capital requirements and my recent experience with Trust Bank. It is also clear to me why the Finanzbank investigation was not completed and the required report not produced . . . From the information now available to me, I can state that there is no doubt that the Askin-led consortium was deliberately misled by Mr Claasen, Trust Bank, Mr Key and Mr Mackintosh by orchestrating the information made available.

That day, at Rhebokskloof, Diedericks was told that he would be sacked and on the next the Askin agreement was signed.

On 15 March 1990, armed with the assurances of the Trust Bank – and it had been made abundantly clear by Askin that their assurances would be relied upon by the English investors – Julian Askin and Hugo Biermann signed a heads of agreement which would, when effected, give them and their associates, who included such first class names as Flemings and Warburgs, plus the Sangster family, control of Duros/Tollgate. It was carefully constructed, with the help of Askin's London advisers, in order to strengthen the Duros/Tollgate balance sheets while giving time for a reconstruction along new lines to be carried out.

Experienced in company finance as he was, it was clear to Askin that the group was over-borrowed. However obliging the banks might be the interest burden was too heavy. He intended therefore to sell off those companies which had limited growth potential and which made the greatest demands on capital, an operation which could only be done over a period of time. The other arm of Askin's strategy was the acquisition of new undertakings, one of which was intended to be Jaton, a British company previously bought into Thomson T.Line.

Trust Bank officials played an active part in these negotiations since Askin insisted that they should support Tollgate in reconstruction as vigorously as they had enabled it to expand. Any injection of new capital must be matched pound for pound by the company's bankers. This they willingly agreed to do, citing again their absolute confidence in Tollgate. The consortium therefore invested R35 million, then about £7 million, a sum reciprocated by Trust Bank, London. The manager there, James Grant, agreed that the bank would match any investment made by the consortium by making loans secured against Tollgate stock. Duros/Tollgate would then issue R60 million debenture stock bearing interest at 14 per cent which would become compulsorily convertible to ordinary shares after three years. Since conversion was compulsory, the debentures were, in effect, deferred equity.

Askin had devised the funding formula with some care. The 14 per cent yield on the debentures was satisfactorily profitable for the London investors, yet sufficiently under the South African market rate (then at least 20 per cent) to give some advantage to the company. The three-year period was acknowledged to be long enough to effect real improvements, while brief enough to give support to the share price, since investors would not have to wait too long to see some benefits accruing. It was therefore important that the Trust Bank was equally committed for the same period, and, by the agreement, Askin could therefore rely on their loan at least until March 1993; or so he thought. Although the new capital was essential, and better than nothing, this was a long way from the R100 million of immediate equity that Diedericks had considered necessary. An equity injection would have been of risk capital, unsecured, entitled to no automatic dividend: the Askin money was secured on the assets, and produced, come what may, a 14 per cent return from the profits of the company.

For their part, as well as the glowing references given by the company's bankers, Askin's consortium had before them the Tollgate's audited accounts for the extended eighteen-month period ending 31 December 1989. At that time Duros was nothing more than a holding company with, apart from a 26 per cent share in S A F Life Assurance Company, its holding in Tollgate as its sole asset. For its part Tollgate held controlling interests in four other publicly quoted companies – Norths, Gants, Entercor and Arwa – which contributed to make any analysis of the accounts difficult. When the results for the period to December 1989 were first announced on 21 March 1990 they showed an operating profit of R15 million, but without mentioning abnormal items, or correctly stating extraordinary items. In the eventual audited accounts extraordinary items of R10.6 million and abnormal items of R15.3 million, together with an increased taxation provision, eventually brought the initially claimed profit to a loss after tax of R26.4 million – in all a good example of the confused state of the group's financial affairs: although it is significant that at the time of signing the agreement, Askin was aware only of Claasen's original inaccurately optimistic figure. Even so, the inflated figures were such that had they not been published at the same time as the news of the consortium's investment the company would have been in serious trouble. This was avoided since the losses could be attributed to Arwa and Gants, and the announcement made that the disposal of certain non-performing divisions (were) at an advanced stage. The shares therefore rose comfortingly, although a dividend was payable only by a very large – R62 million – transfer from the group's reserves.

At least Tollgate appeared rich in assets: after writing R56 million off the balance sheet total R800 million remained. Mervyn Key publicly suggested that the real value was probably double: if that were so then the R35 million which gave the consortium control could unlock R1,600 million of assets – surely a remarkable coup. And Key was also willing to forecast – extraordinarily rashly – that earnings per share would more than double over the next two years. Given that the accounts were audited by properly qualified accountants, Askin's positive assessment of Tollgate's prospects was understandable.

Added weight was given by the fact that Claasen had indicated his willingness to buy out Arwa, his initial investment, which he believed still had good prospects. Askin dissented from this opinion: the manufacture of tights and stockings was a singularly inflexible sort of business, with a constant demand for capital investment in new machines. He had insisted that he would not commit funds to Tollgate if it included Arwa. Taking Arwa out of the Tollgate balance sheet should significantly decrease the borrowing, which was clearly dangerously high, and materially assist in the group reorgnisation.

Probably gritting his teeth somewhat, Johan Claasen paid R42 million in cash for Arwa, which he financed by selling his remaining Duros shares to Askin and Key and borrowing from the reliable Trustbank; Claasen was therefore now no longer part of the controlling consortium, but as part of the agreement, Tollgate guaranteed the loan that Claasen had taken out to pay for his shares, a guarantee that was due to expire on 31 July 1990.

Changes at board level reflected the altered control. With Diedericks and Claasen gone Mervyn Key became the man who represented the link between the former Duros and the new owners and upon whom Askin relied for management information. Hugo Biermann joined the board in October 1990, but played little part in the direction, occupying himself more with new ventures in Britain. He was followed, in December that year by Guy Sangster, whose family interests had done so well by Thomson T. Lines' acquisition of Vernons Pools, Nicholas Soames, grandson of Winston Churchill, Conservative Member of Parliament for Crawley, who moved in very exalted circles, together with the less-well known Nigel Tose and A. S. Wilmott-Sitwell, the son of Peter Wilmott-Sitwell, senior partner of Rowe and Pitman, for many years Tollgate's London stockbrokers. The surviving original directors after Claasen's departure were Mervyn Key, Martin Irish, whose partnership acted as the company's Johannesburg stockbrokers, Michael Lewis and Laurie Mackintosh. Wilmott-Sitwell and Guy Sangster were both taken on by Askin largely as a favour to their fathers. Guy Sangster remained with Nigel Tose in London, but Wilmott-Sitwell had expressed a desire to work in South Africa.

Some personal oddities of the Tollgate board had caused raised eyebrows among the newcomers. Susie Askin had been alarmed when, on their first meeting with the Keys, the Askins had been entertained at a lavish lunch party, given by Mrs Key three days after the birth of her first child – which had implied an unusual level of desire to impress. Similarly, Mr Wilmot-Sitwell was surprised by a lunch given by Mr Lewis at the Johannesburg Rand Club at which the host, having opened a bottle of post-prandial port, threw the cork across the room, crying 'We won't be needing that again.' (Mr Lewis denied the allegation, pointing out that the Rand Club, very properly, decanted its port).

It is customary, and certainly prudent, for any management assuming control of an existing enterprise, to paint as gloomy a picture of the state of affairs as it can get away with. There was no need to exaggerate Tollgate's predicament, as the new owners discovered that something was very wrong and that Tollgate, far from being the flourishing and profitable enterprise described by Trust Bank, was in dire trouble. In May 1991 the results to the year ending December 1990 were published. Askin's statement was uncompromising:

> It would not be amiss, however, to say that we inherited a group of companies that had for some while severely tested the patience and goodwill of its shareholders and bankers. It was a group that was massively over-borrowed, inefficiently managed, totally lacking in strategic direction, and haemor-rhaging from swiftly accelerating losses in many of its subsidiaries. The fact that several of these subsidiaries had been members of the group for only short periods bears testimony to the fundamentally misplaced ambitions and direction of Tollgate at that time.
>
> We bought control of Tollgate because we were of the opinion that the group's difficulties, although considerable, were resolvable and that it owned certain valuable assets and

companies which had sound growth potential. We were also aware that the group's badly damaged reputation and credibility would have to be fundamentally restored. It is our intention to evolve Tollgate into an international industrial holding company, and I am satisfied that the group will soon have a very sound base from which to begin this venture.

From the above, it will be clear that a complete change of attitude and direction had to take place. The group's cumbersome structure, which contained, under the Duros pyramid, five separately quoted companies, has been consolidated into one holding company, which also enjoys a full listing on the International Stock Exchange in London. This structure will result in considerable cost and administrative savings, and allows the group to be controlled with a drastically reduced head office staff. Several senior management changes throughout the group have also been effected. We have conducted, and are still conducting, a necessarily ruthless pruning of the group's loss-making and non-performing assets.

Askin was able, however, to report that his strategy of reducing borrowings had made a good start. As well as selling Arwa, another bad buy had been disposed of by closing Gant's loss-making deciduous fruit canning division. Claasen's cash payment for Arwa had been used by Tollgate to buy a 24.4 per cent interest in Hosken Consolidated Investments. With Hosken's considerable shareholding in Tollgate, and their management of the Tollgate pension fund, the two companies were closely linked. Hosken's chairman, Michael Lewis, had been a director of the old Tollgate company since October 1989 but had joined the restructured group board only in December 1990.

By the end of the first full year of Askin's control it seemed that the drastic measures he had initiated had proved their worth and that Tollgate really had been revived. The surgery had been heroic: in two years, by redundancies and disposals, employment had been reduced from 21,000 to some 2,500. In spite of this the operating profits had actually risen from R26 million to R43.5. More significantly, shareholders' earnings were actually, for the first time, positive, at R13 million after a loss of R18 million the previous year. Even although this profit was wiped out by a loss on 'extraordinary' items of R46.5 million, these items were all related to the costs of disposal of previously inflated assets. The financial press reported that Tollgate, having 'taken the punishment of restructuring on the nose' had 'come in from the cold'.

There were positive indications of future profits as opposed to stopping losses in that, after the year end, Tollgate had made its first overseas acquisition. Jaton Holdings Limited was one of the largest British distributors of industrial fasteners and wire mesh and had produced an operating profit of about £1 million each year for the previous five years. Expected to increase this, Jaton's earnings would do much to improve Tollgate's standing.

Since Jaton had been part of Thomson T. Line and since the Askin interests held a substantial – some 20 per cent – holding in the company, the sale had to be handled with some care and was accordingly sponsored by the highly respected house of S. G. Warburg. The circular to shareholders – 114 pages long – was, at Askin's insistence, constructed to the stringent requirements of the London Stock Exchange and prepared with the utmost care with every sentence weighed and caution uppermost in everyone's minds. Considered as a class four transaction by the Stock Exchange Council, the Jaton acquisition underwent the closest scrutiny. As shown in the prospectus Tollgate's profit had improved further by comparison with the same period in the previous year. Income had more than doubled and resulted in a net income to the stock and shareholders of R5,940,000. Askin's consortium took most of this in the interest on their convertible debentures, but a dividend was paid to the ordinary shareholders of three cents per share. 'Which', the introduction to the prospectus stated, 'reflects the board's confidence in the Tollgate Group's continuing recovery and prospects.' Shareholders could also take comfort from the fact that Trust Bank had confirmed that their facilities extended to the Group remained in place, subject to a review in November 1992.

In March of 1992 the last of the old Tollgate loss-making companies, Tramway Holdings, was disposed of, for R112 million in cash. This strengthened the balance sheet and removed a large chunk of corporate debt and the net asset value per share rose from 423 cents to 651 cents. For the first time the group's structure looked well-organised, rather than the inchoate muddle it had been just two years earlier. Only the fruit-canning operation in Swaziland remained from the original industrial sector. Motorvia was by far the most important vehicle transport company, ferrying used motor vehicles via rail, road and sea throughout South Africa. Springbok Atlas, encouraged by the general relaxation of sanctions after 1990, organised group and individual tours, meshing well with Greyhound Cityliner, operator of the famous long-distance coaches, under the aegis of Entercor, which also included photography, advertising and public relations enterprises. The Jaton documentation had included a note on the interim results that 'the vigorous policy of reducing group debt – which has declined over the last eighteen months from some R390 million to R180 million – is continuing.' Any shareholder, actual or prospective, might believe that Tollgate, and the company's bankers, had every reason to be satisfied.

CHAPTER THREE

The Facts Emerge

Lies, damn lies, and bankers' reports

Behind these encouraging developments, however, all was not going well and Askin was beginning to smell quite a number of rats. One particularly odoriferous rodent was the fact that the Tollgate borrowings were persistently much higher than had originally appeared. Only after a period of some years, and in the course of several searching enquiries, did the fact emerge that Tollgate, far from being the flourishing company that had been described to Askin by Trust Bank, had in truth been in a critical situation, and the facts were well known to the banks. When later put in front of a public enquiry the Trust Bank manager Gerbie Strydom, who together with Koos Morland and others had given such glowing assurances as to the stability and strength of Tollgate, was forced to admit that these were, quite frankly, lies. In March and April 1990 'a very comprehensive investigation' had been conducted by Trust Bank, a 'viability study of the whole Tollgate group', which 'dealt with whether there was the possibility of survival or not'. It concluded, in Strydom's judgement, that Tollgate was in 'deep trouble' and 'a desperate situation'. Without Askin's participation there would have been 'dramatic and drastic consequences for the Bank, either liquidation or something similar.' It was Askin or nothing. Unless Tollgate could be kept afloat, the Trust Bank would probably be brought down; any number of lies would be justified to avoid this.

As a gesture towards propriety the Trust Bank reduced its internal credit rating of Tollgate from (an entirely unrealistic) A A A to the lowest possible grade, A4 – without, of course, telling Askin. Then, in what would be an incredible move for any bank, on 28 March 1990 – two weeks after the Heads of Agreement had been signed – the credit committee of the Trust Bank agreed to a request from Johan Claasen ('known for his ability to take over struggling financial institutions and then turn them round', according to the submission made by Messrs Strydom and Morland) for an extra R69,200,000 of overdraft facility. Tollgate's overdraft was to be increased from R182.35 million to R251.55 million. The reasons advanced were 'during takeover transactions, Mr Claasen was not able to pay much personal attention to the running of an extremely large Group and had to rely extensively on Management' (one must recall that the Managing Director was the worthy Hennie Diedricks) and the 'financial details of certain companies not having been properly researched, has resulted in the Group's critical financial position.' This was from the same Trust Bank executives that were even then assuring Askin of their high regard for Tollgate's management and the healthy state of its business! The application continued: 'A contributing factor has been that the takeovers were partially (*sic*) financed through overdrafts of R50 million. Of this, payment has already been requested for some.' The necessity for Claasen to repay some of his bank borrowings was of course the real reason for his anxiety to sell. But in spite of everything, Strydom and Morland went on to reassure the credit committee, 'The Group is notwithstanding profitable.'

The credit committee agreed, but made their agreement subject to a handwritten proviso that 'approval is conditional on this rights issue (by Askin) going through. If rights issue fails, the facilities will be reviewed immediately'. The message was clear: get Askin's money or the business will be closed and then the position of Trust Bank itself would be perilous. And, when the Sanlam financial interests were merged, Trust Bank and the smaller banking companies becoming Bankorp, a new chairman was sought to unite these previously disparate interests into a major banking operation. This was Dr Piet 'Bible' Liebenberg, who took over in June 1990. He admitted that he 'did not condone the previous strategy concerning the relationship between Trust Bank and Tollgate and ... he in effect acted against the relationship which existed' by dismissing Strydom and Morland.

Liebenberg's admission was made in May 1990 to Hennie Diedericks, to whom he offered the task of managing Trust Bank only weeks after Diedericks had left Tollgate. It was an ironic proposal, given that Trust

Bank executives were even then attempting to blame Diedericks for Tollgate's predicament. Diedericks declined Liebenberg's offer, persuaded instead by his old colleague Dr Danie Cronjé to return to Volkskas, then beginning its transformation to the major constituent of the new bank, Absa, the Amalgamated Banks of South Africa, which in due course would unite under one roof all the Afrikaner banking interests.

Liebenberg had been headhunted from Nedbank by Marinus Daling, Sanlam's man on the Bankorp board, responsible for all Sanlam's outside commercial interests (and today chairman of Sanlam). Daling has been described as 'a belligerent Boer and a staunch defender of Afrikaans' and 'one of the most powerful men in South Africa'. In the next few years he was certainly to be the most active participant in overseeing the policies and strategies of Afrikaner financial interests. He was, naturally, also a senior member of the Broederbond. The intention behind recruiting Liebenberg – his nickname came from his very public religiosity – was specifically to bring some order into Bankorp, and his arrival there signalled a change in policy. The dash for growth was to be abandoned and the incestuous relationship between the bank and Tollgate, its most prominent example, ended – although the bank continued to hold nearly two million shares in the company.

One of the immediate causes for Tollgate's urgent application to Trust Bank for more funds on 28 March was a meeting that had occurred three weeks previously. Michael Lewis was in Hennie Diedericks's office when he was told, for the first time, that the company had to find funds, that same day, to meet a Bill of Exchange which had been issued by Claasen, without Diedericks's knowledge. 'Diedericks's face clouded over. I have never seen him so angry. He was thunderstruck. Then he bellowed "Johan", and he was literally seething with rage, his hands gripping the arms of his chair.'

According to Lewis, Classen knew why he was being summoned (remember that Claasen, effectively Diedericks's boss, had been his underling at Volkskas). Diedericks said to him: 'Johan, I am not a director of Duros any more. I resigned from that company at the beginning of the month. You knew, as a banker you knew, that a Bill of Exchange is sacrosanct. Why have you not made provision to pay it? Tollgate doesn't have the money to meet it and I am not prepared to be involved – this is not my problem.' Claasen, said Lewis, had hidden his face behind a diary. All Claasen could say was, 'Ek is jammer Hennie, ek is jammer.' (I'm sorry.) And then, according to both Diedericks and Lewis, Claasen left the room and essentially left them to cope with the problem, which they did by extending the Bill of Exchange for a further period. Neither the banks, nor any of Tollgate's directors, saw fit to disclose to Askin any of these significant events, enough to shatter the company's stability; it was left until after the new money had arrived from London for the truth to emerge.

Another undisclosed hole in the Tollgate balance sheet had ensured the readiness of Messrs Strydom and Morland to exert themselves on Tollgate's behalf. In June 1988 a total of 75,000 Tollgate shares were allotted to them as a token of appreciation of their assistance, at a price of 200 cents – the current market value being some 800 cents; the two men had effectively been given a present of R450,000. Unable to find an invoice, when the company auditor's queried the payment they were informed that it was merely 'for services rendered'. The 'partnership' which had been boasted of in the *Finance Week* of March 1989 was a partnership indeed! But one that should have brought instant dismissal to the bank officials involved. It was claimed that the then chief executive of Trust Bank, Chris van Wyk, had permitted the two executives to accept the shares, and that such presents were common in the profession. The first is unlikely, and even if true only implicated van Wyk in an improper transaction, while the second is just not so; reputable bank executives to not accept free gifts of this magnitude from customers.

Yet another, more damaging time bomb had been laid in the Tollgate balance sheet. On 11 May 1989 Volkskas had been given a 'put' option, entitling them to demand that 5 million ordinary shares in Duros which they held as a security would be bought back by the company at a price of R5.50. The option was connected to the purchase by Tollgate that month of 17 million Gants shares, which were exchanged for 6.8 million shares in Tollgate. Beset by their bankers, Volkskas, for repayment of outstanding loans, the Gant family required cash instead; Tollgate borrowed the R22 million represented by the current value of the shares, again from Volkskas. In this way the bank transferred their lending from Gants to Tollgate. In order to protect the value of their security

Volkskas demanded to be granted a 'put' option, exercisable at any time in a 90 day period after 1 April 1992: when it was exercised Duros/Tollgate would have to find R27.5 million. To make matters worse Duros had also guaranteed to pay a dividend of at least 90 cents per share in the interim, raising the total sum to R32 million. Half of these obligations were guaranteed by Trust Bank, but were never disclosed to Askin, nor, needless to say, were they revealed to him by Mervyn Key, who had remained on the Duros/Tollgate board. It came to light only in January 1991, when a plan to integrate Duros and Tollgate officially, a complex piece of company restructuring, was ready to be implemented.

Responding to requests from the London Stock Exchange, the Duros/Tollgate company structure had to be simplified. Duros, a publicly quoted company, controlling Tollgate, another quoted company, which in turn controlled other listed companies, such as Entercor, was a prime example of 'pyramiding', forbidden under new regulations for any company having a London quotation. A solution which would meet these requirements was proposed that Duros, together with Entercor and Norths, become subsidiaries of Tollgate Holdings Ltd., which then would become the only public quoted company in the group. It was a complex scheme, requiring much expensive advice and documentation. When this was finally prepared, after being doubtless carefully scrutinised by the professional advisers, who included the London stockbrokers, Rowe and Pitman, and Senbank, the merchant banking arm of Bankorp, the scheme of arrangement was presented to the Tollgate board for signature on 7 January 1991. Once again, the boardroom was the scene of panic and alarm, Askin recorded:

> All the directors were due to attend and we were still waiting for Michael Lewis to arrive. Key burst into my office and told me that the chaps at Volkskas in Johannesburg had just called him. They told him that they would be voting against the Scheme of Arrangement. I was stunned.
>
> I had no idea what he was talking about. Then, for the first time, he told me about the 'put' that Volkskas had against Duros. If we followed the Scheme of Arrangement (in which I was precluded from voting the consortium's

interest), the company against which Volkskas had the 'put' would disappear as a legal entity and Volkskas would be left without recourse. In these circumstances Volkskas would not go along with the scheme. And when we did our sums we realised that Volkskas could block the restructure. My dreams of a grand, attractive London listing were fast disappearing. I had to find a way out.

It should have been impossible that none of those concerned – Mervyn Key, the Trust Bank officers, or the South African professional advisers, had told Askin of the existence of the May 1989 agreement, decidedly peculiar as it was, but, as with other important circumstances, he had been kept in the dark. Some way had to be found, and immediately, out of the current predicament. It was Michael Lewis, chairman of Hosken Consolidated Investments and a non-executive director of Tollgate Holdings who provided, somewhat reluctantly, the solution. As well as owning a 'very substantial' number of Tollgate Holdings shares and shares in the publicly quoted subsidiaries, Hosken also administered the large TGH pension fund. According to Mervyn Key arrangements had already been made with Hosken that they should assume responsibility for the put, but if so Lewis claimed he had never heard it. At the meeting, where 'there was an enormous sense of urgency' Lewis was told by Volkskas that the bank would withdraw its opposition to the scheme of arrangement if Hosken took responsibility for the put. To sweeten the pill, it was proposed that Hosken would be allowed to nominate other persons to assume the responsibility. These nominees would be guaranteed in turn by a Senbank indemnity. Lewis subsequently stated that:

> It was stressed again and again that Hosken was merely required to lend its name to the transaction. Kaiser (Volskas) in particular confirmed that there was no risk to Hosken. I advised those present that if I were to put my name to the agreement on behalf of Hosken, I then as a cautious insurance person I would require Askin, Key and Mackintosh as the nominees to sign appropriate indemnities in their personal capacities to which they agreed.

So convinced by these arguments was Lewis that he volunteered to have his own name included as a nominee, thereby accepting personal responsibility for the put. It was a rash action, which Lewis later had considerable cause to regret.

And yet another very strange transaction known to Trust Bank was a peculiar arrangement entered into by Duros in February 1990, just prior to Askin's agreement, at a time when negotiations were well advanced. Anticipating their resignation from the Duros board Key and Mackintosh entered into a so-called 'restraint of trade' agreement (by which they warranted that they would not work for another similar company) in return for which the company paid a total of R6.6 million, by means of four cheques dated between 1 April and 1 October 1990. These were immediately presented by Key to the Trust Bank's Cape Town branch for discounted payment. In a letter to the branch dated 19 February Tollgate gave an irrevocable undertaking to Trust Bank that the cheques would indeed be honoured at the due dates and that TGH Finance, the actual issuers, would do nothing to impair their value. Again, no mention of this transaction was made to Askin, although it was apparent that, since the shares were registered in the name of Trust Bank Nominees, the bank was fully aware of every aspect. As it turned out, when the two men speedily rejoined Tollgate, after Askin's arrival the payment ought to have been refunded; this necessity was quietly avoided, and the payments retained.

It also appeared that the share price of Duros, at the period when Askin first became interested, was artificially inflated by purchases made on behalf of the directors. In 1989 Johan Claasen instructed Trust Bank to buy any shares that came on the market and financed Mervyn Key to do the same, borrowing more money from Trust Bank in order to be able so to do. Key was also given an interest-free loan of R3.5 million, for which Duros took responsibility, to buy shares. In this way the market price of Duros could be artificially stabilised – and investors misled. Possibly as a method of financing this operation Tollgate paid R275,000 a month to one of Claasen's companies, Cede, during the period July 1989 to February 1990. The bulk of this sum appeared to go to a Claasen Trust account at Trust Bank. A much larger share support facility had been arranged between Claasen and Stewart of FNB on 17 August 1989, whereby R20 million was made available specifically in order that Claasen might 'conclude various degearing arrangements at suitably advantageous prices'. This was, of course, an illegal operation.

As an example of the directors' easy way with money, Key and Claasen had agreed to buy an executive Lear jet aeroplane at the cost of $4 million and paid the first $850,000, which Askin, when he heard of the transaction, was able partly to recover.

Askin was naturally, greatly perturbed by these clear instances of dubious and sharp practice coming to light. Some explanations were offered, but he believed that approximately R70 million had inexplicably disappeared, either by sums of money simply being stolen from the accounts or by substantial overpayment having been made for assets previously purchased. Stories reached Askin of Mervyn Key's office at Duros having looked like a dealer's desk with all the clandestine foreign exchange deals being processed. Key and Mackintosh disclaimed responsibility for most of the irregularities. Askin was instead directed towards casting Diedericks in the role of villain by Laurie Mackintosh, who wrote a memorandum (on 21 February 1992) strongly critical of Diedericks, although concentrating on such relatively minor – in the context of the huge sums that seemed to have gone missing – matters as the purchase of Diedericks' house by Tollgate and the validity of his service contract. Excuses were made, and one problem solved. The payments illegally retained by Key and Mackintosh purporting to relate to their resignations were, it was agreed, to be refunded, but over an extended period.

It was perhaps equally natural that Askin, faced with Key and Mackintosh protesting their own (relative) innocence, would blame the only absent member of the previous management, Hennie Diedericks.

Armed with the advice of the very respectable Cape Town Board of Executors, whose representative W. J. McAdam had joined Tollgate's board at Julian Askin's request in November 1991 together with that of the company's solicitors, Sonnenbergs, and of a leading Cape Town Counsel, Leo Kuschke, the Tollgate board prepared a case describing the misdeeds committed in Tollgate with the connivance of Trust Bank, and draft summonses against Diedericks and the bankers. Before taking any action it was a decided that, as a matter of common sense and courtesy, the bank should be made aware of the facts and their co-operation requested; but by then Trust Bank itself was greatly changed.

Absa emerges

Liebenberg's task of restructuring Sanlam's banking subsidiaries was only the first step towards the ultimate union of all Afrikaner banking enterprises. Like Bankorp, Volkskas had not been without its difficulties. In a similar dash for growth, and pursuing its role as guardian of the Afrikaner tradition, the bank had made some unwise decisions. Without bothering to investigate, carried away by notions of Afrikaner solidarity, Volkskas bought in 1977 100 per cent of the Bank of the Orange Free State (Bankovs) at a wholly unrealistically high price. Hennie Diedericks, who as Volkskas General Manager of Finance had been responsible for attempting to sort out what he termed a 'disaster', believed that the 'problems which came to light after the acquisition ... were so severe that they jeopardised the standing of Volkskas'. On two separate occasions, as a result, Volkskas was obliged to turn to the Reserve Bank for assistance, which Diedericks negotiated on the bank's behalf obtaining 'loans' totalling R16 million. While this sum was minuscule by comparison with later Reserve Bank handouts, Diedericks commented that 'these facilities were not public knowledge and no documentation exists ... This transaction also exemplifies the close connection between the Volkskas Corporation and the Reserve Bank' – the Broederbond in action.

A few years later Volkskas got into even deeper trouble with their purchase of a controlling interest in a publicly quoted company, Bonuskor, which Diedericks was also called upon to sort out. Bonuskor had been founded by Sanlam, who wisely divested themselves of control. By 1985, when Volkskas became involved, Bonuskor losses were running at a rate of R33–35 million at a time when the total profit of the bank capable of being transferred to reserves was R43 million. Once again Diedericks did so well that the board determined that he and Dr P. R. Morkel, Volkskas Group Managing Director, would be 'entitled to rely entirely on their own assessment and judgement' in dealing with Bonuskor. As a result it seemed that within five years it would be possible to convert the loan account of Bonuskor into equity, a considerable relief to the bank (although this happy prospect was dashed by the collapse of the markets after 1987). Much worse news for Volkskas, the foreign exchange adventures of the bank pushed it to the point of being obliged to sell off its own head office.

In an effort to escape from these horrors by diversification and attract new customers, Volkskas bought, in 1990, a former building society, recently converted from a mutual fund to a commercial bank. This was the United Bank, and with it Volkskas acquired a future chief executive, Piet Badenhorst, and a new name, the Amalgamated Banks of South Africa, Absa.

Popularly known as Piet Bliksem – bliksem being the Afrikaans for lightning, but also for scoundrel – Badenhorst was a self-made man, a 'barefoot graduate from Johannesburg's tough Mayfair district'. From a humble Afrikaner background, Badenhorst had worked his way up, as a waiter in a roadhouse, through accountancy articles and a part-time degree at Witwatersrand University. His career had been entirely within the United Building Society which he joined in 1960, rising to become chief executive. He was described by one perceptive journalist (David Gleason, *Financial Mail* 16 February 1996) as 'courageous, unrepentant, autocratic ... conscious of his roots in disadvantage, poverty and religion', but also 'anxious to be acknowledged by a business community dominated by English speakers.'

In its reconstruction Volkskas had the powerful support of Anton Rupert, whose Rembrandt Corporation had a stake in almost every Afrikaner finance house, including the Sage Group, an insurance group whose chairman Louis Shill was to become a government minister. Anton's son, Johan Rupert, had been a director of Volkskas since 1987. A proposal was advanced whereby Volkskas, now Absa, should buy the Allied Bank, another former building society, plus a 50 per cent holding in Sage Financial Services. Against some opposition in March 1991, this was, at a high price, eventually done. The new unit was large and more diversified, but was still nursing some very doubtful assets and remained short of experienced bankers who understood modern corporate lending.

The following year, 1992, saw in March the amalgamation of the two Afrikaner banking groups as Bankorp was merged into the enlarged Absa. Trust Bank therefore became, with Allied, United and Volkskas, an operating division of the Amalgamated Banks of South Africa. Absa was controlled jointly by Sanlam and Rupert interests, who between them had about 50 per cent of the shares held equally (the proportion varied only very slightly from year to year). With the Old Mutual owning some 9 per cent and other strong institutional holdings, individual shareholders represented only between 14 per cent and 16 per cent of the total. Volkskas, that pillar of the old Afrikaner establishment, offshoot of the Broederbond, set the management style for the new bank. As late as 1990 three directors of Volkskas still described themselves as 'farmers' (boeren), reflecting the roots of the enterprise in traditional Afrikaner society; two more were academics from Afrikaner universities. All were quickly dropped from the new, business-centred, board.

By March 1992, when Askin made his *démarche*, Hennie Diedericks had made his way to become a managing director of Volkskas and Trust Bank divisions within Absa. The only exception to the otherwise exclusively Afrikaner senior management at Absa was Bob Aldworth, previously general manager of Barclay's South African enterprise, who after a somewhat chequered career was now general manager of Absa's corporate banking division and a main board director.

Aldworth had joined Barclays Bank of South Africa at the age of 23 with no formal qualifications. He soon became involved in organisation and methods, computer installation, and the development of new products. It was not until 1969, when Aldworth was 38, that he was introduced to banking proper. After a successful period in New York, he became regional general manager for the central Johannesburg area which generated over three quarters of the bank's profits. He did so well that in 1976 at the age of forty-four he was appointed Chief Executive of the South African operations, thus becoming the country's youngest head of any major bank. Aldworth's downfall was almost as rapid. Less than seven years later, he had been fired over an injudicious affair with a bank consultant.

Bob Aldworth's supporters speak highly of his professional judgement, even if his personal life was open to criticism. After a period as chairman of Hill Samuel Merchant Bank, later Corbank, he had been invited to join United Bank in September 1990 at a time when Piet Badenhorst was beginning its transformation into a proper bank. After United Bank and Volkskas merged to form Absa in 1990, acquiring Allied Bank, Aldworth was given responsibility for integrating this new, mainly English-speaking, organisation into the otherwise purely

Afrikaner bank. He became an Executive Director of the merged banks in July 1991, where as the only senior English-speaker, and the only man with high level international banking experience, he was uncomfortably isolated.

It was Aldworth, as director responsible for corporate customers, that Askin first approached with his dossier and the suggestion that his concerns should be discussed with the Absa board before taking further action. Aldworth agreed, and, believing that 'a matter of this magnitude should be dealt with at the highest possible level', arranged a meeting between Askin, Piet Badenhorst, as Absa's chief executive, and Danie Cronjé, his deputy. Dr Daniel Christiaan Cronjé was a very different character from Badenhorst, with nothing of the self-made man about him, but a privileged member of the Afrikaner elite. A banker by profession, with degrees from Potchefstrom University 'for Christian Higher Education', a lecturer in banking and reputed a brilliant mathematician, Cronjé had been with the Trust Bank since 1969 and on the board of the Orange Free State Merchant Bank until that was bought by Volkskas, together with Bankovs, in 1977. Cronjé was a polished organisation man and one trusted by the highest levels of the Nationalist governments. A director of the state-owned armaments organisation, Armscor, Cronjé acted as a financial adviser to military intelligence and regularly attended their 'bush conferences'. As Managing Director of Volkskas, following Dr Morkel's departure (to become chairman of Gants), Cronjé had been a moving force behind the formation of Absa.

The meeting between Askin and the bankers duly took place on 23 March 1992, when Askin related the story of these unexplained gaps in Tollgate's balance sheets. He suggested that as these had taken place when Hennie Diedericks was Tollgate's managing director, and that Hennie Diedericks was now a senior executive with the Bank, that they should consider themselves responsible for at least some of the loss; say R70 million. Cronjé was furious. Askin reported: 'He became very threatening and aggressive. He asked me how I could dare to make statements like that about Diedericks. But Badenhorst promised to look into the matter (although nothing ever came of such investigation).'

Badenhorst's sympathies were similarly altogether with his fellow Afrikaner and Broeder, Diedericks; 'What kind of Englishman,' he demanded of Aldworth, 'is this Askin that he can come into my office and make such statements about senior management without producing a shred of proof?' Aldworth was not surprised; it seemed to him only 'another example of the Afrikaners sticking together and supporting another member of the Broederbond'. Neither Badenhorst nor Cronjé, of course, had any knowledge of what Trust Bank officials may have said in 1990, since at that time Trust Bank was not integrated with the new Absa. The two most implicated men, Morland and Strydom, had already been dismissed, and Liebenberg had left, to become the banking Ombudsman.

But whether or not Diedericks was responsible for the gap in Tollgate's balance sheet something had to be done about replacing the money. Following his policy of never taking any important step without seeking the best advice Askin engaged the services of David Sherwin, head of the international investigatory department of one of the largest firms of international accountants. Askin, who had not been told of Absa's angry reaction, went on to produce a careful proposal to restructure Tollgate. The sums fraudulently or illicitly removed from the balance sheet could not be replaced by normal trading, and certainly not within the three-year period agreement with the company's bankers. In the two years of his control Tollgate had paid some R130 million of interest to the banks now comprising Absa and had reduced the bank's exposure from R435 million in June 1990 to R370 million for July 1992. The group was trading profitably, the cash-flow remained positive and debts were paid – including the bank interest – as they fell due. Aldworth, who was the only experienced corporate banker in Absa, agreed that some form of restructuring of Tollgate was advisable, that the management controls needed reinforcing, and that it would indeed be appropriate for the Bank to make a capital contribution of some R70–100 million towards such a restructuring.

A series of meetings between Absa staff, headed by Aldworth, and Askin's team took place on 6 May, 4 August and 10 and 15 September, after which 'firm restructuring proposals', recommended by Aldworth, were placed before Absa's credit committee on 21 September 1992. As might be expected of a financial plan prepared under the supervision of so distinguished an accountant as David Sherwin and financial advisers of the calibre of the Board of Executors, the final Tollgate proposal was well-thought out and capable of producing a profitable solution.

It comprised the transfer of the property holdings, which produced an income of R12,366 million to Absa, affording to the bank a competitive yield against a debt of R112.4 million. No write-off would therefore be necessary to Absa.

The balance of Tollgate's debt, after one or two relatively minor adjustments, would be converted into five-year redeemable preference shares which would provide Absa with an income that, again, would not necessitate a write-off.

Absa would be required to give a secured overdraft facility of R30 million, whilst Askin would procure a capital injection to buy out minority shareholders. All this should produce annual earnings of some R30 million, of which R24 million would go to Absa in preference dividends and interest.

Initially, according to Bob Aldworth, the proposals were well received, meeting 'with universal support'. But the very next day Danie Brits, head of Risk Management, the department responsible for doubtful debts, told Aldworth that the Tollgate account had been taken over by his department. This action was a clear indication that, whatever the views of the credit committee might have been, a decision had been taken to clear the ground for the company's liquidation. It seemed an absurd decision in view of Tollgate's healthy trading conditions. Aldworth protested 'to write off Tollgate is going to cost us almost R200 million . . . it would be crazy to liquidate.'

Unknown to Aldworth, and to few outside the Broederbond circle, Absa had already decided to put that troublesome customer, Tollgate into liquidation; but no indication of this intention was given to the company. This neglect raises some interesting questions. If a company's continued trading is dependent upon its banker's support, then the intention to withdraw that support involves damaging the interests of creditors and places the directors in most invidious positions. Reciprocally, much responsibility also attaches to the bank, which continued (see pp.95–6 below) to proffer every indication of continued support. Diedericks, who remained until 31 December 1992 on Absa's payroll, was in no doubt that the 'personal animosity towards Askin (which was often expressed openly within Absa and in colourful language by

Badenhorst') was an important factor in Absa's action. The formal decision to liquidate Tollgate was taken on 18 or 19 November 1992 at a meeting between Cronjé and Brits, and reported to a board meeting on 27 November – curiously enough, without any papers, and omitted from the board minutes. In fact, as it later emerged, Tollgate's fate had been settled much earlier.

Ignorant of this intention, in September, October and November Askin was shuttling between South Africa and London attempting to rearrange Tollgate's reconstruction to accord with what he understood to be Absa's requirements. On 4 November 1992 the Tollgate directors agreed a monitoring system whereby Absa would nominate two persons to protect the bank's interests. They would be invited to all board meetings, entitled to receive all board papers and would have control over all income and expenditure. In effect, they would have nearly complete control over the group's activities.

Danie Brits continued the negotiations, but in a much more acerbic manner than Aldworth. Askin related that one meeting towards the end of November ended with Brits telling David Sherwin 'to "get out!" – just like that. When he had gone, Brits turned round and said "Now I just want to tell you something. Mr Diedericks has just been made head of the Post Office and is leaving this bank. And what do you think you are going to do about that, you fokken Engelsman?" And those were his exact words. I just stared at him in complete amazement.'

In spite of such boorish behaviour (and Brits was still, in 1998, a member of Absa's International Banking Divisional board) the restructuring negotiations looked set to continue. One of the by now regular meetings had been arranged for Friday, 4 December. Christo Faul of Absa, who had been handling relations with Tollgate, telephoned Askin early on Monday 30 November to confirm the meeting. He cheerily remarked, 'I am looking forward to seeing you. We are going to sort this thing out', which left Askin and Sherwin, who was present, and by then feeling the strain, considerably cheered. But later, on the same day, Charles Smith, a partner of Sonnenbergs, Tollgate's lawyers, telephoned. He had just heard, from his senior partner, a director of the bank, that Absa were preparing to liquidate Tollgate within the next 48 hours. Askin remembers his response vividly. 'But hang on. I have just arranged a meeting with the bank for Friday!' Smith responded, 'Of course they have. Don't you know who you're dealing with? They specifically asked you for a meeting later in the week to lull you into a sense of security.' It was clear that once Aldworth had been taken off the negotiations these had been nothing more than a complex and expensive pretence.

Had Absa succeeded in obtaining permission to liquidate Tollgate they would have been in complete control, entitled to dispose of the company's assets as they pleased. Charles Smith strongly recommended that such an action be forestalled by the Tollgate shareholders themselves putting the company into voluntary liquidation. Miles Divett of Sonnenbergs agreed that 'if Absa would not respond . . . the directors ought to take control of the situation.' There was no time left to begin negotiations with another bank, which had they been begun in May, when the Absa discussions started, would almost certainly have led to a satisfactory conclusion and the survival of Tollgate. Askin had been, for the second time, deceived by his bankers. Both Trust Bank and the Reserve Bank had deliberately and effectively lied about the real state of Tollgate and Absa had never had any intention of allowing the company to survive.

Rob Walters of the Cape Board of Trustees pointed out to the board meeting that one of the important points to consider was to be more than satisfied that 'nothing to be embarrassed about would come out of the cupboard'. After a good deal of discussion it was concluded that the directors had done nothing for which they could be legitimately criticised, and the decision to apply for voluntary liquidation was taken.

A period of lively activity ensued. An immediate board meeting of Tollgate directors, who themselves could speak for a majority of the shareholders, decided to petition the courts for a liquidation. At two-thirty on the afternoon of the same Monday a petition was accordingly delivered to the Cape Supreme Court, a few doors away from Tollgate's headquarters. While Askin was in court, David Sherwin was working in the company's offices when a breathless messenger from Absa's lawyers entered searching for a director of Tollgate to serve notice of the bank's own petition for liquidation. Baffled, he rushed off to the court, where Absa's barrister, Bertrand Hoberman, was even then opposing Tollgate's petition for liquidation. When the judge realised that Hoberman was actually now in possession of Absa's own petition for the same action that the advocate had just been strongly resisting, the unfortunate Hoberman was reprimanded for what appeared to be a piece of double-dealing, and Tollgate's own petition granted. By then it was late in the day, after the court's normal closing hours.

It is not easy to see Absa's anxiety to liquidate Tollgate as a reasonable banking transaction. The chairman of Absa, David Brink, later claimed that the bank had written off R215 million as a consequence. Bob Aldworth, with access to the papers, believed that the bank's officials were, at the time of rejecting his recommendations, forecasting a loss of very similar dimensions. These were important sums for a bank of Absa's size, and in particular for one that had so heavy a burden of problem debts. When Bankorp was merged into the new Absa, (to join United and Allied Banks and Volkskas) in March 1992, it had a pile of bad and doubtful debts totalling some R5,400 million – at that time worth about £1,000 million – enough to overwhelm such an institution. Faced with similar problems the prudent action would have been to adopt the proven device of forming a 'bad' bank to hold the difficult loans, trading out of them over a period of time, guaranteed by the 'good' bank that would continue the profitable business. Not only would this be to the advantage of the bank's shareholders, since it would avoid their having to accept most losses, it would also the benefit the shareholders, employees, suppliers and customers of those companies which would be obliterated in a liquidation.

'All Hell broke loose' when Absa officials realised that the Tollgate board had got their application in first. Early on Tuesday morning Tony Behrman, a senior partner of Werksmans, Absa's lawyers, made a 'very angry' telephone call to Charles Smith demanding that Askin and Smith fly to Johannesburg and that Sonnenbergs resign to allow Absa 'to put in their own lawyers and liquidators', a demand that was naturally refused. So confident had Absa been that their liquidation application would succeed that they had notified the press and dispatched their staff around the country to take possession of all the Tollgate companies; all of whom had been more or less politely ejected when they made the attempt.

Askin's pre-emptive strike had only limited effects. Absa, with its still huge loans outstanding, was by far the biggest creditor, and, once this was proved, was able to control the process. At this stage Absa seemed to have done nothing grossly improper or illegal. Askin could certainly claim that he had been given an assurance from Trust Bank that his facilities were in place until July 1993, and he had, he fully believed, been in the middle of serious negotiations when the rug had been pulled out from under him. Although this was deceptive, Absa's action was not necessarily on the face of things illegal. Tollgate, it was acknowledged, was unable to repay its borrowings, although the company could claim that interest payments had always been duly made, and that they were operating within the authorised limits. Absa had obtained a winding-up order from the High Court. Following the court's order firms of accountants were appointed as liquidators, the most important being Messrs Glaum and Wallace for Motorvia, and Chris van Zyl of Syfrets for Kyalami.

From that point on it was the responsibility of the liquidators to manage the companies, protecting the assets, negotiating sales either as a going concern or by disposal of separate assets, and to distribute the proceeds to the creditors. These payments were made in order of ranking: preferred creditors, usually the state for taxes, and employees of a certain level, followed by secured creditors, of which the most important was Absa, with the ordinary trade creditors coming a poor third.

Creditors were able to exercise a certain degree of inspection over the liquidators by means of a monitoring committee, but the legal responsibility remained with the liquidators. It was at this point that Absa began to interfere in the process.

Absa flexes its corporate muscles

The facts emerged only three years later. Francis Glaum, one of the Motorvia liquidators, revealed that immediately after their appointment in December 1992, the liquidators were called to a meeting in Absa's offices, with Christo Faul of Absa in the chair. Faul, Glaum related, 'indicated and dictated the procedures to be adopted'; emphasising that Absa required a speedy settlement, and directing – all quite improperly – that the liquidators should scrutinize the directors' actions for possible impropriety – but that this examination should be limited to the period after Askin's takeover. There were to be no injudicious enquiries into what might have taken place earlier. Faul also required that the liquidators should take no decisions without consulting Absa and this requirement was noted in a memorandum signed by all those present, without dissent. Bearing in mind that it is a liquidator's duty to act in the interests of all creditors equally, this was highly unusual and indeed illegal.

An interesting later document (Appendix A) shows how the liquidators were manipulated. The final paragraph (17) is in a different typeface from the rest of the document, including the titles of the signatories. Taken in conjunction with the fact that a space was clearly left for its insertion Absa's hand is visible. The inserted paragraph confirmed the bank to be the only creditor with more than 50 per cent and therefore in complete control of the liquidators.

Absa, it might be noted, publicly denied this, publishing a statement signed by the then chairman D. C. Brink on 3 November 1995 which included the claim that 'Absa does not control the liquidators of Tollgate. Insinuations to the contrary are untrue.' This, given Glaum's chapter and verse, was a lie. Glaum and Wallace both admitted to being directed by Absa, such directions including the imposition of the investigation's time limit to the period of Askin's control.

Absa went further in improperly influencing events; their first chairman, Herc Hefer, was also chairman of the bank's joint auditors, KPMG (in itself something not usual in public companies). KPMG were immediately appointed as investigating accountants first by the liquidators and later by the Office for Serious Economic Offences (OSEO); and, for good measure, KPMG were also auditors of Jaton, the Tollgate subsidiary. This massive conflict of interests, which would not have been allowed in a similar English investigation, made it impossible for KPMG to act as investigating accountants into the part played by Absa in Tollgate's liquidation. Only later did the full impropriety of the bank's – and their auditor's – actions in this matter become apparent.

All this was at least verging on illegality (Glaum later declared that Absa's actions violated section 424 of the South African Companies Act) but what was equally suspicious was the presence of a member of the Office for Serious Economic Offences at the initial meeting, invited there by Absa. Just as they had denied the fact of the initial meeting, the bank later attempted to deny the presence at it of an OSEO official. The OSEO was a statutory body, officially independent, but in fact co-operating in following Absa's agent.

Indeed, it seemed that the bank was not worrying overmuch about getting its money back. To take one example, Jaton, the British company that Tollgate had bought only a year previously for nearly £10 million was sold within weeks for £1.87 million. It was true that Jaton had not lived up to its expectations, but this was due more to a sluggish economy than any fundamental flaw in the company. Even so, this remarkably modest sale figure reflected a valuation based on a management profit forecast: the liquidators accepted this without examination. Within three months the whole year's forecast profit had been achieved, indicating that a more realistic sale price would indeed have approached the £10 million Jaton had cost. The purchasers, SEP Industrial Holdings, saw their share price treble within twelve month's as a result of Jaton's earnings and one independent accountant valued Jaton, in 1996, at between £15–20 million. The *Investors Chronicle* in December 1994 ascribed SEP's rapid profit increase to their bargain purchase of Jaton. If, as certainly happened, Jaton was sold for less than its real value, Tollgate's creditors would bear the loss. Given that Absa was the major creditor, and that the liquidators admitted to clearing every decision with Absa, one might wonder why the bank was so dismissive of the chance to get some of its money back.

Martin Irish, and many others, conjectured that Absa had instructed the liquidators to get rid of Jaton without bothering about the price in order to show that Askin had sold a 'pup' to Tollgate in the first place. If this were indeed so, the smaller creditors would have good cause for complaint. There certainly was something odd about the valuations. David Sherwin had calculated the probable value of Tollgate's assets with the benefit of his own extensive experience and agreed these with Bernard Kaiser, an executive of Absa, as far back as August 1992; nor were these queried in a later meeting between Askin and Danie Vlok, another senior Absa manager. But the estimates produced by Christo Faul on the back of a cigarette box, without consultation, were much lower, and proved to be grossly inaccurate.

Another twist in the bargain basement disposal of Jaton and the unexplained holes in the Tollgate balance sheet unfolded in London.

Guy Sangster and Nigel Tose had not played the most active of parts in Tollgate management, housekeeping in the largely inactive London office whilst drawing £20,000 a month from South Africa. When the parent company encountered cash-flow problems in the summer of 1992 these payments were suspended; £180–220,000 had thereafter inexplicably disappeared from the Swazican London deposit account on which the two former directors were signatories, quite illegally under both British and South African law. Moreover, Tose, together with the Sangsters put in an offer of £1 million for Jaton – so clearly unreasonably low that it was quickly countered by a higher bid.

This was not the only sleight of hand in which Guy Sangster and Nigel Tose were engaged. When Jaton had originally been bought from Ladbrokes, the Sangsters, in order to facilitate the deal, had technically 'bought' £400,000 of physical stock, reducing the overdraft to the sum that had previously been disclosed. Discovering, much later, in the autumn of 1992, that the Sangsters were expecting that this sum should be recovered from Jaton, Askin wrote to the London directors, Tose and Sangster, specifically forbidding any such payment, with a copy of the letter sent to Jaton's London bankers, Barclays. In spite of this the £400,000 was paid from the Jaton account to the Sangsters shortly before the Tollgate liquidation, a circumstance rendered more suspicious since it was subsequently discovered that both men had been talking to Absa, both in London and Johannesburg, since August 1992.

One more strange incident concerning Swazican came to light. On 4 November 1992 the Standard Chartered Bank sent an enquiry to Senbank's Cape Town office requesting 'a full general report on Tollgate Holdings' and, specifically, whether the group was 'good for' an exposure of R.20 million. The enquiry referred to the operations of the Swaziland Canning Co., the only part of the old Gants business that had been retained by Tollgate as profitable. The enquiry was hardly unexpected, being a regular six-monthly check The answer, dated the same day, was from one G. B. O'Shea, Corporate Adviser, Absa:

> The Directors are respectable gentlemen who are well known
> in the market place. Tollgate is regarded as being good for all
> normal business engagements. Code 'C' for your enquiry as

Guarantor for R28. million in total. If given time to pay.
This report is furnished without any responsibility to our
Bank or its officials.
  G. B. O'Shea (Corporate Adviser)

Bank references are, as has been pointed out, notoriously wary, and so positive a response was equal to a clear go-ahead. Although Mr O'Shea was well informed of the Bank's attitude to Tollgate, it seemed that there had been a slip-up. Two days after O'Shea's fax to Standard Chartered Bank he was given an instruction from his manager, Danie Brits:

> *Our conversation of Friday afternoon 6 November 1992 refers.*
> *We confirm RiskControl's instruction that the 'Regskontrolle'*
> *indicator be removed immediately from all Tollgate's and its*
> *subsidiaries bank accounts . . .*

'Regskontrolle' (legal control) indicators on a file meant, according to Absa practice, that any queries on the account had to be passed through the bank's legal department, a sure indication that preparations were being made for decisive legal action. In such circumstances O'Shea's clearance to the Standard Chartered Bank was grossly misleading, but Brits' attempt to shut the stable door after the horse had bolted manifestly collusive, and in fact the Standard Chartered Bank, who had acted on the authorisation, subsequently sued Absa.

Although, with Absa firmly in charge of the liquidation, there was little Askin could do to help, there seemed no reason to leave South Africa for an English winter, but the 'nailing of Askin' took a more serious turn on 6 February 1993. The *Sunday Telegraph* reported the events of that day in their issue of 23 February.

> Shortly after 10 a.m. on a sunlit February morning a blue car containing three men sped through the leafy Millionaires' Row of Constantia Nek, high above Cape Town.
> The car slowed and turned into the dapple-shaded stable courtyard of Steenhuis, the luxury Cape Dutch home of millionaire Julian Askin. From its verandahs an epic view of False Bay rolls out in panoramic splendour. Askin, chairman

of mini-conglomerate, Tollgate Holdings which went bust last December with debts of R300 million (£60 million) was expecting a business colleague when the doorbell rang. 'Must be him,' he thought, rushing from the verandah through the long dining room to the timbered front hall.

But instead of his visitor, three men awaited: plain-clothed inspectors with clipped Afrikaner accents and bulging blazers barely hiding their police revolvers. From the breast pocket of one came a red calling card: Die Kantoor van Ernstige Ekonomiese Misdrywe: the Office for Serious Economic Offences (OSEO).

The three searched every room, from the study to the Askin's thatch-roofed bedrooms on the upper floor. They took away files and papers on Tollgate. An hour later, to a volley of slamming car doors, they left to search the homes of other executives including Alex Wilmot-Sitwell, son of S. G. Warburg director Peter Wilmot-Sitwell, and former director Mervyn Key.

It was an interesting fact that the raid took place at 11 a.m., and accounts of it appeared in the afternoon editions of the Cape Town newspapers which came out at 2.30 p.m.; the OSEO was obviously feeding information to the press.

That this was no isolated incident is indicated by the treatment even then being meted out to the only English-speaker among Absa's senior executives. Bob Aldworth was being made to pay for his support of Askin when on 8 February he was summoned to a disciplinary hearing by Danie Cronjé. He was accused of having defrauded Absa of a sum variously and inexpertly calculated as somewhere between R414,000 and R7,790,000. *Millennium* magazine, in an extensive investigation of Aldworth's case came to the conclusion: 'What is he guilty of? Certainly naivety. Panic unquestionably: he acknowledges that himself. Weakness and poor judgement definitely, for failing – when exercising his responsibility for Allied – to keep at arm's length from a transaction where his own interests were involved.'

In February 1993 Aldworth was particularly vulnerable. He was recovering from a cancer of the throat and was suffering (as he discovered later) from diabetes, but had been wrongly diagnosed two days before the incident, as a victim of Parkinson's Disease, 'I was not reacting logically: I was an impala caught in the beam of headlights at night.' Certainly he did all the wrong things two days later. Admitting (erroneously as it was subsequently proved) the 'theft' of some R400, 000 from the bank, he contemplated suicide but, two days after that, on 12 February, left the country by a circuitous route. Aldworth's wretched physical condition had been exacerbated by the receipt, a few days before Christmas 1992 (and therefore immediately after Tollgate had been put into liquidation), of an anonymous letter. What he read devastated him. Felt-tipped, poison-dipped, it said: 'Who is Bob Aldworth fucking now, now that Sandra van der Merwe isn't around any more? Watch this space for more.' Similar letters were sent to Absa director Piet Liebenberg and Jean Brown, head of Absa's merchant bank.

Equally shattered, and with the spectre of that earlier disaster never far away, his wife Mari called a friend of hers. Her friend said: 'There is someone at Absa who wants to knock Bob down, get him out.'

For the next three years, with his assets and income confiscated, Aldworth lived a penurious existence first in London and later in a Marbella flat, reviled as a 'fugitive from justice'. Only days after Aldworth's flight Askin was given warning that he might well be threatened with even more serious consequences, and without any hope of legal protection.

The fact that the raid on the Askin's home had been reported, in detail, in the afternoon newspapers, indicated that someone was motivated by something rather more than a legitimate desire to establish the facts. This suspicion was confirmed when a 'bug' was discovered on the telephone lines leading to Steenhuis: doubtless a repetition of Aldworth's experience. A few days after the raid Askin was telephoned by a man he had previously met only casually, saying that they must meet urgently, but not in public. The caller (Askin has promised not to reveal his name) was a well-known Afrikaner, a senior member of the Broederbond and came to Steenhuis on the morning of Sunday the 7th. Sitting on the terrace with the magnificent view across the Cape Flats, Askin was warned, very firmly and seriously, that his life was in danger and that there was indeed a conspiracy, among people 'at the highest levels' with him as its target. He should, quite bluntly, leave the country immediately

– and he should not fly by South African Airways. Without revealing his source, Askin consulted his lawyer, Keith Getz. The response was immediate: 'Get out. You cannot afford to take any risks with these people. You're English, too.' This Askin was reluctant to do, but since there was little he could achieve for Tollgate by this time, he left the next day. He recalls

> I left . . . booking my flight on Air France from a call box, leaving my wife with a house party of guests from the UK. I travelled to Paris on 12 February and then on to London. The flight went via Jo'burg where I had an anxious two hours on the tarmac, wondering whether I was being observed. I was enormously relieved when the aircraft took off and even more so when I got back to London. I went straight to a pub – the Antelope – just to get the real feeling of being back in England.

To anyone not aware of the depths to which the South African Nationalist governments and their agencies had descended in the past, Askin's anxieties might seem to be overblown; but it was not the first time that a British subject had been warned to leave under similar circumstances. Alan Crabtree was a senior executive of Trust Bank in 1984 when he discovered an investment fraud involving the bank which he believed amounted to £66 million, and which also involved the government of the Ciskei, a notoriously corrupt Bantustan. Soon after reporting this Mrs Crabtree received a telephone call to say that her husband was a marked man: over 18 months her car was run off the road three times and eventually her brother, a senior police officer, told her that they should leave the country immediately. It was the sort of warning that, in South Africa, cannot safely be ignored. Another journalist told Askin that 'if he had ever met Pat Kenny, he would never have touched Tollgate': unfortunately Mrs Kenny was murdered in 1989. (One prominent opponent of Nationalist Governments told me that he had twice been the target of assassination attempts, one of which had been mounted with the co-operation of the Israeli intelligence services.)

Even in Britain South Africa's covert violence could readily be arranged, as proved by the bombing of the ANC's London headquarters in March 1982. Years later it was revealed that this attack had been personally arranged by the head of the South African police, Johan Coetzee, who imported the bomb-making materials in the diplomatic bag with the full co-operation of the South African embassy in London. Coetzee was instructed by the Justice Minister, Louis le Grange, who must have had the authority of the President and the State Council for so outrageous an action.

Absa soon began to reveal its own readiness to break the law, and to waste millions of Rand, pursuing those who it regarded as its enemies.

The full extent of the bank's manipulations, kept secret at the time and often subsequently denied, only became revealed over a period of years and as a result of legal pressure. The Office for Serious Economic Offences, OSEO, which had carried out the Steenhuis raid, was intended to be an independent judicial department. With considerable pomp Jan Abraham Swanepoel, its director from 1 January 1993, described himself as an Attorney-General and a Senior Consultus; these appointments had been made by President de Klerk's Nationalist government and Swanepoel was himself an Afrikaner. 'OSEO', Swanepoel claimed:

> was established with the objective of conducting swift and proper investigations of serious economic offences. OSEO is staffed by persons with legal qualifications, policemen and Chartered Accountants. This gives effect to the multi-disciplinary approach OSEO adopts in the investigation of serious economic offences or so-called 'white collar crime'.
>
> In terms of section 5 of the Act. I am vested with a discretion to institute an inquiry in any instance where there exists a reasonable suspicion that a serious economic offence has been or is being committed . . .
>
> I regard the independence of OSEO in the exercise of its functions as paramount and something to be jealously guarded. The cases investigated by this office include matters involving persons and entities from the private sector as well as the public sector. The suspects in these matters are more often than not high profile persons and during the past five

years have included politicians from both the African National Congress and the National Party. During my tenure as Director, OSEO has not been subject to political interference by either the previous or the current government. Any form of interference would in any event be vigorously opposed, from whatever source it may emanate.

Accused by Julian Askin of undertaking his investigation at the behest of Absa, which would certainly have been a 'form of interference . . .' to be 'vigorously opposed', Swanepoel was indignant. 'Apart from the fact that these remarks are grossly insulting, they are devoid of any plausibility. It is difficult to fathom what OSEO would have to gain by submitting itself to be used as a pawn by Absa in order to pursue Askin. The allegations', Swanepoel asserted, 'are also inconsistent with the facts. The initial involvement of OSEO in the matter was not at the instigation of Absa. The initiative came from OSEO. On 5 January 1993, an OSEO official, namely Adv. Petrus Marais, made inquiries regarding the collapse of the Tollgate Group. These inquiries were not initially directed to Absa officials. On 12 January 1993, Marais initiated the first contact with Faul of Absa.'

These extracts are taken from an affidavit, submitted to the British High Court, under oath, by Swanepoel on 24 February 1997 and they hinge around a lie. In another separate trial, that of Mervyn Key in South Africa, one of OSEO's staff was cross-examined (on 11 August 1997). Michael John Stavridis was OSEO's forensic accountant in December 1992. According to the transcript of the trial (p. 358) Stavridis was somewhat halting in his evidence as to the origin of the OSEO enquiry. The questions were put by Mr Smuts:

Do you know what the background was to the holding of this enquiry or the decision to hold the enquiry?

'I'm aware who originally made the – the complaint, I think if we can call it that. I – I know – I'm aware of who made the – the complaint and how that was – was triggered, how the investigation was triggered.'

Well, to the best of your knowledge who laid that complaint?

'It was done by a Mr Christo Faul – F-a-u-l. I think he was – he was a – in the legal department of Absa and I think he was in the – I think they called it colloquially their intensive care department. He was a legal adviser for the – their clients that were in difficulty or he was a legal adviser that dealt with Absa clients that were experiencing difficulties.'

The embarrassed Stavridis was then confronted with an affidavit by Petrus Marais, director of OSEO until 31 December 1992, that Marais had met with Adam Harris, Absa's solicitor and Christo Faul to discuss Tollgate affairs in the course of December 1992, a fact confirmed by Marais's sworn evidence (to the Hoberman Commission, p. 358). Asked if he remembered being present, Stavrides stammered.

'I was present at a meeting during – when Mr Faul was president – was present. I think a part of the time Adam Harris may well have been present too. I can't remember that it was December. That's the one thing I can't place.
All right.
'So I – I'm not sure if it's exactly the same meeting.'
But that was then followed by a formal statement submitted by Mr Faul.
'I – I believe so. That would've been necessary.'

He went on to agree that Faul had sent off an affidavit on 22 January 1993 to Marais and Swanepoel. Stavridis' evidence was not the only source of information about the December meeting. Francis Glaum had also been present at this meeting, which he said had taken place within two days of Tollgate's provisional liquidation, that is, in the first week of December. Glaum added that he refused to provide an affidavit to this effect *because he was too scared*. Such nervousness was odd, since Absa's interference had already been publicly conjectured. The *Financial Mail* of 12 February commented:

Advocate Petrus Marais, who is leading the case ... points out that if a person has reasonable grounds to suspect that a serious economic offence has been ... committed ... he may refer it to the director ... by affidavit or declaration.

The *Financial Mail* has learnt that the liquidators were not responsible for any such affidavit. Marais confirms that Absa and other creditors could have been responsible. Absa declines to comment.

It follows from this evidence that the initial involvement of OSEO was indeed also at the instance of Absa in the December 1992 meeting and had not, as Swanepoel had claimed, been at OSEO's own initiative, and begun by Petrus Marais on 6 January. Furthermore, there had indeed been contact with Faul of Absa well before the date of 12 January 1993, the date which Jan Abraham Swanepoel, Senior Consultus and Attorney-General had sworn under oath to be the start of his investigation. A final touch to this episode is that Marais, on leaving OSEO, became a partner in KPMG, the OSEO's auditors, and joint auditors of Absa.

The Hoberman Commission

On 24 February 1993 it was announced that an enquiry into the affairs of Fetlar Foods, a former subsidiary of Tollgate, was to be held under section 417 of the South African Companies Act. Such an enquiry is analogous to those held by Department of Trade inspectors in the UK, a necessary, but basically unsatisfactory, procedure.

Although UK practice has been subjected to weighty criticisms of its inquisitorial nature, the South African variant is even more inequitable. Proceedings are secret, witnesses may not refuse to answer questions, and criminal proceedings may be instituted on the basis of what transpires at the enquiry – all features repugnant to the normal course of justice. As they had done with the liquidations, Absa proceeded to take charge of the commission of enquiry.

The announcement of the first enquiry was followed on 23 June by the appointment of a secret commission, instructed to inquire into the affairs of Tollgate, under the same section, 417. The chairman of the commission was none other than the same Bertrand Hoberman who had attempted to present Absa's petition for Tollgate's liquidation. It was an extraordinary appointment, and one that reflected Absa's influence even on judicial institutions. At the same time an application to sequester and liquidate Mervyn Key's extensive winery was filed by Absa, claiming debts of R20 million. The largest part of the claim did not relate to Tollgate, but to a separate arrangement – another odd 'put' option – between the bank and Key.

Hoberman's conduct of the enquiry, which only ended, under a different chairman, in September 1998, was to become the object of bitter controversy, but Hoberman was essentially a reasonable man. The same cannot be said of Mr Justice Harold Lenin Berman, who heard the preliminary case against Askin. He was certainly provided with enough paperwork: 19 affidavits, all except two from persons unknown to Askin before he made the investment in Tollgate, and, he complained, 'all those other 17 either friends, employees or professional contacts of long standing of Key and Mackintosh, who had been brought into Tollgate by them.'

Some, at least, of the accusations related to a period before Askin had any association with the company, and of the signatures on documents alleged to be his, ten were forgeries. When he offered to have the originals submitted to examination by handwriting experts under the supervision of the British Serious Fraud Office, Askin was informed, after much procrastination, that the originals had been 'mislaid'. Such minor matters did not discourage Mr Justice Berman, who, bustling to his task with great energy, but without concerning himself overmuch with the facts, or examining any evidence, condemned Askin out of hand as a 'rogue and a villain', who was 'patently dishonest as the course of conduct he pursued in the business affairs of the companies with which he concerned himself, which was one of thieving and roguery on a grand scale', demonstrated.

Even in South Africa Judge Berman could not get away with remarks like that and found himself in hot water. Julian Askin subsequently recorded that Berman was 'publicly reprimanded by Judge President Friedman, for his improper conduct and dealing with the sequestration proceedings, which included the giving of a press conference, having a meeting in his Chambers without my Counsel being present and making highly prejudicial remarks to my then South African lawyer, Mr Jeremy Tyfield, of Bernart Vukic Potash and Getz, in a public shopping centre whilst proceedings were in progress.'

Askin's requests for disclosure of documents held by the liquidators, without which his defence against the criminal charges could not be prepared, had been completely ignored. When Judge Berman set a deadline by which Askin's defence must be submitted, his lawyers brought an urgent application to force disclosure of these essential documents.

The day before the court hearing was due the judge called a meeting in chambers. Absa, and the liquidators, were represented both by their solicitors and barristers who had clearly been well briefed. Jeremy Tyfield, Askin's solicitor, only told of the meeting the day before, protested in vain that he should also have been given the opportunity to call counsel to his assistance. At least one of Absa's barristers, Gavin Woodland, apparently agreed, since he was seen to write 'This Judge is mad' on the back of his papers (and was embarrassed, at the end of the meeting, to be asked to return the papers to the judge: fortunately he managed to remove the offending page). But in spite of any possible mental affliction, Judge Berman's decision was firm: Askin would get no papers. Unable to defend himself, Askin was faced with an immediate provisional sequestration of all his assets, wherever they might be found, and was obliged therefore to negotiate a settlement as he eventually did in October the following year.

But not all was going well for Absa, as, for the first time, some of the more-than-doubtful measures taken by their senior management saw the light. Piet Badenhorst had for some time been pursuing a personal vendetta against Kevin de Villiers, chief executive of Allied Bank (incorporated into Absa in June 1991), but who had left, finding personal relations with Badenhorst impossible. In March 1993 Absa brought an action concerning an agreement made between de Villiers, as chairman of Allied Bank, and Peter Mancer, relating to sponsorship for the 1991 BOC solo round-the-world yacht race. Absa claimed that the contract was never meant to be genuine, but was intended to enable Allied unlawfully to claim Income Tax benefits.

The case was speedily dismissed, with costs, by Mr Justice Hartzenburg, who expressed the view that 'this whole case was conducted for the purpose of trying to prove de Villiers liable for something or other and that as such the court process was abused for an ulterior motive.' Accepting the denial of Absa's lawyer, the judge nevertheless added ironically, 'I am still at a loss as to why a public company will go to the lengths to which (Absa) has gone to try and prove to the world at large that, albeit under different arrangements, it had been dishonest.'

Furious at losing this battle, within days Badenhorst's son, Frikkie, had been involved in a raid by tax officials on Mancer's home. It appeared (*Sunday Times*, 4 April 1993) that young Badenhorst had not only accompanied the raids, but had persuaded Mancer's elderly mother that they were personal friends of her son, and that the letter given to Mancer was signed by Frikkie. Almost immediately afterwards, a summons alleging fraud, attempted theft and perjury was served on de Villiers and his former assistant, Patrick Ronan. This action, which was the result of Badenhorst badgering the Attorney-General's department, was too much for de Villiers, who wrote to all directors of Sanlam and Rembrandt the controlling shareholders, and the directors and junior management of Absa. It was effective. Anton Rupert in particular had no desire for the glut of publicity that Badenhorst's antics were creating. Bob Aldworth reported that Badenhorst 'was in a stew . . . he couldn't keep the coffee in his cup.' Piet Badenhorst was indeed due to go. His fight against de Villiers had cost, as well as the adverse publicity, more than R10 million on the single court case.

And these costs contained some very illegal items indeed. Over a period of many months Absa had been tapping the private telephone lines of de Villiers, Ronan and Mancer. According to Aldworth the tapping had been managed

> by a certain Peter Arnold, who paid Dave Miller of the Bruma Lake Spy Shop, who did some of the bugging himself and sub-contracted the rest. Arnold paid his operatives either with bank notes kept for that purpose in a safe in Roy Simpson's office [Simpson was a member of Absa's Loss Control Department, headed by Danie Brink which had taken over the Tollgate account from Aldworth] or via funds channelled through . . . a public relations firm which worked specifically for Badenhorst. [An employee of the firm] was paid cheques by Absa for what was described as public relations services. He then paid them into the firm's bank account, converted the money into cash and paid Arnold.

Not only was the tapping itself illegal, the cost of the operations was nothing less than a fraud on the shareholders of Absa.

The tapes of the intercepted calls were passed daily to Badenhorst who, together with Danie Cronjé and other senior executives, listened to them and read the transcripts. An indication of the current standards of the operation was given by Simpson, who suggested to Aldworth that false information could be fed to Mrs Ronan suggesting that her husband was having an extra-marital affair. 'In the words of Mr Simpson', Aldworth reported, 'his objective in doing so was to "push her over the top". I could not believe that any human being could think, much less act, in this way.' Knowledge of the tapping was admitted by Badenhorst, Danie Cronjé, Mike de Blanche and Alwyn Noëth. Badenhorst went, but Cronjé suceeded him as Absa's Group Chief Executive, and subsequently as chairman, Noëth is Group Executive Director in charge (suitably enough!) of Treasury and Special Services.

As for the trial, de Villiers was found not guilty in March 1995, after Absa had paid an undisclosed, but generally assumed to be large, sum to de Villiers. One other little revealing detail emerged. Absa had arranged for someone to make a spurious telephone call: claiming to be Patrick Ronan, had it been genuine, the call would have been fatal to de Villiers' defence. Fortunately Ronan could prove that he could not have made the call since at the time he was with eight others in a remote Natal state park, Cape Vidal, quietly fishing, miles from a telephone.

The case then became drawn-out and almost farcical as the state sought to prove that Ronan and a party of eight had not visited Cape Vidal: that it was all a fabrication. Oddly, at least in the view of De Villiers and Ronan, the gate log for the day that the Ronan party had arrived at Cape Vidal had disappeared, while the logs for the other days were intact. Oddly too, the state did not call the resort managers but summonsed a man who had worked in the resort in a junior capacity and whom De Villiers had reason to believe was an acquaintance of Absa's Roy Simpson, who was a former Natal Parks Board official.

And Simpson, of course, was the man who had controlled the telephone tapping. Ronan's defence was naturally conceded.

Badenhorst had to go, and in June 1993, after a visit from Johan Rupert and Marinus Daling, with a comfortable retirement package he left, a bitter and sullen man. His departure was little regretted, 'a man' wrote John Spira in *Finance Week*, (28 June 1993) 'who made few friends and many enemies', although the next chairman's report piously recorded that Badenhorst's 'vision and pivotal role in the successful mergers . . . is indelibly recorded in the annals of banking'.

The first chairman of Absa, Herc Hefer, senior partner of the accountants KPMG who had come from the United Group also retired on 31 October 1993 and was succeeded by D. C. 'Dave' Brink. Brink had been summoned to the post in an effort to dilute the Afrikaner image and to distance the bank from the very public iniquities in which Hefer had allowed Badenhorst to indulge. With English as his first language, degrees from both that Afrikaner temple of learning, Potchefstroom, Witwatersrand, the focus of liberalism, and the London School of Economics, Brink could fairly claim to have a foot in both camps and could become quite upset if accused of being an Afrikaner. Bob Aldworth, no particular friend, describes Brink as having 'impeccable credentials' and as a 'highly professional manager and regarded by one and all as a man of probity, in every respect the perfect antidote to what had gone before.' Others might evidence some rather disturbing connections between Murray and Roberts, a firm of which Brinks was chairman, and the bankrupt British motor cycle company Norton Villiers, but Brink was certainly a corporate operator of great skill and experience, and a contrast to Cronjé, his new chief executive.

Absa's share price rose, as Brink and Cronjé promised a new, more respectable, regime. Cronjé was tougher and much more widely experienced than his predecessor. His experience with Armscor had taken him to the heart of the sinister transactions of the apartheid governments. Volkskas, which Cronjé had joined in 1977 had always been Armscor's banker, and its headquarters contained a 'Geheime Kamer' a secret, soundproofed, windowless room to which even such senior executives as Diedericks gained access only once. In that room the most confidential – and the most illegal – deals were transacted. More openly, at least one member of the Nationalist government's terrorist squads has related that money for his operations was collected over the Volkskas bank counters.

Investigations in South Africa which included information given by a senior officer of the Directorate of Covert Collection report that Cronjé was for a number of years,

> responsible for the funding arrangements of the Department of Civil Cooperation (DCC) and its subsidiaries and of other Special Forces units. He controlled both the holding and disbursement of funds allocated for the use of these units and entities and had a complete and detailed knowledge of all the covert organisations and front companies established by DCC.
>
> Cronjé was also involved, with others, in the misappropriation of large sums of money which were abstracted from the covert funds and taken out of the country. He was able to play his part in this because he had sole responsibility for arranging foreign currency transactions in support of covert operations, drawing on accounts which he personally controlled. Some very senior officers, some still serving, others retired, were involved with Cronjé in this activity. There is considerable nervousness among them that if Cronjé is interrogated under the auspices of the Truth and Reconciliation Commission he may disclose what occurred, and the location or ownership of funds which were misappropriated.

Dr Cronjé strongly denies that he was so involved, and traces of illegal transactions during the apartheid years have been carefully covered up – forty tons of sensitive documents are said to have been destroyed – but some proof remains. Take, for example, a transaction between the Armscor Pension fund, Banco Banesto, and Cardoen Industries. On 14 July 1987 Mario Conde, chairman of Banesto, and now in gaol, wrote

> Further to your enquiry discussion between General Malan and Mr Botha has taken place at which it was agreed in principle to retain Banesto as a prime facility for dealings between ourselves and Cardoen Industries.

Further to that our bankers are, in principle, to agree payment of commission(s) by way of Kaneko.

General Malan will discuss/finalise the above arrangements in detail with yourself and Mr Cardoen on 18.8.87

Two years later Mr Hendricks and Señor Conde were on more intimate terms. 'Dear Mario' was sent a copy of a telex from the South African Reserve Bank that an irrevocable credit had been placed at the disposition of Cardoen in the sum of US$200 million of Armscor pensioners' money. This misuse of pension fund assets would, in any other country claiming to follow the rule of law, have earned all concerned prison sentences, along with Señor Conde. (The documents are reproduced as Appendix B.)

Armscor's critics often met unhappy ends. Dirk Stoffberg and his wife were murdered in 1994. Among their effects was a memorandum to a Mr W. Nel of Armscor which detailed the participation of 'Cronjé' in the financing of Armscor through 'Volkskas'. The document was removed by the Special Police Investigation Department, and has since, unremarkably, been destroyed.

The persecution of Askin developed along the lines of that of Aldworth and de Villiers. On 4 July 1993 a warrant was granted enabling OSEO representatives led by Tommy Prins (who had previously carried out the search of Steenhuis) and accompanied by two officers from the Metropolitan Police to search the Askins' Chester Square house. It was the stuff of pure farce. After unavailingly going through all papers and records, which were instantly made available, the OSEO men insisted on rifling through the bedroom cupboards and drawers, before attempting to insist on continuing to search Susie's mother's possessions. This was too much: 'You've already been through my knickers at Steenhuis, Mr Prins, and again today,' expostulated Susie. 'Do you really want to see my mother's knickers too?' It was also too much for the Met, who told Prins that he had gone quite far enough, and showed their South African colleagues the door. They had only managed to find three documents which they could claim to be of interest. In a final note, Major Pearson, who had accompanied Mr Prins, proved his qualities of acute observation when he later described the substantial six-storey house as 'a flat'.

The press enjoyed themselves; it is not every day that Belgravia is raided by the police. Jeremy Woods, a bitter opponent of Askin's, gloated (inaccurately, of course) that Askin was 'badly shaken'. Nicholas Soames, then Minister for Food, was also interviewed and reported that 'the OSEO asked to see me and I did see them for half an hour at the ministry. They were at pains to point out that I had nothing to do with the fraud being investigated.' This claim was absolutely true, in that the offences that had taken place had all been committed before Askin or Soames had anything to do with the affairs of Tollgate, or had been later planned by the original directors.

In the following week OSEO asked the South African court for warrants of arrest to be issued in respect of Askin and Laurie Mackintosh. The most serious charge seemed to relate, not to Askin, but to the dealings that Mervyn Key had been engaging in relating to the Kyalami motor racing circuit. The London *Sunday Telegraph* commented:

> OSEO is probing the alteration of a letter from the Formula One Constructors' Association (FOCA) in London to Cape Town-based Motor Racing Enterprises, a Tollgate company, and, in particular, the role played by South African Mervyn Key who was chairman of MRE and a Tollgate director. In May 1991 FOCA wrote to Key about a five-year contract to stage a Formula 1 Grand Prix at Kyalami, South Africa. The original outlined a deal, agreed by FOCA chief Bernie Ecclestone, head of the McLaren team, under which Tollgate would buy for $US6 million the rights to stage the Grand Prix. The forgery added a sentence specifying 'a non-refundable amount of $US2 million to cover all transport and related expenditure to and from South Africa', to be paid by MRE to FOCA. It was sent to the South African Reserve Bank, which has to authorise transactions involving the exit of corporate money.
>
> FOCA says it never received the $2 million extra payment, made by Tollgate in August 1991.
>
> Judith Griggs of FOCA, who wrote the original letter from London, told the *Sunday Telegraph*: 'We never requested, nor

received, any non-refundable deposit in respect of the staging of the Grand Prix in 1992 or in 1993. The letter with the figure is not my letter and I did not write it.' Police are believed to have traced this money, together with a later sum of $US2.3 million paid for this year's Grand Prix, to Switzerland. Key has been arrested and charged with a series of fraud offences. The outstanding issues to be resolved are who tampered with the FOCA letter; who knew of the tampering; and who benefited from the money.

Mervyn Key later successfully defended himself against these charges. Nevertheless, it was Askin whose arrest had been procured, under the most suspicious circumstances, in Italy.

CHAPTER FOUR

Florence, October 1994

Susie's fightback

Susie was left in a state of shock by her husband's arrest. She could see that this was by no means merely a normal course of legal events. It was now eighteen months since Julian had left South Africa. If the South African authorities had a case against him an application for extradition could have been made either through the British courts, which would have been viewed according to its merits, or during their twelve month intermittent sojourn in Italy. Why wait, and wait until just before the Askins were due to return to London, before taking action? Surely only because the South Africans had been able by then to ensure that the Italians would do as they were asked without enquiring too deeply into the merits of the case.

Faced with her husband's summary imprisonment there was nothing else to do except work through the Italian legal system. Julian had been allowed one telephone call, which he made to alert the London firm which had represented him for many years, Baker Mackenzie. Susie followed this by a personal call to Gerald Cooke, a partner in that firm, and was taken aback when she was asked to confirm that she would be paying the fees because her husband was now unable to. Susie told him that there wouldn't be any fees if Cooke didn't get Julian out of prison and slammed the phone down. When Cooke phoned back after a few minutes, he told Susie that her husband stood very little chance against the South African onslaught. He had spoken to others and was tempted to recommend that Askin give immediate consideration to agreeing to whatever the South Africans wanted and concede to being extradited to South Africa. Cooke did agree, however, to come to Florence immediately.

Fortunately, two old friends, Ronnie and Georgia Norman, who had previously been staying at Scopetino, were still in Florence, and dropped everything to assist Susie. She had also telephoned the British Ambassador in Rome, her local Member of Parliament, Peter Brooke, and another parliamentarian, Mark Lennox-Boyd, a personal friend. British Embassies are often accused of lethargy in rendering assistance to British subjects in trouble, but this could never be said of the Foreign Office staff in Italy during the Askin episode. The Embassy put her in touch with the Florence Consul, Michael Holmes, who agreed to meet the same afternoon. This scholarly, slightly dishevelled, teddy-bear kind of person, who Susie found 'soothing to be with' proved a steadfast friend. Holmes had served in Russia, a good place for removing illusions, and seemed not to doubt for a moment that Askin's arrest had been illegal.

Susie's visit to Julian in prison was made the following day, Tuesday 12 October, at a time when Susie and Julian were grappling with the realities of the situation, convinced that there must be a speedy resolution and that the British Consul and the lawyers could surely obtain Askin's release without much delay. They had no idea that Askin, who had done nothing illegal in Italy, and who had just agreed the settlement of the claims against him in South Africa, could possibly be held for an indefinite period. For a short time the Askins were insulated against the harsh realities of their situation.

Having cleared the vital subject of fees Gerald Cooke arrived on Thursday the 14th. Susie attempted to explain, as best she could, the background, but found the lawyer unreceptive: 'I think he was terrified that he would have to go into the prison the next day. He spent most of the dinner telling me about his own problems at home and his rather shaky marriage and I remember that I felt absolutely flabbergasted that he was telling me about his rather strange marriage and was not really very interested in me, unless he was trying to make his own life sound awful to take my mind off my problems. But I was not very impressed, I can tell you.'

On Cooke's and Holmes' advice Susie had engaged the services of two Florentine lawyers, Avvocati Antonio D'Avirro and Neri Pinucci, who had chambers in a rambling converted palazzo. Susie remembers many hours waiting on the penitential bench for a daily progress report during the next three months, although the language difficulties made communication problematic. She was never totally convinced that the Italian lawyers were fully supportive, recalling after the meeting that, 'They seemed automatically suspicious that anyone who had been arrested by their men in Florence was a crook.'

The lawyers, including Cooke, together with Holmes were allowed to visit Askin in prison on Friday the 15th. Susie was waiting for them outside the main gate:

> Gerald came almost staggering out of the prison, absolutely white, got into my car and I remember so clearly driving back along the road which was to become very familiar to me. And Gerald saying, 'This is simply dreadful Susie, this is simply dreadful,' and my saying, 'Yes Gerald, tell me about it, it *is* simply dreadful.' And he said, 'I don't think I can do anything to help you, I don't think I can do anything about it. I cannot operate for you in Italy and you are going to have to go through the Italian channels now, and you will have to fight this with an Italian lawyer and I don't think there is anything more I can do.'
>
> So I said, 'Well we have been told Julian has to go in front of the judge to have a *perquisizione* on Monday, when they tell you at last why you have been arrested. Gerald, you know he has to go before the judge on Monday, do you not think he should have a representative from England here? After all he is British.'

But her solicitor was not minded to stay, claiming that he could not 'hang around here for the weekend' and was going home.

Susie was torn between the need to get to London to find more effective representation and to stay in Florence to co-ordinate activities there. She would only be allowed four visits a month to Julian, who was due to appear in court on Monday the 18th in order to be formally charged. During the weekend she had the support of two more friends, Henry and Vicky Meakin who had previously arranged to visit the Askins for one of what was intended to be their last weeks in Italy. They accompanied her to Monday's hearing, which was not in the

Questura, but in the Florence courtrooms, an older and more elegant building, with the inappropriately-named 'Jolly Café' tucked away in a corner. Susie recalls:

> On the Monday the Meakins came with me early to the court where Julian had to appear and we sat around and I introduced them to D'Avirro. Jules was late arriving and the court lists had to be altered – typically Italian! When the van eventually screeched to a halt Julian got out, in handcuffs, still wearing the clothes that he had been arrested in the previous Tuesday, nearly a week. He had not been allowed any clean clothes and had not been able to shave. So here was a man six days down the line still standing in these clothes. And when he stumbled out of the van he was dragging his right leg. He looked so awful that Henry Meakin was physically shocked and Vicky burst into tears. They had thought that this was something that could be sorted out very quickly and that people believed I had exaggerated the scene.
>
> He was taken into a side room to be put in front of the judge, and I was allowed to go and speak to him though there were two guards watching all the time. Julian as quickly as possible started to give instructions because it was an extra moment for us to speak. I was going to be allowed to see him only for an hour four times a month – not even once a week, really – so this was an opportunity to have a very quick conversation to tell me what to do. Then he had to stand in front of the judge and be accused of doing whatever in South Africa and the judge said you will be held here pending extradition to South Africa. And that was that and he was put back into the van and driven off, looking extremely ill.

Even though she was expecting the worst, Susie was horrified by her visit to Julian in prison two days later. No prison is agreeable, and this was Susie's first visit to such an institution. There was a two-hour succession of searches and holding rooms on the way in. Susie was thoroughly searched by a 'stout female, tightly corseted into her navy blue uniform'; she was made to undress completely, and her hair and ears were closely investigated. It was like 'being on an alien planet'. When she was finally allowed to see her husband they were both shocked by each other's appearance. Susie was dishevelled and tearful, while Julian was 'very rough indeed'; he had suffered a slight stroke, which had left his right side partly immobilised. He was dehydrated, desperate for something to drink and still stunned by the sudden transformation from the comfortable life of London and Tuscany to the grim surroundings of Solliciano prison.

They were each trying to hold together for the sake of the other. Although determined to put on a brave face, Susie could not restrain some tears; she had to take charge, telling Julian that she would, one way or another, ensure he was freed. They made a pact that she would devote herself to this, while he must hang on, enduring the horrible conditions and the deprivations of liberty, hitherto unimaginable, without breaking down. Askin's health was a serious complication. Both his father and brother had died prematurely of heart-related disease; three years previously he had undergone an angioplasty and was now on permanent medication with regular monitoring essential.

One other thing troubled Julian. He had, after all, been to an English public school, so primitive living conditions were not unknown, and he was a man capable of holding his own in most circumstances; but he really was apprehensive about tedium. One six-kilo parcel per week was to be allowed and Susie should please ensure that this contained nothing but reading matter – English newspapers and books.

Back in London on Thursday evening Susie showed how devastatingly efficient she could be, once they had agreed that 'it was now war'. Immediately in contact with the Foreign Office, she was advised by them exactly what Michael Holmes might do and what he could not properly be expected to do. In the first place he should insist that the prison governor ensure Askin was given proper medical attention. On the same day she had another meeting with Baker Mackenzie. The feeble suggestion – especially stupid since the lawyers had not yet established whether there was any extradition arrangement between South Africa and Italy (and in fact there was not) – was made that Julian should simply offer to return to South Africa. A telephone call to Keith Getz, the Askins' Cape Town lawyer confirmed that, even if bail was offered, there was no guarantee that this promise would be kept: he might have to wait two years in gaol before even being tried. The fact was that respectable lawyers sitting in a London office had no concept of South African realities, of the endemic violence and frequent corruption that still prevailed. She went on to insist that a summary of Julian's case with supporting documents be prepared by noon the following day.

Her diary for that day, Friday 21 October, gives an indication of Susie's activities:

> 8.30 a.m. Spoke to Patrick Fairweather (the former British Ambassador). Staying with Marina Berry – said he would speak to Michael Holmes about talking to the prison governor about getting the doctor to recommend that Julian sees Dr Massi in hospital. Peter Mills sending package of Julian's case history. Patrick Fairweather phoned to say he had spoken to Holmes. Lunched with Anthony Amhurst and described the gist of the case in confidence. Laurence Giovene at Pump Court for conference. Peter Brooke – gave a brief account of the story. Back to Baker Mackenzie for a last chat.

The meeting with Anthony Amhurst was especially significant. It had become apparent that Baker Mackenzie were quite out of their depth with a complicated criminal case involving two foreign jurisdictions. The most they could do would be to ensure that Julian's own affairs were kept in order, to transfer funds to Italy as needed, and to finalise the civil settlement that had already been agreed. It was therefore essential to find lawyers more experienced in such things. The firm of Amhurst Brown Colombotti was an obvious choice. Anthony Amhurst, the suave and elegant senior partner, was of Italian descent, and was already an acquaintance of the Askins.

They reacted with quite extraordinary speed. Amhurst, who had given up smoking, took Susie out for coffee. After the first ten minutes he sent the waiter out for a packet of cigarettes, and sat for nearly three hours, closely attending to Susie's story. The same afternoon he had arranged a conference with senior counsel, Laurence Giovene, qualified in both Italian and English law, who promised a quick response to the problem of the legality or otherwise of the application for Julian's extradition.

On Monday night Susie was back in Florence considerably fortified by the positive response she had received. There pressure from the British authorities meant that Julian was at last allowed to see a doctor on the Wednesday. At the consultation Susie was able to see, but was not allowed to speak to her husband: she found him 'frail and shaky'. Dr Massi's view was that Julian was indeed in a poor way, but that his condition was not life-threatening. Nevertheless he should certainly be removed from prison and allowed to remain under house arrest. His report was passed on to the lawyers the next day, before Susie went for her second visit to her incarcerated husband.

Taking advantage of the four visits a calendar month, and it still being October, Susie managed to get into Solliciano prison once more on Saturday 29th. Thereafter she adopted a pattern of weekly flights between Florence and London.

On the Sunday Susie attended morning service at St Mark's, the English church in Santa Trinita the church immortalised in E. M. Forster's *A Room With a View* as the benefice of the Reverend Cuthbert Eager. The incumbent at that time was, like Mr Eager, 'no commonplace chaplain', but the Right Reverend Eric Devenport, former suffragan Bishop of Dunwich, one of the oldest sees in England and acting Archdeacon in Italy and Malta. Not being without its comic side, the Church of England regarded Florence, whatever views the Pope may have had on the subject, as part of the diocese of Gibraltar until 1992; in spite of this, Anglican priests and the Catholic hierarchy are said to get on well together. A Norfolk man, the Bishop supported Norwich football team, while Julian's loyalties lay with their local rivals, Ipswich Town, which stimulated many lively debates as Eric Devenport became another valuable ally, along with Michael Holmes, in the Askins' struggle. Eric was a source of moral and spiritual support, although, when he brought Askin the Bible for which he had asked, the critical prisoner demanded 'a proper one', and not the modern translation that had been provided.

At the same time that Amhurst was setting the legal machine in motion a less formal defence team was preparing. During his work in South Africa Askin had developed some links with the British intelligence services, and the basement of the Askin's Chester Square house was occupied by a couple who were then working in that field. When they heard from Susie of the events in Italy, they realised that the South

Africans were pursuing at least an extra-legal and quite possibly an illegal course to reinforce their more open effort to procure Askin's extradition, and suggested that Susie meet someone to discuss this.

It was not likely that Susie would ignore any such possibility, and a meeting was arranged in a Berkeley Square basement, where Susie was introduced to Patrick Grayson. Grayson, a former Army officer, had until recently been in charge of the European operations of the world's largest corporate investigation firm, Kroll Associates, known for its work in studying the covert financial operations of the Iraqi Government and for its part in a series of high profile corporate contests including that between Consgold and Minorco. He was now in partnership with Michael Oatley, a former senior officer of MI6, in CIEX Ltd, a consultancy which specialises in the discreet provision of strategic advice and intelligence to very large firms in international aspects of their operations.

CIEX had a great deal more information on South African methods than was generally available. Only some of the full story of South African foreign operations has been revealed over some years, and more is still emerging. Only in 1998, for example, did it become apparent that South Africa had made the biological weapons developed by Basson's researchers available to agents abroad, and that these had almost certainly been used in at least one British assassination, of the anti-apartheid journalist Peter Martin. Admitting the existence of such weapons on the BBC (14 July 1998) a South African scientist described how a sharpened screw driver was impregnated with a poison, the effects of which simulated the symptoms of a natural disease, 'When the – er – person who was to be stabbed was – er – stabbed' – carefully avoiding such terms as 'victim' or 'murder'. While this particular episode dated back to the era of Nationalist apartheid government, there were, as late as 1998, indications that the murder squads continued at work (the murder of Peter de Bruyn in May of that year being one). And Julian Askin was to find out for himself the uncomfortable sensation of being targeted by men who had learned their trade in the Vlakplaas murder squad.

Patrick Grayson told Susie that she was in urgent need of some protection while some investigations were made into who was behind Julian's arrest. The first stage in providing this would be for Susie to relate all the details to a man who was waiting to be briefed, but who had to remain anonymous. Was she willing to do this?

From this point onwards a certain level of discretion is demanded, and some identities are disguised. The man who appeared in the Berkeley Square basement, as it were from the walls, was a burly figure with shaven head, shoulders that merged into his neck and an Afrikaner accent: he was immediately christened 'Bullet head' by Susie. In the four years of investigations that followed, unorthodox and unconventional methods were needed to uncover and counter some dangerously sinister actions: alliances were invoked and prior debts collected in a complex series of operations which involved both the secret services and armed forces of more than one country – and this was funded, commercially and at a considerable expense, by the Askins themselves.

The dangers were real and imminent. Even before Julian Askin's arrest in Italy an attempt had been initiated finally to dispose of him by direct action. Four years later an admission was made by a former South African police officer: his name cannot be revealed, as he insisted that his life would be in danger if it were known. Nevertheless his story was confirmed, and is available in a sworn statement from an eminent South African barrister. He warrants that an approach was made by an identified individual who claimed to be acting on behalf of the 'guys at the Afrikaner Bank', who wanted Askin back in South Africa to be 'dealt with'. By this it was understood that Askin was to be kidnapped, flown to South Africa, transported to one of the farms in the country kept by the Department of Covert Collections and killed (although in fact the outcome would probably have been a 'disappearance' in Italy, or a convenient road accident). The price for this was US$200,000, which would be the largest part of a total cost estimated at between $300–400,000: all was to be planned as a military operation.

The policeman was tempted, but refused: he did not have a suitable infrastructure in place, and had a certain sympathy with Askin whom he considered had been 'screwed by the guys at the Afrikaner Bank'. Had the proposal concerned a 'heavy duty' criminal – a murderer or terrorist – he might have stretched a point. One month later Askin was arrested. Having failed in direct action, 'the guys at the Afrikaner Bank', it would appear, had decided to try another tack. English courts being out of the question an attempt would be made to get Askin returned to South Africa through the good offices of members of the Italian judiciary.

Further evidence of the probability of Absa involvement was provided by Professor John Dugard, who was interviewed on 3 December 1994 by Gerald Cooke. Dugard, professor of law at Witwatersrand University, considered it 'quite likely' that there had been 'a wealth of improper activity at that Bank' and that Askin's accusations were 'almost certainly justified'. He believed that Afrikaners accused of criminal activity were not prosecuted in cases where English-speakers were, and reiterated the close connection between the security apparatus of Nationalist governments and Absa, instancing the use of Absa premises by agents of BOSS for interrogation and for intelligence-related work.

There was another reason why the Afrikaner banking establishment were becoming nervous of what effect Askin's activities might have upon their interests. In April 1994 the first comprehensively democratic elections to central government had been held, with 62 per cent of the votes being cast for the ANC, resulting in a coalition government with a majority of members drawn from Nelson Mandela's party. It would have been possible, and very much according to the practice in other African countries, for the victors to have appropriated the spoils, and turned the Afrikaners – the hated Boers to most blacks – out of the lucrative positions they held in industry, the professions, commerce, finance, the civil service, the military and the judiciary – the last three of which had been almost exclusively Afrikaner. An obvious target would have been the 'guys at the Afrikaner bank', the Boer bankers at Absa.

As it turned out, Mandela's government was impeccably orthodox and conservative. Although cosmetic non-executive board appointments were made, Afrikaner control of the Reserve Bank was left undisturbed, and the finance minister, Trevor Manuel, earned himself international admiration for his willingness to conform to accepted practice. A great deal of money was dispensed by Sanlam in directions where it was thought it would do most good, and black millionaires were created overnight. Any interference which would disturb this delicate order would be very unwelcome, and Askin, it was perceived, was in a good position to provide such interference.

Moreover, it also seemed clear that even the ostensibly legal procedures were initiated and controlled by the unscrupulous and improper actions of both South African and Italian officials. It is sobering to think that, had Julian Askin not been a very wealthy man, then officials, of friendly and (by then) democratic governments would have obtained the illegal incarceration, and possibly the murder of a British citizen.

Susie's next meeting in London was with Michael Oatley, who was now to take charge of the operation within CIEX. As a first step secure communications were essential. Absa's propensity for tapping telephone lines was already established, and Oatley was aware of the extent to which police and officials in many European countries were in South African pay. Susie was therefore provided with a sophisticated mobile telephone which had been developed to prevent the possibility of calls being intercepted. Land lines were afterwards only used when it seemed advisable to feed false information to any possible listener. In the following weeks and months a shadowy network was drawn together to supplement the efforts of official advisers. The Askins' understanding of what was happening to them and how to fight it was enlarged by information and connections developed in South Africa, in Italy, other parts of Europe and in the United States.

Michael Oatley does not resemble the conventional idea of a secret agent: tall, with ferocious eyebrows, he would stand out in any company. He is also unusual among former members of MI6 in that much of his career has been exposed to the public view because of the role which he secretly played across two decades, sometimes with Government approval and sometimes taking a path of his own, in contacts with the leadership of the Provisional IRA. His activities have never been fully explained or admitted but evidently made a substantial contribution to developing the Peace Process which led to the 1998 Easter Agreement and ceasefire. In his early years with MI6 he had been an African specialist, and his last overseas post was in Zimbabwe. From there he would have had detailed evidence of South Africa's covert war to destabilise its neighbours and of the politico-military structure which controlled it. Back in London from 1984 he successively commanded MI6 activities in the Middle East and Europe, supervising the international counter-terrorist offensive, and finished up as one of the service's most senior officers. His and Grayson's shared instinct for vigorous action, and their combined range of contacts, suggested a powerful pair of allies. Neither had any illusions about the Italians.

'Italy', as the *Economist* observed in 1998, 'is not a normal democracy.' Nor, it should be admitted, does the rule of law apply there as it does in Britain. Petty corruption is so common as to be unremarkable, a fact of daily life – see for example, Tim Parks' description of the ubiquitous 'bustarella' (little envelopes containing banknotes) essential in normal contact with the authorities. On a larger scale hundreds of millions of pounds of public money disappear into the hands of the Mafia and its Calabrian equivalent, the Camorra. Brave efforts are sporadically made to indict the more obvious offenders, but are often exposed by such extraordinary events as that in which a group of prisoners actually absconded from the court room itself, through a tunnel which had been excavated to the street outside, an operation impossible without widespread connivance. It is tacitly admitted that Carlo Levi was right when he wrote 'Christ stops at Eboli', and that Italy south of Rome is governable only with the co-operation of criminal bodies (motorway tolls are not levied south of Rome: they would never be collected).

It may be true that for sheer professional corruption at the highest level, France has no equal. (Two thousand five hundred million dollars of Saudi Arabian money went walkabout somewhere in French Government circles in 1974 and has never since been discovered.) The South African embassy in Paris was also found a convenient centre for the intelligence service quartermasters to operate undisturbed. But in Europe Italy is unsurpassed. A survey of the levels of corruption that can be expected, made by Transparency International in 1998, placed Italy at the bottom of Western European countries, on a level with Poland, but more corrupt than Chile, South Africa or Malaysia. In the same year one Italian Prime Minister, Bettino Craxi, had fled the country after being sentenced to eight years' imprisonment for corruption; Silvio Berlusconi, the leader of the opposition, continued unabashed in spite of three prison sentences (which it is highly likely he would never serve) and many more trials pending, including one in Spain. In any other Western European country public opinion would have forced a resignation, but in Italy Berlusconi's crimes were accepted, if not as normal, at least not unexpected. Berlusconi, described by the European anti-trust Commissioner, Karel van Miert, as 'a danger ... to the survival of the democratic system', had as a major financial partner Anton Rupert's Swiss company Richemont.

Even so, when Grayson and Oatley accepted their mission they were told by their Italian friends that if they wanted help they should go, not to Italy, but to the United States. Both legally and illegally, much of the real power in Italy, stemmed from those princes in exile, Italians who had made their way in America.

Before returning to Italy on her weekly visit Susie had to find time to complete the details for the settlement of the civil action brought by the South Africans, which was still hanging fire.

By Friday Susie, joined now by her daughter Charlotte, a great comfort, was back in Florence to be reunited. Saturday saw the arrival of the English QC Laurence Giovene. Giovene's presence in Florence meant that for the first time there was reasonable communication between the lawyers – Cooke had very little Italian, but Giovene was able to talk to D'Avirro and Pinucci in their common language, and with a common background in Italian law. Their first effort was to convince the Florence court that Askin should at least, in view of his uncertain health, be held under domiciliary arrest, although by that time Giovene had been able to satisfy himself that there was, in fact, no extradition treaty in force between South Africa and Italy; but the Italian authorities found it convenient not to be convinced of this. Some of the millions of dollars that South Africa had liberally dispersed during the sanctions period might well ensure that certain Italian officials would be tempted to turn incurably blind eyes to the tedious facts of the law.

There were by now a number of people authorised to visit Julian in prison. Susie was restricted to her four visits a month, but Michael Holmes as British consul was allowed free access, as were Julian's lawyers. With more difficulty Bishop Devenport, who assumed full episcopal garb for the occasion, was able to convince the authorities that as Julian's priest he was allowed to administer to his spiritual needs.

By the time of Susie's third visit, on Saturday 5 November, Julian had achieved a remarkable degree of acceptance with his three Arab drug-dealing cell mates – Abu Emin, at 44, was very much in charge, and as luck would have it, a leader of the large and noisy Arab contingent in the prison. Emin, a short, square and heavily muscled figure, was said to have a turnover of over £25 million a year, mainly in cocaine. He supplied a senior police officer in Rome who had the monopoly of selling drugs in the capital's largest prison: he did not expect to have to serve a long sentence in prison, and certainly he was treated with respect by all, even the warders, generally an arrogant and brutal lot. The other cell mates, Mohamed Ali and Drize, were much younger, content to follow Emin's orders. Askin kept a diary of his prison life, written with considerable difficulty, since any pen he might acquire would be broken by the guards during their frequent searches. Pages of the diary were smuggled out concealed among the papers of his visiting lawyers, whilst Susie supplemented the few letters she was allowed to send by writing between the lines of the newspapers she was permitted to bring to the prison. In his diary Askin records two instances of Emin's exercise of authority.

> November 12: Emin says there is a big fight coming between people of other factions and that he will go for a walk this evening and try and keep the peace. That is where he has gone now in his track suit and leather jacket. He no doubt is tough, hard and shrewd and not a man to be crossed. Everyone treats him with great respect and I expect he has earned it the hard way.

> 11.30 Guard arrives and says I have to collect all my things and I am being sent to another cell. No.4 J. Was devastated. Emin went straight into action and said that I insisted on speaking to the Brigadiere. The guard, though somewhat taken aback, agreed; this brought on all the worries and tension. After half an hour I was summoned to the Brigadiere, and asked to take Emin with me because I needed someone to translate. The Brigadiere turned out to be small and had all the arrogant chippiness of a lance-corporal long passed over, really difficult. And did not look at me once as he shouted at Emin. Emin kept his cool and said that I wanted to remain with them and did not want to go. It was left undecided.

The strange friendship that developed between the Arab drug baron and the Englishman was to prove crucial to Askin's survival. His fellow prisoners were happy to keep the cell 'spotlessly clean' while Askin provided little treats – Mars bars and Coca Cola, savoured in little sips for lunch. Since the prison food was inedible, and the water literally undrinkable, prisoners were allowed to do their own cooking on a camping gas stove in the cell. Privileged by his contacts with the outside world, visits by Susie supplemented by lawyers, consul and bishop, Askin was able to keep his cell well supplied with food and cigarettes, the prison currency. It was a point of honour, and indeed often of survival, that the drug dealers had no contact with the outside world which might reveal to the authorities other members of the chain: Emin, in spite of having in all probability large sums at his disposal, deliberately passed his sentence in seclusion and deprivation – no visits, no mail, no contacts of any kind apart from with his lawyer.

As the only Englishman in prison, and one with no criminal background or experience, Askin was an object of intense curiosity to both inmates and warders, curiosity which sometimes turned to contempt and hostility. Most warders took every opportunity of provoking Askin, knocking books out of his hands, taunting and pushing him, hoping to drive him to retaliate. On the only occasion Askin attempted to use the small exercise yard he was assaulted by two Arabs. 'Jungle Jules' flattened one while Emin dealt with the other; thereafter it was apparent that Askin was under Emin's protection and the 'English prisoner' was left alone. Having let his fair hair grow rather than submit to the prison barber, Askin was christened the *vecchio leone* (the old lion) by his friend Emin, but the notice posted outside the cell described him as Julian Michael Cunning Askin.

Had it not been for the support offered by Emin and his cell mates Askin would have had a very difficult time in prison. Overcrowding was universal – four in a two-man cell, ten in one intended for six. Constant noise, screaming, sounds of pain and conflict as warders laid into prisoners or prisoners fought among themselves – and knives, homemade from cans, were ubiquitous and in constant use. An assault could be organised at one end of the cell blocks and the information carried from cell to cell via the narrow windows within the hour: punishment beatings were inflicted on the stairways, hidden from sight of other prisoners. Supervision was sporadic; the semi-literate warders, recruited from the Mezzogiorno, Italy's impoverished south, were a mixture of vicious thugs and well-meaning simpletons, united in their racial antipathy towards the Arabs who formed the majority of prisoners. No attempt whatever was made for recreation, education or re-integration into society, except occasionally among the prisoners them-selves. It would be misleading to refer to them as convicts. Only a limited form of Habeas Corpus, that basic safeguard of Anglo-Saxon law, obtains in continental Europe. Those imprisoned by administrative action can be held for a full year before any charge is brought, and once a charge is brought can face another long wait before being allowed any form of trial. A great number of the Solliciano prisoners had therefore never been, and probably never would be, convicted of any crime at all.

Askin was surprised to see how even the Italian lawyers seemed nervous of the guards. Patrick Grayson, who contrived access by claim-ing to be another lawyer with visiting cards printed to suit, had no such inhibition: 'he treated the guards like scum, shouting at them in English – "Go away, you silly men" and they went.'

Askin recorded one of the regular searches of the cell:

> November 18: 6am All hell breaks loose. All cells are open and we are bundled out and sent down to a holding room down below. It is dark and as usual the guards behave as if they are all looking for promotion in the SS. It is about 35 minutes before we are called back to our cells. The scene of devastation has to be seen to be believed. There is literally everything ripped apart, all my papers thrown into the corri-dor and I am not allowed them back. My books now all over the cell, their covers off, my writing paper strewn across the floor. Food has been thrown everywhere. TV cord ripped out, food packets emptied, everywhere. The bathroom devas-tated, bedding ripped apart, sheets thrown across the room. I have never seen anything like it. The behaviour of cavemen. All the small things, like salt and pepper have been ripped up and scattered, in an act of stupifying hostility. An interesting spectacle: Emin's clothes, shoes, hauled down and stamped on the ground: he meticulously kept these and now they are dirtied and rubbed on the ground. The clothes hooks we had only purchased days ago have been ripped from the walls

and snapped, the watch on the TV, so we could all see the time, ripped off, its glass smashed – but fortunately it still works. This is a regular search you get once a month or so. The cell was totally devastated and everything broken. If there was a bag of rice they would open it and throw all the rice away. Sometimes it was thrown down the lavatory and as these things were items you bought with precious money it really was heartbreaking.

Even with the battery of expensive legal talent employed by the Askins, and Susie's valiant efforts and courageous support, it was quite likely that Julian Askin might remain in Solliciano for many months – even supposing South African attempts at extradition eventually failed. But the Askins' team was impressive. In England Baker Mackenzie were looking after Askin's financial affairs and putting the finishing touches to the civil settlement, as part of which Absa withdrew all allegations against their client. This was finally signed on 13 October. His defence – and subsequent attack – was in the hands of Anthony Amhurst, with Laurence Giovene as leading counsel.

In Italy D'Avirro and Pinucci were reinforced by a famous Turin lawyer, Professor Vittorio Chiusano, head of the Italian criminal bar, who acted for Giovanni Agnelli of Fiat. The lawyers had jointly reached the conclusion that no extradition arrangements did in fact exist between South Africa and Italy. Such an agreement had indeed been in force between Italy and Britain's Imperial possessions, colonies and dominions, dating from 1873, but these had lapsed when South Africa became an independent republic, outside the Commonwealth, and had never been renewed. This being so, Askin's arrest was illegal, but it was to become clear that at least one Italian court was determined to ignore this fact. What is more, the South African authorities now acknowledge that there *is* no extradition treaty between that country and Italy. It can be assumed, having had so long a period to establish the facts, that this was known at the time. The extradition card was a bluff, played only after the kidnap attempt had been rejected by the South African police officer.

In 1998 the Cape Attorney-General, Frank Kahn, wrote to the Director General: Justice, in Pretoria: 'Your 9/11/3 (R/J) dated 24/2/1998, received on 18/3/1998 (sic), as well as your fax 9/5/3 (R/J) dated 22/4/ 1998 refer ... *As South Africa does not have an extradition treaty with Italy*' (my italics). The letter then goes on to particularise the circumstances under which a person may be extradited from South Africa to another country, under the Extradition Act of 1962. This Mr Kahn was none other than the Attorney-General who, four years previously, had applied for Askin to be extradited from Italy, a country with which he later acknowledged no extradition agreement existed – and that the law governing such cases had been in effect since 1962! While other explanations can be advanced, like that of Dr Johnson when taxed with a lexicographical error, 'Sheer ignorance, Sir!', the Attorney-General's correspondence reinforces the evidence that Askin's extradition application was a piece of flummery. Under its cover Italian judges sympathetic to South Africa could skate over the legal niceties and deport Askin before anyone drew attention to the inconvenient facts.

Italian justice

The immediate legal authority in Italy was the Florence Court of Appeal, a confusing term in Anglo-Saxon law. Its equivalent would be a Crown Court, but one acting at the same time as a prosecuting authority, and it was made clear that little sympathy was to be expected there.

The explanation for the curious attitude displayed by the Florence magistrates was being collected by CIEX's team of intelligence gatherers. In Italy these were represented by two experienced agents who have asked to be known simply as Major Black and Mr White. Both are genial, humorous, powerfully-built and sensible men. Major Black, the senior, concentrated on strategy, while Mr White, very sympathetic and approachable, although speaking little English, proved to be a source of great support to Julian and Susie, as well as providing practical protection. Major Black was not immediately available, and Susie was given instructions to meet Mr White outside a bank in a nearby village. Cautious, she waited with Poppy on the other side of the street while both she and Mr White made sure of each other.

Messrs Black and White were already aware that the Askin's case was being handled at the highest level in Italy. A very senior officer, Gianni de Gennaro, previously director of the DIA, the police department dealing with the Mafia, had taken charge of the case in Rome. De Gennaro had a special relationship both with the senior public prosecutor in Florence, Luigi Vigna, stemming from their work together in the DIA and their membership of the same Masonic Lodge, the infamous Propaganda 2, and with Vittorio la Cava, a senior local judge. This relationship was clear from the outset when Interpol in Rome had telegraphed Vigna (Appendix C), confirming Askin's arrest the same day (11 October) mentioning that 'the South African Authorities manifest great importance to the arrest ... given the amount of money involved and the level of prominence given to the case by the South African intelligence services in the past and at present.' This telegram ended with a note indicating the 'central director of criminal police, de Gennaro was taking personal responsibility for liaison with the Florence judiciary and police.' A copy was sent to one Terry Govender at the South African Rome embassy. Govender was a former member of the South African narcotics squad and security branch, where he worked under Peter Wright, whom, Askin believes, exerted pressure on the Italians to secure his imprisonment.

One reason why de Gennaro was taking such a close interest in Askin's case was the personal friendship of that policeman and the South African ambassador in Rome, Glenn Babb. Ambassador Babb had previously worked as a diplomat, and was at the time a friend of the long-serving Foreign Minister, 'Pik' Botha (although Botha has since strongly condemned Babb's Italian activities). In 1989 Babb had fought the Randburg seat for the National Party (he lost). Significantly, Babb's election agent was the notorious Craig Williamson, one of Police Commissioner Johan Coetzee's best-known spies and most reliable murderers.

Guilt by association is not judicially reliable, but Williamson's appointment as Babb's agent, a very personal relationship, would need much explanation. A self-confessed murderer, Williamson admitted responsibility for the killing of Ruth First and Katryn and Jeanette Schoon, among a catalogue of other crimes. Described as 'all of twenty stone; his head looked tiny, perched as it was on top of all that fat', Williamson was a character no decent person, let alone a diplomat, would associate with. Although he had strong ties with such organisations as the International Freedom Front (a DCC-funded operation) and was a member of the Civil Co-operation Bureau, Williamson followed an individual agenda, including a highly profitable smuggling operation through the Seychelles which he ran in co-operation with Mario Ricci. When Francesco Pazienza, one of the most important Propaganda 2 members, notorious for his role in setting up the Iran-Contra schemes in the United States, and the probable murderer of the banker Roberto Calvi, who was found hanging from Blackfriars Bridge, fled to South Africa he was given refuge by Ricci. Williamson himself is wanted by the British authorities as the principal perpetrator of the ANC headquarters bombing.

Given this network of influence it was reasonable to assume, as in fact it transpired, that Judge Vigna could be relied upon to turn down any case presented by Askin. Any remedy lay only with the Rome Corte di Cassazione, the Supreme Court of Cassation, which was comparable to an Appeal Court in Britain.

Plundering the public purse

Before the case found its way to Rome a proposal was received from South Africa. It came on 25 November. Alan Greenblo, the journalist who had first introduced Askin to the Tollgate director Mervyn Key, wrote to describe the approach: 'The gist of it is as follows (I'm just the messenger): my sources are not convinced that you're as ill as claimed, and tell me it's a ruse to help get sympathetic atmosphere for the extradition defence. They also say that they're convinced they'll get extradition. If you accept this inevitability, they say, it would be better for you to return voluntarily instead and they will intervene personally to ensue that you get bail i.e., that you'll be able to prepare a proper defence from outside prison.'

The suggestion, Greenblo reported, had been made by Tony Berhman, senior partner of Werksmans, a principal firm of lawyers employed by Absa: it could therefore be regarded as coming direct from Absa. Alan Greenblo suggested that it might be that Absa wanted Askin's co-operation in pursuing Mervyn Key who, it seemed, might have been the real culprit in the Tollgate affair: but Askin, writing to Anthony Amhurst on 18 December 1994, said the offer 'should be ignored and treated with contempt . . . as I have not done anything I am of the view that they can – in the words of Shakespeare – get fucked.' When Amhurst, investigating this offer, telephoned Absa's solicitors in South Africa he received confirmation, but also the extraordinary warning that he should not trust Absa an inch – this from their own lawyers!

Other indications existed that questions were indeed being raised in South Africa about the justice of Absa's persecution of Askin.

The Alan Crabtree story attracted much British attention when it was featured in the *Daily Telegraph*, a newspaper which, together with its Sunday stablemate, was beginning to focus on South African financial scandals. Crabtree's plight was further publicised by a BBC television feature. In South Africa the *Financial Mail* described the 'dubious activities' of Claasen, Key and, it was claimed, Diedericks, which had taken place well before Askin's arrival on the Tollgate scene.

Much more damagingly to Absa, an article appeared in the Cape Town investigative periodical *Noseweek*, on June 29 1994. *Noseweek* is a remarkable publication, written, edited and produced by Martin Welz, a lawyer, with the help of journalist Maureen Barnes. It has appeared, somewhat sporadically, since 1993 and has made itself very unpopular among certain sections of South African society, especially those anxious to conceal their activities. Unlike the London journal *Private Eye*, which while uncovering many scandals, has also published some scandalous lies, *Noseweek* is careful to check its facts, and on the rare occasions Welz gets things wrong, apologises. Welz's unparalleled variety of sources made him an invaluable member of the team that Askin and CIEX were later to form in South Africa.

Noseweek's June issue covered both the Aldworth and Askin cases and it pulled no punches.

> Both [Aldworth and Askin] are intelligent and are widely
> respected – at one time they were even celebrated – for their
> ability to handle complex financial matters. Both now believe
> that, because they are 'Engelse', they have been made the
> scapegoats in a vast, Broederbond-contrived cover-up.

Both believe they inadvertently stumbled into a scheme of fraud aimed at plundering the public purse; a scheme which is so vast, shameless and pervasive that they fear they are unlikely to get a fair hearing if they return to South Africa to face their accusers. There are many unsettling reasons to believe they may be right.

The moral and financial collapse in the Broederbond-controlled sector of South African banking and finance is becoming increasingly obvious . . .

Welz continued to point out that the conduct of the criminal charges, which were the pretext for the legal attempt to secure Askin's person by means of extradition:

> [certainly] provide no reassurance! The elderly Judge Berman, (who had from the first shown himself grossly prejudiced) 'is neither physically nor intellectually able to handle a long and complex commercial case which not only puts Askin on trial, but has awesome implications for banking and corporate life in South Africa. In fact, the judge's careless expressions of prejudice against Askin, and his disinclination to put Absa and its cohorts on the line, at least on equal terms, would long ago have led a lesser judge to recuse himself. But then we know from personal experience at *Noseweek* that a sense of shame in judicial matters is not one of Judge Berman's strongest points. Which is a pity – for justice.'

Moreover, Bertrand Hoberman, the lawyer appointed to head the enquiry into the circumstances surrounding Tollgate's collapse, 'was also the advocate appointed by Absa to draw up their application for Tollgate's liquidation, and therefore in the bank's pay. The conflict of interest has since become more blatant: he has already asked Absa's attorneys to provide him with a draft report for his enquiry.'

The *Noseweek* article made direct allegations against the banks now forming Absa. That they, for instance,

> 'did not tell Askin that only three weeks earlier, the MD of Tollgate, Mr Diedericks, had written to the bank asking for

the company to be put into liquidation, as it was unable to meet its commitments to the bank ... Absa, who have taken both Volkskas and Trust Bank into their warm embrace, have certainly continued to keep a tight hand on the liquidation proceedings to ensure that the Bankers' role in events is not investigated. Some of the main players in the Tollgate saga, including Diedericks, were Volkskas employees that worked directly under, and reported to Mr D. C. Cronjé (now chairman of Absa).'

There are many reasons to believe the banks' behaviour, and deals they did while they were in control of Tollgate materially prejudiced other creditors. Askin at that time believed that the directors were responsible for looting between R30 million and R70 million out of Tollgate between 1987 and 1990 – probably on behalf of Volkskas.

If this was so then there would be serious financial consequences. Askin 'has stated that Volkskas and Trust Bank should, if the Tollgate enquiry is correctly conducted, have to pay back R400 million to Tollgate, for distribution to other creditors.' Welz hinted at one of the reasons why the banks were vulnerable.

Most of the problems in Tollgate have their origin in the over-ambitious activities of Afrikaner financial institutions in the late seventies and early eighties. They had become overconfident because of the apparent limitless backing they could expect from Government and the Reserve Bank. The government spent its vast secret Defence Budget through the trusted Broeders at Volkskas and Trustbank – and latterly Absa Bank. So did the Strategic Fuel Fund. All these very secret and suspect deals were done in the secret, sound proof dealing room at Volkskas' head office in Pretoria and were not recorded in the bank's normal records. At one stage the SFF had a R4 billion line of credit at Absa! ....

All the subsidiary companies that were 'taken' over by Tollgate had only one thing in common: they all owed vast amounts of money to Volkskas and Trust Bank – vast amounts of money that they were unable to repay.

These banks then connived at designing some pretty nifty schemes to hide the debts from unsuspecting investors.

By February 1990 Absa's total exposure in the various companies which would ultimately form the Tollgate Group was approximately R650 million. Volkskas managed to get their people into control of Tollgate, which then proceeded to take over these companies – and, of course, their debts, to the bank. Next step was to pay off the bad bank loans by means of extra rights and share issues, which an unsuspecting public were encouraged to buy with optimistic claims about Tollgate's future.

All this put a very different perspective on the claims made by Absa that Askin had pilfered large sums of money. These allegations looked even flimsier after 31 October 1994, when Christo Faul and J. N. Wepener of Absa signed a waiver of 'any claims (actual or contingent and whether direct or indirect) of whatsoever nature which Absa may have against Askin, Mrs Askin or the Groton Trust.' Given this comprehensive statement Absa's continued accusations can only be interpreted as a campaign of unfounded persecution – accusations that nevertheless allowed the Cape Supreme Court to issue an international warrant for Askin's arrest in July.

The supporting evidence for the warrant's issue was prepared by Major Pearson, who had conducted the search of the 'flat' in Chester Square, and contained affidavits as to the misdoings of Key and Mackintosh as well as Askin's alleged crimes. These centred around the complex affairs of the Kyalami racetrack, which had been rendered literally incomprehensible by the manoeuvrings of Key, Mackintosh, McCay and Jooste.

The South African authorities seemed to be working to a timetable in Askin's case. The international warrants for his arrest had been procured in July 1994. The question then arises why, armed with such a warrant, the South African authorities did not attempt to serve it on Askin in London, where he was during the whole of the following month, rather than wait till he returned to Italy, where, as the Cape Attorney-General doubtless knew, no extradition agreement existed. The only convincing answer is that the Italian police and officials could be pressurised in a way that would be impossible in London.

From the South African point of view Italy had the advantage that in prison conditions there might well damage Askin's health in a fairly permanent fashion. Witness one telephone conversation between Mrs Mervyn Key and her sister:

Mrs Key: Did you see what happened to Askin?
Sister: Ja, ja.
Mrs Key: Isn't that amazing?
Sister: It is actually, what, three million pounds?
Mrs Key: No, three million rand.
Sister: No, pounds surely.
Mrs Key: No rand, rand.
Sister: Oh for God's sake; that's nothing!
Mrs Key: It just goes to show what a storm in a teacup it is.
Sister: Ja, but he is still going to face criminal charges.
Mrs Key: Ja, but that too is all trumped up you know.
Sister: Did he have a heart attack?
Mrs Key: Ja, he did.
Sister: But he has been in all this time.
Mrs Key: Ja, I know. With two North African gentlemen who apparently asked for favours.
Sister: Oh God. Oh God!
Mrs Key: According to good sources, that is why he is so ill.
Sister: Oh no.
Mrs Key: So he has probably got Aids now.
Sister: Oh shit. Oh God.
Mrs Key: Terrible, hey. You don't wish that on your worst enemy.
Sister: Terrible, that is really sad. But I don't either . . .
Mrs Key: I wish it on Absa though.

And another conversation between Mervyn Key and Laurie Mackintosh:

Mackintosh: I was very interested in that newspaper article on Mr Askin.
Key: Wasn't it interesting?
Mackintosh: God, he's had a stroke.
Key: Ja, well I don't believe that story frankly. I think it's just

a lie. But I hear from Rupert Wragg and he's asked me to have lunch with him tomorrow

Medical care in Italy is, to be generous, patchy, and that in prison considerably worse than it would have been in Britain. Askin was taken for an electro-cardiograph in the prison hospital. The person carrying out the examination – Askin was assured he was properly qualified – had to prop up an instruction manual on Askin's stomach while trying to find out how to work the thing. Askin finally lost patience and refused to carry on. He also refused, distrusting the safety of the operation and the reliability of the test, which might have proved anything the authorities wanted them to prove, to have a blood test in the prison. If this was needed, he insisted, it must be done in a proper hospital and under consular supervision. He also refused, in spite of much shouting and abuse, to take the Valium that was insisted upon (although, for the sake of quiet, he became adept at pretending to swallow the pills).

But in spite of such treatment Askin's condition had not greatly deteriorated after his first stroke, after he had made the difficult psychological adjustment of coping with an indefinite period of arrest with possible dire consequences at the end. Patrick Grayson and Michael Oatley, who had some experience of behaviour under stress, were both deeply impressed by Askin's light-hearted courage in very difficult circumstances.

The thrust of Askin's attempts to secure legal redress was through Professor Chiusano's appeal to the Supreme Court in Rome, a process which it was estimated would take some months. The events of 23 December were therefore entirely unexpected. Julian was gloomily awaiting the last meeting with Susie before Christmas, which she was to spend in England, but instead of his wife the two Florence lawyers, D'Avirro and Pinucci, appeared, obviously bringing good news. They had rushed to the prison, straight from the courtroom, where documents had just arrived from Amhurst, translated into Italian and covered with the Italian Embassy's official stamp. These were translations of the agreement made with the liquidators, proving that the allegations made against Askin by them and Absa had been withdrawn following the reluctant settlement he had made in October. There was little alternative for the Florence magistrates other than to authorise Askin's release from prison to house arrest.

Prison procedures meant that this could not, in fact, be effected before the next day. As it happened the British Consul, Michael Holmes, was in the prison Governor's office when the news came through: he described how the Governor's face dropped with disappointment. Before being allowed to see Susie, Askin was treated with more than usual discourtesy, and given a particularly thorough body search. For much of the time allowed to them the Askins sat in stunned silence, hardly daring to believe that something would not intervene to prevent his release.

CHAPTER FIVE

Wondrous Deceitful

'(The Italians) for the most part are both grave and ingenious, but wondrous deceitful in their actions.'

WILLIAM LITHGOW, *Rare Adventures and Painfull Peregrinations.*

Release?

Askin's cell mates had no such reservations: by the time he was returned from the meeting with Susie a party was being organised by the three happily grinning Arabs. By the time the special risotto and fried chicken, served with Coca Cola, the Château-Lafite of prison life, a score of well-wishers had packed into the cell. Considering that most of them had still years of their sentences to serve Askin found it extraordinarily touching.

His Christmas Eve release was unceremonious. Disregarding the guard's objections, Emin insisted on accompanying Askin to the door of the cell block – an indication of the Tunisian's influence. Pushed into a van with another prisoner, Askin was refused his passport, but before the van got through the main gates a brown paper package was thrust into his hand containing it.

Julian remembers every detail of the journey to prospective freedom. Once outside the prison his fellow passenger began a stream of invective at the guards, which no amount of banging on the van doors would silence. Only when the van stopped did the shouting also cease, and when the recalcitrant prisoner was finally bundled out the cursing began again, until one of the guards jumped out after the man, who prudently disappeared.

At Tavernelle, the nearest small town to Scopetino, the prison van handed Askin over to the local *carabiniere*, who accorded him the sort of treatment that would have been more appropriate to a convicted terrorist than a man who had just been released from prison. Two cars were required, one with Askin and two troopers, the other with four men, all armed with machine pistols. Susie, who had just stopped at a petrol station, saw the procession sweep past at high speed and had to rush off in pursuit. Arrived back at the farmhouse the urgency was forgotten and the drama relaxed: machismo having been satisfied and 'face' preserved, the *carabiniere* hung around to smoke and enjoy the view, while the Maresciallo (Sergeant in charge) quite civilly requested Askin's signature to a document and wished them both a Happy Christmas. Before taking himself and his squad off, leaving Askin free to take his first bath in three months, the Maresciallo observed that he and his colleagues were in the habit of eating their spaghetti between 8.30 and 9.00 in the evenings, with the implication that should Askin choose to absent himself, that would be a convenient time.

Even had Askin been the rogue that the South African press and Mr Justice Berman had described there was nothing to prevent him leaving. His passport had been returned, Absa's accusations withdrawn, his very considerable wealth freed from any threats of litigation, and Susie's handsome Constantia house restored. They could have returned to London and taken up their life there, or anywhere else in the world with the exception of South Africa, in great comfort. But Askin had signed that piece of paper, committing him not to leave the property until the case against his extradition had been decided by the Supreme Court in Rome, and he was a man of his word. The Supreme Court hearing was due on the 17 January, and Professor Chiusano was convinced that their verdict could only result in Askin's being unconditionally liberated. In the meantime they could enjoy an unexpectedly happy Christmas, with Charlotte coming over to join them.

Gathering clouds, however, were visible upon the horizon. It was not likely that de Gennaro would tamely accept Askin's new status. Immediately on hearing of Askin's release he shot off a fax on 29 December, under the heading 'Precedenza Assoluta' to the Florence Court demanding confirmation of Askin's release, and adding 'since this department must adhere to the demands for great haste being telephoned by the South African ambassador in Rome', if the news were true he would expect an answer with 'maximum urgency'. There was still much confusion about the legal position. On 16 December an 'urgent' fax had been sent by the assistant clerk of the Florence Court, Wilma Bedussi, to the Italian Ministry of Foreign Affairs, asking for clarification 'as a matter of urgency' as to exactly what arrangements for extradition existed between Italy and South Africa. This was rather late in the day, more than two months after Askin's arrest. The answer, which only arrived on 27 December, was equivocal and only given as an opinion; that the Anglo-Italian treaty of 1873 was still in force – which would have meant inevitable diplomatic discussions.

Seizing the opportunity, on the very next day, la Cava ordered Askin to appear in court at the earliest opportunity, on 9 January 1995. But any encouragement the Italian Foreign Ministry might have given to the Florence bench should have been dampened by a letter from the British Foreign Office to Amhurst Brown Colombotti confirming that in fact, since South Africa left the Commonwealth in 1962, any previous extradition arrangements ceased, and that previous to that, South Africa as an independent Commonwealth Country would have relied upon its own extradition agreements: and these did not exist with Italy. It followed that the Italians could not agree to extradite Askin to South Africa.

Nor was it likely that the South Africa would refrain from more direct action. While in prison, guarded by Emin and his friends against any possible attempt on his life by a well-bribed guard or prisoner, Askin had been reasonably safe, but the farm was isolated, with easily interrupted communications, an ideal place for abduction. Major Black and Mr White moved quickly into action, and Julian, who had previously only heard of them from Susie, was impressed. Mr White, with an immense array of electronic instruments, swept the house and the telephone lines without finding anything unusual. Nevertheless a start was made on the installation of infra-red cameras and television monitors that should reveal any attempt at intrusion. Julian had taken the precaution of hiding his passport in Daisy's grave, where the only likely disturbance was from Clara, the horse, who had taken to making pilgrimages to her friend's last resting place.

Major Black stayed with the Askins, being joined by Anthony Amhurst on 28 December. Black is an impressive personality with a natural air of authority. He is not in the habit of carrying weapons, explaining that any armed criminals he may meet in Italy are likely to be well-financed and trained, and that they will always have the initiative. The British method, he believes, of only arming trained policemen when they know that they can themselves take the initiative is much safer. But Mr White has no such inhibitions, and carried a 9mm self-cocking pistol, while Franco was an able shot with his sporting rifle and shotguns: and for all outside communications the Askins relied on a secure mobile telephone rather than the land-line.

In spite of the lawyer's confidence, Askin, who knows what the South African authorities can be capable of, remained concerned that they would find some way around to a favourable outcome when their case came up at the Supreme Court on 17 January. Professor Chiusano, that most eminent authority on Italian law, was dismissive. The Corte di Cassazione was the highest court in the country, and no inferior jurisdiction could possibly defy its ruling. Indeed the Florence Court had already behaved illegally by imprisoning Askin, and both the public prosecutor Vigna and Judge la Cava would be committing professional suicide if they ignored the Cassazione's authority.

But that eminent lawyer Professor Chiusano was greatly mistaken in his assessment of the Florence judiciary. When the news of the Supreme Court's verdict came through as expected, on 17 January Askin's instinct was to leave Italy as soon as soon as was legally possible. The Corte di Cassazione's (on this occasion headed oddly enough, by Mr Justice Giuseppe di Gennaro) judgement was clear: Askin had been improperly arrested. The Professor however advised patience, to wait until the actual piece of paper – which the Florence court had been ordered to hand over to him recording the Supreme Court's decision – had been produced.

The South African Ambassador in Rome, Glen Babb, was better advised. On the 18th, the day following the judgement, he told a South African journalist that Askin would remain under arrest, regardless of what the Supreme Court might say. And indeed, that night, two heavily armed *carabiniere* officers came to the farmhouse: one was carrying a sub-machine gun and both behaved threateningly, insisting that Askin was going to be re-arrested and demanding that he sign a document they had brought with them. Fortunately Major Black, who had been staying with the Askins, chose that moment to appear, his natural air of authority supplemented by his identification. Askin recalled: 'The two *carabiniere* offices snap to attention, their faces ashen, their demeanour utterly transformed.' They explained to Mr Black that they were acting under orders from their Maresciallo, who had been instructed by the public prosecutor, Vigna. Major Black, who was convinced that they had come to arrest Askin and haul him back to prison, irrespective of the Supreme Court's decision, despatched the policemen in short order, although they refused to give their names, and took with them the piece of paper they brought for Askin to sign.

Since it was becoming more than apparent that the Florence Court of Appeal intended to pay no attention whatsoever to the Supreme Court's instructions, and that he had no physical proof of their decision, a messenger was despatched to Rome to obtain a copy of their judgement for Askin. Before his return the *Carabiniere* Maresciallo arrived at the farmhouse with a set of documents from the Florence Court demanding Askin's re-arrest. It was an incredible situation. Public prosecutor Vigna had obtained an *ex parte* injunction from Judge la Cava, who unblushingly maintained that he had received no order from the Supreme Court, and that indeed he knew nothing of any hearing having taken place in Rome.

Searching for an explanation for this extraordinary disregard for the due processes of law, one has to choose between poor official communications or uncommonly effective private channels. On 18 January Ambassador Babb had confidently forecast Askin's re-arrest and days later the Florence judges had, quite illegally, obliged. Professor Chiusano was incredulous at what he described as 'totally shameful behaviour', but could do nothing except to put the case once more before the Supreme Court, which would involve another delay. But before his appeal could be heard, the Florence magistrates had the opportunity to try again, which they immediately did by summonsing Askin to appear before them on 24 January. Professor Chiusano was worried by these developments, and not for purely legal reasons. In that respect he was absolutely confident that Askin's case was rock solid, but it was apparent that they were being opposed by powerful and unprincipled people who had been caught out in the course of some highly irregular activities. Precautions were essential, and Susie Askin would be well-advised to spend less time in Italy.

Evidence of the 'Get Askin' plot in South Africa was by then steadily being discovered by CIEX. There were strong suspicions in the intelligence community that the South African diplomatic privileges in Italy were being abused, and information began to be made available both in Africa and Italy. It was explained to Askin that his co-operation in exposing the links between de Gennaro and influential South Africans would be much appreciated, and would warrant the support of more than one intelligence service. By the second week in January 1995 one South African effort was uncovered in the shape of a sophisticated intercepting device placed on the telephone line leading from Scopetino. The voice-activated recorder was concealed in a junction box and a telephone pole a couple of kilometres from the farm, opposite the little church of Santa Maria. Hoping that someone might come to remove the recorder the Askin protection squad enlisted the services of Italian policemen from a town outside Florence, who could be relied upon not to be controlled by the Florentine magistrates. Had they discovered anyone, they would have been able to make the arrest, and the charge, in another judicial area, but, disobligingly, no one turned up. After four days, the surveillance was abandoned and the recorder removed. It was a day too soon, for the next night the telephone wire was cut in two places by an acetylene torch, in an effort to make it seem that there had been a lightning strike, which would have enabled an investigation to be made as to why the recording had stopped working. But the device was by then back in England for analysis. It proved to be a sophisticated receiver/transmitter, made in Israel, a country whose intelligence forces had for many years co-operated closely with the South Africans, but all the identifying numbers had been erased.

As an extra precaution in controlling their dangerous prisoner the local *carabinieri* held a duplicate set of keys to the farm's entrance gate; the Askins countered this by fitting a device which made the duplicate key ineffective, but allowed the gate to be unlocked from the house, giving those inside time to dispose of any potentially embarrassing visitors who might be spending time with them. The discovery of some of these visitors could have been unfortunate, since they included two former members of the SAS who had been recruited to plan a possible escape route if the South Africans embarked on desperate measures.

They surveyed all the border crossings, and developed fall-back plans which included an escorted passage on skis – Askin being a competent skier.

The legal task remained however that of avoiding Askin's appearance before the prejudiced Florentine court until confirmation of the second application to the Supreme Court had been received. He had been summoned to another appearance before the Florence judges on 24 January, which might well have resulted in immediate extradition. Entirely illegal though that would have been, legality did not appear to be a concern of that section of the Italian judiciary.

The preferred method of escaping such a dangerous appearance was for Askin to plead illness, for which substantial evidence could be produced. His stroke in prison had left him with a poorly functioning right leg and arm, which he attempted to strengthen by taking a painful walk round the property twice a day. Moreover, his heart condition remained sufficiently serious as to render any shock dangerous. His physician, Dr Pieri of the Florence cardiological hospital, accordingly prepared a certificate to that effect after a careful examination.

When, on the morning of the 28th the local Maresciallo arrived to arrest Askin, Major Black, there for the occasion, handed him the certificates, with a letter of the apology from Askin: these were duly delivered to the Florence court. Susie, who attended the hearing herself, reported Judge La Cava to be furious and having to be sternly reminded of his position by Professor Chiusano. Reluctantly, la Cava agreed an adjournment until 28 February.

That same night, the telephone lines were again cut. More bodyguards were moved in, commanded by a retired colonel of the *carabinieri*. Askin sat up with them for most of the night, watching the boundary fence through the infra-red cameras, and making regular patrols of the border. Apart from one hare, a wild boar and a fox, no intruders were discovered, but in the morning the Italian telecom engineers arrived, unsummoned, to repair the 'fault'.

Again, the question arose: how far were these expensive precautions necessary? The Askins' Florence lawyers were dismissive: indeed, Dr D'Avirro had little faith in his client's innocence, having been heard to say to a third party that Askin was 'a crook' and having made no secret of his suspicions to Susie. But Chiusano, much more experienced, was worried, and rightly so. The sources in New York insisted that there was constant danger of violence, and three years later hard evidence came to light proving how grave the threat to Julian Askin had been when it seemed to the South Africans that the legal processes needed some assistance to produce the 'right' answer.

Askin's doctors had been accurate in describing his health as 'poor'. On Saturday morning, 25 February, he had another heart episode and was rushed to the emergency cardiac wing of the Florence public hospital where he was put under intensive care. Although his condition stabilised quite quickly, his own practitioner, Dr Pieri, told him that he must stay in hospital under observation until Thursday or Friday the 2 or 3 March. This would naturally have prevented, once more, his appearance scheduled for 28 February.

This would have been a serious setback in the energetic campaign being waged by the Florentine police and officials to oblige their friends in Rome and South Africa by, somehow, getting Askin removed from the scene. They accordingly took immediate action. Within an hour of Dr Pieri's leaving his patient an orderly arrived to remove the drips from Askin's arms; he was followed by a doctor and nurse, whom Askin had never seen before, who confirmed that he was to be discharged, and that Susie would arrive to collect him. They claimed – although the ward had many empty beds – that the hospital was full.

Askin was by then convinced that something sinister was afoot, and his suspicions were correct. Judge la Cava had learned of Askin's admission to hospital through one of his informers within minutes of it happening. He had thereupon written to a Dr Graev, an acquaintance of his at the hospital, asking him to give an opinion that Askin was malingering and was in fact fully fit. A copy of this letter has since come to light, as has the obliging Dr Graev's certificate, stating that 'the patient's condition is not such as to render him totally incapable of attending the hearing' – an equivocal enough statement, which it needed to be, since Graev never even saw the patient on whose condition he was reporting. Once liberated from his drips Askin, who by now was suffering from a blazing headache, staggered into the nurses' room and demanded that he should see copies of all the examinations or notes that had been made since he arrived in the hospital The nurse, who was the one who told him to get dressed, refused, but the infuriated

Askin, to put it in his own words, 'turned it into an opera' and the nurse, unable to find anyone to back her up, finally submitted, showing him the files. Askin, who had been used to papers in Italy going missing without good cause, removed all the documents he could, managing to do this before he was told to report himself to the police office. (Unusually to English ideas of medical practice, every large Italian hospital has a police office staffed twenty-four hours a day.) The policeman he found there was a reasonable being who spoke enough English to make it clear that Askin had to sign a document, after which he could immediately go home. Susie could drive him, and he was assured there was no official reason stopping him from returning; he was simply being discharged from hospital.

This seemed somewhat surprising since Askin had been given to understand that the condition of his house arrest was that he should go nowhere without an escort of the *carabinieri*. When this point was put to the hospital policeman he shrugged it off and said that as far as he was concerned there was no problem and the Askins could drive home on their own, an explanation they were prepared to accept. Fortunately for them, just at that moment, the telephone rang. The policeman handed it over to Susie saying that it was 'Dr Manzoni for you' – a name that neither of the Askins recognised.

It turned out that 'Dr Manzoni' was in fact Mr White, who had, using his own methods, found out what was going on and was even then in the hospital car park calling from his car phone. There were, it seemed, two police cars lying in wait, one outside the hospital and one on the road to the airport. This last point was significant since in order to get back to the farm the Askins had to pass the airport. The police were waiting for them to do just that, when they would immediately be arrested on the pretext that they were attempting to escape as they were headed for the airport. Mr White confirmed that it was quite unlawful for a man under house arrest to travel anywhere without a police escort.

The plot was clear. If Askin was arrested on this pretext he could immediately be taken to court in front of the prejudiced judge and an extradition order recommended against him. Since Susie would also have been arrested as a conspirator in Askin's flight he would immediately be robbed of his most effective defence. It was only Mr White's intervention that avoided this.

Finally the hospital police telephoned the Tavernelle police to arrange for Askin to be collected. They agreed to do this rather reluctantly, saying that in the meantime the Askins should wait in the police office. Much sooner than had been reasonably expected, (they must have been lurking somewhere near the hospital), two officers, one in uniform and one in plainclothes arrived. The two *carabinieri* told Susie that she could follow in her car and agreed that they would wait for her in the road outside, giving her time to collect her vehicle from the car park. Askin continues:

I got into the car with the two officers and almost immediately a heated argument took place between the two men. They drove out and waited for Susie, but when she arrived one of the officers got out and said to her 'You cannot come with us.' They told her to drive home immediately.

My wife told me later that the policeman had also told her quite firmly that she was not to follow them, and had explained this by saying, 'We are taking your husband to the doctor'. My wife obeyed this instruction and immediately left to drive back to Scopetino. I was now feeling even less well and was alarmed at the sudden change of advice and aggressive tone of the officer's voice to my wife. The *carabinieri* then drove me to another part of the hospital and pulled up outside a building. The plainclothes officer went inside, and about three minutes later returned with some folded papers and a brown envelope. He held the papers separately, outside the envelope, as if the papers had either not yet been placed in the envelope or had been withdrawn from it. As we drove off, he turned the inside car light on and read the papers out aloud to the uniformed man. They both laughed on a few occasions as he was reading it out. I did not know what they were reading but the plainclothes man, who spoke a little English, turned to me and said, 'They've fixed you now, Askin. You're going back to South Africa.' His comment produced further laughter from both men. I was staggered by this and became extremely anxious about what they might be doing, particularly as they had asked my wife to return to Scopetino.

The route back to Scopetino leaves the autostrada at the Firenze Certosa exit. When the police car shot past that point Askin expostulated that they were going the wrong way, but was ignored. The next exit, Firenze Sud was also passed at high speed, and Askin began to get really worried. Wherever the *carabinieri* were taking him, it was not back to the farm.

The effect of this was to make me hyperventilate. I said again: 'To get to San Donato you should have taken the Firenze Certosa exit.' The plain-clothes man turned to me and grinned and said, 'Askin we go the tourist route. It is none of your business.' By now I was extremely concerned and my chest was becoming painful. I was already beginning to think that I was being taken somewhere else other than San Donato, particularly as they had insisted that my wife went home and did not follow us. I repeatedly asked where they were going and all my questions were ignored. This served only to heighten my state of anxiety.

The officers drove on, and just before the next exit, some 18 kilometres further on (Inchiesa), I protested again. At the last second, the car swerved off the motorway on to the exit slip road. The officer drove the car at speed up to the toll booths, then braked hard, did a sharp turn and headed back towards Firenze. I was thrown around the back seat and this produced further laughter from the two officers.

By now I was breathing very rapidly and felt physically very uncomfortable and was extremely worried about what was going on. The officers clearly thought it was amusing but I did not. I was worried that they were not going to take me to San Donato and were going to take me somewhere else. The whole thing seemed highly irregular and I felt I was being deliberately intimidated for reasons I could not fathom: I already felt a great deal worse than I had when I left the hospital.

Dr Pieri had prescribed some emergency heart pills, so I decided that I ought to take one. I did this and it seemed to lessen the pain slightly.

A few minutes later a call came through for the officers on their car radio. It appeared as if they were being asked where they were. Their demeanour changed, as if they had been given an order. I believe this was the voice of a senior officer or their commanding officer from the Tavernelle *carabinieri* station. I say this because my wife had become alarmed by my absence and had phoned Avvocato Pinucci to express her concern. In response Avvocato Pinucci phoned the *carabinieri* in Tavernelle to ask what had happened to me as I had been picked up at the hospital some while ago and had not yet arrived back at Tavernelle. My wife had been back at Scopetino for nearly one hour. Avvocato Pinucci said that both he and my wife were worried about what might have happened.

By the time the officers finally left me at Scopetino I was feeling extremely unwell, was out of breath and very tired. After I had been at home for a few minutes I had to take another emergency heart pill and went to bed.

Two hours later I was still in a very tense state, felt very unwell, and was lying in bed. My wife managed to obtain Dr Pieri on the telephone, and explained my condition to him. He decided to come out from Florence immediately. He arrived at about 10.30p.m., by which stage Susie had left for a meeting with Avvocato Chiusano in Firenze. Dr Pieri examined me and said that I was in a particularly hypertensive state and should take a 'complete rest'.

Dr Pieri confirmed that under no circumstances should Askin attend the court hearing the following day. Professor Chiusano, already on his way from Turin, was positive that even if Askin had been well enough it would have been foolish of him to attempt to attend the court on the 28th. Michael Holmes, the British Consul, would indeed be present, armed with letters from the Foreign Office confirming that the extradition treaty that had existed between Britain and South Africa had in fact lapsed in 1962. Chiusano agreed that this constituted an undeniable proof that there was no legal method for extraditing a British subject from Italy to South Africa, but, he went on, the prosecutor and Judge already knew this full well. In his opinion they would simply pay no attention to the British Foreign Office or Her Majesty's Consul. They had already disobeyed an order from the Supreme Court in Rome and were quite capable of disregarding this evidence. What he was anxious to do was to have a statement of their behaviour read formally into the court record. After that he would seek another adjournment until the Supreme Court had heard Askin's appeal.

The *carabinieri*, who included the same pair who had taken Askin on the wild drive the previous night, arrived the following morning at 7.30 a.m. and were given the doctor's certificate. This had no effect on Brigadiere Amerosso, who shouted at Susie that her husband was in perfect health, 'as good as a ripe peach' and that he had a letter from Doctor Graev to prove it. Losing his temper completely the Brigadiere 'started hurling insults and invective' at Susie. His orders were to get Askin to court even if he had to drag him from his bed. Susie countered by saying that Professor Chiusano had confirmed that it was illegal in Italy to drag someone from their bed into court against the evidence of a doctor's certificate. At this point Major Black appeared and attempted to calm things down. Susie in spite of the early hour telephoned the London lawyer Laurence Giovene who confirmed to the Brigadiere that it would be illegal to attempt to arrest Askin under those circumstances. Another shouting match ensued.

The Brigadiere slammed the phone down and went outside, where the other officers were waiting. He told Susie that he would drag Askin to court whatever the bloody law said: he had his orders. Major Black advised the officer to call his superior officer, the Maresciallo. This sobered the Brigadiere up a bit and he made a call from his car, not forgetting to shout another insult at Susie before he did so. Major Black said that in all his experience of the *carabinieri* he had never witnessed such behaviour: somebody, somewhere, he insisted must be being paid a considerable amount of money.

After about forty minutes the Brigadiere returned to the house alone and asked to see Askin. His face was red with rage and frustration. He marched into the bedroom and barked in English, 'Will you come to court or not?' Askin replied that he would like to do so, but was feeling unwell and had been told not to move by his doctor. The Brigadiere exploded and repeated the question. It was precisely what he had been told to ask and Askin must reply with a Yes or a No. Nothing else. Askin refused to answer and instead wrote a letter which he handed to the Brigadiere asking him to give it to the Judge. In the letter Askin expressed his wish that he could be in court and apologised for not being able to be there. The Brigadiere stamped out, telling Askin that he would be back for him shortly. At the bedroom door he turned and said that it didn't matter anyhow: the Judge had every intention of starting the hearing without Askin and would extradite him.

After another tense forty-minute stand-off in the garden where the officers lounged about smoking, the Brigadiere called them in suddenly and they drove away.

Susie rushed into Florence to meet the British Consul. They had problems finding out which court the hearing was to be held in, but bumped into Dr Tonni, the ultimate Head of the Florentine Judiciary, whom Michael Holmes knew. Susie was introduced and Dr Tonni invited her and Holmes up to his office while Mr White, who had been shadowing them, made himself scarce. Dr Tonni said that he had been told that Askin was South African, and not a British subject. He seemed surprised at learning the facts and obligingly tried to find out where the case was being tried, which did not seem easy. When eventually its location was discovered it appeared that the hearing was being held in camera.

Susie and Holmes headed off for the court, but as they crossed a courtyard they were intercepted by Avvocato Pinucci, who had just come from the court. Judge la Cava had indeed attempted to start the hearing without Askin, but had been sharply brought to heel by Professor Chiusano and been forced to adjourn the case until 4 April. This constituted a welcome victory for the professor and for the Askins, who now had to hope that the Supreme Court hearing in Rome would take place before the revised date. By starting without Askin, Judge la Cava had also made a mistake, since at any future hearing Askin would not have to appear unless he specifically so wished. The Judge would have to write to Askin asking him if he wished to appear in court or not, but he was under no legal obligation to do so. It had turned out exactly as the Tavernelle Brigadiere had predicted. Judge la Cava had intended going ahead with the hearing, with or without Askin being present, ignoring any evidence, and ordering an instant extradition: proof, were further proof needed, of the powerful influence that certain South Africans could exert in Italy.

Much to everyone's surprise, the following morning (Wednesday 1 March) Brigadiere Amarosso, who had been so offensive the previous day, turned up wreathed in smiles. Julian Askin recorded:

> He asks if he can go inside and see how the patient is feeling. The Brigadiere enters Askin's bedroom with a massive smile and a warm greeting. Askin sits open-mouthed while the Brigadiere waxes lyrical about the weather and expresses great concern over Askin's health. The face is smiling but the eyes are ice cold. Askin's ticker almost goes haywire again out of surprise. After a couple of minutes, the Brigadiere wishes Askin every good bit of luck and health and turns on his heels. At the door he tells Susie that Italian weather is so much better than the English. During this whole episode the Askins have not said a word to one another. They fall about laughing after his departure, wondering what on earth it can all be about. Franca the maid comes in, having heard all this. Her daughter goes out with this *carabiniere* and says he's an arrogant bastard and this is the best thing she has ever heard. Franca says she is certain he has been told to apologise, and spends the next ten minutes roaring with laugher. The Askins can't believe it.

It turned out that Mr White had used his influence on the senior *carabinieri* officer in the Florence region, who exploded with wrath at this treatment of British citizens who had committed absolutely no offence in Italy, and ordered the Maresciallo to ensure that his junior officer made an immediate personal apology. Then, the next week, Michael Holmes was able to tell Askin that the British government had finally agreed to make an official protest, the first in more than twenty years. It being judged undiplomatic to attack the conduct of the Florence judiciary directly, the protest centred on concerns that South Africa was improperly attempting to interfere with a British citizen in Italy. The protest was not well-received at the Italian foreign office, but it was grudgingly agreed that something should be done.

Whilst things were looking up for the Askins, it was understood that it was precisely when legal methods did not seem to be working for the opposition that illegal and violent methods were most likely to be used. If, as was surely likely, the Supreme Court repeated its earlier decision on the hearing, which had now been fixed for 28 March, then Askin must not wait for written confirmation, but immediately leave the country. A well-planned clandestine exit was therefore necessary.

Although the Hereford squad was still available it was decided not to use them, but to make the operation one of informal Anglo-Italian intelligence co-operation. The object was to achieve the safe delivery of both Askins to London, together with all items of value from the cottage, it being presumed that the Florentine judiciary were likely to confiscate these. Getting Susie back was relatively easy, her departure having been arranged ten days previously to avoid suspicion. On the morning of the 28th, Franco, the gardener, drove Susie to the airport (for his own safety he had not been told of the plans). Apart from one policeman seeming to take an interest in Susie's luggage – an enormous quantity even for Susie Askin, who does not travel light – her departure went without a hitch. Once back in London Susie telephoned the cottage, with a conversation, which had been well-rehearsed for the benefit of the telephone-tappers. Askin confirmed to her that he would wait in Italy until the Court papers had been received, when they would cele-brate together with a short holiday on the Amalfi coast, and then settled down alone, to wait for the telephone call from Rome that would announce their victory. He recalls:

> I cooked myself a lone meal of pasta, using up most of the spices that would have otherwise been left behind. I made the hottest penne arrabiata of my life. It occurred to me only after I'd eaten that it might not have been the ideal meal to consume just before a tense night and a long car journey!
>
> At 8.45 p.m. the news came through, 'The court has freed Askin again'. There were no conditions, I was as free as any other man. The ruling against the Florence judiciary was stronger than ever before. I was illegally and unlawfully arrested and imprisoned the first time. To have re-arrested me specifically against the instructions of the Court in Rome

served to redouble the Court's censure of the action of the Florentines. I was to be made completely free immediately and unconditionally. It was a massive smack in the nose for the South Africans and their Italian friends.

I phoned the news through to Susie. She opened champagne, and I attacked a bottle of Chianti. I felt an amazing sense of relief. My departure could now be in no way considered illegal. I would be leaving without the actual Court papers in my possession, but that was a mere technicality. I will have committed no offence upon Italian soil. The danger was if the Public Prosecutor in Florence intended to have me re-arrested yet again and was keeping my movements under observation. This was thought by everyone to be highly probable.

Shortly before midnight a call came through from Mr White that Askin should now leave. It was the ideal time to move, being the period when the police shifts change, ensuring that a thirty-minute gap when the retiring shift are completing the paperwork and the newcomers settling down to their first espresso. Julian Askin must take advantage of this opportunity to leave the farm and get beyond the borders of the Florence area. He collected his travelling kit (of which the most important item was dog Poppy) and made his way to the road, where he was to meet with the first car, driven by a colonel of the *carabinieri*. Much to his horror, he walked into a police car, but a smiling face assured him that the colonel had merely borrowed it for the occasion. Askin should have no worries, but sit up and enjoy the view.

They stopped in a lay-by before the autostrada entrance, Askin being transferred to a fast car being driven by Major Black. Another car, driven by Mr White, was to lead. This had been specially prepared, equipped with an extensive array of electronic gadgetry which, among other things, could access any police radio network between Florence and the Italian border. If any police unit seemed to be showing an undesirable interest in the convoy Mr White could send out an emergency signal recalling all police cars in that area to their base.

As it turned out, the trip went without a hitch, except that Major Black, bored with the motorway speed of 140kph, dashed ahead to his more habitual speed of 180kph, before Askin pointed out that they had overtaken their scout car. In true Italian fashion, a solution was reached whereby both travelled at breakneck speed, but with Mr White's electronic marvel being allowed to stay in front. Crossing into France at Ventimiglia, selected as the best place to avoid suspicion, they were met by Michael Oatley, who then drove non-stop to Calais, where they arrived the following evening.

Reflections

At no time did an Italian court consider the charges against Askin. All they concerned themselves with was the validity or otherwise of the extradition request which the South Africans were so assiduously pressing. Both the Florence prosecutor and judge assumed Askin's guilt without question. Many in South Africa, have done likewise, and fought doggedly against Askin's attempts to obtain a hearing in an English Court! It is therefore worth while briefly examining some aspects of the case against Askin.

Since the charges expressed by Judge Berman in the original warrant for arrest issued in July 1993 were substantially those listed by the liquidators in their civil claim of October the same year, some can be quickly dismissed as referring to events which happened before his arrival or to the activities of other directors. In arriving at the settlement made in October 1994 the liquidators, including Absa, accepted this, and accepted the much smaller sum of R2,900,000 (equal then to about £500,000), in place of their original claim of R 23 million.

Askin has always maintained that even this greatly reduced sum was not in fact owed by him. Tollgate did not resemble a normal, permanently established and stable company. Throughout Askin's period of office it was in a permanent state of flux, disposing of large businesses and acquiring others, reorganising and regrouping: the reduction of staff from 20,000 to 2,500 is an indication of the scale of this change. All this restructuring was done by Askin personally, travelling between Cape Town and London. Askin did not even have an office to himself, sharing Mervyn Key's desk in Cape Town. Informality was the keynote of management. Meetings were frequent, but unstructured. Never a professional hands-on manager, Askin acted as a financier and entrepreneur relying on professional firms of lawyers and accountants, which he employed freely, to advise and guide. In a stable company most of this work would be done a good deal less expensively by the firm's own accountants and legal department, but Tollgate never had a structure that permitted this. In particular Tollgate never had a finance director or comptroller, an authoritative senior figure who would have ensured that records were always up to date. As executive chairman, Askin's contract allowed a generous discretion in expenses, which it was agreed could be set against his salary if these were not properly chargeable against the company. Askin had, at the time of the takeover, in March 1990, agreed an annual salary of R520,000, to escalate in accordance with inflation, but that personal expenses could be set against this, in order to avoid paying tax. Such an arrangement, which would have been illegal in Britain, was permissible in South Africa and was accepted by Tollgate's auditors. Thus a number of payments made during the course of the year from company funds were carefully recorded and at the end of the accounting period would be charged against Askin's personal account and deducted from his salary – which he often did not draw. Inevitably, if trading was suddenly halted, as it was in the liquidation, there would be a number of such loose ends floating about in the accounts. It was these that were, quite properly, debited against sums owed to Askin by Tollgate, such as his pension contributions, and reflected in the October 1994 settlement.

Although they included some striking items, dear to the heart of journalists and judges, such as the charter of aeroplanes and helicopters and the payments of air tickets for family and friends, the total sum claimed by the most ingenious methods the liquidators could contrive did not exceed some £120,000. But one major charge attracted attention. This was the accusation that Askin had diverted millions of dollars from Tollgate to a personal account of his in Switzerland The facts, although very different, are exceedingly complicated.

The Kyalami race track had ceased to be used for Grand Prix racing during the period when South Africa had been subjected to the international sporting boycott. When it became clear that racing would once again be permitted it was necessary to reach agreement with the Formula

One Constructors' Association (FOCA). The chairman of FOCA, Bernie Ecclestone, suggested that Askin met his colleague, Max Mosley. At the meeting, Mosley explained that FOCA were owed some $US1–2 million from the previous contract and that this sum would be written into the new contract. Further, since the contract would be with a Tollgate subsidiary, and FOCA were apprehensive that the South African authorities might at any time impose restrictions on the export of currency, they wanted an irrevocable personal guarantee from someone non-resident in South Africa, who would not be affected by such controls, that payments would indeed be rendered punctually.

This Askin agreed to do and signed such a guarantee on 12 April 1991. In this he agreed to meet the relevant obligations of Motor Racing Enterprises (MRE), the Tollgate subsidiary responsible for Kyalami. He accordingly opened an account with Credit Suisse in Geneva (no.760349/52/1) in his own name and with the approval of the Tollgate directors. This account would act as a vehicle for payments to FOCA and receipts from MRE: which in fact happened for the Grand Prix season of 1992 and 1993.

Askin's willingness to oblige was to some extent part of his character: if he saw an opportunity for a good profit he did not shirk from the responsibility, but also because he relied completely on Mervyn Key to control the MRE business. After all, Key and Ecclestone were old associates who worked together in Kyalami until 1985 and indeed had been joint owners of the track: and Askin's Swiss financial transactions were all, he insists, properly disclosed and recorded by the auditors.

Kyalami had not done well in the period of sanctions, but by 1989, with the prospect of sanctions being lifted, Key had already, according to Johan Claasen, negotiated with FOCA the return of Kyalami to the international circuits, and FOCA officials had checked the condition of the track. The profit for Tollgate was certainly potentially good, since Key had also arranged that South Africa Yellow Pages, the telephone directory advertising organisation, would sponsor the new Grand Prix, committing R40 million over a three-year period, which they would be enabled to write off against profits for tax purposes.

The affairs of MRE/Kyalami were very much the personal concern of Mervyn Key and David McCay, one of the earlier directors of Duros/Tollgate, who resigned that position in 1989. Seven years later, in February 1996, McCay was put in the position of having to defend himself against charges brought by Tollgate's liquidators. He admitted at the trial that in 1986 he had formed, together with Mervyn Key, a company called MRE(Pty) in which each man held 45 per cent, the remaining 10 per cent being owned by Laurie Mackintosh. In a series of extremely evasive answers McCay demonstrated an extraordinarily cavalier attitude towards business.

> Q: You just signed whatever was put in front of you?
> *McCay*: I think that is common practice in business ... I have never read the articles and memos of any company in my life ... of what relevance is it?
> Q. How much money did you lend ...
> *McCay*: I haven't a clue ... but hundreds of thousands at a time.

MRE (Pty) was joined in December 1987 by the Kyalami International Circuit Ltd (KIC) and Kyalami Entertainment Enterprises (KEE), both again jointly owned by McCay, Key and Mackintosh in the same proportions. All these companies were audited by Tony Jooste, a relative of Mr McCay, and his personal accountant. KEE was the company that had the right to repurchase from Amaprop, which it passed on to KIC, who in turn used it as security for a R3.9 million loan from FNB's always helpful Manager, Dave Stewart.

These companies did not appear to be very active, to the extent that Jooste wrote to the South African tax authorities saying that MRE was 'dormant' and had ceased trading in the year ending February 1989 and that he had no means of contacting the shareholders to establish their wishes: this was, of course, a lie. The company's only asset, Jooste claimed, was the helicopter used by Key, McCay and Mackintosh, and their former colleague Christo Wiese.

The events that followed were quite extraordinary. In June 1988 Duros a publicly quoted company, whose board Key had joined the previous year, agreed that its subsidiary, Entercor, should buy that 'dormant' company for R6 million, at that time equivalent to some £1,100,000. At the same time Entercor would be given a lease of the racetrack by KIC, for an initial period of nine and a half years, with an option to extend for a second ten years. For this Entercor would pay R7 million, described as 'a contribution to the cost of repairing the circuit', which had to be spent through the landlords, KIC. In all the equivalent of £2.7 million came from Tollgate, and, with the exception of R2 million withheld as a tax reserve, was immediately pocketed by Key and McCay. At his trial McCay stated, 'If my memory serves me right, Macgregor took a million, Mervyn took five, I took five and two was left behind.' This incredible transaction was, he claimed, approved by Christo Wiese, who said, 'it looks like a very nice deal.' Asked if it was true that the agreement made in the name of MRE was one in which it purports to sell a business, a business which according to its own audited financial statements it does not own, McCay could only answer 'Yes'.

Another facet of this deal was that Trust Bank had lent the R13 million to Tollgate to permit the transaction: McCay's share went straight into his account at Trust Bank, Key's to his at FNB. Both banks were aware of the whole business. And this was not the end: in February 1989, KIC, which had already granted a lease of the track to Entercor, transferred the option to purchase from Amaprop back to the third company, KEE, owned by the same principals in the same proportions. KEE then sold the property itself to another Tollgate subsidiary, Arrowgate, for R12 million, some of which would have had to be repaid to FNB in order to release the guarantee which they held on the option. That option was in fact not exercised until late in 1991, until which time Amaprop remained the registered holders of the land, the sale and resale of which had enabled R25 million to have been filched from Tollgate – and all before Askin ever began talks with the directors, a fact which does not seem to have troubled any of his accusers.

It was presumably in an effort to disguise the real nature of some of these transactions that Julian Askin's signature was forged to some documents in order to suggest that he may have profited from these earlier transfers.

The topic of forgery also emerged in McCay's evidence to the Hoberman Commission, where (p. 5335) he denied the authenticity of a signature that was meant to be his.

One example of a forgery was discovered in a covering letter purporting to come from Judith Griggs of FOCA, on 23 May 1991, addressed to Mervyn Key. A comparison of the original and the forgery reveals two major differences. Firstly, the original refers to the 'execution of a collateral agreement by virtue of which payment of the fees under this Agreement is ensured by bank guarantee'. This refers to the Swiss account which Askin duly and properly opened. Secondly, the forgery contains a paragraph, 'Furthermore, as outlined to you, a non-refundable amount of $2 million is payable to cover all transport and related expenditure' – clearly the $2 million which Mosley had referred to. Significantly, while both the original and the forgery have a paragraph beginning 'Furthermore, and as advised to your Mr Askin today . . .', the inserted forged paragraph is 'as outlined to you' – i.e. Mervyn Key, with no reference to Askin.

CHAPTER SIX

Askin and Some Allies

Home again

On 29 March 1995 Julian Askin arrived safely in Chester Square, to the enormous relief of Susie. The fact that he had left Italy legally as a free man did not stop his enemies from expressing their fury. The South African *Sunday Times* reported that 'Former Tollgate boss evades net'. By 16 July Cherilyn Ireton, in the same journal reported that Askin 'was defiantly mixing with the rich and famous in London . . . playing in a golf competition with his horse-racing buddies', going on quite falsely to declare that Askin had been 'declared *persona non grata* in Italy'. The Florence magistrates, in spite of being twice overruled by the Supreme Court, had not given up. In the face of clear evidence that no extradition treaty existed between Italy and South Africa and that Askin was not in Italy but in England, in opposition to the Supreme Court order, the local judges, on 11 July, solemnly declared that Askin could legally be sent to South Africa. Merely to clear Askin's name, a third, expensive, application to the Rome Supreme Court was needed.

Realising that it was inevitable that the Supreme Court would merely repeat its previous decision, and probably with some strong words about the behaviour of the Florentine judiciary, South Africa's reliable Italian friends were ready with a countermeasure. Before the case was due to be heard, in December 1995, an Attorney-General, Esposito Vitaliano, tried to force through a quick hearing, without notifying Askin's lawyers. The move was thwarted, but it was discovered that, oddly enough, Vitaliano had recently been on holiday, together with his family, in South Africa. Shortly afterwards two South African policemen were discovered attempting to persuade an officer of Scotland Yard to take action against Askin. That too was settled by a diplomatic lawyer's letter on 25 January 1995 to Brigadier Fourie, the South African High Commissioner's police representative in London, after which the affair subsided.

After his harrowing experiences in Italy Julian Askin was a changed man. Whereas before his arrest he had felt aggrieved, he was now implacably angry. He had experienced, in the most personal way, the effects of Afrikaner hostility, and the great power that could be marshalled against him. Before his experiences of South African persecution in Italy Askin's intention had been only to pillory South African misdoings by writing a novel and beginning the recovery of some of the money he had lost. Far from having benefited from any alleged 'frauds' Askin had lost his original investment of some two and a half million pounds and been forced into paying too much on the civil settlement: as much again would they have to be spent on fees and expenses. Askin was now bent on complete exposure of the continuing sinister machinations which still operated under President Mandela's new South Africa as they had done in the era of apartheid. From being an open, optimistic, incautiously trusting man he had become suspicious to the extent of near-paranoia. His initial hopes of a new dawn that had been raised by Mandela's release in 1990, and reinforced by the new Government of National Unity appointed in April 1994, were severely damaged. Still, with a considerable fortune and a great deal of experience at his command, he could prove a dangerous Nemesis: from now on no holds were barred, and the intelligence resources of CIEX were deployed to procure evidence for his eventual riposte.

There had been many developments since Askin had left South Africa in February 1993. After his departure Susie had spent some time at Steenhuis, liaising with the Askins' Cape Town lawyers and preparing the house for short holiday lettings. The reaction of sympathy to Julian's predicament had been widespread; more than two hundred letters expressing support had come from their friends, one of whom sent Susie a cheque for ten thousand pounds. But she was both surprised and disappointed at the behaviour of some of Julian's former colleagues. Nicholas Soames, who had been well-rewarded for his participation in Tollgate, with a generous salary and a chauffeur-driven car provided for his personal use in London, had not even telephoned to express his sympathy when Julian had been imprisoned. Guy Sangster, whose family had made so great a profit by their participation in Thompson T. Line had certainly lost a small percentage of that in their Tollgate investment. Sangster had also been offended when he had been dropped from the Tollgate board by Askin (at, it should be said, the insistence of the London institutional investors, who felt that the board did not give the impression of sufficient professional gravitas). He began a campaign of denigration against his former chief, which was sometimes carried to a ludicrous extent.*

The Sangster family had been for many years a favourite subject of gossip. Guy's father Robert, was famous for the ease with which he had spent a considerable fortune on entertainment and racehorses (he lists his winning horses rather than his wives in *Who's Who*) and had made a point of ensuring that one, perhaps the most noted, of gossip columnists, presented a frequent and favourable picture of his activities (although such journalists, it is said, make more money by accepting presents to keep the donors *out* of the news). This was Nigel Dempster of the London *Daily Mail*, one of the notorious London tabloid newspapers. Often known, not necessarily affectionately, as 'Dumpster' or 'Humpty', Mr Dempster's 'devotion to the cause of the thrice married pools heir' roused the derision of *Private Eye* (11 August 1985). 'Sangster boasts to me that he featured in Humpty's little "Mail" column no fewer than 105 times in the past five years, and when not writing about the tycoon himself, Dempster drools over Sangster's wives and daughters instead.

'Just think what all this delicious PR must be worth.'

An example of Mr Dempster's concern for accuracy and his adherence to the Sangster family's interests can be seen in his article in the issue of December 16th 1993, headlined 'Askin, the "rogue" rents out to Peter' (*Daily Mail* readers were expected to know that this was Mr Dempster's familiar reference to Charles Stanhope, Viscount Petersham). In the article Steenhuis was described as being built in 1992 when in fact construction began in 1989, with the family moving in the following year. (A matter of some importance since the claim had

---

* An interesting detail is that Sangster subsequently claimed to have been a director of Thomson T. Line, a successful company, which he had not been, and denied membership of the Tollgate – a bankrupt company – board, which he had indeed enjoyed.

been made that the house was built with money abstracted from the Tollgate shareholders. Had this been so, the Tollgate liquidators would certainly have sued Askin, but like so many allegations against him, this was completely unfounded.) Nevertheless, the article claimed that 'Among the investors in Tollgate, Askin's company, was the family of leading racehorse owner and breeder Robert Sangster, who lost £6 million of which £1.2 million was a direct loan to Askin for a joint venture which he refuses to acknowledge for a personal debt.' And, as an illustration of the perennial exaggeration of the luxuries of Steenhuis, the accompanying picture, entitled the master bedroom, shows the sitting room – the bedroom being the more modest attic above. Julian Askin also believes that Guy Sangster had been in contact with Absa, since in the latter half of 1992 he suggested to Askin that a personal guarantee should be substituted for the corporate debt – a proposal that Askin naturally declined.

Dempster's source in Cape Town was Rupert Wragg, who received payments of £300–400 in return for information about the Askins. In pursuit of one of these payments Wragg telephoned Susie during one of her visits to Steenhuis in October 1993, ascertaining that she was intending to return to London the following week. It may have been an entire coincidence, but the lawyers acting for the Hoberman Commission of Enquiry got wind of this and had a subpoena prepared demanding Susie's appearance before them. Fortunately the subpoena was entrusted to a lawyers' clerk who had better things (a rugby match) to do that weekend. Susie was made aware of the subpoena and warned that it would be used to keep her in South Africa, ensuring that she was made to assume responsibility for her husband's alleged debts, that her movements were being monitored and that she would be well advised to leave immediately. This she did, driving to the airport with only a handbag as luggage as if to meet someone. When service of the subpoena was attempted on the Monday Susie was no longer there. But the liquidator did succeed in obtaining a temporary lien on Steenhuis *and the dogs* which was only discharged in the following year.

Chris van Zyl, of Syfrets, appointed as trustee in the interim, was unable to account for the removal, during his period of office, of many of the most valuable and easily removable articles that had mysteriously disappeared from the house, a loss which could not be claimed from the insurers. Susie had also had to deal with one extraordinarily petty incident. Her brother's house in Cape Town had been flooded, and she had sent him some electric heaters to help the drying out. The trustee had interpreted this as theft of the assets (having done nothing at all about the real, very considerable thefts) and sworn out an arrest warrant against the unfortunate brother, which had only been withdrawn after lively expostulation and the formal signature of the settlement agreement.

After the Askins had settled the suit the liquidators had brought, in October 1994, Susie was able to use Steenhuis, with her mother and Charlotte as regular visitors, but it was still judged too dangerous for Julian even after his release in Italy to return to South Africa. His only hope of a safe hearing lay in ensuring that a case should be brought before an English court.

Susie had particular reason to complain of Guy Sangster's behaviour. On the day following the police visit to Chester Square on 1 July she received a letter from Guy Sangster, asking her, in a friendly enough fashion (he signed it 'love, Guy'), if she could call in at the office he maintained in Knightsbridge. Although she was feeling decidedly off-colour, having had an operation to remove a malignant melanoma only that morning, Susie agreed readily enough.

She was given an extraordinary reception. Sangster was with Nigel Tose, another former director (it will be recalled that both men had continued to pay themselves handsomely from the Swazican funds), who asked her if she was carrying any recording device. Since there is little enough of Susie, and the T-shirt and jeans she was wearing left no room for concealment, it was an absurd as well as a grossly uncivil question. Sangster – 26 years Susie's junior, the proud possessor of a single O level from Harrow – spat out a series of nonsensical threats: he would have the Askins driven out of town, they would not be allowed to go to any race meetings at which the Sangster family would be present, they must not visit any restaurants which the Sangsters used and, significantly, 'We'll get Dempster to rubbish you'! Not to be out-done, Tose, who over the last few years had made tens of thousands of pounds from following Julian Askin's lead, finished by declaring, 'We'll not stop until we have your husband put in prison.'

Susie, in spite of feeling the effects of her operation, countered spiritedly; these young idiots didn't have the courage to say anything to Julian, and were attacking her instead. She left Tose and Sangster speechless, but the campaign of harassment continued.

The determination of the Afrikaner establishment to 'get' Askin had been enthusiastically backed by certain parts of the South African English press. All newspapers may be subject to pressure from advertisers, but most reputable journals contrive to maintain a decent editorial independence. Not so with the *Sunday Times* of South Africa. An article published on 16 October, 1994, by a team of three journalists, Jeremy Woods, Glenda Nevill and Cherilyn Ireton, gloated over Askin's situation. It was packed with innuendo; the pleasant but inconsequential rented Italian farm cottage became a 'luxurious hideout' situated in the midst of some of the country's most 'prized wine-producing slopes'. A 'luxury Mercedes Benz, bearing foreign number plates' – which happened to be that of Signor Grassi, the landlord – 'was parked in the grounds'. Askin was a 'fugitive' with a 'posh ... R5 million home in London's exclusive Belgravia, furnished with expensive antiques and paintings'. The article appeared under the banner headline, 'We find Askin's hideout'. It was hardly much of a secret, since the Askins had been renting the Italian farm, and openly entertaining a constant stream of friends, since the previous year. Scopetino was described as a 'Tuscan villa where SA tycoon walked into a trap after fleeing UK' – doubly deceitful since the Askins had been moving frequently between Italy and London.

The story contained a gloating claim by Tommy Prins (who had carried out the knicker-drawer searches in Steenhuis and Chester Square), now described as head of the Cape Town Office for Serious Economic Offences: 'Knowing Askin travelled to his Tuscan home regularly we set our plans accordingly. We were aware of his movements in London, we knew exactly where he was, and when he went to Italy. We monitored his movements for twelve months.' The implications of this statement from a responsible official are disturbing. Given the intense interest evidenced by the protracted surveillance, the South African authorities must surely have discovered that there was no extradition agreement with Italy, and therefore no *legal* means of extraditing Askin. The delay can only have been due to the need to establish the *illegal* arrangements. Askin had to be harassed and frightened into not asking awkward questions, and the Afrikaner establishment was therefore mobilised to do this. Incidentally, the scale and duration of the OSEO effort, which must have been very expensive to the South African taxpayer, gives some idea of the espionage activities of the South African authorities in England: activities, naturally, unknown to the British police.

In the anti-Askin campaign the South African *Sunday Times* was an enthusiastic collaborator. 'Steenhuis or Pollsmoor?' was the introduction to a column by Woods on 27 November 1994 (Pollsmoor being the prison where Nelson Mandela spent the latter part of his sentence). Although what was purported to be recorded was the decision by the Supreme Court *not* to impound Askin's property following the settlement of creditors claims (at R2.9 million, a far cry from many of the figures bandied about) the tone was savage in its presumption of guilt.

> Askin back in Steenhuis? Steenhuis or Pollsmoor?
>
> That seems to be the choice of residence. For fallen whizz-kid Julian Askin if the long arm of the Office For Serious Economic Offences is successful in bringing Askin back in cuffs to face the music over his crashed Tollgate empire.
>
> Pollsmoor, or somewhere like it, is the obvious favourite if Mr Askin, accused of fraud and theft of many millions, is kept in custody here.
>
> But the decision by the Supreme Court this week not to sequestrate Askin was influenced by his wife Susie buying Tollgate liquidators' claims against her husband totalling some R3 million.
>
> Steenhuis, the Askin flash, fake Cape-Dutch home built on Constantia Nek with views across the Constantia Valley is allegedly owned by Mrs Askin.
>
> But the popping champagne corks of the good life at Steenhuis must seem a far cry for Askin now as he languishes in custody in a Tuscany prison, fighting an extradition process.

This was only two days after the *Cape Times* of 25 November had reported the fact that 'Absa bank, which has placed the Tollgate group in liquidation, waived all claims of "whatsoever nature" against Mr Askin.' And that nothing in the agreement would constitute Askin's admission of 'any negligent, reckless or fraudulent act or omission'. When Askin left Italy, after the Supreme Court had declared in his favour for the second time, Jeremy Woods reported that Askin had apparently 'slipped through a legal loophole'.

Perhaps the finest example of journalistic hyperbole – and inaccuracy – was Charmain Naidoo's article in the *Cape Times* of 29 January 1995. Again the Askins were described as buying the site for their Constantia house in the summer of 1990, when in fact it had been done the previous year. Other splendid solecisms included references to 'a lifestyle straight out of Nero's Rome', 'Turnbull and Affer' (*sic*), 'Germyn Street' (*sic*), 'Verve Cliquot' (*sic*), and to how some members of London's financial élite would get up and leave unfinished dinners at Bibendum's or Pont de la Tour when Julian walked in. This was all pure fiction, together with the words of an anonymous 'friend', who said 'I've been to Badmington (*sic*) Estates, the most pretentious place in the world, but I was more intimidated in Suzie Askin's house. Much more.'

Even while he was still under detention in Italy Askin was preparing an assault on his South African detractors. Some of the South African press, unlike the *Sunday Times*, did not follow Absa's line uncritically. The *Financial Mail*, *Weekend Argus*, and, pre-eminently, *Noseweek*, were prepared to dig out the facts. Another influential editor, Hugh Murray, made a journey to Florence on behalf of the monthly magazine *Millennium*, to discover the truth for himself, a visit which led, over the next two years, to an extensive and serious coverage of many aspects of the Tollgate affair. Under the names of '*Leadership* and *Millennium*', but with the same staff and editor, a number of detailed, well-researched articles were published between April 1995 and August 1997 which inexorably brought new evidence before South African readers. The effort was not without cost to Murray, who lost much advertising revenue and eventually had to suspend publication.

The faith of those who were beginning to accept Askin's version was bolstered by a television programme that appeared on South African 'M-Net,' in March 1995. Jeremy Woods, predictably, poured scorn on Askin's 'silver-tongued ... plausible performance.' But the effect was damaged by the acquittal, in March 1995, of Kevin de Villiers, which left Absa having had to admit the charges of illegal telephone tapping, and the complicity in it of Cronjé, now their chief executive.

During the original recording of the television programme Askin made a claim which was subsequently cut from the transmission

> Q. If one looks at the major insolvencies ... liquidations of companies ... all involving substantial debts to banks in the Absa group – how has this bank survived?'

> *Askin*: Well, I'm led to believe that they were only able to put Tollgate into liquidation – which I said should never have been done, as a bank's last priority should be liquidation – because they were given an enormous loan by the South African Reserve Bank, undisclosed, and at a very low rate of interest. In fact when I went to see Johan Rupert about it, he told me that the loan did exist – it was over a billion rand – and that his father resigned his directorship of the Reserve Bank as a result of this secret loan. It is terribly wrong that a commercial bank should use subsidised money to put a business into liquidation.

Johan Rupert had by then taken over from his father Anton much of the responsibility for the family's extensive shareholdings, which included, as well as the huge Rembrandt Tobacco Company, some 25 per cent of Absa equity. Askin and Johan Rupert had met on 6 September 1993 at Rupert's London house. In the course of their conversation it had been revealed that the SARB had advanced R1,000 million to Trust Bank to deal with all the write-offs that its lending policy had made necessary, including that of Tollgate. This transaction had been made without the knowledge of the SARB board, an action which had led to Anton Rupert's resignation. The elder Rupert put it about that his resignation had been due to a potential conflict of interests but the real reason had been his anger at this immense intervention. Askin believed, and Johan did not disagree, that the liquidation of Tollgate would never have taken place without the generous support of the South African Reserve Bank which had enabled Trust Bank/Absa to survive. This issue was to assume much greater importance in the coming months.

Other events were helping to cause informed opinion to look questioningly at Absa. Kessel Feinstein, who had taken over as Tollgate Holdings' auditors in 1990, challenged the whole legal basis of the Hoberman Commission, insisting on taking their case to the Constitutional Court. Hoberman himself had become to see that the true facts of the Tollgate liquidation did not match the picture that Absa and its lawyers had painted. In July 1994 Hoberman received a truculent telephone call from Mr Borman, the senior partner of Miller Gruss, known to Hoberman, both professionally and socially, for many years. Borman was described by Hoberman as 'extremely angry at the fact that I was proposing to investigate the claims and securities of Absa. He spoke very loudly and sounded overwrought. He spoke so loudly that my wife who was sitting nearby could hear most of what he said. He castigated me for not having discussed the matter with him first.'

It was unusual enough that a solicitor, however senior, should presume to address a prominent barrister in such terms, but to attempt to bully a Commissioner into favouring one party to an official enquiry was thoroughly improper. Some powerful pressure must have been exerted on Borman, exacerbated by the fact that it was he who had suggested to Absa that Hoberman should be appointed to the enquiry, presuming him to likely to be compliant to the wishes of the bank. Borman was doubtless embarrassed by his nominee daring to question Absa's case. Hoberman recorded: 'I must say that I was thoroughly shocked by this outburst from Mr Borman who has since been palpably hostile towards me in my dealings with him.'

Borman having failed to intimidate Hoberman, other tactics were employed. Within days the Cape Bar Council were told that a complaint had been received by Gauntlett and Woodland, ostensibly barristers for the liquidators, but who were proving themselves consistently attentive to Absa's requirements. The complaint had nothing to do with the present case, but related to a previous one in which the two barristers had been opposed by Hoberman. It was a technical breach rather than a serious impropriety, but one deeply embarrassing to Hoberman, who was fined R1,000, then about £200. The Bar Council's proceedings, which were meant to be confidential, were immediately leaked to the press, and widely reported. The timing of the complaint leaves little doubt that it was Absa's punishment for Hoberman's disobedience.

In an episode which was later to assume a greater significance, Hoberman, troubled by the reprimand from the Bar Council, sought the counsel of Judge Gerald Friedman, Judge President, a former teacher and friend of his. Explaining his situation, and submitting all the relevant documents, Hoberman asked the judge whether it was proper that he should continue to head the commission of enquiry. If no one objected, the judge decided, it was 'perfectly acceptable' that Hoberman should continue with his task; but this had now assumed a new character. Within a year of its establishment the Hoberman enquiry had developed from the searching review of the Tollgate directors' presumed iniquities, orchestrated by Absa, into a stand-up fight between Absa and the liquidators – the same liquidators who had signed up at the beginning to be obedient to Absa's orders – and Hoberman himself had become persona non grata with the bank and its advisers.

Chris van Zyl had sold his business to Syfrets, the old and highly-regarded Cape firm. Syfrets was owned by Nedbank, giving van Zyl an added encouragement to square up for a fight against Absa. Throwing their weight about, Absa had asked for a general meeting of creditors who would be invited to agree amendments to the liquidators' instructions. These would (as summarised in the *Weekend Argus* 1–2 October 1994):

> Remove the liquidator's right to take anyone to court – for example, for ignoring a subpoena;
>
> Put a stop to any public inquiry;
>
> Require all questions to be put in writing in advance, with the provision that written answers may be given and there would be no cross-questioning;
>
> Oblige anyone who wanted a witness called, including the liquidator, to pay the costs of the resulting inquiry and
>
> Require the liquidator to set out in advance the issue he wished to investigate.

Syfrets, convinced that these would constitute an infringement on the rights both of the liquidator and of other creditors, maintained that Absa had arranged the repayment to itself of 'well in excess' of R100 million just before Tollgate had been placed in liquidation. If so – and it was strongly denied by Absa – this would be tantamount to fraudulent preference.

Van Zyl's solicitor, Peter Whelan, believed – and more evidence later emerged than was apparent at that time – that as far back as 1989 Trust Bank, now a constituent part of Absa, had knowingly done business with an insolvent company, Tollgate. If the bank had, at that time, enforced the security on R650 million of debt the company must have defaulted, which event would, given the size of the exposure, have resulted in Trust Bank's own downfall. Strictly speaking it could be said that as long as a bank is prepared to support a debtor, then that debtor is not insolvent, but in this case Trust Bank could not realistically enforce its security: had Tollgate gone under then Trust Bank itself would have failed, since the sum involved was greater than the bank's total capital. As a consequence, it could be argued that Trust Bank, during this period, was effectively running Tollgate, masterminding illegal and improper transactions, controlling and signing cheques and reducing Tollgate's indebtness to themselves from R600 million to R200 million. This, the liquidators believed, was a fraud on behalf of the creditors and so were contemplating suing Absa for R400 million.

They were, however, experiencing problems in collecting evidence and had asked Hoberman to be allowed to participate in the Section 417 enquiry over which he was presiding. Although Hoberman initially agreed to the request, Absa objected: the liquidators were therefore expelled from the hearings, being told that everything they had been given was confidential and could not be shared with anyone. Frustrated, the liquidators then instigated a legal move which would have resulted in a public hearing. Absa were therefore obliged, since they were constantly highly nervous of any publicity, to agree to widening the enquiry to include the liquidators. In February 1996 the liquidators begin to insist that Absa's own activities be examined by the Hoberman committee. They believed, and could produce solid evidence to that effect, that Absa had procured for itself preferential treatment in the run up to the liquidation at the expense of the other creditors.

Pressure on Absa was building up from other directions. After Kevin de Villiers' triumphant acquittal of all the charges Absa had caused to be brought against him, the chairman, Herc Hefer, left suddenly without a successor being appointed. At the annual general meeting the board pointedly congratulated Cronjé and the management, which was, correctly interpreted as an indication that Badenhorst was about to be disposed of. Julie Walker of the South African *Sunday Times* commented: 'Absa's chief executive of the day, Piet Badenhorst, had a history of treading on smaller people . . . Now Mr Badenhorst has retired from Absa and races pigeons in Florida [a suburb of Johannesburg] while Mr de Villiers is still in the heart of Johannesburg's business.'

Another of Absa's bad bargains was also moving into the limelight. While Askin was having his every movement watched the unfortunate Hennie Diedericks was having an equally rough time. On 1 January 1993 Diedericks took up his Cabinet-approved position as managing director of the Post Office, a very senior and well-remunerated appointment – and at the same time resigned from the Broederbond, which he had so proudly joined as a young man. 'They told me it was a cultural organisation. Instead they were running the country.' Within five months of his new appointment Diedericks's world began to crumble. On 13 May OSEO raided his Constantia home, as they had that of Askin, and equally found nothing of import. In spite of this the raid was well-reported and extremely embarrassing, as allegations of possible fraud continued to be published. By November 1993 he had to spend two weeks in a psychiatric clinic recovering from nervous collapse. His health was not improved by a series of appearances before the Hoberman Committee. These quasi-judicial committees, where ordinary rules of evidence and judicial procedure do not apply, can be alarming to the robust. Diedericks complained, 'It was the most unfair interrogation. Questions were random, it was so aggressive. They expect you to answer, without records or papers, questions about matters from five or six years ago.'

By February 1994 it was clear that Diedericks could not carry on with his Post Office job.

In June 1994 a claim was made by the liquidators that Tollgate's 'course of uncontrolled acquisition' had caused a 'staggering increase of interest-bearing debt.' Between June 1987 and December 1989 this had, it was claimed, shot from R10 million to R373 million: a period, of course, *before* Askin even began to look closely at the company and one during which Diedericks had been, for some considerable time, in executive charge.

Diedericks found himself in a very unpleasant situation. It was four years since he had left Tollgate, well aware of the doubtful conduct of Key and Claasen, but reasonably confident that Askin, who should have been aware of the situation, would have long since ironed out, or at least made public, any problems. Two years back in Volkskas/Absa top management, succeeded by two years at the head of the Post Office, Diedericks assumed he had a settled, and prosperous career. He now knew otherwise. Events climaxed when on 29 June 1994, a sheriff's officer came unannounced to Diedericks's office to inform him that the Tollgate liquidators – which in effect meant Absa, his former employers – had applied for a sequestration order. He had five days to defend a claim of R19 million. Volkskas, the bank which he had saved from disgrace, faxed a notice that his bank accounts were frozen and his credit cards cancelled. His lawyers demanded a down payment of R250,000 before undertaking any defence.

The *Cape Times*, informed as usual by Absa and ignoring the presumption of innocence, headlined 'R19 million fraud'. The whole of Afrikaner society pulled down its shutters. His wife was told, by the wife of a 'very senior member of parliament' that Hennie was 'a crook', and that she should leave him; they were asked to remove their daughter from her school; their son was publicly humiliated by a lecturer at his university, Stellenbosch, who also called his father 'a crook'; and the pastor of their church told the family they would no longer be welcome.

It was too much for a man who attached great importance to his reputation and his respected place in conventional Afrikaner society. Struggling for a couple of months, Diedericks finally gave up, took to the bottle, and checked into an hotel with the intention of suicide – an intention so apparent that the hotel staff telephoned his home, bringing his wife Alta rushing to the rescue. She obtained a court order to send Hennie to an alcohol addiction recovery unit, the Hesketh King rehabilitation centre. Here the unhappy Diedericks experienced almost a religious conversion, helped by the fact that he was secluded from his financial difficulties and protected, by the court order, from any further action by the liquidators.

Six months later, in February 1995, he was discharged, cured. His first action was to appeal to his old colleague Danie Cronjé, now chief executive of Absa, insisting on his innocence and recalling his past contributions to Volkskas. At least, in the subsequent interview, Cronjé came clean; when the two men met on 1 March Cronjé stated directly and in so many words, that Absa were not going to allow any of their officials to be questioned on the Tollgate affair, which, if they were not careful, could cost the bank a write-off of R200 million.

Cronjé was taking a risk in washing his hands of Diedericks, for Hennie's eighteen years with Volkskas meant that he knew where all the skeletons were buried, and these included one, mouldering relic of Cronjé's own. In 1984 Cronjé had been senior General Manager in charge of International Finance. It was a difficult time, with the value of the rand sliding. Many Volkskas customers who had foreign debt obligations faced large losses, but the bank's advice to them was to stick it out, waiting for the rand to recover. This never happened. Cronjé attempted to solve the problem by what seemed a sound plan to obtain external funding at the same time as increasing the profits of this division. This was to borrow eurodollars, which were available at low interest rates, lending them on to Volkskas' subsidiaries at a very much higher rate, who could then lend the dollars to other customers. Such an operation was normal enough, but no experienced banker would have assumed so great a risk relative to his capital: the normal course would be to 'cover' the exchange risk by buying forward dollars for at least a fair proportion of the whole.

Unfortunately for Volkskas, Cronjé had misjudged the situation. In 1985 the Chase Manhattan bank refused renewal of its loan, President Botha disappointed investors' hopes in his damp squib of the 'Rubicon' speech, and the rand tumbled to half its value against the dollar. Cronjé's scheme had cost the bank R280 million – some six times its forecast profits for that year – and Diedericks was implored to find a solution, to remove the loss from the sight of the SARB and the public. If the bank had been obliged to reveal its loss it might well have been forced to liquidate.

An attempt was made to allow the loss to be carried forward by selling the eurodollars (and their consequent loss) to a hitherto dormant company, Volkskas Industrial Financing, which was lent money by the bank in order to do so. Volkskas Industrial Financing not being a subsidiary, the loss could be moved off the Volkskas balance sheet, enabling it to produce respectable 1985 figures. As well as depositors and shareholders being kept in the dark, the foreign lenders of the eurodollars were not informed of these manipulations.

The device was only modestly successful: after a year the eurodollar loss had declined only by R40 million to R240 million. Another solution had to be found. The Volkskas board attempted to do this by proposing the illegal device of revaluing all the bank properties to create a fictitious reserve (in spite of its illegality this was agreed by the auditors Aitken Deloitte and by the Finance Minister, Barend du Plessis – naturally a Broeder). Diedericks pointed out the inadvisability of such a step, and propounded a more ingenious route.

Volkskas' Pretoria head office was valued in the balance sheet at R24 million. A stroke of the pen enabled this to be upgraded to an estimated value of R124 million producing a handy surplus of R100 million. The Volkskas subsidiary, Volkskas Centre Pretoria (VCP), which actually owned the building, was given a loan of R93.618million by Volkskas, which was then used to pay a dividend of R93.618 million. This windfall was used to offset Cronjé's loss on foreign exchange (which tax credits had reduced to R122 million).

The only snag with this was that, should this transaction be reflected in the balance sheet, it would appear that the Bank's head office had been sold, which would stimulate awkward questions. VCP was then sold to another company, Lifegro Insurance Ltd, again structured not to be a subsidiary company and therefore not appearing in the bank's consolidated accounts. This convenient enterprise was jointly owned with Anton Rupert's Rembrandt Group, with Volkskas having an option to re-purchase its head office for R2 million, less than 2 per cent of its claimed value, which had nevertheless been agreed as the artificial sale price.

Altogether a most ingenious device and one of which Diedericks was justly proud; but it was an arrangement which could never be disclosed to the public, or confidence in the bank would have been destroyed. Cronjé himself had described Diedericks as 'both brilliant and the group's top troubleshooter', a reasonable enough description, especially in the light of another, more recent, situation in which Diedericks and Cronjé had been involved.

This was in the first half of 1991, at a time when Cronjé was managing director of Volkskas with Diedericks as his deputy, in the run-up to the merger with the United Bank. 'The losses in Volkskas,' Diedericks wrote,

> were an enormous problem and frustration and reflected on the bona fides of the Volkskas Group in entering into a merger agreement ... and immediately thereafter started showing enormous losses. There were various sessions with Cronjé, Stegmann [J. A. Stegmann, director], van Vuuren [J. L. H. van Vuuren, director, Bankfin] ... and with the auditors [Aitken and Peat]. The question that had been raised was to what extent did management, the board of Volkskas and its auditors understate the position of Volkskas as at 31 March 1991. In doing so they misled United ... *It was a serious problem.* We never got to the bottom of it because nobody was prepared to admit that they made a mistake but the events were of such magnitude and of such a dilemma that the whole focus then moved on to how to overcome it and it was again left to me to sort out the mess – which I did. We changed the whole accounting policy of the Absa Group relating to the provisions of bad debts with the full support and eager co-operation of the auditors.

Having in these ways saved Cronjé's skin, Diedericks was furious when a man whom he had considered as a personal friend refused, three years later, to help at so vital a time. He put to Dave Brink, the new chairman, who had not been personally involved in any of the previous events, the suggestion that they should co-operate in defending themselves against Askin's criticisms. Brink was emollient, but refused, leaving Diedericks to complain that he had 'made the mistake that his former colleagues at Absa Bank were his friends. It now became clear to him that they were totally ruthless.' In particular Diedericks felt that he had 'become a threat to Dr Cronjé. He feels uncomfortable in my presence of being responsible for bailing him, my senior, out of situations which he was basically involved in creating and on top of which he had no answer of solving himself.' As a result Diedericks believed that 'it would suit (Cronjé) finally to make certain that I would have no credibility left in future to be able to refer to these circumstances which could lead to his own detriment and downfall.'

Recognising, however, that his immediate problem had to be settled – he had been told by his lawyers that Adam Harris of Miller Gruss, representing Absa and the liquidators, had received instructions to 'wear Diedericks out' – Diedericks agreed with the liquidators that a payment of R375,000 would fully satisfy their claim of R19 million. As with Askin, this payment of a tiny fraction of the original claim was accompanied by a complete clearance. From that time, September 1995, he was free to fight back, and the enemy was clearly identified as his old employer, Absa.

The alliance forms

When he heard of Diedericks's actions, Askin realised that, far from being at daggers drawn, the man he had previously accused and reviled was actually on the same side, persecuted by the same joint enemy, and suggested that Diedericks should come to London to discuss possible co-operation. Diedericks took some convincing, remembering bitterly Askin's original accusations. Only after several telephone calls to his lawyers would Hennie agree to talk to Julian, and then to come to London for discussions.

On 30 July 1995 Hennie Diedericks arrived at Victoria Station to be met by Julian Askin. It was, astonishingly enough, the first time the two men had met, and they now encountered each other in unpropitious circumstances. Journalists Hugh Murray and Paul Bell reported in *Millennium*:

> they shook hands and exchanged commonplace civilities about the lateness of the hour and pleasant journeys. Under the skin however, both men were seething with curiosity, extreme suspicion and latent hostility.
>
> Askin had publicly and – it is now clear to him – unfairly, branded Diedericks a thief – 'I was the guy who shafted you,' Askin has frankly told him – and Diedericks, for whom, as a consequence, life since 1993 had become the stuff of nightmare, was hugely aggrieved. 'Even so,' says Diedericks,

ASKIN AND SOME ALLIES

'for me it was not that important to judge Julian's character. Rather, I needed to fill in certain gaps about his dealings with Trust Bank and later Absa, and about his management of, and experience at, Tollgate. But I was feeling good. I had always believed it was possible a break might come, when such chances come in life, one must take them.'

Askin, on the other hand, was convinced that there must have been a time – after Diedericks left Tollgate to return to Volkskas – when Diedericks would have joined the Absa chorus seeking to discredit him. He also feared that Diedericks had been so badly beaten about by the Absa-directed liquidators of Tollgate that he might have caved in and come to London as an agent for Absa, in order to find out what Askin was up to. And Askin himself had gone through so much that he had become conditioned to a high degree of paranoia. As Diedericks himself says, 'anything was possible'. At the same time, however, Diedericks felt a certain relief: while he had come to the embrace of a putative enemy, he was no longer completely alone.

Both men started by being suspicious. Diedericks was uncomfortable in the opulent surroundings of Chester Square, and Askin was still in the distrustful mood induced by his Italian experiences. He noted in his diary, 'H. D. is wary, but seems willing enough. He speaks with a thick Afrikaans accent and claims to be embittered and thrown aside by Absa.' Not convinced that Diedericks was sincere, and fearing some sort of trap, all the meetings with Diedericks were secretly recorded. Askin was taking no chances and himself made notes of their discussions.

For the first day's talks on Monday 31 July he recorded:

> The day is heavy and goes slowly. Hennie D. is reluctant and not forthcoming. Everybody [the solicitors, Anthony Amhurst and Stephen Morris were also present] is unimpressed and concerned. He doesn't seem to have brought information or be really concerned to get into the heavy stuff. This might be early days; he might be intimidated; it might be a set-up as well, which worries everybody. We don't think so, but it's not impossible. He says he was in the Salvation Army clinic for six months, not for drink but to

straighten himself out. Lunch at Mimos. He has rugella salad and veal chops. Drinks Gavi quite happily. Wonders how you get your photo taken at Mimos.

In evening JA takes him for a pint at the Antelope then to dinner at Santini. HD drinks Felluga Pinot Grigio and eats courgette flowers and osso buco. JA asparagus and P. Pollo Santini. HD still very cautious but warming up a bit. It is going to take time and HD confidence will have to be earned slowly, it seems. HD mentions that he might not wish to return to SA that he's worried about criminal prosecution et cetera that he could be arrested upon his return and that he wouldn't be able to afford any bail and would therefore be put inside and couldn't talk to anybody. JA not convinced: it seems a little too pat. AA and JA had both thought earlier that his likelihood of being pursued criminally was slight because it would only raise the profile of Absa, which could hardly be their intention. JA leaves HD at 10.30.

Askin then went off on a holiday leaving Diedericks in London for a series of meetings with Amhurst and the CIEX team, during which a careful record was produced. Diedericks' precision, his knowledge of the Afrikaner financial establishment, and the weight given by his long experience of South African banking, were to become the backbone of the evidence against Absa.

When the story of the meeting was published, along with a photograph of the two men walking in Chester Square, Absa executives were incredulous. Believing the whole thing to be a fabrication, they had the photograph closely examined to see whether it was a composite image.

During his stay in London Diedericks met Martin Welz of *Noseweek*, and was forthcoming on a number of subjects connected with Tollgate. Gants, the food processing company acquired by Tollgate, had got into difficulty largely by following Volkskas' advice on foreign exchange transactions. To make matters worse for the Gant family their own estate, Lourensford, was included in the security. The Gants' urgent need for cash to repay their loans from Volkskas led to Duros underwriting the 'put' option described on pp.78–9, the true cost of which was never revealed in the company accounts. The difference between the purchase price of R21.2 million stated in the accounts and the actual R33 million needed for the 'put' explained at least part of the Tollgate missing millions.

Yet another of Absa's victims was deciding to make common cause with Julian Askin. Claasen had every reason to be aggrieved by Absa's treatment of him. He had perhaps been overconfident when he bought Arwa, prominent though it was in its industry, but without any management depth or the modern machinery needed to be competitive. From the first Trust Bank had assured him of their continued support, as they did Askin, but by March 1990 it had become vital to the bank that Claasen should buy Arwa from Tollgate. Askin had made it very clear that he would not invest unless Arwa was removed; and without this the true facts of Tollgate's desperate situation would be revealed and the bank, in all probability, ruined.

After Claasen took personal control of Arwa from Tollgate he discussed the company's prospects with his old friends Morland and Strydom, in June 1990, who agreed a loan of R39 million to fund the acquisition from Tollgate. This was in spite of the fact that Strydom had reported to his managing director, Chris van Wyk, that Claasen would not be able to pay interest on this loan, which would only be made for 'special reasons'. Essentially, according to a Trust Bank document 'the only reason we are prepared to put Mr Claasen in a position to take Arwa Corp Ltd. out of Tollgate' is to reduce our exposure. The original Afrikaans minute of 27 June read, '*indien ons nie vir Mr C. instaat stel om AG uit de Tollgate stal te neem nie, die regte uitgfte v. R90 million, wat noodsaaklik is om ons blootstelling mit Tollgate en Duros te veminder, deur die mat sal val.*' 'Both these applications granted, not on their respective merits, but in order to ensure that the intended investment to be made (by Askin) and the rights issues ... would not be jeopardised.' Strydom agreed that this was 'an essential step to save Tollgate to save (our)selves'. Save, to some extent, Trust Bank, it did but at Tollgate's cost, since Tollgate had agreed to guarantee Claasen's debt – another R39 million of obligation unknown to Askin. In addition Trust Bank provided a R50 million overdraft to Arwa.

On 3 August 1990 Gerbie Strydom was obliged to write to Gerrie Barnard. 'There appears to be total confusion over what precise facilities the group has with us ... We have been,' he admitted, 'too inclined [in the past] to have verbal discussions with the two of them [Key and Claasen] and then later not to have anything really on paper . . . Gerrie you have informed me this afternoon that MK has had so many meetings with people at head office that people do not know precisely what is happening day to day. This is no excuse . . . it is your duty to find out exactly what was discussed.'

On 25 July 1990 investigating accountant H. G. Meyer wrote to H. van der Merwe of the credit department:

> The situation surrounding in particular Tollgate Holdings exposure is worrying, viz R201 million, against R243 shareholder funds . . . Our exposure to Arwa is however also a big problem . . . We cannot trace any correspondence on this guarantee [the R39 million in respect of Arwa]. Our legal department should look urgently at this and say how we should react

Although in August 1990 Trust Bank attempted to reduce the agreed overdraft Claasen was taken aback when, on 5 September, a lunch with van der Merwe was cancelled, and replaced by a confrontation. Claasen was told that he must sell the business he had bought, with the full co-operation of the bank, five months previously.

He was appalled:

> I emphatically rejected the proposal and said to Mr van der Merwe that I wished to refer him to our previous meeting, about the undertakings given to me by Mr Strydom on the restructuring of Arwa and that I was here to make a presentation to them on how this could be done to the benefit of both parties. Mr van der Merwe then asked me a very peculiar question i.e. can I produce documentary proof that the Bank had given me the undertaking to restructure Arwa. I was completely surprised at this question.
>
> I answered him that I never worked on such a basis in the past with the Bank and I never had any reason to have done so. I had no reason whatsoever to mistrust or not believe an undertaking given to me as a chairman of a large company by a senior official of a large banking group.

I then asked Mr Strydom to confirm to the meeting what he had told me on which he denied that he had ever given me an undertaking to restructure and reschedule the debt position of Arwa. On his answer I then asked Mr van der Merwe if he can explain to me why this transaction was approved and the finance given to me by the Bank in the first instance if it was not bankable, and why did they leave it to such a late stage without notifying me that they never intended to fulfil their obligation.

The guarantee that Tollgate had given was due to expire in December and van der Merwe wrote on the original report his instructions, 'Issue Summons now on the R39m. guarantee, before the 31.12. 90 because there cannot be a problem.'

Desperate to achieve a solution before the Tollgate guarantee expired, the bank called the loan. On Christmas Eve 1990, at six in the afternoon, Claasen was notified that he had to repay the R39 million by 10 a.m. on 27 December – a difficult task, given that both Christmas Day and Boxing Day were Bank Holidays. Effectively that gave the unfortunate Claasen ninety minutes of a working day. He was therefore obliged to surrender his assets, including his holding in Arwa. The bank lost no time in selling the Arwa hosiery division to the FSI group, which controlled W & A, Arwa's principal competitor, whose previous interest had been stifled by opposition from the monopolies authority. But the price was a long way from the R33 million that W & A had offered for the hosiery division alone the previous year – the whole enterprise was sold to W & A for only R9.3 million: and it might be noted that the chairman of FSI was Mr Jeff Liebesman, who also happened to be a director of Senbank, Trust Bank's affiliate in Bankorp, and that W & A had been allowed to run up a debt of R1,000 million with Senbank. Claasen was indignantly furious: he had, with Trust Bank's active encouragement, bought a company for R42 million which he had been forced by the bank to sell to a company owned by one of its directors only a few months later, for a price well below its true value.

Worse was to come. The Mr H. van der Merwe who had been responsible for the Arwa account and who had made the original agreement with Claasen, had given instructions for the summons to be issued and had negotiated the sale to W & A, left the bank to join W & A as deputy chairman shortly afterwards, receiving a joining bonus of R5 million. And a few months later W & A sold its hosiery division, together with Arwa, to the American Kiwi Brands Corporation for R200 million: of this, R65 million was in respect of Arwa – a profit for FSI of over R55 million within a year (less, of course, Mr van der Merwe's little perquisite). Mr Liebesman had not done too badly but Mr Claasen had lost a fortune. And, to add more profits to the bank, Tollgate had been forced to honour their guarantee. In all, Trust Bank had made R100 million through a carefully planned campaign of chicanery.

Pursuing his task in the liquidation of Tollgate, Eugene Wallace, Motorvia's joint liquidator had been attempting to reach agreement on a settlement of their claims against Claasen. When he had got wind of this Christo Faul of Absa was furious. It was Absa's policy to force Claasen into bankruptcy in order to make it impossible for him then to litigate against Absa – as he had good ground for doing. Christo Faul instructed Absa's solicitors, Werksmans, to write to Wallace's lawyer, Miller Gruss, reminding them of the minute – the illegal minute – that the liquidators had signed at the onset, committing them to follow Absa's instructions. Judging this an empty threat, since Absa could hardly expose their own unlawful action in demanding the agrement, Wallace refused, and settled with Claasen.

Absa's actions in alienating Glaum and Wallace had now provided the Askin side with two more valuable allies, who in the coming months were able to divulge some of the bank's glaring irregularities.

Hennie Diedericks was soon followed by another visitor to Chester Square. Bob Aldworth recalls; 'On Friday, 13 October, I received a telephone call that was to mark a turning point in my life. It was from Julian Askin . . . now hell bent on clearing his name and pursuing Absa to the ends of the earth.' Askin wanted to include an affidavit from Aldworth in the case he was beginning to prepare, and was willing to pay all expenses. Aldworth had good reason to be aggrieved by his treatment by Absa. After his flight from South Africa he had been living with his wife Mari in a London bedsit, on the edge of penury. His pension from Barclays was frozen in South Africa, and he recalled, 'on the best of days we were living on £10 a day. I remember once being down to our last £5 when an envelope arrived, unsolicited, with some money from a friend. Maybe it's true that He kept an eye on those who are in trouble.' The Almighty obliged to an extent, enabling the Aldworths to move, in December 1994, to a rented flat in Marbella.

Aldworth was in no position to do much immediately in the joint defiance of Absa. As Diedericks had done, Aldworth spent many days in discussing his case with Askin's solicitors, but

> at the end of our sessions, I started feeling extremely unwell: I was suffering from shortness of breath and my energy was badly depleted. Askin suggested I visit his GP, who took one look at me and sent me to a cardiologist who had me admitted to a clinic on the same day. My legs were so swollen by then, I could hardly walk. I spent 10 days in the clinic, during which time 21 litres of water were drained out of me and I lost about 20kgs in weight. The cardiologist gave me about six months to live, which, it now turns out, was rather a pessimistic view. Askin picked up all the bills and I am forever grateful to him for this.

But the alliance between Aldworth and Diedericks had one useful effect. While Aldworth was in hospital, Diedericks worked out that in his estimation as a professional banker, Aldworth had no liability towards Absa. Armed with this thought, and the results of a preliminary meeting between James Ramsay, Aldworth's solicitor, and David Brink, Absa's chairman, at which Brink showed himself willing to be reasonable and conciliatory, Aldworth decided to return to South Africa on 14 January 1996. On arrival, and with something of a flourish, he announced, 'I am returning to South Africa ... to face head on and counter the allegations which have been made against me, demonstrate my innocence of any criminal wrongdoing and ensure that truth and justice prevail.'

He was to be disappointed. At their first meeting Brink had changed tack. He had spoken to Absa's executives (not, as he had previously promised to Aldworth, the Board, who might well have taken a very different stance), who had convinced him that they should not attempt to settle amicably with Aldworth ... And Brink added, 'Bob, even if you go to trial, and are found not guilty, I will always consider you guilty' – a remarkable display of prejudice from one who was 'something of a legend' and 'regarded highly for his commitment to business ethics'. Although a free man, allowed bail, Aldworth found himself on the old legal treadmill, defending any action for fraud. It was only in 1997 that he finally, and successfully, won his case, but his evidence was helpful to the dossier Askin was preparing.

CHAPTER SEVEN

Safety at Sea

A brotherly helping hand

The reference made during the conversation between Johan Rupert and Julian Askin mentioned on p.171 to a rescue operation, commonly known as a 'lifeboat', instituted by the South African Reserve Bank on behalf of Absa was to become the central point in Askin's case against Absa. His researches into the management and policies both of that bank and of the South African Reserve Bank, and the misdeeds that were uncovered became the eventual cause of turmoil and scandal in the South African financial world. The Governor of the Reserve Bank found himself accused of deception amounting to fraud in collusion with pillars of the financial establishment and his executives and colleagues in enriching themselves at the expense of the public. Many international firms were obliged to attempt answers to a lot of awkward questions, the South African government established two commissions of enquiry, and the currency came under considerable strain.

It was in February 1992 that the possible existence of large sums of money being provided by the South African Reserve Bank to Absa was first mentioned. In a fashion that was to become commonplace, it was immediately lied about. Questioned on the subject by a reporter from the South African *Sunday Times* the Reserve Bank Governor, Dr Chris Stals, flatly denied it: 'In view of the stories going around, I would like to say that the Reserve Bank had nothing to do with the Absa transaction.' Since then this statement, and others made by Dr Stals, have been shown, many times, to be false.

In analysing the motives for what followed it has to be made clear that all parties concerned – the directors, and major shareholders of the Reserve Bank and the banks assisted by that institution – were, almost without exception, Afrikaners: and such Afrikaners were highly likely to be Broederbond members.

It would be misleading to posit a Broederbond 'conspiracy' over-shadowing every action that helped Afrikaner enterprises. There were, in all probability, few formal meetings of office-holders in the Brotherhood evolving co-ordinated plans of campaign; eighty years of working together for the advancement of the Volk's interests sufficed. In much the same fashion as Masonic Lodges can work in local communities or in police forces, like-minded people, brought up in similar traditions, co-operated to advantage each other. Whilst there are doubtless many petty scandals that Freemasons might prefer not to have disclosed, it is probably true that 'Freemasonry's great secret is that it allows middle-class, middle-aged men excursions into the unfamiliar territory of flam-boyant sentimentality without calling their sexuality into question' (Nick Paul, *Noseweek*).

But the Broederbond differed from the Masonic movement in several important respects. Firstly, its members had formed the great majority of *every* South African government for more than half a century, and had therefore established virtual monopoly of policy-making. This power was reinforced by a similar degree, amounting to unquestioned control, of the police and armed forces, with a powerful representation in the judiciary. Then, Broeders were committed to a narrow national-ism (no member, for example, might marry an English-speaking woman, send his children to an English school or university, or be divorced) which could amount to the sort of contempt and hatred expressed in Brit's epithet 'fokken Engelsman'. Moreover, many Broed-ers had been deeply involved in illegal transactions during the whole period of sanctions, when the line between legality and Afrikaner patri-otism had been largely expunged. And, at all times, there were decent, pious and responsible Afrikaners increasingly concerned about the future of their country under the Nationalist policies of apartheid: but such men, like Diedericks, were tending to leave the Broederbond, if indeed they had ever been members.

Change was also moving within the Brotherhood. Nationalist policies of Afrikanerisation had opened new opportunities for Afrikaners to assume positions of power, and able and increasingly well-educated

Afrikaners had not been lacking to fill them Through the executive committee, with its sub-committees and study groups, the Broederbond had for years formed a virtual research foundation for Nationalist governments. Its leaders were among the first to accept the inevitability of change. Pieter de Lange publicly advocated black participation in politics, and Chris van Wyk, was among those prominent businessmen who attended secret meetings with the ANC. He was followed by Roelof Meyer, who took up the discussions with Cyril Ramaphosa which unblocked the conflict between the Nationalist government and its opponents between 1992 and 1994.

Until 1990, when it became advisable to make a gesture towards the approaching majority by appointing two token non-executives, all the directors of the South African Reserve Bank were Afrikaners. Even after 1990 all the executive directors appointed by the government under the Reserve Bank Act still remained Afrikaners: C. L. Stals, the Governor, C. J. de Swardt, G. W. G. Browne, M. T. de Waal, J. J. Fourie, and – a name to remember, C. H. (Christo) Wiese, Mervyn Key's old partner.

It was a situation impossible to parallel elsewhere in the world. Although Afrikaners represented only one twelfth of the population, and controlled perhaps one quarter of the financial institutions, every director of the Central Bank was an Afrikaner, as were almost all its senior executives. Searching vainly for an example, one might try envisaging a Federal Reserve Bank where all the directors and most of the directors were Hispanic, or a Bank of England staffed entirely by Welsh-speakers, carrying out its daily correspondence in that language: but the imagination boggles. The doors of 370 Church Street Pretoria stood wide open as a refuge for troubled Afrikaner financiers and there was much traffic through them.

Dr Stals, who became the central beleaguered figure in the drama, had served with the Reserve Bank all his working life, since 1954. He had worked under all the Nationalist governments since that of Hans Strydom, when he had seen apartheid installed and flourish and the Afrikaner laager eventually crumble under international and internal pressure. Coming from the Broederbond aristocracy – his father, A. J. Stals, had been chairman of the Bond – his actions showed him to be devoted to the interests of the Volk. Father and son had acted as keeper of the Bond's financial secrets – which under Chris Stals had been assisted by the destruction of an enormous quantity of possibly embarrassing documents.

Wide powers were delegated to both the Governor (President in Afrikaans) and Deputy Governors (Vice-President); since the Reserve Bank had control over all foreign exchange transactions, which could result in large profits, few were prepared to cross its senior executives. Even the bank's non-executive directors were in a position to exercise great power: if, of course, they were told what was really going on.

The South African Reserve Bank is, like many other institutions in that country, not quite the same as similar organisations in other parts of the world. It continues to be privately owned, but in an almost nominal fashion. With only two million shares in issue, the permissible dividend, if pegged at 10 per cent, reduced the market capitalisation to something like R2 million. Shareholders are allotted one vote for each 200 shares held, with a limit of 50 votes, even for those institutions which may have a number of individual shareholders. It is therefore impossible for shareholders to take decisive action.

Private ownership of a central bank is not unprecedented; the Bank of England was only nationalised in 1948, but the Bank of England took some of its responsibilities rather more seriously than did the SARB. Although governors of the Reserve Bank carried out the normal duties of central bankers – controlling money supply in the interests of the economy – and sometimes very successfully, there were significant differences. The Reserve Bank appears to have exhibited a remarkably casual attitude towards one of the most important of its responsibilities, the formalities of exchange control upon which the whole question of currency policy depended. Dr Stals, for example, considered that four inspectors, only two of whom were qualified, were quite sufficient for this task.

Others did not agree. An enquiry headed by Mr Justice Harms, on the whole anodyne in its conclusions, reported in March 1989 that bank officials did not read applications for foreign exchange critically, if at all, and that there was little effective control of foreign exchange transactions. Nico Alant, writing in the *Mail and Guardian* of 30 April 1998, considered that this lack of concern had led to 'massive abuse of our foreign exchange reserves and a burden on our criminal justice system'. The Transvaal Attorney-General's office was reluctant to prosecute major infractions since it would be obliged to attribute at least half the blame to the Reserve Bank itself. When an interdepartmental conference attempted to investigate massive frauds, to the extent of thousands of millions of rands, the Reserve Bank representatives were required to leave before the potentially embarrassing meeting began.

The Reserve Bank was, throughout the period of Nationalist governments, prepared to go much further in breaking the law in the interests of the apartheid society. The ease with which illegal foreign exchange transactions could be made was revealed in a speech made by General Tienie Groenewald, former head of military intelligence in the South African army, to the American Conservative Caucus. Groenewald, extolling the virtues of South Africa, told his audience 'Any foreigner can, with no restriction, either bring money into South Africa – whether it is hot money or not, does not matter – bring it in or take it out.'

This inefficiency was not the result of gratuitous neglect, but reflected South African government policy. As the doctrine of Total Strategy was implemented the Reserve Bank was drawn into the underhand measures needed. Any pretext of an even-handed and judicial control of currency regulations and capital movements was abandoned. Companies engaged in 'sanctions-busting' were assured of the necessary permission, and many other applications concerned only with private gain were allowed to slip through the net. More seriously, secret funds used by Nationalist governments in both external and internal destabilisation and downright terror tactics, developed a culture of secrecy and deception, which traumatised normal diplomatic life, and the structure of public morality.

Although a privately owned institution, the SARB is obliged to remit any surpluses over the 10 per cent dividend to the South African Treasury. In the year ending March 1992, for example, a net profit of R155.1 million was made. After a transfer of 10 per cent of this sum to reserves, the whole of the remainder, over R139 million, was paid to the government; the shareholders' dividends amounted to only R200,000. The corollary of this arrangement was potentially lethal. Should it be proved that the Reserve Bank had acted illegally to reduce its profits, it might follow that the Board was responsible for such a shortfall in taxpayers' potential receipts. Leaving aside the personal responsibility of the directors, the thought that the Reserve Bank might be called upon to refund sums which ran into hundreds of millions of rands was a point that was indeed subsequently raised with some energy and which provoked violent reactions.

Broeders, too, were the recipients of the SARB's generosity. The two main banking groups which had formed Absa in 1992 were Sanlam's Bankorp and the Broederbond's own creation, Volkskas. Although Sanlam had begun in a different Afrikaner tradition, that of the more internationalist Cape rather than the isolationist Transvaal, over the years Sanlam's board had become almost as purely Broederbond-controlled. Members of the board were almost all loyal brethren; their vice-chairman, Wim de Villiers, also chairman of their great mining company, Gencor, was the most vocal sponsor of the disastrous 'total strategy policy'. His colleague, Marinus Daling, was one of the Bond's more prominent members.

It was not unusual for the same individuals to be both donors and recipients. Piet Liebenberg, who was to negotiate the deal with the Reserve Bank that saved Bankorp, became Director of the South African Revenue Services, where he was faced with explaining how his activities resulted in the loss of over R1,000 million to the Revenue (he resigned rather than have to make the attempt). Anton Rupert, whose interests held a controlling interest in 25 per cent of Absa shares, was on the board of the Reserve Bank when the 'Lifeboat' was launched. He was succeeded, in April 1992 by Mervyn Key's old colleague, Christo Wiese, chairman of the Boland Bank, which had previously also been succoured by the Reserve Bank. Of the great Afrikaner capitalists only Rupert's views on the Broederbond were doubtful. According to Wilkins and Strydom (*The Broederbond* p.428) he had wanted to resign from the brotherhood because 'he thought the Bond's narrow Afrikaner image could damage his image as an international businessman', but was dissuaded by the chairman, Dr Piet Meyer. Rupert remained outstanding among South African businessmen of any race in his capacity for strategic thought, and had many years before abandoned his original Fascist sympathies. He continued to take an independent line, and showed himself capable of angry criticisms of the other Afrikaner concerns but he was never averse to acting in the interests of the Afrikaner Volk as a whole, provided they coincided with those of his own concerns.

It has to be remembered, when reviewing the SARB's policies, that these were formed in three phases, merging one into the other. During the first period, which petered out between 1987–88, the doctrine of total strategy had been broadly supported by Afrikaner business, although there had been expressions of marked discontent ever since the disappointment of the Rubicon speech. During this period it was generally believed to be necessary to close ranks in support of the government policies, seen as essential to the Volk's interests. Any help the SARB might give to Afrikaner business would be a patriotic duty, with questions of propriety or legality falling into subordinate positions. Critical comments from the right-wingers, protesting against any reform to the apartheid system which they cherished, were comparatively rare among senior businessmen (most of whom were, as English-speakers, even more sceptical about Nationalist policies, and all of whom were having to cope with the damaging economic effects of apartheid ideologies).

As it became apparent that the piecemeal approach of President Botha was not going to work, (Coloureds and Indians spurned, in different degrees, the cardboard assemblies that had been allowed them), a different answer had to be sought. A real dialogue with the black majority was now accepted as essential. When this was begun, with senior Brothers often taking the lead, and international pressure eased, evading sanctions became less important, but, if anything, the vital need to export capital to safe havens abroad increased. The future loomed murky and uncertain, the currency was perilously exposed, Swiss francs and dollars were eagerly sought.

Allied to this demand for secure foreign nest-eggs was the pressing necessity to cover up the huge sums which had already been deployed abroad for use in sanctions-busting or destabilisation (not forgetting the odd acts of terrorism). While it was acknowledged that these might be less called upon in future the existence of such funds was comforting to imperilled politicians and officials. At this time, and especially in the four painful years that followed Mandela's release in February 1990, most whites assumed that a deal could be done to protect their interests, but few were willing to rely on it. The most optimistic were those Nationalists, like President de Klerk himself, who were convinced that they held the economic levers of power, and that any political settlement would leave their happy situation unaffected.

As a precautionary measure, cosying up to potential black leaders began. The Reserve Bank hurriedly appointed, for the first time, some non-Afrikaner Directors – O. E. H. M. Nxumalo (1 December 1990) and Deenadayalen Konar (28 July 1990) – but their function was akin to that of cavalry in warfare – purely decorative: management remained firmly in Broederbond control. Sanlam, more to the point, ensured that a company, New Africa Investments Limited (NAIL), floated on the Johannesburg Stock Exchange in August 1994, with the object of increasing black participation in commerce and industry – 'empowerment', in the current jargon – created instead instant black millionaires. These fortunate gentlemen, who might reasonably be expected to show proper gratitude, included the chairman of the African Bank, Sam Motsueyane, who was given nearly R18 million worth of shares, and Dr Franklin Sonn, the Ambassador to the USA who received R8.9 million. Marinus Daling joined the party, celebrating Mandela's release by drinking champagne with his appointed successor, Thabo Mbeki, and claiming 'loss of political power has freed us . . . politics can never be a real and lasting source of our Afrikanerdom.' The Reserve Bank governor agreed: 'The ideals of optimal growth, low inflation and a rising standard of living will not be achieved without adequate progress in the field of political reform.'

1994 brought with it increased concern about the future of the economy. The Nationalist government of President de Klerk had managed to keep the economy on an even keel better than many had expected, and the Reserve Bank under Dr Stals, exercising a tight monetary control, had contributed greatly to this end. But with ANC ministers now in charge, could the new government be relied upon to face down demands from its supporters for short-term improvements to their own living standards at the expense of stability?

South Africa's Gross Domestic Product, which had slumped alarmingly in the disastrous year of 1992, had since shown positive growth. Abandoning its previous, never unanimous or enthusiastic, advocacy of widespread nationalisation and doctrinaire socialism, the ANC in power had showed itself as comfortingly conservative. The Reserve Bank had done much in reassuring the Finance Minister, Trevor Manuel, enabling him to resist the pressure of more radical cabinet and party colleagues and restraining what might be disastrous inflation and loss of confidence internationally. Admiration for the genuine achievement of Dr Stals and the part played by the Reserve Bank in so doing did much to buttress his position when much less admirable tactics began to be exposed. This they began to be from 1995 onwards.

Politics, it was true, would never be the real and lasting source of Afrikaner power, but economics were still relied upon to preserve the hegemony built up by half a century of Afrikaner Nationalist governments.

It was therefore imperative to ensure that Nationalist-controlled enterprises remained intact. The English-speaking banks had retained much of their international character and could rely upon support from the USA and Britain: but the Boers had few respectable foreign friends (although the huge sums of money squirrelled abroad could buy much influence – the links with criminal and government intelligence services were kept in good working order) and Boer banking was uncomfortably exposed. There was however, the all-Afrikaner Reserve Bank to bolster them up.

The first *identifiable* (although certainly by no means the first) instance discovered in the records of the Reserve Bank subsidising Afrikaner Banks begins with a letter from the Managing Director of Bankorp, G. C. (Stoffel) Erasmus, to Dr de Kock, the then Governor of the Reserve Bank, dated 10 April 1985. It was a confession of failure and an appeal for help. Referring to a meeting held with de Kock and his deputy, Dr Stals, on 29 March, Erasmus explained that the Bankorp subsidiary, Mercabank, had problems with 'a great part of its asset portfolio'. Too large a proportion of the bank's advances and investments were producing little, if any, return. In another three months, by the end of June the bank would not be able to pay interest to its depositors.

Nor could these non-performing assets be simply written off: the bank had not enough in its undisclosed reserves to enable this to be done. The directors were therefore obliged to abandon their efforts to recover any loans which might entail writing down the dwindling capital. Liquidation or receivership, Erasmus argued, was out of the question. The effects on public confidence would be too drastic. Would the Reserve Bank therefore please oblige with a loan of R300 million?

It was nonsensical, the economic philosophy of Mr Micawber, hoping that someday something would turn up. Without writing off bad loans any new money injected into the bank would only add to them. Incompetent and insolvent borrowers would have to be given more credit until something did turn up.

Erasmus blamed the 'sharp decline in the economy' for the trouble, but the date of his letter is significant. In July 1985 the Chase Manhattan Bank refused to roll over $US10 million of loans due to mature in 1986. A month later, after President Botha's disappointing Rubicon speech, Governor de Kock spoke of 'utter disaster'. No upturn was visible on the horizon that might offer some hope of succour to Mercabank or its controlling shareholders.

Bankorp might be only a relatively small bank, but it was Afrikaner through and through. The history of Bankorp begins with a partnership between the three pillars of Afrikaner financial might – Volkskas, Sanlam, and the government (in the shape of the Industrial Development Corporation) – in the merger of Central Merchant Bank and City Merchant Bank which formed Mercabank. Somewhat later Sanlam bought a controlling interest from its partners, acquired a string of minor, now defunct banks, including Sasbank, Johannesburg Bank and the Federal Bank, renaming the whole Bankorp. When in 1977 Bankorp, reluctantly, and under pressure from the government, accepted responsibility for Trust Bank (see p.57) and, according to a memorandum later prepared by the Reserve Bank, Sanlam took the decision to change from being a passive shareholder to an active controller of their banking businesses

Their takeover of Trust Bank was made possible, it would appear, by what might have been the first secret intervention of the Reserve Bank to assist the Afrikaner banks. In the files of the Bank can be found minutes of a meeting held on 7 September 1989 between SARB and Bankorp, which refer to Bankorp's takeover of Trust Bank twelve years before as having been accompanied by an unquantified measure of support, 'Die SARB het hier bystand verleen'.

The motives for so doing, and for the secrecy which still surrounds the transactions, were largely political. Trust Bank had been presented as the enterprising, shiny new face of Afrikaner capitalism, and could not be seen to be faltering. As for liquidation, that was quite impossible. Too many senior figures in the Cape National Party had their finger in the till – the Mondorp case was notorious – and the facts that would emerge in a liquidation had to be suppressed.

At this stage Sanlam also controlled 63 per cent (Boland Bank held the balance) of Mercabank, which described itself as a merchant bank. That term covers a wide range of very different institutions, ranging from such venerable eighteenth-century foundations as the London Accepting Houses, to fly-by-night two-men-and-a-cat money lenders. Mercabank's chief claim to be taken seriously as a bank lay in the strength of its controlling shareholder, Sanlam, with assets of some R70,000 million. Its lending portfolio consisted mainly of advances to property developers and industrial companies, with investments in unattractive quoted shares – the good ones having already been disposed of.

Mercabank's managing director, Dr Charles Ferreira, had already approached Dr Stals of the Reserve Bank, but was told to stop discussions. The Reserve Bank had already been obliged to support Trust Bank and could not be touched again, or not just yet.

In any other country the usual practice would have been to require the controlling shareholder either to produce the necessary funds – which Sanlam was well able to do – to put the bank into liquidation, or write off its own share-holding in order to enable other interests to restructure the bank. Not so in South Africa. Afrikaner solidarity demanded that Broeder should stand by Broeder, but with public money rather than their own funds.

In his application to Dr de Kock, Erasmus suggested a very strange and indirect method of payment. The Reserve Bank loan would not be made direct to Bankorp but to an intermediary. This was to be the Monkor Trust Investment Corporation, owned equally by Sanlambank and Boland Bank, and later given the more manageable name of Bank-Bol. As well as a convenient device which might help the Reserve Bank to recover its money in a liquidation, the arrangement had the merit of allowing both Bankorp and the Reserve Bank to hide the transactions in their balance sheets. Depositors and shareholders other than Sanlam were not therefore to be told that Mercabank was, on its own admission, teetering on the brink of failure and dependent on outside help. And competitors were to be placed at a disadvantage, since the proposed loan was at highly advantageous rates – 3.5 per cent at simple interest at a time when prime bank rate was of the order of 12–14 per cent. Mercabank would be given a handsome income for three years, which would help the profits (and the share price) but would have no effect on the essential matter of improving the capital and reserves.

The Reserve Bank sent a reply on 30 May, which was, it must be said, a little sniffy. It was signed, not by de Kock but by the senior vice-president, or deputy governor, C. S. Stals, who had also been present at the first meeting with Erasmus on 29 March 1985. This particular letter (Appendix D) forms a valuable piece of evidence in the case against Dr Stals. Writing on 24 February 1998, in an indignant effort to defend himself against some well-founded criticism, Stals wrote, 'You apparently did not take account of the fact that I was not involved in the initial discussions in April 1985 or in 1986, when the original decision was taken to provide assistance to the Bankorp Group. I only became involved in 1990' (see Appendix E). The files of the Reserve Bank themselves provide clear evidence to the contrary. Dr Stals was not only present at the first discussions with Ferreira and Erasmus but signed the letter of offer.

In that letter Erasmus's request was only partly agreed. The advance would be restricted to R200 million with interest at 3 per cent. Repayments were to be monthly, with full restitution no later than 31 May 1990. The loan was to be used to buy approved Government stocks, deposited with the Reserve Bank. Since at that time the interest on such stock was some 15 per cent, Bankorp were in effect being given a present of 12 per cent on R200 million over five years. If this was to be repaid over the period as required by the Reserve Bank the total would equate to some R60 million; not enough, by a long way, to cope with Bankorp's dire necessities.

Inevitably, Bankorp were soon back with their begging bowl. On 20 March 1986 Erasmus wrote again to Dr de Kock. No monthly repayments had in fact been made, and Bankorp now had R387 million of problem loans – not having the capital to write any off, they had perforce been carried on the books, paying no interest and adding to the debts. Sanlam had produced R39 million as a loan, but at 7.5 per cent, a compromise between the Reserve Bank's generosity and the going rate. Sanlam's policy holders were restive: it was no business of an insurance company to be investing in high-risk situations, and few riskier companies were in a riskier situation than that in which Bankorp found themselves. Delay had only made things worse.

But Erasmus was sure he could rely upon the Broeders, and hoped for more than just cash. An indication of the confidence Bankorp reposed in the willingness of the Reserve Bank to stretch several points was evinced by his astonishing request that Sanlam would not be forced to sell its majority interest in Mercabank under 'disadvantageous' conditions, and also – which was remarkably candid of him – for their advice on how to cook the books. The auditors were becoming suspicious; as long ago as 1982 they had to be given 'a strong letter of comfort' from the shareholders, Bankorp and Boland Bank, to enable them to sign off Mercabank's accounts. When inevitably Sanlam was forced to go to the public for a rights issue, some explanations of the Reserve Bank's assist-ance would be looked for; but these could not honestly be given without exposing the critical situation in Mercabank. Some suppression of the facts – delicately expressed as 'the handling of the situation' – was necessary and the Reserve Bank's co-operation would be appreciated.

Dr de Kock sent a fairly dusty answer on 18 April 1986. The extra R100 million would be granted, on conditions. First, that Boland Bank should be freed from any responsibilities towards Mercabank: it was to be unconditionally Sanlam's baby. Second, that repayments must be made in order to clear the account by 31 May 1990, although a repay-ment holiday was granted to 1 June 1988. As for the impudent request that Sanlam be protected from having to dispose of its shares, and advised on how best to present matters to the public, these were refused. Bankorp would have to invent its own lies.

Again the support offered by the Reserve Bank was not nearly enough. Mercabank was not illiquid (short of ready money, which could reason-ably be remedied by a loan) but insolvent, unable to pay its debts as they fell due or to obtain the means of so doing. This had been so at least since 1985 and probably, given the 'strong' letter of comfort, since 1982. In these circumstances, and in default of re-capitalisation, the law required that such a company should be wound up. This was fully appreciated by all concerned in Sanlam and Bankorp. In a document reporting Mercabank's position on 31 March 1987 the share capital, reserves and hidden reserves together amounted to R82 million (of which R56 million was not disclosed). Anticipated write-offs and losses, not included as a contingency reserve totalled R162 million. Looking ahead ten years another R105 million loss could be expected: and all this with no repayment of capital or interest to the Reserve Bank.

June 1987 saw yet another appeal by Erasmus. In contravention of the previous agreements Bankorp had not been able to pay off any of the principal or even meet the interest on the due dates. In his answer C. J. Swardt, the Registrar of Banks, approved a cosmetic adjustment whereby Mercabank, having bought the assets of Sanlambank, changed its name to Santambank. The Reserve Bank allowed repayment of the R300 million loan to begin only in April 1990, to continue thereafter at the rate of R50 million per year.

In the context of Bankorp's troubles it was worse than useless. By going to the public for one rights issue Sanlam had effectively shot their bolt, at least for the time being, and without fresh capital the burden of debt could only grow worse.

The speed with which this happened was substantially increased by Dr Fred du Plessis's drive for growth in that other branch of Bankorp, Trust Bank. Du Plessis's death in a motor accident in March 1989 brought Attie du Plessis and Marinus Daling on to Bankorp's board, and the recruitment in April the following year of the new broom Piet Liebenberg to sort out the confusion in the bank. April 1st was the trigger date on which, under the latest agreement, Mercabank (now Sanlambank) was due to begin repayment of the Reserve Bank's R300 million. Since no payments at all, either of principal or interest, had been made in the previous six years, in spite of successive agreements, it can have come as no surprise to anyone when on that date Bankorp confessed that its subsidiary, yet again, was unable to pay.

The approaching default was in fact well anticipated. Bankorp was due to release six-monthly results in February 1990, which, if properly prepared, would have had to confess the true state of affairs. This was not in fact done, but the results published on the 28th of that month included the statement that Sanlam would in the future take shares in lieu of cash dividends. Since this was one of the conditions later attached to the lifeboat it is clear that at least an outline agreement with the Reserve Bank had been reached as early as February.

Daling, du Plessis and Liebenberg could claim to be newcomers to Bankorp (although Daling and du Plessis as long-serving directors of

Sanlam were undoubtedly aware of the bank's dire straits) but the Governor of the Reserve Bank was now the same Dr Stals who had authorised the first rescue in 1985. Liebenberg's formal approach was followed by an investigation which showed that Bankorp was unprofitable, that at least 48 per cent of its assets were non-performing, and that no progress had been made with liquidation of the bad debts. In view of the fact that Bankorp executives had been reporting regularly to the Reserve Bank, and that their meetings had been carefully minuted, these revelations can have come as no surprise to Dr Stals, but the Governor put on the requisite show of shock and horror.

The investigation presented, Dr Stals considered, with doubtful accuracy, the prospect of a bank failure which could cause 'a serious threat of contagion' to the whole of the South African financial situation. If this was so it was an illustration of the Reserve Bank's own folly in allowing the situation to get out of hand and its failure to take any effective action. It was more than straightforward incompetence; from the beginning the successive attempts to help out the Afrikaner banks had been accompanied by dissimulation and deceit, which were about to be compounded and continued. As an emergency step to enable the matter to be arranged away from the public gaze, Bankorp was given an extension of the repayment to 1 August.

This situation, it must be remembered, was well developed while Trust Bank officials were attempting to lure Askin into Tollgate with assurances of a glowing future. On that critical date, 1 August, the leading lights of Afrikanerdom were convened to arrive at a solution, or, perhaps more correctly, to formalise a solution that had already been agreed some months previously. Dr Stals chaired a meeting which included Johannes Antonie Lombard, son of the Broederbond founder, Ivanhoe Makepeace Lombard, Barend Petrus Groenewald (both deputy governors), Johannes H. van Greuning, Registrar of Banks, Piet Liebenberg, executive chairman of Bankorp, W. H. J. (Hennie) van der Merwe, chief executive of Senbank, Marinus Daling and Attie du Plessis, representing Sanlam, and brother of the then finance minister Barend du Plessis.

It is worthwhile reflecting on the future careers of some of those present. Liebenberg was sacked after less than two years in office. Van Greuning was packed off to the World Bank before revelations of his inept and deceitful performance in the affairs of Cape Investment Bank became public. Van de Merwe was none other than the individual who enriched himself so neatly at the expense of the unfortunate Claasen. The meeting of these interesting characters reached the conclusion that the picture that emerged 'was rather desperate', and that something more drastic must be done than the previous attempts to tinker with Bankorp's chronic problems.

Before describing the Reserve Bank's plan to rescue Sanlam and Bankorp it is useful to see what had happened elsewhere, for Bankorp was not the only South African bank in trouble. Other rescues, among them Rondalia Bank and Pretoria Bank, had occupied the Reserve Bank's attention. All were, it should be noted, Afrikaner banks. To this rule one part-exception exists. Nedbank was at least Dutch rather than British in origin, but its main qualification to be a lifeboat passenger had been that its most embarrassing debtor was that arch-Afrikaner Louis Luyt. All these interventions were kept strictly secret (the full story of Merca-bank's successive rescues is told here for the first time). One other instance, however, slipped through the veil, that of the Cape Investment Bank, which also applied for help in 1990.

The Governor as Father Christmas

The details of the relations between the Reserve Bank and the Cape Investment Bank were only squeezed out over a protracted period, but exactly paralleled those that existed with Bankorp. The Cape Investment Bank (CIB) had been established only two years previously by the Afrikaner Pickard family, and shortly afterwards merged with Corbank, the former Hill Samuel business, whose chief executive was Laurie Korsten. Its trading policy was simply to make money as quickly as possible, which it attempted to do by initiating an altogether excessive amount of 'off-balance sheet' business – being essentially speculation in quoted securities. With adequate control, as part of a much wider business and in appropriate sums, this is an acceptable operation for any bank, but CIB had gone much further. With a capital of only R35 million their traders were speculating as much as R1,000 million, chiefly on Eskom stock, (the electricity generating and distributing company), and to such an extent that their year end balance sheet to 30 June 1990 showed a totally fictitious solvent situation.

In presenting the accounts the CIB chairman reported 'a difficult but gratifying year characterised by achieving forecast results, rapid expansion, and therefore uncertain environments and the resultant strain on people and the organisation.' In cold fact, as Mr Justice Nel reported in a subsequent investigation, the bank was insolvent; there had been numerous offences committed by the directors, and an unqualified report was only avoided by a R50 million gift from the SARB. When rumours began to circulate about the Cape Investment Bank's status the SARB had shown its sympathy, which took the tangible form of buying CIB stock at an unrealistically inflated price – R500 million in October 1990. It was not enough.

In the year 1990–91 losses continued at the rate of R500,000 a month, which totalled for the year nearly R6 million. This was too much for the bank's auditors, whose tolerance so far had been extraordinary, but who were now finally insisting on appending a note to the accounts. Such a note would describe the losses and explain the situation, but inevitably bring about a collapse in confidence and the speedy demise of the bank.

The SARB stepped in to prevent this in December 1990 with a wholly artificial transaction. In a letter dated 10 December 1990 Dr van Greuning, in his capacity as Registrar of Banks, wrote from the Reserve Bank to Mr Pickard.

> The Governor of the South African Reserve Bank has given his approval that a loan should be made available to your bank to 'Compensate' for the losses that have been incurred on off-balance sheet assets.
>
> This special aid action is being launched to prevent a further shock being caused to financial markets. Your auditors have insisted that these losses must be published as a note to your annual accounts dated 30 June 1990, which will result in your depositors and clients possibly losing confidence in your bank.

Van Greuning's post had been created in the 1990 Banks Act, and carried with it important responsibilities. He had to approve all banks' directors and senior management, together with their controlling shareholders. Bank directors had to assure the Registrar of their awareness of the relevant legislation and their own personal liability. Annual meetings had to be convened between a bank's board, its auditors, and the Registrar, at which meetings the auditors' report to the internal audit committee (on which the non-executive directors sat) was considered. All excellent devices, but almost all, it seemed, ignored.

The solution advanced by the Reserve Bank was that it should lend R300 million to the CIB at a nominal interest rate of 1 per cent. The Reserve Bank then 'borrowed' the same sum back, at a much higher rate – 17.2 per cent. The period of the 'loan' was calculated to enable CIB to earn enough to get it out of trouble. The difference between the borrowing and lending rates was essentially a straightforward present from the Reserve Bank to the shareholders of the Cape Investment Bank. As such, given the obligation of the Reserve Bank to remit its surpluses to the South African Treasury, it was also a donation from the South African taxpayer. Although the arrangement followed the lines of that offered to Mercabank in 1985 the conditions were more generous; there was no repayment of interest or programmed repayment of the principal. Indeed, since this was offered at a merely nominal rate its eventual repayment was a relatively minor matter.

Given the highly suspect nature of this artificial transaction it was essential that it should be kept secret. In order for this to be done the whole transaction had to be completed before the SARB's own year end, which was the end of March: it was, but only just in time, on 28 March. The fictitious loan did not therefore need to be disclosed to the shareholders of the Reserve Bank, or to Parliament. The CIB auditors cleared the accounts without a qualification and depositors in the CIB could therefore continue to believe in the safety of their money.

By far the largest of these deposits was that of the Rail Commuter Corporation (RCC), which amounted to R242 million of a total of some R300 million. This body had been established to subsidise the fares of commuters – mostly black – who had been forced by the apartheid rules to live at considerable distances from their place of work, and whose low wages made the cost of travel a heavy burden.

Since its beneficiaries were black, its money provided by government, and its board not representative of the business community, the Rail Commuter Corporation was not a significant power in the financial world, and the Afrikaner Nationalist government of F. W. de Klerk was still in power.

In December 1992 the RCC, responding to the rumours which were circulating, enquired of the Reserve Bank about the safety of their deposit with CIB. A meeting was held at the Reserve Bank at which Dr van Greuning, who was meant as Registrar to superintend the conduct of South African banks, expressly decided, with his colleagues, not to tell the truth, but to give a false impression. The RCC's representatives were therefore solemnly assured that their money would be safe. Three months later the CIB was bankrupt and the RCC's money lost.

This was not before one other neat piece of self-enrichment. It is an axiom that a bank in distress should be helped by other banks. In South Africa the Reserve Bank was willing to do this for an Afrikaner bank only if another Afrikaner bank was willing to offer brotherly help – hence the fusion of Bankorp and Volkskas. An attempt was therefore made by the Reserve Bank to interest another small bank, Prima Bank, in taking charge of CIB. Once again, the Reserve Bank sought some way of deceiving the public, and arranged for Prima Bank, on 16 April 1991 to be given a device commonly known as an 'American option' which carried a built-in guaranteed profit. This enabled the directors – the Afrikaner directors – of Prima Bank to receive R5 million for their agreement, ostensibly in order for them to purchase shares in a rights issue. Three days later CIB collapsed and the five million had disappeared.

The demise of the CIB was the subject of two enquiries. The first, undertaken by Mr Justice Rabie, was to consider the complaint of RCC, and was held in secret, but the facts emerged. Judge Rabie agreed that a simulated transaction, such as the SARB's 'loan', was equivalent to a fraudulent transaction, but he said nothing. The judge, knowing that fraud had been committed, remained silent: such negligence, irregular for any officer of the court, inexcusable for a senior judge, was an excellent example of Afrikaner solidarity. Dr van Greuning, who had himself authorised the simulated transaction, and assured the RCC of the CIB's solidity, claimed 'a depositor has a duty to establish for himself at the bank how well the risk is managed and what the bank's position.' In the fantasy world of Dr van Greuning, anyone putting money in a bank should go to the premises and insist on investigating for themselves what went on. Mere reliance on accounts approval by distinguished professional firms, or on the statutory responsibilities of the Registrar at the Reserve Bank, or even personal enquiry at the offices of the Reserve Bank, were not enough.

Audited accounts would have been little help for both internal and external audits of the CIB were perfunctory. Banks are meant to have powerful audit committees, composed of non-executive directors, intended to keep a watchful eye on the activities of the executive directors. Leslie Stephen Phelps, a well-known accountant, helped with this function in the CIB from 1990. He took his duties lightly, admitting 'I don't think, (the audit committee) ever held a meeting from the time I was appointed'. (Nor, for that matter, did the credit committee, as Bob Aldworth discovered when he was invited to join the board.)

Mr Phelps went rather further than ignoring doubtful activities: he initiated at least one himself. His family trust borrowed nearly R2 million to fund his purchase of CIB shares, and a company in which Mr Phelps had a considerable share holding borrowed over R4 million for the same purpose. When Phelps was questioned at the secret enquiry by barrister Sam Aaron he was dismissive, and went on to implicate other banks.

> *Aaron*: 'You have loans totalling R4.5 million and there is not even correct documentation in place to show who the debtor is, what the terms of the loan are. And you happen to be on both sides of the transaction. I would be very embarrassed about that.'
>
> *Phelps*: 'It wasn't my responsibility to put the documentation in place.'
>
> *Aaron*: 'You are saying the bank must go whistling for its money after a shell of a company?'
>
> *Phelps*: 'The deal was struck on that basis, Mr Aaron.'
>
> *Aaron*: 'Is that fulfilling your fiduciary duties as a director of the bank?'
>
> *Phelps*: 'Mr Aaron, that was the deal that was struck.'

Aaron: 'Do you consider that to be an adequate basis on which a director can borrow money from a bank?'

Phelps: 'Yes. Mr Aaron, I think it is not an unusual practice for banks to finance shares on that basis. I've done three other transactions with other banks, two with Senbank and one with Finansbank on almost an identical basis . . . or shares in Rusfurn, shares in Unidev and shares in a company called ABS Management. Bankers do take these chances yes.'

The Reserve Bank had hoped the whole business of its 'loan', and the gift made by buying shares at an inflated price, might be kept secret. When Dr Stals was eventually forced to admit the facts, first to the Parliamentary Select Committee, and later to Mr Justice Nel's commission of enquiry into the Masterbond collapse, he was unapologetic. It was not the duty of the Reserve Bank to tell the truth about a bank's status to a depositor, even one so important to society as the RCC. Moreover, if the truth had been told in December, the RCC would have tried to take its money away and forced the liquidation of the bank. At which time – although Dr Stals did not say so – creditors would have found that in December 1992 that they could rely on the Reserve Bank's 'loan' of R300 million – enough itself to pay depositors.

But then the whole deception would have collapsed. The SARB and Dr Stals were still hoping that the Reserve Bank's secret support would get the CIB through another year, at the end of which another set of doctored accounts could be produced. During this period they hoped a different solution could be found, which might well have been the merger, sufficiently well-dowered, with Absa. And, after all, as the ineffable Dr van Greuning went on to say, 'Ordinary depositors should not know everything that goes on in the banking system, this will shock the trust in the banking system.'

Dr van Greuning, in fact, could to a great extent be blamed personally for the CIB's troubles, since he had recommended one A. Swartz as Chief Executive of that bank. Since Mr Swartz had been warned off the Johannesburg Stock Exchange it was an eccentric choice. In the armed services it is the custom to remove useless, unpopular, or downright dangerous officers by posting them elsewhere. Dr van Greuning, who was criticised by Mr Justice Nel for 'a serious dereliction of duty' was sent to the World Bank, where among other activities he co-authored (with E. Folkerts-Landa) a paper entitled 'The Case for Regional Financial-Market Infrastructure in Africa'.

The directors of the RCC, honourable men, were furious at the deception that had been practised upon them, and prepared to sue the liquidators for the release of their deposit. Since this action would have had the effect of making the whole matter public, it could not be allowed by the SARB. Just before the case was due to be heard the Finance Minister intervened and persuaded the Minister of Transport, Piet Welgemoed, to bring about an arbitration whereby all participants were required to sign secrecy agreements. That was the enquiry conducted by Judge Rabie, which, when the veil of secrecy was lifted, was shown to have provoked some unusual candour.

Judge Rabie, who had been Chief Justice at the time of Muldergate and therefore well-acquainted with skulduggery, rejected the description of the Reserve Bank assistance as a 'loan' (it would have been extremely difficult not to). Dr Stals was dismissively cynical: 'Yes, we're going to help him . . . but now how do we do so? We can, like Father Christmas, make an inscription in our books and say we made a donation of R15.37 million to this Institution. This is what it really boils down to, to an important extent.' But if this was to be done, what explanation could the Governor offer to his shareholders? It was a markedly different story to that which Dr Stals gave the Hoberman inquiry when eventually forced to appear there. But Rabie went on to rule that since the loan was no real loan, the Reserve Bank was entitled to have its money back; which was the conclusion that the minister and the bank both wished him to reach. But since this could not be admitted to the shareholders Dr Stals and his directors deliberately dressed up the grant as a loan in order to mislead the shareholders. Even Judge Berman had ruled, in 1987, that 'A disguised transaction is in essence a dishonest one.'

Since the Bankorp lifeboat was so closely paralleled by that given to the Cape Investment Bank, the comments made by Mr Justice Nel on the CIB during his later investigation into the collapse of Masterbond can be taken to apply, *pari passu*, to the conduct of the Reserve Bank towards Bankorp. In the report published in November 1997 Judge Nel found the evidence given by Stals 'startling', an example of the belief that the end justifies the means, and the resultant disregard of the principles of fair presentation and substance over form. Dr Stals' credibility was called into question; 'It is obvious that important aspects of the evidence of Dr Stals (as reflected in Hansard) is contradicted by the evidence which was led in the "secret" Prima Bank inquiry.' Moreover, the Reserve Bank's conduct had dragged down some of the best-known accounting firms – Deloitte's and Cooper's local affiliates – into complicity in the deception of the shareholders and public. Nel summarised his views with such stern forcefulness it is difficult to believe that Dr Stals remained in office:

> The standards set by the Reserve Bank by its philosophy that the end justifies the means and the apparent acceptance thereof by the auditors concerned, could only have a negative influence on the auditing profession in South Africa.
>
> The auditors were members of some of the most prestigious internationally affiliated auditing firms whose members are amongst the leaders of their profession. Leaders who are also perceived to be responsible for the setting and maintaining of ethical standards and generally accepted accounting practice.
>
> The extent to which the auditing profession has been influenced by these standards set by the Reserve Bank is obviously debatable. What is not debatable is that any such influence should be eradicated.

The offer made by the SARB to Bankorp, although much larger, followed the pattern set by that made to CIB. The terms were set out in a letter dated 3 August 1990, and remarkably liberal they were. Previous efforts by the Reserve Bank to ensure that Bankorp repaid the money advanced were tacitly abandoned. Everyone concerned knew that repayment would never be made: Dr Stals was indeed acting as a Father Christmas. The support, which at that time totalled R1,000 million, was in two parts. R600 million was to be used by Bankorp to buy government securities, which at that time yielded an interest of some 20 per cent. All this interest would accrue to Bankorp, and repayment would be made simply by handing the securities back. Whether the market price of these stocks had gone up, or down, Bankorp would not be responsible. In addition R400 million was to be lent at a nominal rate of 1 per cent. The profit between this and the yield on a gilt-edged security would, again, accrue to Bankorp.

There were limits set to the Reserve Bank's generosity. The annual grant, coyly referred to as 'interest help', would be limited to R150 million, and assistance was to cease when Bankorp capital and reserves had reached R1,500 million – an estimated total aid of R800 million. On the other hand, this R800 million would remain for the most part with Bankorp. Only 20 per cent at most was liable to be repaid to the SARB. So expressed, in spite of the attempts to disguise the assistance as a 'loan' it is clear that at least R640 million (say £142 million) was to be a straightforward gift from the SARB – and therefore from South African taxpayers – to the shareholders of Bankorp.

Although structured in a similar way to the earlier loans the Reserve Bank had clearly learned not to expect too much from Bankorp, The interest at 1 per cent was nominal and there were to be no management changes demanded, it presumably being hoped that with du Plessis, Erasmus and van Wyk gone, and under the new direction of the stern and unbending Liebenberg, the existing executives would perform less unsatisfactorily. Above all the great bulk, if not all, of the 'loan' was not repayable; it was a gift, pure and simple.

In this way, the Bankorp lifeboat reflected similar terms to those offered to the Cape Investment Bank. One major difference however was that the Bankorp grant was specifically related to a list of 'doubtful' debts, which were specifically designated. Of these Tollgate was one of the largest, but not the biggest. Two other firms, Rusfurn and W & A, the company that had been the recipients of Trust Bank's generosity, owed more to the bank. When later forced to disclose the terms of the lifeboat Dr Stals insisted that 'only losses that already existed or were anticipated on June 30 1990 and that were reported in the list, could be written off against income specifically generated for this purpose.'

Clearly, it was to Bankorp's advantage to ensure that the list of bad debts was as comprehensive as possible, and accordingly one of Liebenberg's first moves had been to urge the senior general managers to highlight all the group's risk exposures. Subsequently Hennie van der Merwe instructed the managers to bring forward all potential bad debts as soon as possible in order to maximise the amount that the Reserve Bank and Sanlam would have to provide in support. 'We are going to clean up this lending book', he exclaimed. The managers obliged with such alacrity that the final total was more than double the first assessment. The manna from heaven had to be made as profitable as possible.

The treatment accorded to the shareholders by the Reserve Bank was noteworthy. According to the practice in other countries, it is the interests of *depositors* that central banks protect by means of emergency aid. *Shareholders* are meant to bear the brunt of losses; it is after all their risk capital, and their responsibility to have appointed adequate management. But other countries do not have pressure groups wielding the sort of power that the Afrikaner lobby exercises in South Africa. In the CIB every effort was made to protect the (Afrikaner) shareholders, with the depositors' interests being, very deliberately, jeopardised. The Bankorp rescue ensured that the shareholding Broeders had their interest specifically safeguarded by the Broeders in the Reserve Bank. Sanlam by that time held more than 90 per cent of the shares in Bankorp. On paper, in the 1989 Bankorp accounts, shareholders' interests amounted to R387.64 million: in 1990, after the SARB rescue, these had risen to R681.9 million: a year later they were shown as R1300.9 million – all figures far lower than the eventual assistance provided. Sanlam had its investment saved by the Reserve Bank; it was not even required to forgo any dividends, but simply to reinvest them, in that way avoiding the payment of tax on the money they would otherwise have received. Other shareholders would continue to receive whatever cash dividends the bank saw fit to issue. And among these shareholders were the directors of Bankorp.

It is difficult to be sure of the extent to which the non-executive directors of Absa were clear as to the implications of the Reserve Bank lifeboat; what is certain is that they were anxious not to let the news escape, to the extent of deciding at their meeting on 27 November 1992 not to minute details of the arrangements – which was itself a criminal offence. That there were guilty consciences in the Reserve Bank is proved by minutes of the Governor's meeting on 27 March and 1 April, which recorded that the management 'felt uneasy about making this sensitive information about the aid to Bankorp available even to members of the Audit Committee. The matter was consequently not placed on the Agenda for the discussion of the Audit Committee'. If not precisely criminal, this is directly contrary to the whole intention of proper controls – and this in the bank meant to be responsible for imposing such controls.

When, eventually, after repeated denials and evasions, the truth came out, Dr Stals attempted to represent gifts made to Bankorp as entirely normal central banking practice, such as that made by the Bank of England during previous British banking crises. It is worthwhile examining one of these, to see how this comparison is erroneous and misleading.

Some six months before Bankorp's first application to the Reserve Bank, in October 1984, Johnson Matthey Bank (JMB), in London, found itself in similar difficulties.* Like Trust Bank, JMB, a fully authorised bank, was a wholly owned subsidiary of a publicly quoted company, Johnson Matthey, a major operator on the bullion market and one of the 80 largest UK companies. Unlike the South African Reserve Bank, the Bank of England had much experience in dealing with such matters, dating back at least to 1890, when the merchant bank, Barings was the object of just such a rescue.

When matters came to a head at Johnson Matthey Bank the Bank of England was able to step in with practised speed.

> On 1 October 1984 JMB was bought for £1 by the Bank of England: directors left and were replaced by Bank nominees; new management was provided; the clearers put up £75 million, the Bank £100 million towards reconstruction, and the police were called in later to investigate possible frauds.
>
> A loan book of some £400 million, of which £310 million were classified as bad or doubtful, and provisions of £220 million indicated to be necessary, were revealed. Good management, combined with financial resources sufficient to soak up the losses, produced results, and is enabling the business to survive for either sale or an orderly liquidation. In the long run it is even possible that the whole of the extra cash provided might be recovered.

* *Uneasy City*, Frank Welsh, Weidenfeld & Nicolson, 1986, Chapter 8.

Given what was to happen in South Africa certain aspects of this rescue deserve comment: a. It was completely transparent and public. b. The shareholders lost the whole of their investment. c. The directors were dismissed. d. Possible frauds were investigated. e. Other banks contributed to the rescue. Even so, the arrangement was subject to criticism.

> An alternative course, which would have been possible at no cost to the taxpayer, would have been to insist that the shareholders of Johnson Matthey PLC assumed responsibility, with the assistance of their own bankers. As it was, the NatWest was dragooned, not without understandable peevishness, into supporting the rescue; its support might have been more enthusiastic if the Bank of England had adopted the course of providing a standby credit to NatWest ensuring that the shareholders ultimately paid, rather than, in effect, going the whole hog of nationalising JMB. As a result the shareholders of JM PLC are doing very well indeed now the incubus has been removed; shares stand at 180p and on a price/earnings ratio in the twenties, indicating a fair degree of optimism. What is more, a potentially dangerous signal has been sent out: however small and scruffily managed a bank may be, so long as it is a 'proper' bank, the Bank of England will not allow it to fail.

The same writer also commented, prophetically enough, considering the final Baring's collapse of 1994: 'In the context of the wildest outburst of activity by new and untried organisations the City of London has ever seen about to occur, [the "Big Bang"] this message will encourage ventures that should be very firmly repressed. Many other managers will shortly find themselves in the same position as those JMB executives who, pressed for results, took unwarranted risks.'

The South African Reserve Bank's actions were different in many respects from those of the Bank of England. No attempt was made to bring the other South African banks round to support Bankorp, and for very understandable reasons. Not being part of the Afrikaner network, Standard Chartered and FNB would have certainly asked some awkward questions and almost certainly insisted that shareholders contributed much more in recapitalisation, and that decisive management changes were made; in short that a professional job was made of the restructuring. Almost certainly too they would have insisted on more transparency, and not agreed to be party to the auditors misleading the outside shareholders. The Afrikaners were determined to stick together. Governor de Kock had refused to guarantee that Sanlam would not be forced to dispose of their shareholding disadvantageously, but his successor was willing to go to great lengths to support the majority shareholders. The shareholders' interests, far from being wiped out, were actually fostered, the directors were left in place, the banking community was not called upon to help, and false and misleading information was put before the public.

CHAPTER EIGHT

Some Truths Emerge

Unprofessional and reckless management

Forcing the Reserve Bank out of its self-imposed silence on the subject of lifeboats was the first result of Askin's campaign, but more directly relevant to his complaint against Absa was the link between the lifeboat and Tollgate's liquidation. It might well be that Absa and Sanlam should eventually repay the billions they had received from the Reserve Bank to the South African Treasury, but this would not help Askin to recover any of the money he and others had lost in Tollgate's liquidation. Should it be proved however that Absa had acted uncommercially, protected by the Reserve Bank lifeboat, there might well be a remedy in law.

Hennie Diedericks led the fight in South Africa, supported by Hugh Murray and Paul Bell in *Millennium* magazine. The third of their articles published in October 1995 contained some damaging accusations levied by Diedericks against Absa. Recounting the details of a meeting held with Cronjé, Brits and Badenhorst on 19 November 1992, Diedericks said:

> They reiterated that they wished to press ahead for a liquidation of the Tollgate Group. They expressly stated that they could afford to take those steps because of the accommodation from the Reserve Bank. I had the very clear impression from both Dr Cronjé and Mr Brits that they had already made up their minds as to the way forward. Thus, it was clear to me that any comments which I might make would make no difference to their opinion as to the way forward and their decision to liquidate the Tollgate Group. Mr Brits

[chief executive of the risk management department] made it clear that he had no good word for Mr Askin. Mr Brits worked under the direct instruction of Dr Cronjé. In general terms, the attitude of Absa was very aggressive towards Mr Askin. I found this surprising since, as noted above, Trust Bank/Absa had restructured and given assistance to the W & A group of companies and to the Russells furniture group, and Mr Askin had over the last two years reduced the Tollgate group's liability to Absa and serviced the interest.

Absa was not prepared to assist in a similar way with reference to the Tollgate Group notwithstanding the fact that Mr Askin had expressed a willingness to invest more if the right package could be agreed with Trust Bank.

I am of the opinion that Absa, through its unprofessional and reckless management . . . placed the Tollgate Group, its management and directors under unreasonable strain. I also believe, due to the fact that the lifeboat facility was readily available, that a non-commercial decision was taken in liquidating the Tollgate Group in order to recoup the investment Trust Bank/Absa had made in the context of the partnership banking arrangements. If Absa had not received the accommodation from the Reserve Bank they would have been forced to treat the Tollgate Group in a proper commercial fashion and to reach an agreement for its survival and future prosperity. All things considered, Absa had no option but to try to discredit Askin. Dr Cronjé, Mr Brits and Mr Badenhorst knew full well that Absa and a number of its officials ran the risk of being sued if Mr Askin ever discovered details concerning the accommodation from the Reserve Bank. They needed to ensure that if Mr Askin ever complained, nobody would believe him.

In summary, it is quite clear to me that as a consequence of the safety net provided by the accommodation from the Reserve Bank, Absa were encouraged to act in an irresponsible manner with reference to the Tollgate Group.

Without this accommodation from the Reserve Bank any sensible bank would have ensured that it did nothing to impair the value of the assets against which it was lending. However, with reference to the Tollgate Group, it suited Absa to charge as much interest as possible and to maintain the exposure of the Tollgate Group as short-term borrowings for which it could charge very high rates. Then, when the Tollgate Group went into liquidation, the intention was that Absa could simply walk away from the problem with no loss. Rather, the problem would be one for the other banks [notably, First National Bank and Standard Chartered], and the other creditors of the Tollgate Group.

Such accusations drew blood, in the shape of an indignant announcement on 11 October 1995 by Absa rejecting 'defamatory statements' made by Diedericks as 'dubious in the extreme, as it is obvious that no considerations of public interest required such publication at this time.'

This odd qualification unwittingly reveals something of the arrogance that pervaded Absa's reactions. Why should any publication be determined by what is in the public interest? The press is not part of the civil service, nor any financial institution only open to attack if it is 'in the public interest'. Absa showed little concern for the public interest, or that of shareholders or employees, when it used unprincipled methods to cheat Claasens over Arwa, or, as shall be shown, to liquidate Tollgate to its own advantage. The arrogant asumption was that the public interest was identical with Absa's interests; 'L'État, c'est moi'.

Apart from characterising the salient points of the offending article as 'ridiculous', Absa's statement offered no argument but only abuse (it is a good old legal maxim that, in the absence of a good case, one abuses the opposing party).

> Absa wishes to express its outrage at the article and to record its repudiation of the allegations made against Absa in the article. We ask the public to appreciate that because of current and threatened future litigation [including threats now quoted by Askin and Diedericks themselves] Absa can only become involved in dealing with scurrilous falsehoods such as those published by *Millennium* through the proper legal channels.

Absa has nothing to hide in the Tollgate history and will participate in public discussion of the matter as soon as the legal processes have run their course.

Absa had already recorded its reservation of rights against anyone publishing defamatory material on this subject, Absa is considering its legal position on whether to take immediate steps in respect of defamatory articles which have been published.

Diedericks replied by giving information to Chris Steyn for her article published in the *Weekend Argus* of 14/15 October. The *Argus*, part of the Independent Newspapers group, showed itself less susceptible to Absa pressure than other journals, especially the *Cape Times*. Diedericks had some significant things to reveal about Absa:

Mr Diedericks told Spectrum (the *Argus*'s investigative unit) that Mr Cronjé had called him to a meeting in March this year, in response to the impassioned letter from Mr Diedericks imploring Mr Cronjé to defend him against charges levelled at him by Tollgate's liquidators.

On March 1, said Mr Diedericks, he was called to Mr Cronjé's office at 6 p.m. He said Mr Cronjé told him 'directly and in as many words' that Absa did not want the liquidators to see the bank's officials with Mr Diedricks and that, if Absa was not careful, it could cost them a write-off of R200 million. Mr Diedricks alleged Mr Cronjé added that, since Mr Diedericks had resigned from Absa, they owed him no loyalty.

According to Mr Diedericks, Mr Cronjé used words with the 'clear effect' that he was doing him a favour, and that he was running a risk to be meeting with him as it could have created a 'delicate' situation between Absa and the liquidators.

And in one of the letters to Cosab's [the South African banking Ombudsman's office] Mr Liebenberg [former chief executive of Trust Bank], dated March 22, 1995 he wrote that his repeated written and personal requests since June 30 1994, to Absa and Mr Cronjé, to unfreeze his banking facilities, had been refused on the grounds that it would damage the bank's relationship with the liquidator.

If Absa maintains its stand that any support of me could damage the relationship with the Tollgate liquidators, then I have to conclude that I am, for sinister reasons, being sacrificed for the sake of own-interest relationship with the relevant liquidators.

In a later letter, of 25 May, Diedericks charged: 'Absa is suppressing fundamental information in connection with Trust Bank's involvement in the Tollgate debacle and is incriminating me through that. Thus the conflicting interest situation has already been created by them. To now try and play "holy" is devoid of all reasonable logic.'

Mr Diedericks vowed last week to survive. 'If they think I will go away and keep quiet they are making the mistake of their lives. I can now, with the help of international lawyers, prove that all the allegations against me have been fabricated, or are ridiculous misrepresentations,' he said. 'I am not negotiating from a position of guilt.'

He warned that, after 18 months of persecution, the fight back was only just beginning: 'This is the first shot. What is to follow is going to be more traumatic . . .'

David Brink, Absa's chairman, responded by continuing to abuse the other party, with an advertisement on 3 November which reproduced Diedericks's letter to them in which he had asked for Absa's help in joining him in an action against Askin. Askin was dismissed with Judge Harold Lenin Berman's remark that he had engaged 'in thieving and roguery on a grand scale', but Brink gave the bank's own version of the decision to liquidate Tollgate. It included a number of inaccurate statements and at least one untruth: 'Absa does not control the liquidators of Tollgate and insinuations to the contrary are untrue.' Quite possibly, since Brink was not on Absa's board at the time, the chairman was unaware of the arrangements imposed on the liquidators by Chris Faul, but no one in Absa offered any emendations which might have saved the chairman from propagating a lie. Abundant evidence to contradict Brink's very public claim existed to prove Absa's insistence that the liquidators agreed every step with the bank. Mr Brink also showed his shaky grasp of legal principles when he referred to Askin as 'a fugitive from justice' and referred to his 'alleged innocence'. This was an extraordinary defiance of the principles of the presumption of innocence, but one that had ancient South African antecedents. British colonial officials were scornful of the local magistrates' assumption that any 'Kaffir' was guilty until proved innocent.

One section of the advertisement was particularly interesting since it acknowledged, for the first time, the existence of the lifeboat.

Tollgate and the Support Package

1.1 The Board of Absa accepts that in line with accepted international banking practice and as had been done for other South African banking institutions, Bankorp received financial assistance from the South African Reserve Bank (SARB) in August 1990. When Absa took over Bankorp in September 1992 the support package already formed part of the net book value on which the transaction was based. Absa is not in a position to disclose any details of the support package.

1.2 The articles referred to above insinuate that Absa cushioned its Tollgate losses by manipulating the support package (referred to by *Millennium* as 'the lifeboat') provided by the SARB and that it acted without conscience because of the security offered by that cushion, and, in particular, chose to liquidate Tollgate at an inopportune time for inadequate and improper reasons.

1.3 The fact is that none of the Absa losses in Tollgate was charged to and/or paid for by the support package. Absa during the year ended 31 March 1993 wrote off R215 million in respect of Tollgate. This write-off below the line is contained in note 2 to the financial statements

1.4 The decision to liquidate Tollgate was unaffected by the support package and was taken in terms of normal banking practice.

It was not enough. The *Financial Mail* struck some damaging blows the same day:

Extraordinary events have taken place: yet another S417 inquiry is now taking place – quite unnecessarily, in secret – and the Commissioner, advocate Bertrand Hoberman, acted on behalf of Absa first in preparing Tollgate's liquidation papers and then in opposing a liquidation brought by Tollgate's directors (Absa is Tollgate's largest single creditor). Also it seems the inquiry is confined to investigating actions and events within specific dates, a limitation which invites immediate suspicion. A private home was seized and has since been returned; large sums to settle civil claims have been paid, arrest warrants against Askin for fraud and theft are still extant; he was imprisoned twice in an Italian jail, illegally says the Italian Supreme court: an ambassador is closely linked with some of these events and so, apparently, are the security services of two European powers and South Africa. All that is missing is novelist John le Carré's spy master George Smiley.

None of this is amusing. It is tacky in the extreme. More than this, it has an unfortunate impact on South Africa's international image. The possibility that actions may be launched in the British High Court against Absa and others must now be regarded seriously.

Also important is the allegation – as yet unconfirmed – that Absa received a Reserve Bank lifeboat of R1bn. It is now being said this sum, a gift to an ailing banking group at the expense of the taxpayer, could have been as much as R4bn. Given the recent bail-out of African Bank it is only right that the extent of the Bank's assistance be made public.

If the international confidence in South Africa's financial system is not to be impaired, only a public cleaning of what looks ominously like the Augean stables will do. Either the S417 inquiry must be opened or a commission of inquiry must be appointed.

This Tollgate/Absa issue won't go away in a hurry. The Reserve Bank has some answering to do – in public please, as befits a democracy. The irony is that, as the country took the Bank's medicine (high interest rates, tightening money supply) in a supreme effort to defeat inflation, so a lifeboat of unknown size (and profound priming effect on money supply) was provided to a select institution. And banking regulators, especially former Registrar Hennie van Gruening, now with the World Bank, need to provide some answers too.

Here is real work for the Truth Commission. Unfortunately, it will probably be impelled to look elsewhere. This is a pity. How systems and regimes are financed is the key to the past. The actions of security forces and their antagonists may be compelling but they are of little account in the grand scheme of things. Balance sheets are always more important than generals.

This protracted public exchange had the effect, much desired by Askin, of opening up, to a limited further extent, the deliberations of the Hoberman commission leading to public sessions in which Diedericks, Stals and Cronjé were allowed to advance their points of view.

Such transparence was not allowed without demur. No objections were raised by the representative of the First National Bank and the Standard Bank. Jeremy Gauntlett, on the other hand, representing both the liquidators and Absa – a potential conflict of interest which would have been extraordinary anywhere except in South Africa – put forward objections at some length, although without excessive clarity. He described the opening of the session as 'an exercise in prematurity' and was supported by Mr Rubens, who objected to certain 'gratuitous and irrelevant evidence' – a submission by Bob Aldworth. Commissioner Hoberman was confused when told that Mr Rubens was representing both the liquidators and Absa – leading for the latter and acting as junior to Mr Gauntlett in representing the liquidators – yet another example of the South African gallimaufry of conflicting interests. 'No doubt,' Mr Gauntlett submitted, 'the public is very interested in allegations made about the Broederbond, about the Reserve Bank, about lifeboats, about Absa's ineptitude or complicity or everything else in the last days of the Raj,' but suggested that in open session 'information might come out that would be prejudicial to our unresolved investigations and the claims which we are in process of formulating.'

Eventually, and somewhat grudgingly, in his own inimitable language, Absa's counsel accepted that Diedericks's evidence should be heard in public. 'In the light . . . of that ruling of a truncated ambit of evidence for Mr Diedericks as opposed to the otherwise unqualified one set out in your letter . . . and in the light moreover of the attitude evinced by major creditors in the group to the liquidators of Tollgate, at this stage the liquidators of Tollgate wish to say nothing further in relation to the procedure which you have adopted.'

Hennie Diedericks's appearance before the Hoberman Commission on 22 January 1996 marked a turning point in the history of the Tollgate affair. He was not an ideal witness, sometimes hesitant, in the grip of a bad cold, often resorting to Afrikaans in place of a less-than-perfect English. But the essential worth of the man shone through, and his acknowledged experience gave weight to his utterances; Hoberman, too, although not the most brilliant of lawyers, was able to appreciate Diedericks at his full worth. As a managing director of Volkskas, and of Trust Bank (Absa later attempted to deny this, saying that Diedericks had merely been an innominate executive), and in charge of Tollgate for two years, there was no one in as good a position to have full knowledge of all the relevant facts.

As the hearing was in public, to be reported all over the South African press, Absa and the Reserve Bank's actions were at last forced out into the open, to be explained as best could be contrived.

On one point only in his evidence was Diedericks open to criticism, and then only on a matter of scale. He suggested that Absa's charging too high an interest rate had been a major cause of Tollgate's failure. It was true that Absa had consistently deducted interest from Tollgate's accounts at more than the agreed rate, and an investigation was held as a result of which the bank eventually restored R800.000. The investigation was however limited to the trading of a single subsidiary over a short period; Askin estimates that the true total ran into tens of millions.

But the main thrust of Diedericks' evidence was concentrated on the lifeboat issue. He was quite clear that the lifeboats – and there had been many launched – were quite contrary to the British practice. After describing, in Afrikaans, what British practice was he confirmed that the Bank of England's method was to offer only 'a hard loan with very fixed conditions on it'. Furthermore, unlike the procedure commonly adopted in Britain the SARB assistance was not transparent, and depended on State money with the taxpayers remaining in ignorance of what use had been made of their cash. Diedericks explained the mechanics, accurately if not too clearly.

> Q: The extraordinary profit ends up with the commercial bank at the expense of the Reserve Bank?
> Diedericks: With the commercial bank at the expense of the Reserve Bank. So that income should have been collected over here.
> Q: By the Reserve Bank?
> Diedericks : By the Reserve Bank. That is Treasury's money and that is indirect taxpayers' money which has now been creamed off for the benefit of this entity ... Now that is completely, as you understand now, contrary to what is the going procedure at least in the Bank of England. There's no loan and I venture to say, Mr Chairman, no balance sheet of any one of these entities ever shown any commit-ment, no loan, no nothing has been indicated through those balance sheets. So there was no loan. It was a free hand-out.

Moreover, Diedericks suggested that the assistance had been given with-out the knowledge of all the SARB directors, although he went on to suggest – entirely correctly, as it transpired – that the Sanlam directors knew all about it.

In addition to claiming that the SARB support was improper – and he might have added, illegal – Diedericks maintained that in the absence of such assistance, Tollgate would not have been liquidated. This was indeed the nub of the question, and Commissioner Hoberman attempted to clarify the evidence (p.4986):

> 'Mr Diedericks, can I just sum up your evidence as I under-stand it up until now. I understand you to say that Absa would not have liquidated the Tollgate group, were it not for the fact that it had the benefit of this accommodation from the Reserve Bank?'
> 'Correct.'

'It would not have liquidated the Tollgate group, were it not for the fact that it knew that any loss that it would suffer as a result of the liquidation would be paid for by public funds?'

'Correct.'

He added that while at Absa he had gained the impression that such was the dislike of Askin, that no proposals he could make would be accepted (p.4987). 'Certainly I have the impression from the comments made by Dr Cronjé, Mr Brits and Mr Badenhorst, that regardless of any proposals which were put forward by Mr Askin with reference to the reconstruction of the Tollgate group, Absa were intent in any event in putting the Tollgate group into liquidation.' And Badenhorst had dismissed Askin as 'a cocky little Engelsman'.

Although cross-examined aggressively by Gauntlett and Rubens, Diedericks stuck to his guns. 'You don't need to test my credibility and attack the messenger. Look at the documents, look at the facts.'

This last was a sore point. As a secret enquiry, the papers of the commission were jealously guarded, and Diedericks was about to ask that Absa produce documents that both he and they knew would be embarrassing to the bank. His solicitor, Richard Marcus, interrupted the cross-examination to ask that his client be given documentation to enable him to answer Absa's charges. Pondering this application, Hoberman began to appreciate that the force of Diedericks's evidence was causing him to reconsider his previous acceptance of Absa's statements.

Bertrand Hoberman had been appointed at Absa's behest as a reliable and biddable lawyer. But even the supposedly obedient Commissioner had been led to believe that Diedericks's claim that the lifeboat's existence had enabled Absa to proceed with liquidating Tollgate should be examined – especially since he accepted that Absa's lawyers 'were inclined to dismiss' these allegations. Diedericks's request that supporting documents be produced was the subject of discussion over some weeks, opposed by Absa but strongly supported by the Standard Bank's lawyers. Hoberman, growing ever more suspicious of Absa's good faith, instructed that these documents should be produced for Diedericks, giving him the facts he needed to face Absa's lawyer's cross-examination.

But Absa had no intention of letting Diedericks into the witness box; he had done enough damage already.

After these damaging accusations it was essential that the SARB should, also in public, attempt to refute Diedericks's allegations as to the impropriety of their assistance to Bankorp. It should also have been necessary for Absa staff to proffer their own explanations of Diedericks's accusations made regarding the Tollgate liquidation, but while Dr Stals of the Reserve Bank accepted that he must make a personal appearance, Absa remained coy and evasive of any public debate, making one last effort to abort the whole procedure.

On 23 February Hoberman was telephoned by Ivan Levy, a solicitor representing the Standard Bank, to ask that the session at which Dr Stals was due to give evidence, scheduled for the next working day, Monday 26, should be postponed, as one Mr Mervyn King was seeking to negotiate a settlement 'between the Banks'. King was a director of FNB and generally well-regarded. When asked to telephone Hoberman, King did so, and repeated his request for an indefinite adjournment of the enquiry. Hoberman was not minded to agree, and was suspicious that an outsider had attempted to intervene to halt the investigation. He could not imagine that King had taken the initiative himself, and telephoned Cronjé for his comments. Cronjé replied that he had been told by his subordinate, Brits, that King had indeed offered to attempt a mediation between the rival claims of the banks, to which Hoberman answered, 'Who is Mr Mervyn King that he now takes the initiative. Perhaps you could tell me who is he?' – questions which Hoberman later admitted would have been more accurately put as, 'Who the hell is Mr King that he should want to interfere?'

It is indeed very difficult to believe that King's approach had not been at least discussed with, if not prompted by, Absa, concerned at the imminent appearance of Dr Stals before the enquiry, and the prospect of so many cats being released from their bags. But it failed in that Hoberman, rendered even more distrustful of Absa, decided to plough ahead with his investigations

Dr Stals' lecture

Dr Stals' appearance before the Hoberman Commission was a majestic event. It is not every day that the Governor of a Central Bank has to defend himself against serious accusation made by another experienced banker, and Dr Stals acquitted himself with gravitas. Although he had been asked to send an advance copy of his speech to Hoberman, he did not do so, and on 26 February 1996 Dr Stals read a long and dignified paper to the Commission, which addressed none of the issues that really mattered. The obvious however was stated frequently, and at length. Gently taken through his evidence by his counsel, Mr Seligson, Dr Stals flatly contradicted Diedericks. 'Like the Bank of England, the South African Reserve Bank made loans, not gifts or grants or anything like that, they are loans with definite security and repayments. We have the same very strict requirements, we have loans, we asked for securities, the loans were repaid, so I don't think the impression should be created that the Bank of England does it one way, we did it differently . . .'

This perversion of the truth in a statement given on oath to a statutory body was of course made before Dr Stals' admission that the CIB 'loan' was nothing more than a gift had been made public, a fact which the Governor must have trusted would never see the light of day. After reading the paper he left the enquiry in stunned silence. Not having seen the paper, and having to rely on whatever they had been able to garner from the wordy presentation, no one felt able to ask any questions. They had not been helped by the fact that Stals had read his paper in Afrikaans, a language in which many of the listeners were not entirely comfortable, and which was not the common language of the country's business.

The speech was stately enough, but totally misleading. 'Be that as it may, in most countries in the world, including South Africa, monetary policy cannot be implemented successfully without the presence of sound and well-managed banking institutions, operating in most cases in and through efficient and effective financial markets, and trusted at all times by the public. The effectiveness of the central bank's monetary policy is therefore to an important extent dependent on the existence of sound individual institutions.'

An acute listener would have noticed some fuzzy logic. 'It should, in all circumstances for example, be taken into account that the alternative, that is not to provide assistance to a banking institution in distress, will also have adverse consequences for taxpayers, particularly if it happens to be a large banking institution serving thousands of individuals and businesses in the community.'

In tedious fact, taxpayers as a class may or may not be disadvantaged in providing assistance or withholding it. Depositors, borrowers, share-holders and employees, will be affected, but not taxpayers. Only a prosperous bank, paying taxes on its profits, will benefit taxpayers The inconvenient opposite point, that money given by a central bank which would otherwise have gone to taxpayers – and a very great deal of it went in subsidising Bankorp – is an absolute, perfect, and definitive loss to the taxpayer. (To say nothing, for the moment, about the deception practised on the taxpayer by disguising the character of the subvention.) All this was airily dismissed by the Governor as 'a debatable issue which will rather be left aside'.

Giving examples of other countries' assistance to banks, Dr Stals instanced the enormous, highly publicised assistance given by the French and Spanish governments to Crédit Lyonnais and Banco Banesto respectively, while failing to point out that the banks' management and shareholders were forced to pay the price and that the transactions were painfully transparent. Certainly Crédit Lyonnais was assisted by the French Government on an enormous scale – and much to the annoyance of the European Commission. However this was done with maximum publicity and the management was, very publicly, replaced and charged with criminal offences. Moreover, Crédit Lyonnais was owned by the state, so there was no question of benefiting shareholders. None of the cases quoted by Dr Stals in any way resembled the outright gifts that the SARB made to the shareholders of Afrikaner banks.

The fact that Dr Stals was able to quote other banks as examples only highlighted one essential difference: these transactions had been public and transparent.

Dr Stals laid down eight points that he considered could be derived from the practices followed universally by central banks. My comments follow.

1. Financial assistance is applied very sparingly, and as a general rule only when a particular case provides a threat of contagion of the whole banking system.

In fact, SARB acceded to every request made to it. As long, that is, as a request came from an Afrikaner bank. Or, at least, all the support operations were given to Afrikaner banks: it might have been that only these banks were sufficiently badly managed to require help. When the African Bank got into trouble in October 1995 no lifeboat was launched. Nor can it be argued that Bankorp's likely collapse threatened the whole banking system. Bankorp was a relatively small bank and had a single powerful shareholder, Sanlam, with a massive stake. But Sanlam was part of the Brotherhood.

2. Protection of depositors is a major consideration that must be taken into account, especially by central banks that have to operate in a vacuum where there is no public system of depositor protection.

Considering the way in which, by choosing the time to withdraw its loan to CIB, the Reserve Bank lost R200 million of the RCC's deposit, this is breathtakingly impudent.

3. Confidence in the banking system must be preserved, without providing open-ended support for mismanagement, fraud or internal inefficiencies in banking institutions.

Almost invariably it is management's fault when banks are in trouble. The replacement of failed management is essential. Yet in 1994 *all* the members of Absa's executive committee had been on the board of one of the constituent banks during the whole period of the trouble. Cronjé and Noëth were both involved in the Badenhorst telephone tapping affair. The constant series of aid given to Bankorp between 1985 and 1995, a period of over ten years, can only amount to providing open-ended support for mismanaged and fraudulent institutions.

4. Arising from the foregoing, financial assistance emanating from the central bank/government must, as far as possible, serve to protect depositors and not shareholders of banking institutions.

The shareholders of Bankorp/Absa did very well indeed out of the Reserve Bank help. They were not required to write down their shareholdings, and, quite astonishingly, continued to be entitled to receive dividends throughout the whole period. Moreover, one shareholder, Sanlam, was placed in a position of holding privileged information denied to other shareholders. And any directors who had share option facilities were able to continue with them, which anywhere else would be both shameful and dishonest.

> *5. In order to assist the banking institution to overcome its problem, the central bank may provide a loan at a nominal rate of interest, or perhaps provide guarantees for raising low interest rate loans from other institutions.*

But the Reserve Bank help was only disguised as a loan, as the Governor admitted to Mr Justice Rabie. It was, in fact, a straightforward gift.

> *6. The assistance must be conditional upon remedial action that will lead to recovery and may often require a change of ownership, of senior management, and even of the structure of the affected institution.*

An interesting point. There was indeed 'a restructure of the affected institutions'. Bankorp was bought by Absa, but Dr Stals adamantly maintained that this had nothing to do with the lifeboat. Few can be convinced. As for the ownership, Sanlam continues to be the major shareholder. Senior management continued placidly uninterrupted.

> *7. There must be possible exit for the central bank from the assistance programme, perhaps only after the credibility, creditworthiness and public trust in the institution have been re-established.*

Any rescue of a bank would almost always involve the rest of the country's banking system. This was never even attempted with Bankorp. The only answer was to merge with the other equally groggy Afrikaner bank, Volkskas. The proper alternative would have been to involve First National Bank and Standard Chartered, non-Afrikaner banks, who would certainly have insisted on uncomfortable action and embarrassing disclosure.

In the initial agreement an exit for the Reserve Bank was necessary, although it amounted to only 20 per cent of their gift. 80 per cent remained, permanently, as a subsidy to the shareholding of Absa. Eventually, the whole of the Reserve Bank's munificence was allowed to remain in Absa.

> 8. *It may in certain circumstances be necessary to keep the assistance package secret, particularly if disclosure could be counter-productive and defeat the objective of the exercise.*

Well, yes, 'in certain circumstances'. But the Reserve Bank still attempts to keep all its lifeboats very much under the cloak of secrecy: and secrecy when it is used to cover fraud is never allowable.

The Governor's summing-up may be judged against the above observations. 'These are generally the considerations that the Reserve Bank applied in providing assistance to South African banking institutions in recent years. The Bank is of the opinion that, if tested against those criteria, the assistance it provided to the Bankorp Group and later Absa was justified in terms of such common practices applied in this regard by central banks in the rest of the world.'

There are some other rules of practice which would, I am assured, be agreed by the Bank of England and that should be added to the ones Dr Stals enumerated, but so signally failed to follow.

1. A lifeboat should have strict time-limits. As soon as the troubled bank has recovered, the assistance should be repaid. If it does not recover, it should be closed. While the period of the SARB assistance is not known (it may well have started a quarter of a century back) it certainly continued for at least ten years, and the assistance was never repaid.

    It is unheard of that a bank which has amalgamated with another bank, thereby acquiring stability, capital, solvency and liquidity, should continue to receive a lifeboat which would only enhance the financial benefit of the bank newly created through the amalgamation. Such a scheme no longer constitutes assistance to an ailing bank, but is a straightforward abuse of the system in order to place taxpayers' funds into the pockets of the individual shareholders.

2. Confidentiality does not constitute a licence to mislead. The bank's financial statements – and those of the Reserve Bank – must reflect the income and assistance received, together with the obligation to repay. The CIB story indicates the lengths the Reserve Bank went to in order to avoid this disclosure.

3. Before any other action is even contemplated, the rest of the financial community should be asked, indeed required, to lend their support. In the whole history of the Reserve Bank's operations this was never done when it was an Afrikaner bank that was in trouble. Nedbank's lifeboat was supplemented by the Old Mutual's contribution of equity, but the troubles of Bankorp were sheltered from the world by an Afrikaner security blanket, paid for by the taxpayer. It might also be remarked that closing down a bank is standard procedure. Administrators are appointed, profitable divisions sold, and bad debts vigorously pursued. This could have been done in 1985 without causing more than a ripple. The Reserve Bank's procrastination only made matters worse.

Did the Reserve Bank's actions constitute, as both Judge Berman's and Judge Rabie's opinions indicate, a fraud? The Reserve Bank 1989 Act allows the bank to make loans against the provision of adequate security. But what was put in place was no loan, but a simulated transaction so disguised as to enable it to be publicly described as a loan, rather than a straightforward gift of interest income. That this would be considered fraudulent is evidenced by a South African judicial precedent. Skjelbreds Rederi A/S and Others v. Hartless (Pty) Ltd 1982 (2) SA 710 (A) Erf 3183/1 Ladysmith Pty Ltd and Another v Commissioner for Inland Revenue 1996 (3) SA 942 (A), where on page 952 the court says the following:

> A disguised transaction . . . is something different. In essence it is a dishonest transaction: dishonest, in as much as the parties to it do not really intended to have, *inter partes* [between themselves] the legal effect which its terms convey to the outside world. The purpose of the disguise is to deceive by concealing what is the real agreement or transaction between the parties. The parties wish to hide the fact that their real agreement or transaction falls within the prohibition or is subject to the tax, and so they dress it up in a guise which conveys the impression that it is outside of the prohibition or not subject to the tax. Such a transaction is said to be *in fraudem legis* [in fraud of the law], and is interpreted by the courts in accordance with what is found to be the real agreement or transaction between the parties.

One more point. When the merger between Bankorp and the Volkskas group was finalised in 1992 a further agreement was entered into with the South African Reserve Bank, confirming the provision of the lifeboat, with Absa substituted for Bankorp. But – and this is significant – the original condition that the agreement would end once Bankorp's assets and reserves reached R1500 million (subsequently amended to R300 million) was dropped. Had it not been, the assistance would have had to be terminated then and there.

Dr Stals' speech was reported in the South African financial press with varying degrees of credulity. David Gleason was perceptively critical in his report (8 March).

> A week ago the SA legal system suffered the equivalent of collective laryngitis, unusual among those given to verbal diarrhoea.
>
> The occasion was the S417 inquiry into Tollgate and the event was the testimony delivered by Reserve Bank Governor Chris Stals. Stals spoke for hours. Not once was he interrupted or asked a single question. Counsel were spellbound. It was a

performance which demonstrates that the art of oratory isn't dead.

Gleason recalled that in an earlier article he had suggested that the loan should be repaid and 'those directors responsible for the mess, be called to account for their negligence'. Both demands were entirely in accordance with normal practice. But nothing had happened. 'Instead, Stals has said – on oath – that the loan was repaid.' Which, of course, it had not been. All that had happened was that the SARB had 'deemed' the loan repaid – i.e. accepted the fact that it hadn't.

'This is, of course, a disgrace. Unsuspecting taxpayers have hosted a hoax.' Sanlam, as major shareholder and in management control should have been required to accept full responsibility, or to lose its investment.

> We cannot, we dare not, turn a blind eye. Accommodations have been made which negate official responsibility, Tax-payers' hard-earned pennies have been thrown at impecunious bankers who are then absolved from the need to repay – or even account in public for their wilfulness.
>
> I must ask, therefore, whether the silence in Cape Town is mute acquiescence. And, while I am at it, I would like to suggest that it may behove the governor to revisit the meaning of the word 'repaid'.

Although a good deal more respectful, Deon Basson's series of articles in the *F & T Weekly* made the same point. Fred du Plessis, whose drive for growth had encouraged the Bankorp management to issue massive bad loans was not only executive chairman of Bankorp, and chairman of its subsidiaries Santambank, Senbank and Trust Bank, but executive chairman of Sanlam and Federale Mynbou. With its own chairman so exposed to personal responsibility for Bankorp there should have been no way in which Sanlam could avoid meeting its obligations towards Bankorp rather than relying on the taxpayer.

This point was, understandably, not addressed by Stals at all, but some revealing off-the-cuff remarks of the Governor were recorded. *Business Day* of 27 February reported: 'Claims by Diedericks that the assistance was a free handout to Bankcorp read like an Agatha Christie

novel and indicated confusion between the Bank's activities at the discount window and its role as a lender of last resort.'

This was the same Dr Stals who had joked about being a Father
Christmas, and described how the present to CIB had to be disguised
as a loan.

Little attention however was paid to the central question of whether
the Reserve Bank had acted at all legally. At this time the Rabie report,
which stigmatised the CIB assistance as fraudulent had not been published. Deon Basson did report the views of an academic, Felix Oelkers,
that the Reserve Bank did not possess the 'right' to rescue banks. The
former Deputy Registrar of Banks, Carel Oosthuizen, while not going
so far, did outline a number of steps that must be followed before
assistance could be given. These included a solvency investigation, a
due diligence study by independent experts, and a political assessment
by government, none of which took place before the major Bankorp
rescue. Basson also pointed out the fact that most other commentators
preferred to ignore that 'the combination of "Afrikaans" banking groups
with Afrikaner shareholders assisted by a Reserve Bank loaded with
Afrikaner directors adds an ethnic flavour to the furore.'

Twelve years after the Johnson Matthey affair the Bank of England
had not changed its views. Speaking in Hong Kong on 26 October 1996
the Governor, Eddie George, put it clearly:

> Where there is systemic risk you cannot pick and choose,
> supporting some institutions but not others ... That would
> introduce a serious competitive distortion and moral hazard:
> When we do consider extending 'last resort' support, we
> will explore every option for a commercial solution before
> committing our own resources. We will look to major share-
> holders to provide support; We will try to structure it so that
> any losses fall first on shareholders, and any benefits come
> first to us. Our terms will be as penal as we can make them
> without precipitating the collapse we are trying to avoid, and
> we aim to provide liquidity: we will not in normal circum-
> stances support a bank we know at the time to be insolvent.

Why Tollgate was killed off

The truth about the Reserve Bank's support operations is only now emerging, but the effects they had on the liquidation of Tollgate became apparent more rapidly. As Diedericks had claimed at the public hearing of the Hoberman Commission, the lifeboat not only made it profitable for Absa to liquidate Tollgate: the company's demise became inevitable.

The revised, third, lifeboat that had been officially launched in August 1990 soon proved, like all its predecessors, unable to cope. A year later, in September 1991, a fourth instalment of aid was given, on the same basis as the other. The 'assistance' given by the Reserve Bank was increased to R225 million a year for five years, a total of R1,125 million – more than £200 million, even in the depreciating South African currency: and of this huge gift only some 20 per cent, at most, would ever be repayable. Without such an injection the merger between Bankorp and Volkskas/United into Absa would never have been possible: and in the mechanics of restructuring Tollgate was a vital component.

During the first period, the run up to Liebenberg's approach to the Reserve Bank in June 1990, Tollgate's continued existence was essential. At the end of 1989 Tollgate owed some R380 million – and occasionally even more – to Trust Bank, (and another R70 million to its other bankers). That R380 million was very nearly equivalent to the whole of Trust Bank's shareholders' funds (R387.4 million in June 1989) and over half of the parent company, Bankorp's, shareholders' funds (R689 million). The loan was secured to Trust Bank against Tollgate shares. If these were to lose their value, then a sum equivalent to more than the whole of Trust Bank's equity capital would have been jeopardised. In such circumstances, the liquidation of the company, which would also have uncovered a great number of very doubtful transactions implicating Trust Bank officials, would have been inconceivable.

Bankorp and Sanlam, holding over 80 per cent of the shares, were well aware of the impending crisis. There was a flurry of boardroom activity. In May 1989 Marinus Daling and Attie du Plessis, both able and ambitious 'Sanlammers', were appointed as directors of Bankorp, being faced with the already burgeoning problems of bad debts and muddled controls. Chris van der Walt, chairman of Bankorp was replaced in January 1990 by Derek Keys, the unctuous but sure-footed Minister of Finance in the last Nationalist and first 1994 coalition government. His was a stop-gap appointment, and his replacement by Liebenberg was announced in March 1990, although Liebenberg did not take post until 4 June. At the next level Kobus Roets was replaced as Managing Director of Trust Bank by Chris van Wyk. He lasted only until July the following year.

In May 1990 the Registrar of Banks, the egregious Dr van Greuning, gave his assent to the transfer of all the assets and liabilities of the two Sanlam subsidiary banks, Santambank and Senbank, to Trust Bank. This was the start of the rationalisation which reached its conclusion with the formation of Absa. In his letter Dr van Greuning confirmed 'the Reserve Bank confirms further that the arrangements as set out in our letter dated 20 March 1990, regarding the loan to Santambank, remain unchanged.' It would therefore appear that yet another Reserve Bank loan existed which has never been publicly admitted.

The three-page letter of 3 August 1990, which sufficed to put the R1,000 million aid package into effect was only supplemented by more formal documentation in an agreement dated 3 September 1991, by which time discussions between the shareholders of Bankorp and Absa as to a merger were already under way. The formal agreement confirmed the original understanding that the money made available was related to a list of doubtful debtors as they existed at June 1990, totalling some R1,635 million (and which, when compared with the publicly stated shareholders' funds, after Santam's contribution of R550 million, is a devastating figure). This schedule, a vital document, included Tollgate in the sum of R250.7 million and Arwa (guaranteed by Tollgate) for R95 million.

In other words, at the same time that Trust Bank, and the Reserve Bank, assuring Askin of Tollgate's health and strength, were preparing to finalise their part of his consortium's takeover, Bankorp's loan book was being presented to the authorities as a 'doubtful' debt. In fact, the 'doubt' amounted to a certainty, since the Reserve Bank was prepared to give Bankorp enough money to write off their loans. That this was so is confirmed first by the internal memoranda passing between bank officials at the time, and quoted on pp.75–6, and secondly by Hennie Diedericks, who was informed of the whole situation in his conversation with Liebenberg in April 1990. Liebenberg acknowledged that the Toll-gate loans were indeed the subject of discussion between Bankorp and the SARB and that he had been assured of the Reserve Bank's support. And finally, confirmed by Dr Stals himself when he made it clear that the list of doubtful debts presented to him included 'only losses that already existed or were anticipated on 30 June 1990'.

Just before the final absorption of Bankorp into Absa, Dr Stals wrote again to Liebenberg, on 27 April 1992. There had been some discussion as to whether the schedule of doubtful debts as at 30 June 1990 might be changed. Stals rejected the idea:

> The support that the agreement provides is based on the doubtful debtor schedules as at 30 June 1990 and which is annexed to the agreement. The replacement of debtors on the schedule by replacing it with other debtors which existed on 30 June 1990, change the basis on which the support amount has been determined and similarly affects the agreement between Bankorp and the SA Reserve Bank. We are thus of the opinion that the replacement of debtors is in conflict with the support package.

But he went on to say:

> As far as the impression unintentionally has been created that replacement of debtors are acceptable, the Reserve Bank is presently prepared to accept replacement of debtors on the schedule. To provide a fixed base to the agreement, it is necessary to compile before 31 May 1992 a new schedule, listing the names of doubtful debtors as at 30 June 1990, and to adjust the agreement (not the support amount). The contents/construction of the new schedule have been left at your discretion. It is accepted that it is not possible to provide for exact amounts and that there will be deviations on the estimated amounts. It does not mean that the initial esti-mated amount of R1635 million, provided by the Reserve Bank and the shareholders, will be increased.

On the amended schedule of debts provided for, Tollgate was not included.

It is true that, according to proper banking practice, Tollgate was *not* a non-performing debt. Since Askin had taken charge in June 1990, all interest payments, which amounted to a total of nearly R200 million, had indeed been promptly met and that cash-flow continued positive. But neither Trust Bank nor its successor Absa was much concerned with proper banking practice. As far back as June 1990 it had been decided that Tollgate had to be finally dealt with. Discounting the absurd explanation that the omission of Tollgate from the March 1992 list was due to Absa's confidence in Askin's management, the only possible reason was that the Absa board had already written off its liabilities to Tollgate. These had been taken off their hands by the Reserve Bank.

Those two essential conditions had been fulfilled. The debt had to be provided for, and therefore due and payable without further notice, by 31 March 1992, and actually called by December of that year. Tollgate had therefore to be disposed of before that date. If Tollgate was then still in existence, the R350 million specifically provided by the Reserve Bank was due to be repaid to them, an impossible thought for any Absa executive to entertain. That R350 million was equivalent to one third of the bank's net earnings. Tollgate simply had to be liquidated before the due date, and Askin was merely strung along until a convenient excuse could be found.

And November 1992 would have been the first date when Trust Bank, or its successor Absa, could have forced Tollgate into liquidation as long as the company continued to generate enough cash-flow to repay the interest on the due date – and this continued to be so until the final day's trading. Since the interest due was not actually handed over to the bank, but merely deducted by them from the company's accounts, it would have been impossible for Absa to have pretended otherwise. Moreover, Tollgate was trading within the limits authorised by Absa. Even at the date of liquidation the overdrafts allowed by Absa totalled R297.96 million, with the sum actually drawn being R292.03 million – R5 million *below* the authorised limit. But the decisive reason why an earlier liquidation was impossible was that Trust Bank had given an undertaking to the London Stock Exchange, essential to the takeover of Jaton in November 1991, that Tollgate had sufficient working capital facilities in place. That undertaking expired on 19 November 1992.

There were other indications that Trust Bank was secretly making arrangements for an eventual liquidation. In January 1991, following their action against Johan Claasen, Trust Bank required a guarantee that Tollgate would repay its facilities by 31 March 1992. When Askin objected – he had Trust Bank's assurance only months earlier that his facilities were in place until June 1993 – he was expressly reassured that the reference to 31 March 1992 was for 'bank internal reasons only', and that Trust Bank stood by its earlier engagements. Relying on this verbal assurance, made by Etienne du Toit and Hennie van de Merwe, the unsuspecting Askin signed an undertaking to repay by March 1992, and was reassured when that date passed with no mention of repayment being demanded. But the undertaking remained in force, a time bomb that could then, at any time after that date, provide Trust Bank with an immediate trigger to bring about Tollgate's liquidation – but always only after 19 November 1992. And it was that undertaking of Askin's to repay on 31 March 1992 that was eventually used by Absa to liquidate Tollgate.

Protected by the SARB's lifeboat against the whole of their exposure to Tollgate, Absa's strategy was simple. As long as the company was trading, the bank would draw off as much as it could in interest and consolidate whenever possible its position as secured creditor. Then, as soon as possible after 19 November, liquidate. On no account should any extra money be allocated to Tollgate, as Julian Askin's restructuring proposals required: that would be self-defeating, since in order to take advantage of the SARB's support the company had to be terminated before 25 December 1992. The window of opportunity for Absa was extremely narrow.

They used it well, taking whatever action would assist the bank in maximising the yield from the inevitable liquidation. On 19 November Dr Cronjé, working with Danie Brits, wrote to Hoskens exercising a 'put' option held on Tollgate shares, so converting an equity position, useless in a liquidation, into debt, which would be covered by the lifeboat. It was therefore extremely embarrassing when, on 4 November, Standard Chartered Bank asked for a banker's reference on Tollgate. There was no alternative other than to bite the bullet and lie, warranting their fellow bankers that the company was good for R20 million, while being prepared to assure the courts that Tollgate had been in default since March.

Well before this, while negotiations were still being pursued with Askin, as he thought in good faith, Absa executives busied themselves with preparations for liquidation. On 2 September 1992 Egbert le Roux wrote to Estienne du Toit, who had been monitoring the Tollgate account: 'Despite Johan Smit appearing to have done a security audit, I believe we might ask him to confirm the cross-guarantee situation in the group. So we are justified in looking at a group situation and therefore will not be confronted with holes in our security situation . . . certain securities have apparently now been put in place. If liquidation is considered the effects of this should be borne in mind – viz the possible setting of them aside.'

The benefits to Absa went further than merely being given the R350 million which it had claimed to the S A R B as a doubtful debt. They would also be entitled to claim on the same basis as any other creditors in the liquidation. In addition the R350 million included contingent liabilities, which were otherwise fully secured and on which no loss was eventually suffered; these amounted in total to over R100 million. This they were effectively paid twice over. Then, since the Reserve Bank had structured their support as a fictitious 'loan', which was 're-lent' to the Reserve Bank, Absa were responsible for the net interest they received of 15 per cent, a total of R1,125 million. This was never declared, and the tax never paid. Of the R600 million was thus improperly retained nearly one third related to the Tollgate debt.

In all, by putting Tollgate into liquidation, Absa probably earned themselves an extra R500 million over and above their loan: not a negligible profit, and one to which the bank's earnings from Tollgate during the period July 1990 to December 1992, when Askin was in charge, could be added. These amounted to nearly R300 million – R170 million in interest, plus R125 million by the reduction of the opening borrowing figure.

It was equally vital that no hint of the bank's intentions should leak out. Askin, if he knew he was faced with a complete negation by Absa of their existing agreement, would have had time to make alternative arrangements. Given his record, and the resources he could muster, the agreement offered by F N B to provide facilities to Tollgate, the fact that all the companies were trading profitably, and the eight months he had wasted negotiating with a bank that never had any intention of reaching an agreement, he could almost certainly have raised enough capital to ensure Tollgate's continued trading.

Was there any truth in Dr Stals' contention that the existence of the Reserve Bank lifeboat had nothing to do with the formation of Absa? The question then to be addressed is what would have been the situation in Bankorp without the Reserve Bank's gift?

At the end of 1991 shareholders' funds stood at R1340 million in the published balance sheet. Since this was after the secret Reserve Bank aid of R1,125 million, the position would have been – had the lifeboat never been launched – that shareholders' funds would have slumped to R215million – surely a hopeless position. Absa paid R1287 million for Bankorp, a little less than the disclosed asset value (the price was actually negotiated by Hennie Diedericks, who managed to reduce the sum paid by R100 million). It is unbelievable that Absa would have paid anything approaching that sum without Reserve Bank support, and that therefore the deal as structured could never have been done. The existence of the lifeboat was essential to the successful merger of the two Afrikaner banks and was only made possible by disregarding the accepted rules of central banking, and then energetically attempting to hide what had been done.

For confirmation, the situation of Arwa presents itself. Arwa's debt to Absa was an almost exact parallel to that of Tollgate. At the same time, between April and June 1990 when Askin was finalising the Toll-gate takeover, Claasen was making his arrangements to fund Arwa, at Arwa's instigation, as a necessary precondition for Askin's intervention in Tollgate. Hennie van der Merwe, who was responsible for the negoti-ations with Claasen (and who did so well for himself later) was one of those present at the initial launch meeting, and ensured the inclusion of Arwa's debt on the non-performing list. Within days of the agree-ments being made, Arwa was doomed. R95 million was noted on the Reserve Bank's list as a bad debt from Arwa, which would be provided for in full from the lifeboat facility.

There was therefore no incentive at all for Absa to get a respectable price for the sale of Arwa's hosiery division. It could be, and it was, passed on to Arwa's rival company controlled by Lieberman at a modest figure, and quickly disposed of at its real value, giving so satisfactory a profit to a director of Absa, so comfortable a berth for one of its senior executives and so welcome a windfall to the bank.

CHAPTER NINE

Sinners and Bankers

Hoberman delenda est

January 1996 seemed to have marked the beginning of the disintegration of Absa's case against Askin. Battered by the short careers and subsequent denunciation of Piet Liebenberg and Piet Badenhorst, who only contrived to serve three years between the pair of them, the bank found its new chairman Dave Brink was not forceful enough to hold the fort when the Tollgate enquiry began to fall apart. Bertrand Hoberman, having disappointed his patron Absa's expectations of unquestioning obedience, was falling out of favour. 'I don't think I am Absa's favourite person at the moment, I don't think I have been ... for quite some time', he admitted to Paul Bell and Hugh Murray of *Millennium* in January 1996.

The order originally establishing the Hoberman commission on 23 June 1993 authorised the Commissioner to summon specified individuals before the tribunal; they included the Tollgate directors, but also the 'relevant persons or officials' of, among others, Absa Bank. It was only with the greatest difficulty and after much equivocation that the bankers appeared. Similarly, item 7 of the order requires that 'all documents, records and papers in their possession, custody or power' of such persons should be produced. Hoberman was to meet with a determined resistance when he attempted to gain access to Absa's records, and the attempt was to result in his own dismissal.

Over two years of hearing evidence had elapsed before Hoberman's suspicions began to focus upon possible faults within the bank, when he ordered that Absa's claims to have secured lending against Tollgate should be investigated. Diedericks had presented a detailed study with quantities of supporting documents, indicating, 'it is clear that from November 1990 the Bank [Absa] secured its position at the expense of other banks and creditors.' Liquidator Chris van Zyl, working independently had already asked for these to be investigated. Together, amounting to some R250 million, Absa's claims to security, if overturned, would substantially weaken the bank's potential dividends. The decision to investigate, Hoberman said, 'met with enormous resistance – you can imagine ... There was a lot of unhappiness about that in certain quarters.'

There was much unhappiness too among the management of Absa when Hoberman insisted on seeing for himself the Bank's files, and was not put off by evasive stories about documents being mislaid. By the end of March none of the specific documentation that Hoberman had ordered should be made available to Diedericks had been produced and the Commissioner was getting impatient. He had the legal right to insist on documents being made available to him, and accordingly instructed Max Levenberg of Werksmans, acting for Absa, to procure that these be produced 'no later than 20 April'. Four days after his deadline Hoberman had received nothing better than 'photocopied snippets' from the minute books, which were quite useless as evidence.

After the usual prevarication, Absa asked Hoberman to come in person to Johannesburg to examine the board minutes in order to satisfy himself that the extracts from the documentation, which was all that had so far been made available, included everything relevant. This he did, accompanied by the forensic accountant on his team, Alan Greyling, on 2 May. They were shown only the minute books of the Group Executive Committee. Astonishingly – or perhaps, given the facts, not – they found no reference to the liquidation of Tollgate. The failure of one of the bank's biggest customers, which represented a potential loss equal to some £50 million, one which would have devastated the bank's profits, was not even officially discussed.

Naturally enough, Hoberman was 'highly suspicious', and made his suspicions clear to Christo Faul. Furthermore, he recorded

> It was obvious that I was not impressed with Mr Faul's explanation, given to me when I queried the absence of minutes, that the decision to liquidate the Tollgate Group

was a mere management decision. I was aware of an affidavit sworn by Mr A. R. M. Aldworth which refers to the fact that, for example, Mr P. J. Badenhorst (then the chairman of Absa) had indicated to the Board that there would be no disadvantage to Absa if the Tollgate Group was put into liquidation because of the existence of the lifeboat.

Indeed, I asked Mr Greyling if he could suggest the name of some other person who was a Director of Absa whom I could approach for more information in this regard. He suggested that I telephoned Mr W. G. Boustred which I later did. When I eventually spoke to Mr Boustred, I obtained the firm impression that he had anticipated my telephone call. He denied that the lifeboat had any relevance.

It is significant that according to the evidence of Mr Faul, it was on the evening of 2 May 1996 (visit to Jo'burg) that he, Mr Brink (then the chairman of Absa) and Dr Cronjé came to the conclusion that I was biased against Absa and that application should be made for my recusal.

I myself found it extremely surprising that in a major institutional organisation such as Absa, there was apparently so little documentation dealing with the liquidation of the Tollgate Group in respect of decisions taken by the Board and Executive Committee of Absa. The lack of documentation at Board and Executive Committee level raised my suspicions. The timing of my pressing for this documentation (and the heightening of suspicions in connection therewith as communicated to Mr Greyling) and the subsequent application for my recusal as Commissioner was more than coincidental.

It was at this stage that certain difficult facts, such as the imposition and the speedy removal of the 'regskontrolle' tab on the Tollgate accounts at Absa began to emerge and suspicions of Absa's conduct burgeoned. Diedericks's efforts at forcing disclosure from the bank were now helped by an unhappy creditor, Hennie Bredenkamp, director of K & M Civils, a construction enterprise owed more than R2 million for work done on the Kyalami racetrack. A robust character, he describes himself as a 'bedondere padmaker' (cantankerous – or rascally! – road-maker). Bredenkamp as a proven creditor had been given all the documentation and transcriptions amassed during nearly three years of sittings. Reading these and following the enquiry in pursuit of his missing millions Bredenkamp had become convinced that there was a great deal of explanation due, and not, in the main from Askin. Henceforward Bredenkamp enrolled with Aldworth, Diedericks – to whom he made available certain documents when it proved impossible to obtain these elsewhere – Claasen and, increasingly the liquidators, to be among those who supported Askin's actions against Absa. His considerable weight was also put behind Chris van Zyl's efforts to overturn Absa's securities.

Although some less important hits were acknowledged – Absa conceded that it had overcharged Tollgate some R800,000 on the interest that had been deducted from the company's accounts, the dispute resolved itself into two separate arguments. Had Absa, as alleged by van Zyl, falsified its claims to security and had the SARB lifeboat been applied to make possible the liquidation of Tollgate?

The last was strenuously denied by Christo Faul, who had been given the unenviable task of public spokesman for Absa. Faul, at that time described as senior consultant for risk management, stated that he had been made responsible for deciding whether Tollgate would be reconstructed and, if so, how it might be done. He told the Hoberman enquiry that he recommended the company's liquidation, since, among other 'facts', Askin had said that the investors were not prepared to re-capitalise the company. This was certainly not so, for Askin's supporters in the City of London were willing to consider any proposals he might have advanced – had the bank been prepared to discuss these. Diedericks's evidence was scornfully dismissed as that of an 'unstable' man who had attempted to play off one side against the other. In common with all other Absa executives, Faul continued to deny that the 'lifeboat' had anything at all to do with the decision on liquidation.

Diedericks's evidence attracted widespread attention, but that given by a former colleague of his passed almost unnoticed. Askin had always suspected that some, at least, of Tollgate's missing millions had been shifted abroad: there had been descriptions of Mervyn Key's desk looking like the office of a foreign-exchange dealer. On 22 February 1996 Key's old colleague David McCay gave evidence that one of Key's companies, Davgro, later Drive-tech, 'had at some time in the late eighties set up "Invicta Panama", and that was at the behest of the strategic Supplies Commission (SSC) that was to put some 400 or 500 million into rubber and bearings and silk and all sorts of nonsense in case of sanctions ... So at quite a large cost we set up Invicta Panama, structured a deal with Nisha Airwo, which is the trading house ... whereby a certain amount, I think 8.3 per cent of the purchase price was trapped in Invicta Panama. About two years ago', McCay continued, 'the Reserve Bank said would we please unwind it'. McCay wanted half a million dollars to do so, 'so the Reserve Bank says keep it'.

In addition to this frank admission of how illegal activities were carried out with the connivance of the Reserve Bank, McCay told another interesting story of how he arranged foreign investment. This was in the shape of a company, Table Investments, to be established in the Caribbean and administered by a local firm, Pim Goldby, as 'a conduit for investment into South Africa in the olden days when we bought the Rand Merchant Bank in May 1979. Owen Horwood at a lunch with Dr Rupert and his son Johan and me, laughingly he said of course it would be very nice for us to have the overseas investment into your bank openly. So we had the 1976 riots and things were a little bit hairy. So Johan Rupert and I went overseas ... and we finally got Bank [indistinct] the fourth largest bank in Switzerland to invest openly'.

To the question 'Pim Goldby must have been acting on the instructions of somebody?' McCay answered, 'No, no, the ... I don't know, I mean I don't know how they set up their structure', which all gives a scent of how Afrikaner financiers and their English-speaking friends managed things 'in the olden days'. While no documentary proof exists of such transactions, McCay's revelations do add weight to Askin's contention that before his time Tollgate's accounts hid many sensitive secrets. 8.3 per cent of even $US400 million is some $US35 million!

Press comment was becoming increasingly critical of Absa: an article in the *Financial Mail* of 16 February by David Gleason was uncomfortably on target and in the political arena the ANC recommended that there should be an investigation, with prosecutions of those found guilty. On 25 February Aldworth claimed R7.6 million in damages from Absa: and the following day Dr Stals gave his evidence to the Hoberman Commission, in public.

It was the beginning of a bad time for the Governor. On 13 February the international value of the rand began to slide. By the end of March it had depreciated by 9 per cent and the decline continued. Four months later the rand had lost another 11 per cent. In his annual report, published in August, Dr Stals said that this decline 'could hardly be explained or justified in terms of these basic economic fundamentals. Unfounded rumours, speculative transactions and negative views of the South African socio-political situation, forced the exchange rate of the rand to a value which now surely does not reflect the true economic potential of the country.'

Tollgate and the certainly not 'unfounded' rumours concerning the lifeboat were beginning to have national effects. Worse was to come.

Perturbed by the criticism, Absa asked for three days of the Commission's time in order to put their own case. It turned out to be a fiasco. On the first day for which all the lawyers and their clients were arrayed, Simon Ridley, the general manager in charge of finance, did little more than hand over a paper. On the second day (21 March 1996) of Absa's requested three, Dr Cronjé gave evidence for an equally short time.

When Dr Cronjé was examined by the Hobermann Commission he was asked who were the other Absa officials who participated in the decision to liquidate Tollgate. In reply he prevaricated. 'It was the Executive Committee who were authorised to decide, but this authority had been delegated to him, together with the chairman, acting on the recommendation of Mr Brits, Mr Christo Faul.'

Asked if the lifeboat featured in the decision he answered simply, 'no'. The same answer was given to the question, 'Did you believe at the time when the decision was taken to wind up the Tollgate Group, that the Tollgate exposure would be written off against the lifeboat?' Hoberman then asked how Dr Cronjé believed that the write-off would be dealt with in the bank's accounts, and received the peculiar response that, as Deputy Managing Director who had just assumed responsibility for one of the biggest commercial losses to befall the bank, he 'assumed that shareholders' funds would be used for that at some stage or another'.

Cronjé denied again that the lifeboat played any part in the decision, and repeatedly that there was no cut-off date for the list of bad debts. In evidence he alleged that:

At the board meeting on 27 November 1992 the Board was appraised of the possibility of there being an orderly liquidation of the Tollgate Group. There was also discussion at that meeting of the need to make substantial additional debt provision of approximately R200 million in respect of the Tollgate Group . . . these provisions were necessary, whether or not the group was put into liquidation, because of the precarious financial position of the group. Final decision . . . taken by Mr Brits and myself on 30 November the decision was a management decision, and not a Board matter.'

After he had been told that Faul, who was due to take up the third day of the Commission's time, was ill, and would not be coming, Hoberman was indignant and asked Cronjé 'bluntly' if the bank had anything to hide. Cronjé replied, 'We have nothing to hide.' It did not satisfy the Commissioner, 'Well, I must tell you that it isn't the impression I have been getting. I was told yesterday that Absa would not make available to me certain documentation. Are you aware of that decision?' The monosyllabic answer came, 'Yes'.

Absa was also beginning to discover that incessant bad publicity could bring worrying financial consequences. On 27 May David Brink announced that an international share offering was to be sought, and that authority had been gained to issue up to 5.6 million new shares. Within two weeks the project was dropped amid rumours that the bank would not be able to meet the standards of disclosure demanded in London. These were angrily denied by Brink, denounced as 'absolute tripe and nonsense' claiming that the market had softened (which it had not in that short time). The fact remained that Absa was not able to press ahead with its financial plans.

During the exchange of views in the press Mr Christopher Kemble, of ING Barings, Absa's London advisers, went out on something of a limb, claiming that the lifeboat was 'definitely not the reason. We went into all of that in detail and on the advice of our lawyers concluded that it was in the past, had been disclosed and had no material impact on Absa as of now.'

Well, it is true that the lifeboats had been launched some years before and that their existence had been – very reluctantly – disclosed, but the question had already been asked – what if the Finance Ministry just asked for their money back?

David Gleason in the *Financial Mail* of 16 February had advanced one suggestion: 'It is time therefore for someone, especially the previous owners of Bankorp [Sanlam] to repay the benefit and the lifeboat derived from taxpayers' largesse. Until that is done, Sanlam should eschew dividends from Absa.'

Although not at the time taken seriously, the real prospect that their 25 per cent holding in Absa might entail substantial penalties later began to loom large. It was clear to Absa that Hoberman, now thoroughly suspicious and in possession of much material that the bank would have preferred to keep undisclosed, would have to go. Hence Absa's attempt to have the enquiry shelved by Mervyn King's mediation. When this fizzled out, on 8 May, the morning Diedericks was due to appear in public to argue his case before the Hoberman Commission, armed with the information so painfully obtained from Absa, the bank struck. An application was brought by Absa's counsel demanding that Hoberman be dismissed, claiming that he was 'hopelessly biased' against the bank. It was a massive insult, made without any warning, in public and without any consultation with the liquidators who were already indignant. This was the second occasion on which they had prepared for their advisers to be present during the whole of the three-day period it was expected to devote to Diedericks's evidence. But Absa had already been given a bad enough time during the previous appearances of Cronjé and Ridley, transitory though these were, and were not going to risk appearing in public in contest with a now well-informed Diedericks.

Mr Rubens, who had previously acted for both Absa and the liquidators, was now speaking only for Absa when he accused the Commissioner of bias and prejudice, and failing to challenge any evidence advanced by Absa or the Reserve Bank. Hoberman was indignant:

> Mr Rubens I must say that I have grave doubts whether this application of yours is *bona fide*. The reason I say that is that a week ago I called upon your client to produce certain minute books and I asked for those minute books to be produced here in Cape Town. The response that I got was a letter from our attorney inviting me to come to Johannes-

burg to inspect the minute books in Johannesburg. Now all the conduct that you complain of, to the extent that it's factually correct, all that conduct had taken place long before then. I would have thought that if this application was bona fide, that your response to my request that you produce the minute books to me would have been put everything on hold, we're going to bring an application for your recusal. On the contrary I'm invited to come to Johannesburg to look at the books. I think that this application is no more than a charade which you are playing out for the benefit of the press and the application is refused. I also want to tell you that there is no basis whatsoever for your perception that I'm biased against Absa and I want to give you my assurance that I am not biased against Absa. Are you now in a position to proceed with the further questioning of Mr Diedericks?

Mr Rubens replied: 'No.'

Aldworth later related that a senior counsel had told him that 'There was no way in the world that Absa was going to take the opportunity to question Diedericks. He was waiting for them. He gave the impression of a man going to a party, a party to which he had been looking forward for a long long time.'

Equally, perhaps even more so, Absa would go to very great lengths to prevent the Commissioner, of all people, making public the bank's lies and prevarications. The case for Hoberman's refusal went forward to a court hearing, for which Hoberman produced an affidavit describing his 'trouble' at discovering that minutes of Absa's board and group executive committee held no mention of the decision to liquidate Toll-gate prior to a minute of 26 February 1993. Even that belated reference did nothing but take cognisance 'of the fact of the liquidation and the write-off of R215 million'.

Faul's explanation that the decision to liquidate a client, regardless of the extent of the exposure, 'was a management decision and not one taken by the board' is, frankly, incredible. Banks do not allow their management to write off such sums, that amount, as R215 million did, to some 5 per cent of the shareholders' funds, and indeed the authority delegated to Absa's executives did not permit this. But even if true, Faul's story only showed up the board control of his bank to be appallingly lax.

The liquidators were solidly behind Hoberman, believing it essential that the enquiry continue, and that 'there were other transactions, impeachable dispositions and the possibility of liability under Section 24 of the Companies' Act' that could be charged against Absa. Glaum told Diedericks that Absa stopped the enquiry so that it could not 'look at the role played by the big boys. In panic somebody swung their gun round and tried to shoot the Commissioner.'

Askin sues

And in London too the clouds were gathering. Askin had already, on 12 March (the time was determined by the fact that any action would have to be commenced within six years of the original investment, a period which would have expired on 16 March 1996) launched his action in the courts against Absa. The writ of summons accused Absa, Bankorp, Strydom and Morland of fraudulent and/or negligent misrepresentation and conspiracy to defraud, and Cronjé and Badenhorst of conspiracy, and of procuring or inducing the actions of the first defendants. Particularly in view of their unfortunate experiences with law courts, Absa had shown great reluctance to let any of their executives appear before any tribunal. They could be sure to fight hard against the possibility of having to do so in an English court, where the judges could be expected to be less amenable, and would attempt to insist that the case should be heard in South Africa.

Askin's initial case was gradually being bolstered as others began to ride alongside, stimulated by Absa's unpopular efforts to have Hoberman dismissed. This could only lead, and was already leading, to further delays, expense and causing the prospect of any payment being made to the creditors to recede even further. On 9 May Glaum had a long talk with Diedericks in which he disclosed that two weeks before the liquidation in December 1992 visiting Absa executives told James Thompson, Managing Director of Motoravia, of their intention, adding that they wanted themselves to buy 52 per cent of the company. Armed with this prior information Thompson was able to prepare for his own bid for the company.

The following day, 10 May Askin spoke to Gerbie Strydom, the former Trust Bank executive who, together with Koos Morland, was beginning to prepare his own revelations. On the same day Johan Claasen launched an action against Absa and Hennie van der Merwe, who had done so well for himself over the sale of Arwa to its rivals. Claasen claimed R54 million in damages, which, considering his losses, was not excessive.

It was, presumably, the growing pressure on Absa that led Denis Worrall to make an attempt to smooth matters over. Worrall had for some years acted as a bridge between national governments and international appearances. As that rare bird, an English-speaking Nationalist MP, and a not-undistinguished academic to boot, Dr Worrall had been banished from South Africa for daring to suggest that at some unspecified future date blacks might have a degree of parliamentary representation. He served only two years of his sentence as Ambassador to Australia before being transferred to London, where he made a brave effort to present the reasonable face of Nationalism. Telephoning Askin, Worrall said that he had met 'at a very high level' with Absa and that he had 'made a telephone call to somebody in importance in this matter' which Askin took to be Anton Rupert. Dr Worrall explained that he had been mandated by both Diedericks and Aldworth to resolve their disputes. But this could not be done without Askin's co-operation. Askin, said Worral, was the key to the situation. There was, he added 'a general helplessness at Absa regarding Askin'. They simply didn't know what to do about the situation any more, or how to get out of it. He was in 'no doubt' that they wanted a settlement and that one could be agreed.

Askin's reply was non-committal. Worrall had exerted himself to convince Askin not to make it a 'Boer–Brit' struggle, which, as Askin's support was coming from such Afrikaners as Diedericks and Claasen and increasingly from the liquidators, was certainly not his intention. It remained true however that Absa had inherited all the traditions of the Broederbond-controlled banks and their management, often themselves former Brothers, were implicated in the illegalities that had been so common.

In July Askin's lawyers served writs in the London High Court on

Absa, Bankorp and named executives, which included Cronjé and his predecessor Piet Badenhorst, alleging fraud, misrepresentation, material non-disclosure and wrongful indictment. In a personal statement Julian Askin said, 'I have been described as a fugitive from justice and I have long said that I would be prepared to face any charges brought in a British court. I am now seeking justice for myself in a British court.'

The Reserve Bank was also coming under heavier fire. On 6 August the *Financial Mail*'s cover carried a portrait of Dr Stals captioned 'The Beleagured Governor and the Rand'. The *Mail and Guardian*'s headline (26 July) was 'Stals Stays Tjoepstil' (dead quiet). Criticising the 'Governor's apparent decision to opt for silence', the paper suggested that 'a proper response would be for a full judicial enquiry to investigate this tale' (of the secret decision to hand out money to an ailing bank).

It was by then known that Bob Aldworth's account of his struggle with Absa would appear in book form, and would certainly contain much critical material. When, a few days prior to publication, Absa demanded that Miller Gruss cease to represent the liquidators, it seemed that the bank was thrashing around in panic. This move was apparently made because after three years Absa had decided that there was an intolerable conflict of interest. The immediate effect was to push the liquidators, Wallace and Glaum, more decisively into the Askin camp.

The Infernal Tower, under Bob Aldworth's name but substantially re-written by Jeremy Gordin and Benjamin Trisk, appeared early in October. The book covered not only Aldworth's story, but those of Askin, Diedericks and Claasen in relation to their treatment by Absa. It was an immediate success, and stimulated more criticism of Absa. 'And these men ask to manage our money' was the title of one review by David Gleason, who went on to say that the book 'reveals sinews of wickedness which left me worried and thoughtful about the depths of the malaise which grips South African business and bankers. Where else, in God's name, is it possible to read that really serious bankers tap the phones of their employees and devise scurrilous actions deliberately designed to make women believe that their husbands are being unfaithful?' Gleason wrote of a 'web of deception, duplicity and dishonour.'

At least Absa were able to claim one victim when on 18 December Judges van Zyl and Conradie decided to accept Absa's petition to sack Bernard Hoberman.

Their decision was in keeping with the judicial standards previously set by Judge Berman. Absa's claims were swallowed, hook, line and sinker, in spite of much evidence to the contrary, although the judges were probably never shown the relevant papers. They decided there was no merit in Diedericks's meticulously prepared charges, which were dismissed as 'certain allegations attributed to one Diedericks, a former managing director of Tollgate' – never mentioning the highly relevant fact that Hennie Diedericks had also been a managing director of both Volkskas and Trust Bank, and a senior executive of Absa. 'Bankorp', the judges decided, 'was to supply a list of debtors as potential "passengers" on the lifeboat' whose debts would be written off against the financial aid covered by the 'lifeboat'. Tollgate was at no stage such a "passenger" and no portion of its debts was ever written off in this way'

The judgement was heavy with innuendo and loaded remark. Aldworth was 'an erstwhile banker'; Hennie Bredenkamp was 'one Bredenkamp', although Cronjé was respectfully alluded to as 'Dr Cronjé'. 'Devious allegations of impropriety and irregularities committed by major role players in the financial and banking world . . . gave rise to an almost hysterical response . . . it must have become clear, at a very early stage of this investigation, that the allegations relating to the "lifeboat" were wholly unsubstantiated, irrelevant and devoid of merit.'

It was clear that the judges had not spoken to brother Rabie, who could have told them of the 'simulated' transaction in the CIB case, nor looked up Berman's ruling that such a transaction was fraudulent. But it was good, comforting encouragement to Absa at a time when this was much needed. On 18 December their erstwhile counsel and present bugbear, Hoberman, was sacked and retired from his legal practice, an embittered and disappointed man. His replacement was the ancient Mr Justice Browde, who apparently then settled down to a good sleep, with no sign of progress in the enquiry being visible for some time. It was an appointment much to Absa's satisfaction; the bank volunteered to pay for the expenses of the enquiry, which included the fees of Mr Browde himself.

But Absa's victory was pyrrhic. Too much had already come out of the closet and more looked certain to follow. On hearing the news of the judgement David Gleason recorded (*Finance Week* 15 January 1997) that his 'blood pressure went into orbit ... These are judges who don't much care for a probing press ... the impression I have is that the press must report what those in authority told it'. Judge van Zyl had said that Hoberman should have cautioned himself against the 'lifeboat hysteria.' Gleason commented, 'here is a judge who had taken it upon himself to disregard an event of major importance'. The cloak of secrecy which had surrounded the whole subject was nothing more than a 'charade'.

Aldworth's trial was still to come, and Absa's charges against the unlucky Aldworth had been prepared in March 1993. Aldworth surrendered himself in December 1995, when a fairly speedy trial might therefore have been expected, especially since, in February 1996, the Witwatersrand Attorney-General's office had told Aldworth they would only be proceeding with one charge. Each South African province has its own Attorney-General, at that time all appointees of Nationalist governments. Standards of performance vary considerably, but none appear very proficient. It has taken five years for Mr Kahn, Attorney-General of the Western Cape, who would be responsible for any action against Askin, *not* to get a case to court. In an effort perhaps to improve his performance, Mr Kahn approached the counsel acting for Tollgate liquidators to assist in drawing up charges against Askin: very properly the counsel refused such a gross conflict of interest.

His colleague in Johannesburg was luckier. When a charge sheet was eventually presented to Bob Aldworth's lawyers in May 1996, it was so inaccurate and incoherent that it was forthwith rejected by them. Five months later, in October, ten months after Aldworth had first presented himself to the courts, a second, more professional, charge sheet was produced. It then emerged, after much prevarication, that the charges, presented in theory by a senior law officer, had in fact been drawn up by none other than the lawyer who was acting for Absa in defending Aldworth's civil action, and who had obviously been given documents by Absa that were not available to the Attorney-General. It further transpired that this work had been paid for by Absa's solicitors, Routledge and Macullum. It was a totally improper and unjust situation that ought never to have been countenanced; and Aldworth was told that his trial must be postponed again, until early the following year.

Similar delays, feebly explained, were appearing in the case against

Askin. Although the barrage of verbal abuse continued, although more intermittently, no progress was made in formulating charges. These remained the bulky, but poorly prepared accusations that had had prompted Judge Berman's remarks and secured Askin's provisional sequestration, none of which, it was well-understood, would bear the light of legal scrutiny. The failure to make any real attempt to extradite Askin was increasingly manifest, although many journalists failed to appreciate the point.

In June 1996 the indefatigable Jeremy Woods wrote, 'the South African office of Interpol is renewing its efforts to bring former Tollgate boss Julian Askin back to South Africa ... A report on Julian Askin was completed by the Office for Serious Economic Offences nine months ago and handed to Cape Attorney-General Frank Kahn, who then started extradition proceedings. Kahn was quoted as saying, "We would like the British to be more co-operative. Negotiations have been going on through the relevant channels".'

Three months later Linda Ensor reported (28 October) 'The Western Cape Attorney-General's office is proceeding with its application to have ... Julian Askin extradited from the UK.' A staff member, Billy Darner, 'could not indicate when the application could be brought'. This, it should be noticed, was *three years* after the original allegation, a period in which Askin had been subjected to a series of scurrilous attacks.*

It seemed that after another two years nothing had been done, indicating that the Cape authorities knew full well, but would not admit, that they had no case. Askin's detractors chose to ignore the fact that on 10 October the Corte di Cassazione finally decided, as it had done on the two previous occasions, that his arrest was illegal. The only legal way forward for the South African authorities remained the application to the UK for the extradition that they were so unwilling to pursue.

The chances of this ever happening, which had not been improved by the scandal of Absa's tampering with the state's case against Aldworth, were diminished further by another legal blunder on the bank's part. A case alleging credit card misuse had been brought by them against a

---

* It later transpired that the excited noises made about Askin's arrest being handled through Interpol were groundless. A senior source within South African Interpol confirmed that Askin's name had never appeared on any Interpol list in 1993/4 or since. Woods and other journalists were simply being fed stories by Absa and their friends in the legal system.

travel agent, Lee-Ann Moch. In her defence, Miss Moch subpoenaed Piet Badenhorst. When the sheriff's officer's arrived at his home with the summons Mrs Badenhorst told them that Badenhorst was dead and produced a death certificate – which turned out to be that of Badenhorst's father. Diedericks, who was assisting Miss Moch, confirmed that he had seen an Absa document on which Cronjé had scrawled 'Hang her', and had in his possession another bank internal document which said 'Fuck him' in reference to another Absa client, a medical man. These interesting snippets can be compared with Absa's statement in its annual report that it conducts its business 'with uncompromising integrity and fairness so as to promote complete trust and confidence' and that its relationships 'with the regulatory authorities, clients, competitors, employees' etc. were conducted in accordance with the Council of Bankers' code of good banking practice.

Absa was in continuing trouble with the liquidators, who were by now convinced that the bank had secured themselves at the expense of the other creditors. In July 1997 David Gleason returned to the charge. Protesting against the secrecy imposed by Commissioner Browde, he remarked that Absa's conduct – the bank had applied, as was their wont, to have the liquidators' lawyer removed – was 'getting to be a procession which smacks of a persecution complex or concern that issues may emerge which some parties believe better left buried.'

Absa's increasing unhappiness was evinced by David Brink's remarks in another of Millennium's articles, 'Sinners and Bankers'. On the deception of Askin at the time of the Tollgate acquisition, chairman Brink claimed 'for a banker to say to a potential buyer, just watch out, you're about to buy a load of crap, well, that is just not done', a remark which shows either gross ignorance or cavalier disregard of banking decencies, as well as that inelegancy of expression that seemed so common among the bank's senior executives. Another comment that 'I don't think the SARB has even given a lifeboat to an insolvent bank: it does so to address liquidity problems. Solvency must be there. The Reserve Bank wouldn't behave imprudently' betrays breathtaking innocence on the part of Mr Brink. Trust Bank was not just insolvent: it was dead in the water before the Reserve Bank's lifeboat was launched.

CHAPTER TEN

Absa in the Ascendant?

Absa go to market

Hoberman's dismissal removed one major irritant from Absa, offering the prospect of calmer waters ahead for 1997. Signs that the Askin network was falling apart were also beginning to appear. In his deposition to the British court, as part of the case he had launched against Absa, Askin had quoted Christo Wiese of the Reserve Bank reporting that Piet Badenhorst had vowed to 'fuck Askin up'. Hugh Murray, editor of *Millennium*, who had recorded the remark and passed on this information to Askin, was worried: it wasn't just Wiese who was retailing Badenhorst's views:

> This was a global, or it you like, a Southern Africa discussion. I mean I can tell you it was a bloody . . . it was a bad joke. And I can tell you that everybody knew that and you put Christo Wiese's name in that story, you could have put anybody's name. You could put Johan Rupert, you could put Steinmetz, you could put Hennie Diedericks, you could put Johan Claasen, you can put Hugh Murray, you can put Paul Bell, you can put Ken Owen, and you can put any of these guys, Nigel Bruce, any one of those guys will have said substantially the same, coming from which ever side of the bloody fence you might care. So they all reflect the one thing, which is that Piet Badenhorst was walking around saying he was going to fuck you up.'

Wiese, while he did not deny having told Murray of Piet Badenhorst's expression objected to being singled out as an informant, and he was in a powerful enough position to make life uncomfortable for Murray, who continued:

> Let me just say to you right now, that I couldn't give a continental of what comes out of those tapes. I will tell you he will deny it and I will have to have nothing to do with it. And that's all there is to it. What'll happen there, very simply is that you will actually alienate yourself from everybody who has ever been remotely interested in championing your cause because we happen to believe in you. But I can tell you that belief will disappear down the bloody plug very very quickly . . .
>
> . . . I've been hung out to dry by every bloody guy in Afrikaans business. I'm hated and loathed by Johan Rupert now . . . I've lost an enormous amount of bloody money as a result of this thing. If I say enormous I can't believe it. I mean when we totted up the bloody contracts, it's pushing nearly two million since this thing began. Two million is a serious margin in this little business of ours. And you can kind of . . . I have actually stuck with this thing because I've believed you and I've never done anything underhand.

Murray was referring to the advertising revenue his publication had lost as Absa's friends had cancelled contracts. The combination of these losses and the fears of libel actions meant that *Millennium*, which had been of great service to Askin's cause in revealing so much of the chicanery of the 'guys at the Afrikaner bank', could not be depended on in the future.

Absa, on the other hand seemed brimming with self confidence. The speedy action in securing the removal of Hoberman before he had the opportunity to refer to the missing minutes had been successful. The new Commissioner, Judge Browde, was successfully discouraged by the bank from reading through the previous papers which included many unanswered charges against Absa. Acting for Absa, their solicitors, Werksmans, assured the Commissioner that acquainting himself with the facts would be a waste of time; their barristers, Jeremy Gauntlett and Gavin Woodland, would feed the judge with what information they considered relevant; an assurance which the aged judge apparently accepted.

As they had done at the beginning of Hoberman's tenure of office, Absa attempted to quell the liquidators' independence by instructing them that there were to be no conversations with Browde except in the presence of an Absa representative. That initiative was less successful, since, for their part, van Zyl objected strongly and Wallace declared his intention to insist that both the lifeboat and the influence of Absa in the Tollgate liquidation must be investigated.

Claasen was dealt with, for the moment, by Absa's saddling him with a R200 million claim, with the obvious intention of making it impossible for him to continue fighting his own case against the bank. The summons, issued on 21 January 1997 alleged that during Claasen's tenure of office in Tollgate, which was defined as being between 3 June 1987 to 13 June 1990, various offences were committed. These included false statements to the Reserve Bank relating to the purchase of the Lear executive jet aircraft, and failure to repay Motorvia for the initial instalment. Ironically, as Absa must have known, it was Askin who, when the aeroplane purchase transaction was discovered, ensured that the money was repaid. Other allegations included one that Claasen and Diedericks, in July 1989, paid Key R36 million to ensure the maintenance of the Tollgate share price. A second irony was that this was done with the connivance of Trust Bank officers. Altogether, Claasen was accused of defalcations to a total of 'at least R200 million'.

It can scarcely have missed the attention of Absa's board that these were exactly the offences that Julian Askin had been taxed with, and that they all occurred before he took control and without his knowledge. Absa were also claiming that which they had earlier indignantly denied, that Diedericks was implicated with Claasen in the very offences of which Askin stood accused.

Other moves were, however, being made. At the beginning of January, Michael Oatley, accompanied by Susie, went to Cape Town to begin investigations on the ground.

The new strategy was for Askin to adopt a low profile while CIEX found other sources of information which might be helpful in the case that was being pursued against Absa in London (and which Absa were strenuously attempting to have transferred to South Africa). Oatley had, in his previous service in Southern Africa, gained the confidence of some officials in the South African government and intelligence services, and was able to begin collating much varied information, some of which was highly relevant to Askin's proceedings. These began to flow encouragingly quickly when a Durban lawyer, who had been defending people on drugs charges, had discovered that the anti-drugs unit of the South African Police had been used as a cover for sending 'rogue cops' to work abroad on undercover missions. The considerable financial resources needed were channelled from government sources through, first Volkskas, and then through accounts held in the merged Absa.

Other sources, including the proceedings of the Truth and Reconciliation Commission (TRC) Archbishop Tutu's striking device for avoiding either trials or revenge attacks, produced information regarding financial undercover work. The TRC has been reluctant to bring economic crimes within its purview, a task for which it is badly equipped, but other witnesses had given useful information. Dr Pasques, a civil servant seconded to President Botha's office, formed the company 'Adult Education Consultants' which was to be the cover for the Defence Force's Secret Operations, including military destabilisation and the training of terrorist groups – an ironic form of adult education. At least R165 million of state funds was moved through Adult Education Consultants in the five years before 1990: all of which was done through the Volkskas accounting system. During the trial of Colonel Eugene de Kok, the chief of the Vlakplaas murder squad, it emerged that one of his front companies, 'Honey Badger Arms and Ammunition', had contracted with Absa's chief of security, Brood van Herden, to provide guards. The bank's office furniture store was therefore under the paid protection of the Vlakplaas hit squad: there were no attempted break-ins.

Another senior military intelligence officer, Mariette Hartley, working under the alias Karen Lessing, channelled funds supplied through Dr Cronjé to other front companies, in this instance to Creed Consultants and Topman. Hartley/Lessing was a director of Longreach, a prominent front company, which operated from the Duros building in Sandton, Johannesburg. One of the best-documented operations arranged through these front companies was that code-named 'Marion', which resulted in the murder of the UDF leader Victor Ntuli and twelve others in Janaury 1987. 'Marion' was authorised at the highest level in a State Security Council meeting held on 3 February 1986: it is worth noting that Ambassador Glenn Babb was a member of the State Security Council. Another discovery that appeared at this time was the existence at Volkskas of a block of intelligence services accounts, one of which was denominated 'Executive Services', run by five managers working under chief general manager Jan C. Marais.

Oatley's other main task was to gain access to the South African government in order to ensure that the results of his work were known. Relations at that time between Trevor Manuel, well-settled into his cabinet post, and Dr Stals of the Reserve Bank continued cordial. President Mandela had given up much day-to-day responsibility, moving into his role as world-statesman and regulator of party dissensions. It was Thabo Mbeki, deputy president, due to succeed in spring 1999, who was head of the government.

Mbeki is very much a second generation ANC leader. His father, Govan, who had served a long prison sentence with Nelson Mandela, was an aggressive communist, and it took some time for Mandela and the elder Mbeki to appreciate each other's qualities. Both his parents, prosperous middle-class Xhosa, were educated in Lovedale, that remarkable multi-racial (until Nationalist governments intervened) school.

Thabu was prepared for leadership first at Moscow University followed by a degree course at the almost equally left-wing new university of Sussex. With an impressive personal charm allied to his sure-footed skills as a negotiator, Mbeki was able to bridge the gap between the ANC activists in the townships (and even in the disgruntled guerrilla bush camps) and white politicians and businessmen. Even Pieter de Lange, chairman – although a remarkably enlightened one – of the Broederbond, was susceptible to Mbeki's persuasive qualities, while relatively liberal businessmen such as Gavin Relly of Anglo-American found him a relaxed, pipe-smoking kindred spirit. No one had done as much as Mbeki to bring about the 1994 settlement other than Mandela himself, and his agreement was essential to any possible settlement of the war between Askin and the Afrikaner bankers. Gaining the confidence of the Deputy-President, without at the same time making enemies of other ministers and civil servants was to be a long, but ultimately very successful operation.

One hopeful prospect however was opening up in that contacts were established with the ANC and with the South African Communist Party. For seventy years South African communists had been torn between following the Moscow party line and the imperatives of Marxist dogma and the hard realities of South African politics. Although many, like Govan Mbeki and Joe Slovo had remained faithful Stalinists through the period of the gulags and of the invasions of Hungary and Czechoslovakia, others had abandoned formal Communism, but all had been active against apartheid. More cohesive and often better educated than the ANC activists, Communists emerged with credit in the post-1994 world of South Africa, in contrast to their fellows in other countries which had experienced the collapse of Communism.

It seemed that the ANC and SACP had successfully penetrated military intelligence as far back as 1983 and had been able to collect many critical documents. Their intention was to leave these undisclosed until the Truth and Reconciliation Commission had finished its work towards the end of 1998, when hundreds of criminal prosecutions would be started against those who had illegally amassed money abroad. At least two specific investigations had already been initiated – that concerning Wouter Basson and another into the Helderberg air crash where it is thought that the plane, carrying 159 civilian passengers and crew, was also loaded with ammonium perchlorate, a highly volatile additive for manufacturing rocket fuel.

More immediate, and pregnant with future trouble for the 'guys at the Afrikaner bank' was the enactment of the Special Investigating Units and Special Tribunals Act of 1996. Under the terms of this act, in March 1997, a special commission was established under Judge Willem Heath to investigate possible fraudulent acts in the public sector. Heath was a younger Afrikaner, twenty years junior to such other judges as van Zyl and Conradie or Rabie. Born in Boksburg, near Johannesburg, he had been appointed to the bench in 1988 in the last years of the old apartheid regime and served on the Bisho court, in the Ciskei Bantustan. He had made a reputation there as a firm and courageous judge – one of his judgements was the reversal of a decree which had given immunity to the police and soldiers involved in the 1990 Bisho massacre, which opened the way for a number of successful prosecutions. Another judgement formed a landmark in South African judicial history when in 1992 he ruled that a man may be charged with the rape of his wife. A quiet, self-contained man, Heath was a member of the Church of the Latter Day Saints, the Mormons, and had no share in the classic tradition of the Dutch Reformed Church-Broederbond establishment which had lain at the core of Nationalist policies.

The commission was given wide powers of selection, investigation and subpoena. Specific investigations had to be permitted by presidential ordinance, but, in the earlier days at any rate, there was no question of this being refused. Once the evidence had been collected the case was presented, not through the creaking machinery of the ordinary courts, but to a special tribunal which could impose the seizure of assets, including overseas bank accounts, and order money to be repaid to the taxpayer. In its first year the astonishing figure of 90,000 cases had been brought to the commission's attention, and some had been already processed.

The actual reimbursements made had not been great – the best-known being the investigation into the Ciskeian auditor-general's office, where, a few weeks before the elections, the results of which would signal the end of Ciskeian independence, 92 staff members awarded themselves considerable pay increases and promotions. Heath referred the matter to the tribunal, insisting that the amounts overpaid should be refunded. The sum saved was estimated at R4 million, but it could be argued that much greater future savings had been made. When the prospect of very large recoveries from the Reserve Bank, Absa, and its shareholders came into prospect, the Heath Commission was bound to show a lively interest.

There had been criticism of the commission's powers, as taking the bread from the mouths of deserving lawyers and by-passing normal police proceedings although the word 'normal' could hardly be used with any accuracy to describe South African policing. These were countered by the fact that while conventional actions might from time to time ensure successful prosecutions, there was no mechanism for restitution to be made. The judge argued that in Germany, for example, administrative courts of control such as his tribunal had existed for centuries before being suspended by the Nazis, who wanted no restraints on executive power. Since Heath was determinedly 'colour blind', there was also a rising tide of nervousness among some ANC members and sympathisers who were doing well out of their new access to the gravy boats, a nervousness that was to become more noticeable as the commission proved itself effective.

President Mandela, however, who had no tolerance for corruption wherever it might be found, gave a boost to Judge Heath's work and indicated the direction it might take when speaking at the funeral of an ANC member in August. 'We are not dealing with an individual or just a small group of criminals. We are dealing with experienced political criminals in command of huge resources ... We are dealing with a highly co-ordinated network of people deployed in state organs.'

For the time being, however, Absa was in the ascendant, and in June 1997 felt confident enough to launch another funding exercise similar to that which it had had to abandon twelve months earlier. This was to be an offer for sale of some 18 million ordinary shares at a price of $US6.64 each, which made a total of $US120 million, a very significant sum for Absa. Three years of rising profits enabled such an offer to be made, although the profits for 1995 and 1994 had shown only the most modest advances since 1993.

	1993	1994	1995	1996
Net income after exceptional items (R million)	684	666	774	1026
earnings per share	126.6	109.3	133.3	196.1

These figures, incidentally, give the lie to chairman Brink's excuse for withdrawing the previous year's projected offer: the earnings growth since 1993, less the 7 cents per share, with 1994 actually showing a considerable drop in earnings, simply did not justify a public offer. And there was all that distressing publicity.

The 1997 offer was entrusted to Merrill Lynch International, together with ING Barings, Deutsche Morgan Grenfell, Hongkong and Shanghai Banking Corporation Investment Bank, UBS, Robert Fleming and J. P. Morgan. These are some of the best names in international finance:

Merrill Lynch, 'the thundering herd' is the world's largest broking firm. ING Barings, Deutsche Morgan Grenfell and HSBC Investment Bank combined the weight of the new owners with the experience of those banks they had rescued from distress or failure – Barings, Morgan Grenfell and the Midland – while UBS and JP Morgan were internationally prominent. (It is noteworthy that Barings and Morgan Grenfell, two of the oldest and most-respected London banks, were given no lifeboats to save them from failure: it was, as it should have been with Bankorp, up to the banking community to step in).

To Hennie Diedericks and others it was unthinkable that Merrill Lynch, a firm which in the United States prides itself on the opportunities for advancement given to American blacks in its programme of positive discrimination, should be financing the financial bastion of apartheid, which had been accused of so many dirty tricks and even, occasionally, convicted. Danie Cronjé and Alwyn Noëth, of telephone tapping fame, were prominent in the list of executive directors. A third, Caspar Louw van Wyck, was found by the Supreme Court to have been responsible for bringing an action which was rejected since his executives had been proved 'such accomplished liars'. This concerned Absa's attempted denial of a contract that existed with one David Hirsch; it was only when – in an echo of Hoberman's action – Absa were forced to produce their minute books that the existence of a meeting (attended by van Wyck) that all had been denying, was proved. Of a fourth executive committee member (there *were* only six) Jean Jacques Brown, *Noseweek* wrote on 21 March 1998 that his conduct was 'not only dishonest; it was probably criminal as well'. But since Judge Sutherland's decision on van Wyck was only reached on 30 July it was too late to affect the Merrill Lynch offer document which appeared on the 15th even had that company wished to do so. It is however noteworthy that Absa did not include the David Hirsch case in their list of those they were fighting.

Diedericks accordingly wrote on 3 June 1997 'as a concerned South African' to Guy Dawson, in charge of the issue at Merrill Lynch:

> During 1992 I was appointed Chief Executive of Volkskas Bank and Trust Bank, the principal operating divisions of Absa Bank Ltd. I left the bank at the end of 1992 to take up the position of Managing Director of the South African Post Office.

You may or may not be aware that Absa is being sued in the London High Court for fraud and misrepresentation. Preliminary matters have commenced in the High Court today. It is my understanding that in affidavits and exhibits submitted to the London High Court, it has been claimed that Dr Danie Cronjé, the current Absa Group Chief Executive, was the only man entrusted with the holding and disbursements of funds allocated to the Directorate of Covert Collection (DCC) and South African Special Forces. These funds were apparently administered from Absa Bank accounts and are to become the subject of investigation by the Truth and Reconciliation Commission which is investigating the crimes of the old Apartheid State. In affidavits and exhibits entered into the court, it is apparently claimed that Dr Cronjé has extensive knowledge of all the covert organisations and front companies established by the DCC. As you may be aware, many of these front companies were involved in numerous acts of murder and destabilisation which have already been reported to the Truth and Reconciliation Commission.

As a previous Chief Executive of Volkskas I must emphasise that I had absolutely no knowledge of this and am horrified to think that the Bank could have been used for such appalling purposes. It reflects most unfortunately on the many loyal and long serving employees of the bank.

He went on to remind Dawson of the appointment of the Heath commission:

You may or may not be aware that a Special Investigating Unit created under Republic of South Africa – Act No 74 of 1996 (Proclamation – 14 March 1997) – has been requested to investigate the controversial secret rescue package or 'lifeboat', which the South African Reserve Bank extended to the Absa Group up to 1995. The allegations are that it constitutes an unlawful and gross misappropriation of state related funds (in excess of R2 billion) and lends itself to uncommercial decisions by Absa which led to devastating unnecessary losses for certain of their customers. This matter will most likely enter the international arena in the near future.

You may or may not be aware that Dr Cronjé is presently under investigation by the Attorney-General of Gauteng for statutory perjury.

(This was a reference to the fact that Dr Cronjé had asserted in a formal affidavit that he had never been a director of Volkskas; this was untrue, and had been claimed by Dr Cronjé to have been a mistake.)

Diedericks reminded Mr Dawson that only the previous day the Tollgate liquidators had petitioned that Absa claims be set aside and concluded:

> I am writing to you to urge you, to establish whether these claims have merit and to examine the documentation submitted so far to the London High Court. It is my understanding that further corroborative documentation will be surfacing over the coming months.
>
> I am concerned that should you go ahead without establishing the facts of these matters, South Africa's attractions as a potential investment area for international investors will be damaged.

It is believed that Diedericks's written approach (to which he received no answer) was supplemented by a personal and authoritative briefing given to the London chairman, Christopher Reeves, but it is not clear that any investigative work at all was done by Merrill Lynch, in spite of the warnings received. Certainly no mention was made of the publicly acknowledged role of Cronjé and Noëth in the telephone tapping incident, nor any mention of the role that Volkskas had played in the whole business of financing illegalities throughout the apartheid era. When I attempted in June 1998 to talk with Mr Dawson, or with Richard Silverman, in charge of corporate relations, neither letters nor telephone calls were answered. The City of London being usually a courteous sort of place, this was unusual and can be taken as a sign that Merrill Lynch were decidedly reluctant to discuss the matter. The question why invites some unpleasing conjectures.

Certainly Julian Askin's letter to all the city firms implicated in the Absa issue ought to have caused some discomfort. In it he said: 'We live in a world of corporate governance where shareholders have an expectation that the Board of Directors will ensure at all times that management does operate with clean hands. Its need to do this becomes even more relevant in a new South Africa which seeks to take its place on the international stage.'

Not that the offer document was sparing in its revelations of the cases brought against Absa: by Claasen, by Diedericks to the Heath Commission, by Gilbey's Distillers, by the Premier Group, and by other unnamed plaintiffs. These were all dismissed as without foundation: on the lifeboat question the bank claimed that it 'is satisfied that its conduct, and, so far as it is aware, Bankorp's conduct, in relation to the "lifeboat" has been entirely proper.'

It is true that the Merrill Lynch placing of Absa shares was not, as the City phrases it, a widows and orphans issue, where security and transparency are essential, but rather aimed at sophisticated, large-scale investors who could be assumed to have a fairly relaxed attitude towards questions of morality. Nevertheless, the City of London generally prefers that the decencies should be observed.

The Absa share issue was successful, and in fact oversubscribed, although in one of life's little ironies it lost a good deal of money for those who bought the shares. A year later Absa shares were trading for the rand equivalent of just over four and a half dollars; Merrill Lynch's investors have lost about $35 million of their $120 million, and look like doing rather worse in the future, which must make it one of that firm's less happy recommendations, and go some way towards explaining their reticence.

Absa in court

Absa's good fortune in the matter of their cash influx was reinforced by two reverses for Askin. In the first, his case in the British High Court against Absa was dismissed. His lawyers had hoped to convince the judge that it was not only right that the case should be heard in London but that a safe hearing could not be expected in South Africa. The court was not so persuaded, and ruled that the case should be transferred to South Africa. It was conceded that the English courts could have jurisdiction, but that the balance of convenience indicated that South Africa should be preferred.

The English bench of judges (the Scottish system and habits are markedly different) has its peculiarities. Judges are appointed for life, as long as they behave themselves (*quamdiu se bene gesserint*) and the standard of acceptable behaviour is generously stretched. Only in exceptional cases are judges asked to leave (one, in the last fifteen years). Discourtesy, eccentric sentences, and such minor matters are dealt with by a quiet reprimand. In this way English judges are insulated to a high degree from government pressure and therefore able to act independently, often indeed in opposition to the expressed wishes of the executive.

They are also, as a class, remarkably difficult to bribe. Many have accepted considerable financial disadvantages in moving from the bar to the bench: a good barrister or solicitor earns many times the annual salary of even the most senior of judges. Since English law relies to a high degree on precedent – the decisions of previous judges – the bench is much attached to custom, and reluctant to abandon traditional modes. When trial by battle was abolished in the 1820s judicial views were raised in its defence, and the continued attachment to wigs and robes is a notable feature of an English court.

With the expansion of the British Empire, English common law has spread over the world. The United States accepts common law as the foundation of its system, and most Commonwealth countries, including India, have followed. Judges from Commonwealth countries – especially, it should be said, white Commonwealth countries – are regarded with motherly respect by English judges: at least given the benefit of the doubt! As part of a great tradition Commonwealth lawyers take pride in their passage through the Inns of Court and often through the ancient universities. Mohandas Gandhi, Pandit Nehru, Jan Smuts and Martinus Steyn are only some of the leaders who qualified as English lawyers. At least two of the most senior and respected of British judges, members of the judicial committee of the House of Lords, are South African by birth, refugees from apartheid law.

South African law differs from that of England in many civil matters, where it follows the Roman-Dutch system, and recognises some features of traditional customary law. But in criminal practice the law in South Africa, which owes much to the Rose Innes family, is parallel to that of England. English judges, especially those with no experience of South Africa, tend to assume that similar standards of judicial behaviour apply.

In this they are mistaken. During the nineteenth century, in Cape Colony, the bench was active in restraining colonial excesses and in preventing many abuses of the non-white population. Blacks and whites were punished in the same way for the same offences, dangling side by side from the same gallows in the days of public executions. This was never so in the Dutch-speaking republics and very rare in the other British colony of Natal. After the Act of Union judicial practice tended to become more partial, although as late as 1950, a Supreme Court was able to mount a spirited defence of non-white rights against governments determined to introduce apartheid legislation.

With the insistence by successive Nationalist governments in packing every branch of the executive with Afrikaners the judiciary was not spared. English-speaking judges became rarer, and fewer of these felt able to stand up for common law rights. Law, it was claimed with some justification, was decreed in a sovereign elected assembly, and it was the duty of the judiciary to give effect to this law following the clearly-expressed desire of parliament. Many Afrikaner judges continued to uphold more liberal principles – the Treason trial of 1956–61, mounted as a show trial by the Fascist sympathiser Oswald Pirow, pressed on for five years and ended in farce when the Afrikaner Judge Rumpff dismissed all the charges, and Nelson Mandela walked free.

Over the near half-century of apartheid governments white, and especially Afrikaner, society tightened into its laager. English judges tend, even today, to be recruited from a small segment of the middle classes, who frequently adhere to the same standards and accept similar values. Under apartheid, South African judges were even more homogeneous.

Askin was disappointed when it was ruled that the case could not go ahead in England, but he was given the right to ask for an appeal against the judgement, so the war continued.

The next engagement was on 29 October, when the right to appeal was considered. It met with the same lack of comprehension. When it was stated that Absa was the largest bank in South Africa an immediate mental comparison was made with Barclays, in British minds still the big South African bank. To those without much knowledge of South African history the close interweaving of the apartheid state and the Afrikaner banks was incomprehensible. Nor could the English judges think too badly of their Italian brethren; one knew what happened in countries like that! But in spite of it all Askin was given the leave to appeal one more time, with the case to be heard some time the following year.

One valuable ally however dropped out. Hugh Murray of *Millennium*, with Paul Bell responsible for most of the investigative work, had striven consistently for two years to bring the facts to light, and generally adopted a sympathetic attitude to Askin, Diedericks, Claasen, and, later Hoberman in their complaints against Absa. But in the issue of August 1997 Murray made a sharp about-turn. Threatened with a legal action his financially stressed publication could ill afford, he published an apology to Glenn Babb, who had been accused in the magazine of 'curious behaviour' which seemed 'decidedly unambassadorial'. Murray had been obliged to settle this for R40,000, and was looking financial dissolution in the face. As part of the settlement he had been obliged to publish an editorial not only retracting any slurs on Babb, but also judged it prudent to withdraw his previously expressed support for Askin, justifying this by accusing Askin of not providing him with facts to support his previous articles, especially that concerning Babb. Maureen Barnes commented in *Noseweek* with heavy irony:

> In a lengthy and convoluted diatribe Murray, in the guise of intrepid reporter confessing to an honest error, ditches Askin and his cause and repudiates the months of enthusiastic support he gave to the businessman. In the midst of his vituperative attack on his former friend – thinly veiled in mea-culpa rhetoric – Murray reveals that he published material in *Millennium* on matters for which he had not seen any evidence. Then he does the journalistically even more unthinkable. He blames his source for this oversight, denouncing him in tones more reminiscent of a betrayed Victorian spinster than a hotshot publisher.

It is tempting to speculate on the nature of the pressure which brought Murray to perform this despicable act. But whatever the reason or incentive, he has made Askin's contention that he is unlikely to get a fair trial in this country more valid than ever.

Another development was emerging, more encouraging to Askin and potentially extremely dangerous to Absa. More well-documented cases of fraud had been disclosed in South Africa than was reasonable, many said to implicate members of the government or senior civil servants. On 7 November 1997 Mr Justice Hendrick Nel, sitting with Judge R. Cleaver and Mr H. D. Collier produced his report on the 'Affairs of the Masterbond Group and Investor Protection in South Africa', requested some years previously by President de Klerk. Unlike Merrill Lynch's offer of Absa shares, Masterbond was very much a widows and orphans affair, and the collapse of the company in 1991 had ruined many small investors. The Commissioners went, as their mandate required, well beyond the administration of the Masterbond group, and of the banks most closely associated with it, the CIB and the Pretoria Bank. Inevitably (dealt with on pp.204ff), there was widespread fraud and lax administration within the companies, but the real sting of the Nel report lay in its revelations of the serious faults in the regulatory infrastructure.

The sins of the Registrar of Banks, Dr van Greuning, have already been discussed. Nel drew attention to his counterpart, the Registrar of Companies, whose official powers 'created the dangerous delusion that shareholders, investors and creditors of companies are protected by this office . . .' whereas in fact 'the Companies Office has become little more than an antiquated filing room.' There were no inspectors employed, all prospectuses reaching the office merely being stamped and registered by a clerk, which constituted an open invitation to fraud.

As for the 'saga of dishonest or inefficient auditors', it was 'difficult to believe that some of the auditors concerned . . . could have been so inefficient or blatantly dishonest.' The Attorney-General came off almost as badly. Following critical reports on Masterbond a case for prosecution was submitted to the Attorney-General during August 1986. *Three years* later, on 6 July 1989, the Attorney-General informed Masterbond that there would be no prosecution. During this period the Attorney-General had conducted no examination into Masterbond's activities and was therefore in no position to reach such a conclusion. One asks whether this is gross inefficiency or collusion?

Judge Nel was brutally forthright. 'Prosecution of white-collar criminals had become a farce. Save for some high-profile accused, Attorneys-General do little to ensure prosecution. The reasons are lack of staff, incompetence and a general lassitude.' But it was none of these reasons that had prevented, over a period of five years, Attorney-General Kahn from bringing charges that might justify Askin's extradition: it was the fact, mutely acknowledged by the passage of time, that there was no base whatsoever for such charges to be formulated.

The Nel commission did not stop with analysing past misdeeds, but continued sitting in an endeavour to outline a structure in which fraud would be less easy. Their conclusions will doubtless form the subject of much debate, and of these not the least radical is the establishment of formal interest groups. These might consist of suppliers, customers, minority shareholders or others having a legitimate claim to be kept informed of a company's affairs. Such groups, it is proposed, would have the power to appoint their own auditors to produce parallel reports which could supplement those of the auditors appointed by the company's directors. Had such a system been in existence at the time of the Tollgate liquidation, or of the Reserve Bank's lifeboat to Bankorp, the progress of events might have been very different.

CHAPTER ELEVEN

Nemesis Looms

A complex charade

Towards the end of November South Africans, or at least those who read newspapers, are thinking more of the approaching summer holidays than business, and Judge Nel's report took some time to filter through into public consciousness. It was over a month before even the livelier journalists pointed out some of the startling conclusions (and, since the report was more than a thousand pages long, some little time was needed to study it).

Reaction, when it came, was sharp. Brendan Templeton and Jeremy Gordin described the Commission's findings as 'a blistering attack on those elements of the South African financial system designed to protect investors.' Dr Stals' 'startling' evidence and his 'Jesuitical' explanation of the Reserve Bank's donation was duly noted. Deon Basson reported in the *Financial Mail* of 9 January 1998:

> In the dying days of 1997 the first report of the Nel Commission landed on my desk . . .
>
> The report is a well-researched document that will soon become a standard 'reference work' with a long shelf life. It will be used by lawyers, accountants, politicians, academics, students, regulators, consumer groups and journalists . . .
>
> Auditors will increasingly come under the spotlight. I want to focus now on a situation where auditors are compromised unnecessarily by the 'system'.
>
> I refer to the so-called simulated transactions (lifeboats) entered into by the Bank with certain banks. The Nel Com-

mission mentions Cape Investment Bank, Prima Bank and Bankorp.

Technical details about these transactions have been published before, so I won't repeat them.

What is important, though, is the accounting consequences of these transactions. Though each transaction created an income stream, not one was ever accounted for . . .

But the problem is there has never been a proper framework for the public disclosure of these simulated transactions. Disclosure to date has largely been the result of public pressure or Section 417 inquiries following the liquidations of banks or their debtors.

The Bank has consistently sheltered behind Section 33 of the Reserve Bank Act which prohibits it from giving details about its clients (banks).

It's time to formulate clear policy requiring the bank and the banks concerned to publish details about the simulated transactions as soon as the crisis has passed.

David Gleason, who had been following the whole story closely and critically, was acerbic. Remarking the mysterious R5 million payment made to the Prima Bank directors, Nel had said: 'it is obvious that important aspects of the evidence of Stals (as reflected in Hansard) are contradicted by the evidence which was led in the secret Prima Bank inquiry'. Gleason commented:

This is legal shorthand for saying either Stals dissembled when he gave evidence to Parliament or his officials lied under oath during the Prima Bank 417 inquiry.

The lifeboat loans to Bankorp/Absa are dealt with at length. Stals told yet another secret 417 Commission of Inquiry, this time into the affairs of Tollgate Holdings, that the loans made to Bankorp and Absa between 1985 and 1995 were at all times recorded in the (Bank's) books, were regularly audited by the Bank's internal and external auditors and were included in the published financial statements of the Bank.

Given the finding of Judge Rabie that these were not loans but simulated transactions, this suggests Stals and the Bank's compliant auditors put in place a complex charade which was swallowed by the Bank's directors.

It is now beyond dispute that these disclosures were handled in a manner which ensured they were cloaked from public inspection. And Nel pointedly makes it plain that 'the auditors of the recipient (Bankorp and Absa) would also have been aware of the true state of affairs.'

At the same time a possible solution to the lifeboat scandal, as it had now become, was being canvassed. Absa was by now proved, beyond any reasonable doubt, to have benefited from an enormous, and probably illegal, gift of taxpayers' funds. Would it not be prudent, and avoid much unpleasantness if restitution could be made in some elegant fashion, such as funding a 'People's Bank' for South Africa? This could be a non-profit making operation, funded by Absa, with some contribution perhaps being made by Nedbank and their controlling shareholders, the Old Mutual, the only other beneficiaries of lifeboats (as far as was known, since the truth about all of these useful vessels has yet to be revealed).

Indications were emerging from Absa that such a move might be welcome. Speaking to that invaluable intermediary, the cantankerous roadbuilder Hennie Bredenkamp, Christo Faul had asked for a written report (on 25 November 1997) recommending 'how the Tollgate Holdings affair might be handled! into the future'. A few weeks later Bredenkamp had a long meeting with Kobus Roetz, the former managing director of Trust Bank. Roetz had said

that there was great confusion and apprehension within Absa at present. They didn't know how to deal with, or get out of, the implications of the secret lifeboats. They were also afraid that there were too many skeletons that might come out with it. Matters were not going well at Absa. There were additionally major computer software and hardware problems and staff had been forced to work throughout the Christmas period in an attempt to correct matters and cover them up. The senior man involved had resigned. Brink was glad to leave the chairmanship of Absa. He had attempted to act as a Mr Clean, but had become increasingly compromised by 'the skeletons that were falling out of just about every cupboard he opened. Brink believed that he was becoming tainted and getting further out of his depth. The new executive Board appointments bring in four more Broeders around Cronjé. The latter has no strategy or policy other than trying to keep the lid on absolutely everything in the hope that Absa can outlast and outspend any opposition.

There were also sound political reasons for Absa's anxiety. The once-solid Afrikaner laager was disintegrating: the National party splitting, F. W. de Klerk resigning from the coalition government, and new alliances being formed. Political pressure within South Africa was building up as interest in the damning criticisms of so important an institution as the Reserve Bank were disseminated. Hennie Diedericks had been approached towards the end of September 1997 by Bantu Holomisa and Roelof Meyer to brief them on the subject. The first important National Party member to convert to the acceptance of majority rule, Meyer had been a key figure in joint negotiations with Cyril Ramaphosa which led to the entente between Mandela and de Klerk.

One of the seven National Party ministers in the 1994 coalition government, Meyer had become disenchanted at the lack of National Party unity, allying himself with 'General' Holomisa. Head of the Transkei Defence Force, Holomisa was regarded as one of the most able and least corrupt members of the Transkei government. In 1989 he headed a coup against the little-regretted government of that homeland, and began negotiations for its reintegration into South Africa, but found himself also out of sympathy with the ANC. Holomisa and Meyer were about to commence the formation of a new political party, and wanted Diedericks to provide them with information regarding the lifeboat, which they intended to use to criticise both the Nationalist government for allowing it, and the new government for doing nothing about it.

Ex-President Botha seemed to embody the old order's decay as he sulkily refused to appear before the Truth and Reconciliation Commission. It was an extraordinary spectacle. Anywhere else in Africa a displaced and largely disgraced politician (there is no doubt as to Botha's active and enthusiastic participation in the most heinous activities of the Total Strategy, confirmed by the Truth and Reconciliation

Commission's report in October 1998) would either be living in luxury abroad, or dead. In South Africa Botha continued to live in comfort, on a state pension, able to use any legal methods of avoiding punishment. The re-named Broederbond had reverted to assume the character of its less rigid predecessor, the Afrikanerbond, and its restrictions on membership were relaxed, but a hard core of members continued at their regular meetings – that at Easter was the most important and closely-guarded. With many difficulties still strewn in the way the new South Africa was inching forward.

President Mandela, having shed the incubus of Winnie Mandela (also condemned by the TRC), was happily married to Graca Machel and settling into the role of a much-admired international elder statesman. At home his great personal authority was deployed to support Thabu Mbeki, upon whom was devolving the greater part of government work; a responsibility he was carrying with unruffled aplomb.

The Askin campaign was able to begin the new year of 1998 on an optimistic note. Michael Oately was now commuting almost weekly between Africa and London, reviving his old African ties, discovering new sources of intelligence and, a matter of prime importance, establishing communications with the government. For these to be effective it was necessary that CIEX should be able to marshal a weight of convincing evidence to prove beyond doubt that the Reserve Bank had acted illegally and that there was good reason to insist on a settlement.

Expert advice was sought on the mechanics of lifeboats from Sir Kit McMahon, who had been Deputy Governor at the Bank of England since 1980 before becoming chairman of the Midland Bank. A forthright Australian, who had been an Oxford don before moving to the Bank of England, Sir Kit had an unparalleled practical and theoretical knowledge of the subject. McMahon's opinions were reinforced by those of Ian Watt, former head of the Bank of England's special investigation unit, who had gained particular knowledge of some nefarious banking activities as a member of the Volcker Commission which enquired into the fate of Holocaust victims' assets.

From a central banker's point of view Sir Kit was unequivocal: the South African Reserve Bank's actions were completely unacceptable as international practice. There should have been an insistence on management change and the position of directors: it was quite wrong to disguise a gift as a loan. Repayment should have been insisted on and was now due. Ian Watt was equally strong, particularly on the question that directors, who knew about the scheme, had been given share options: he believed that repayment should be enforced by the South African government.

A meeting was held on 19 January to discuss possible action with CIEX's South African professional advisers. Pierre du Toit, senior partner of Arthur Andersen, is the antithesis of a conventional accountant. Large, given to wearing Mandela-shirts of somewhat decided pattern, du Toit has strong opinions on the proper conduct of business, which he can reinforce with great professional skill. Eberhard Bertlesman, in contrast, is quiet and understated, leader of the Pretoria Bar. A second-generation Afrikaner of German origins, he was approached to join the Ruiterwag at the age of 22. It was not a wise move for the junior wing of the Broederbond to have made to a staunch and uncompromising opponent of Nationalist government's apartheid policies. Bertlesman had been active in the opposition to the National Party and had, unusually for a career lawyer, stood as an opposition parliamentary candidate in the 1977 elections. His involvement with human rights campaigns had led to a number of threats which increased when he became involved in a campaign to have General Hendrik van der Bergh, head of the infamous Bureau of State Security BOSS, prosecuted. That effort led to Bertlesman's car being daubed with red paint and the words '*iy vaan vrek*', which may be translated as 'you will die (like a dog)'.

Among Bertlesman's anti-government clients was the Afrikaans newspaper *Vrye Weekblad* and its editor Max Du Preez. *Vrye Weekblad* had been the first to reveal Captain Dirk Coetzee's revelations about the Vlakplaas murder squads. Bertlesman had also acted for the family of Anton Lubowski, a personal friend, Dr David Webster, another Vlakplaas victim, murdered in 1988, and for the man who was now Justice Minister, Dullah Omar. Bertlesman was therefore well acquainted with the machinations of the apartheid security services, and could speak with authority, an authority recognised by Judge Heath.

Contacts were also made with former members of the security services, co-ordinated by an interesting character, code-named 'Pavarotti', who was on friendly terms with the most senior of cabinet ministers. Since by co-operating some of those who gave evidence risked, quite literally, their lives, names are here often disguised, with sources glossed over altogether. Using the wealth of information that was coming to hand, Bertlesman was able to prepare a detailed case that could be brought against both the Reserve Bank and Absa, corporately and the directors individually. In due course this work paved the way for actions to be brought by the Heath Commission, and put, as it were, all the Askin/CIEX cards on the table. Their work had to be able to stand up to any expert evaluation, as in due course it would.

The Law's delays

One section of the community delighted by the Tollgate liquidation, and its attendant dissensions and scandals, was the legal profession. Since February 1993 dozens of lawyers had been guaranteed a steady income, as solicitors and barristers representing interest parties, and as judges and commissioners. 1998 saw some of the cases reaching a conclusion, although others still dragged on.

Hennie Diedericks's action against Absa claiming R30,800,000 in personal damages was potentially very worrying for the bank. Headlined as 'A matter of honour,' Jeremy Gordin described the background, and gave an excellent portrait of Diedericks.

> Anyone aware of the events behind this move will know there is more to the matter than merely money; it's about a man's honour.
>
> Diedericks is – not to put too fine a point on it – a living caricature of an Afrikaner banker. He hails from the Waterberg, hauled himself up banking's corporate ladder by his bootlaces and from 1984 to 1992 was a member of the Broederbond. His manner and dress are conservative.
>
> He also has a mind like a computer and an unwavering gaze. He reminds you of a comment once made by a junior officer about an Israeli general called Yoma Efrai: 'When we needed to construct a very straight road in the Sinai, we simply asked Efrai to lie down on the sand because he's so straight, a man of probity'.

Whatever the result of the case, it seemed that Absa would have to face that which they had always dreaded, and avoided at the last minute by their application for Hoberman's dismissal: their executives would be confronted with the formidable Diedericks in open court.

That particular ordeal had again been avoided, and once more at the last moment, in the matter of Aldworth v. Absa. Aldworth, eventually fined R100,000 for what was essentially a piece of laxity rather than criminality, had brought an action against Absa, alleging unfair dismissal. Absa, always looking to get in a counter-blow, had applied to the Rand High Court to have Aldworth declared a non-resident, which if successful, would have resulted in his being obliged to pay R250 thousand in costs. When in February 1998 the application was dismissed Absa threw in the sponge, settling out of court, paying Aldworth R1,086,000 in damages (which included a counter-claim from Absa of R415,000). It was a moral victory for Aldworth, and the end of a very difficult period for him, but of wider importance was the light which the episode had shed on Absa's very murky practices. The telephone tapping, the Geheim-kamer, and the frequent evasions and brutalities had indelibly smeared Absa's public image.

The bank's spokesman, executive director Bert Grieser, did his best to provide an explanation. 'Absa', he said 'were advised that the substantive reasons for Aldworth's dismissal were sound in law but procedurally flawed,' in that they did not conform with the Labour Relations Act. 'Now,' rejoiced Mr Grieser, 'a full and final settlement had been reached and the book on the Absa Aldworth case is now closed'. This was so in that Aldworth was now able to drop out of the news – much to his relief – but the damage to Absa, whose virulent accusations about Aldworth's behaviour were still recalled, was lasting. Aldworth, whatever Absa might say in mitigation, had won.

Mervyn Key, too, found himself legally absolved from blame when he was acquitted in December 1997 at the end of a lengthy case. First arrested on 15 March 1993, the day after a successful Grand Prix race had been held at Kyalami, Key was accused of fraud, foreign exchange contraventions and forgery. When his case finally came to trial Key defended himself with much skill – he was a very able lawyer – and complete lack of scruple. Following the example of Absa's instruction to the Hoberman Commission to concern themselves only with events *after* 1990, when Askin appeared, the prosecution faithfully charged Key only with offences said to have been committed during that period, although abundant evidence existed, to the public knowledge, about earlier irregularities.

Key's weakest point concerned the very complex events in and around the Kyalami race track. To cover these, and the associated accusations of forgery (one recalls the evidence found in Key's house that he had been practising other people's signatures) Key invented a complex, and entirely untrue story. Askin, he said, claimed to be short of money, having had difficulty in paying capital gains tax to the UK Inland Revenue. Gratefully, therefore, he accepted a loan of one million pounds from Key in order to be able to make the investment in Tollgate. The money, Key claimed, had been won by his father in an Australian lottery, an explanation akin to that frequently put before courts, 'I won it at the races, M'Lud'. Key had not, it seemed, found it necessary to tell his father that this loan had been made, or to admit to him that it had not been repaid on time, or to have any communication at all with the unlucky old gentleman on the subject. Unfortunately, no record of the loan existed, but a brave effort had been made to 'reconstruct' a schedule of the transaction.

Furthermore, it appeared that the (non-existent) loan had been made through Longdon, a company owned by Key. This company actually did exist (and as Askin understood, had been formed with the participation of Christo Wiese, Bernie Ecclestone, Max Mosley and the Gant family). Longdon was situated in the Isle of Man, and apparent difficulties were found in making its records available. To thicken the mixture Key claimed that a power of attorney had been given to Askin in July 1990 by the directors of Longdon. This document, happily, was produced to the satisfaction of the court.

Armed with the power of attorney, Key continued, Askin was able to divert another million pounds to Max Mosley of FOCA, who had, it was said, also suffered losses, this time at Lloyd's, not at that period an uncommon event. When this was discovered by the auditors it was 'promptly repaid' by Askin. Key also made considerable play with Askin's negotiations with FOCA which resulted in the establishment of the Credit Suisse account through which payments from Kyalami, guaranteed by Askin, were made.

Understandably, the judge found it difficult to work through this tangle of events, but allowed himself to make some very peculiar remarks. At the start of his findings the judge asserted 'that each and every count alleged by the state is based upon an alleged common purpose on the part of the accused, Askin and Mackintosh.' The judge went on to confuse Askin with Key. In such ways the trial of Mervyn Key was turned into a trial of Julian Askin 'in absentia', without his being able to give evidence or contest statements. It was a travesty of the normal course of justice, but not one entirely abnormal in South Africa.

As well as a number of factual errors, for example citing Julian Askin as chairman and chief executive officer of Tollgate, which latter he never claimed to be, the judge accepted much uncorroborated and inherently improbable evidence, without making any attempt to procure either documentation or to summon witnesses. Max Mosley could, for example, have testified that the whole story of a loan from Askin was false. Similarly, Key claimed that Askin suggested that a payment of $US2 million should be made to a Geneva company Allsport/Geiss, which had been created by Bernie Ecclestone in 1985 to hold all advertising rights on motor racing circuits run by Mr McNally. The court made no attempt to discover the truth of this not unimportant, but absolutely untrue, claim. The truth, had anyone wished it to be known, of the Swiss transactions could have easily been ascertained through the bank accounts or by reference to Mr Ecclestone.

The facts behind the various allegations was as follows: Askin never had a power of attorney from Longdon and had never met anybody associated with it. He knew nothing about Longdon other than it was the vehicle through which Key-related investors had invested into Tollgate.

To the judge's sweeping statement 'There is nothing improbable about Askin having loaned the money to Mosley as a result of his having suffered a loss at Lloyd's,' Askin replies:

It is totally improbable: did the court even establish that Mosley was a Lloyd's name? I have never conducted any business with Mosley. Other than one meeting where he explained that Key owed Ecclestone money from the previous Grand Prix and that this amount had been built into the latest contract, I know nothing of Mosley's affairs. I am certain that had Mosley been asked to comment on this he would say exactly the same. I met Mosley a second time when he came to South Africa to watch the Grand Prix in 1992. Nobody ever sought to get an affidavit from Mosley which would confirm Key's statements as lies.

Showing some difficulty in distinguishing between fact and allegation the judge averred, as a fact, that: 'the alleged loan to Mosley was in fact later disclosed to the auditors and was promptly thereafter repaid by Askin'. Askin dismissed this as 'Complete rubbish. I have never loaned Mosley anything. It cannot be that there is anything in the audit regarding this. And what evidence could there be that I had paid money back to Mosley? It's absurd and so easily demonstrable as a lie.'

Indeed, Askin claims to have never negotiated with FOCA: 'I made a brief visit to Ecclestone merely to say that as chairman of Tollgate I was prepared to ask the Reserve Bank for a guarantee, and tell Ecclestone that it could take some time. He later spoke to Key. It was from that meeting that the suggestion that I put up a bridging guarantee emerged. This allowed Ecclestone to place Kyalami on the official FOCA list for a Grand Prix.' Apart from that occasion, Askin continues, he met Ecclestone only socially, at the Kyalami race track. As for the alleged loan from Mr Key senior, Askin dismisses it as 'absolute rubbish'. He had no capital gains tax problems in the UK, and the alleged reconstruction of the transaction was, like the power of attorney, nothing more than a common forgery.

At the close of the trial, confirming that it was to a very high degree Askin who, in the eyes of both the prosecution and the judge, was in the dock, the senior prosecutor, Billy Downing, told the press (*Cape Times* 18 January 1998) that consideration was being given to the extradition of Askin and Mackintosh and that 'the extradition decision has already been taken regarding Askin'. Incredibly, this reputable legal official went on to say that the Cape Attorney-General, Frank Kahn, has 'successfully applied for Askin's extradition from Italy some time ago, but he fled the country before the order could be carried out.' Downing must have known that the exact opposite was true. The Italian supreme court had specifically – three times – refused extradition, and Askin had left the country entirely legally.

Moreover – as has been explained on pp.129–30 – the Attorney-General himself knew and acknowledged that Askin could never have been legally extradited from Italy. There was no extradition treaty. In his letter (ref. CUL/98/0002) dated 21 March 1998 Kahn specifically states the fact 'South Africa does not have an extradition treaty with Italy'. All the talk, which had emanated over the years from the Attorney-General's office, was so much flummery. There was no way that Askin could be brought to South Africa, on the by-now entirely discredited charges; but illegal methods were still being vigorously pursued, and these could be traced back to Absa.

Prominent among apartheid's executioners was Lieutenant Abram 'Slang' (snake) van Zyl, a member of the Vlakplaas murder squad and of a sinister military hit squad known as Region 6 of the Civil Co-operation Bureau. This was formed in the late 1980s and consisted of former policemen, virtually all of whom had been members of the infamous Brixton Murder and Robbery Squad. They were led by Colonel Staal Burger and included, as well as van Zyl, Ferdie Barnard, the assassin of David Webster, Calla Botha and Chappies Maree. Region 6 has been well described as 'highly organised, skilled and utterly unscrupulous unit operating outside the law against South African citizens who were assaulted, killed, or terrorised for no other reason than that they were opponents of the government.'

One of van Zyl's more absurd but less lethal assignments was climbing into Archbishop Tutu's garden in order to hang an ape foetus on a tree, the intention being to accuse the archbishop of witchcraft. Van Zyl's murders have never been fully documented, but testifying before the Harms Commission, Snake acknowledged that the Civil Co-operation Bureau 'claimed to operate against all "enemies" of the state, from the left to the right of the political spectrum', although van Zyl professed rather 'a soft spot for rightwingers'. Jaques Pauw quotes him as saying: 'Personally, I must say, I preferred leftists as targets rather than rightists.' However, he conceded that the decision to murder people had never been easy. It had to be avoided at all costs, but unfortunately circumstances demanded that such action had to be taken from time to time. The action of the CCB, he said, was 'for me, for you, I'm talking about the whole of South Africa.'

At the inquest on Anton Lubowski, van Zyl was named as being amongst nine *prima facie* accomplices who had arranged the killing although the lawyer had been murdered by an Irish mercenary, Donald Acheson. They included Burger, Botha and Maree. At the trial a graphic indication of the grisly absurdity of the Vlakplaas terror squads was Acheson's admission that he had been instructed to kill 'a prominent liberal newspaper editor by putting poison into her personal sanitary towels or toothpaste.' Van Zyl was also given responsibility for an attempt on the life of Dullah Omar, now (1998) Justice Minister. In his admission to the Harms Commission van Zyl's selected assassin, 'Peaches' Gordon, related how he attempted to poison Omar's medicaments. A few weeks after his confession Gordon's mutilated body was discovered; the key witnesses to his murder were shot as they left a police station (TRC report vol. 3, chap. 5, p. 28). Van Zyl left no live evidence.

Van Zyl's preferred hit man was Warrant Officer Chappies Maree, described as a 'psychopath' who took real pleasure in his work. It was some indication of Absa's close relations with the nastier aspects of Nationalist apartheid governments that when van Zyl and Maree were sent into pensioned retirement both these disreputable assassins were able to set up detective agencies employed by Absa. They were also willing to undertake rather more serious tasks than that of guarding Absa offices. It was van Zyl, acting on behalf of 'the guys at the Afrikaner bank', who was behind the attempt described in Chapter Four to have Askin kidnapped from Italy in 1994, and it was van Zyl, as will be seen, who was asked to organise another murder attempt in 1998, when the pressure on Absa was stepped up.

Not just one, but several bombs are ticking

Public interest, now the Browde Commission had gone underground, focused less on Absa than the Reserve Bank. Judge Heath reported in January 1998, during a presentation made to the Justice Department, that an unidentified member of the public had asked his unit to enquire into the circumstances of the lifeboat. Gerhard Visagie, the unit's chief legal adviser, warned that the mere fact of reference did not necessarily imply an investigation would follow: 'it means that we will look at the essential facts. We would also have to consult internationally as the lifeboat scheme is internationally accepted. The question however, is whether this was a real lifeboat situation.' Whether the unit went further, he added would depend 'on whether President Mandela will issue a proclamation authorising the unit to continue investigating the matter.' The question was now in political hands, and both the Reserve Bank and Absa began to exercise their influence to keep Heath from looking further.

Eddie George, the Governor of the Bank of England did not help the Reserve Bank's case when he made a speech in Pretoria the following month in which he stated:

> The central bank would not normally be involved in a significant financial risk. However, in a situation where the failure of one institution could bring down other – otherwise viable – institutions, the central bank may need to consider acting in the role of lender of last resort to the failing institution, which might expose the central bank to financial loss.
>
> The central bank safety net is not there to protect individual institutions from failure. It is there to protect the stability of the financial system as a whole. In the absence of a serious systemic threat, the right course would be to allow the institution to fail.
>
> There can be nothing automatic about 'lender of last resort' assistance and, if rendered, the terms should be onerous, especially as it involves the commitment of public money.'

All of which, of course, was precisely what the Reserve Bank had not done.

But the major scandal erupted following a long and well-researched article by Bill Jamieson in the London *Sunday Telegraph* on 22 February, 1998 headlined 'South Africa's dirty banking secrets'. Clearly well-informed as to what had been going on in CIEX's office Jamieson wrote:

On the basis of reports now in the hands of the South African cabinet, the country's Reserve Bank and Dr Chris Stals, its governor, are on borrowed time.

The explosive details of the reports could undermine South Africa's financial standing. If Stals is forced to quit over the affair, the Rand could go into a tailspin, plunging an already weakened South African economy into deepest gloom.

Not just one, but several bombs are ticking.

First there is a detailed report recently completed by Justice Nel into the collapse of the Masterbond Group and investor protection in South Africa.

Then there is an investigation by Justice Heath into the misappropriation of state assets; a continuing inquiry rumbling away in Cape Town on the lending policies of Amalgamated Banks of South Africa, the country's largest retail bank, and papers calling for a new system of banking and financial services supervision.

Now there is the latest and most explosive report on the situation. In the past two weeks Thabo Mbeki, South Africa's deputy president, is believed to have received advice from leading outside experts, including former Bank of England officials, that there should be wholesale reform at the central bank, that Stals should be replaced, and that the government has a good legal case to recover the billions of rands used to prop up South Africa's banking system in the early nineties.

According to bank sources in Davos and Johannesburg, fresh evidence presented to the government by Sir Kit McMahon, the former Deputy Governor of the Bank of England, and Ian Watt, the Bank's former special investigator, takes issue with the Reserve Bank's defence that the lifeboats were conducted in conformity with international practice.

It suggests the actions of the Reserve Bank fitted no acceptable international pattern and were illegal. It argues that the personnel and directors who took part in the lifeboat arrangements, together with the auditors who approved misleading financial statements, could be liable to legal action. It also suggests that the lifeboat money should be repayable

– as it is in internationally acceptable support operations.

Three other sensitive issues are thrown up in the train of these investigations.

First, were the gains enjoyed by shareholders in the banks who were in receipt of secret support not effectively made possible by the use of public funds, and thus reclaimable?

Second, what of the director and senior managers of the banks who gained through personal shareholdings and share options? Should these not be subject to some claw-back by the government?

Third, what might be the legal liability of US investment bank Merrill Lynch which last summer was the lead sponsor of a $120 million global stock offer by Absa knowing at the time that investigations into the receipt of lifeboat funds were under way?

Jamieson's article created a great stir in South Africa. The suggestion that the Reserve Bank had done anything remotely wrong was indignantly, and predictably, denied by Dr Stals. Even more alarming, however, was the rumour that the 'latest and most explosive report' had been commissioned by Thabo Mbeki; this too was denied by Professor Jakes Gerwel, the Cabinet Secretary. Attempting to find an authoritative comment on the charges, Janice Warman of *Finance Week* approached Roger Alford, of the London School of Economics. Dr Alford was not too helpful: 'Propping up a bank with a few million pounds worth of loans which may convert into higher income and make them solvent – that cost is really quite small compared with closing the doors and calling in the loans, given the shock to depositors and other depositors in other banks. However, illegality is another matter.' But he added that the Reserve Bank's action 'would seem to be a reasonable pursuit of general central banking objectives ... But not if South African law forbade it – and as long as it took the form of loans which were paid back.' And of course, the aid given did not take the form of repaid loans, but of outright gifts, while the legality of the action remained in question.

Alec Hogg, now formerly of Absa, was scornful. Approached by Krisjan Lemmer of the *Mail and Guardian* (27 February), the most authoritative South African newspaper, Hogg trashed the report, concluding, among other things, that it was a 'product of poor research and ignorance'. But, warned Lemmer, 'Since the scandal exploded in the early 1990s, Absa has spent a fortune trying to persuade the South African public that the Reserve Bank's actions were entirely normal. The man at the front of this propaganda war was Alec Hogg, who left Absa last year to host a daily financial news show on SAFM, Market Update. Hogg rarely has a bad word to say about Absa on the show – not surprising since he also hosts a financial programme on SABC TV that is sponsored by the banking group.'

The Reserve Bank produced an eleven-page press statement which recounted in injured tones:

> The Reserve Bank has been unable to establish the source of the latest attempt to discredit the Bank and its senior officials in the eyes of the international financial community. Neither the principals who commissioned or prepared the so-called 'explosive report' referred to in the article, nor the persons who allegedly provided evidence (Sir Kit McMahon and Mr Ian Watt, respectively former Deputy Governor and former Special Investigator of the Bank of England) contacted the Reserve Bank to establish or verify the facts of the matters raised in the article. The two South African Commissions, chaired respectively by Judge Nel and Judge Heath, referred to in the article also never approached the Governor of the Reserve Bank formally for an explanation of or information on the assistance provided by the Bank for good reasons to the banks mentioned in the article. As a result, the accusations in the article are totally without substance. It is hoped, however, that this unfounded attack will be recognised as such.

Given the facts, their explanation was hardly convincing. Financial assistance, the Bank argued '... is only provided to solvent banks in financial difficulty when there is a reasonable chance that the assistance will enable the banks to overcome their financial problems.'

But what was the truth? Mercabank and Bankorp were nowhere near being solvent: they were teetering on the brink of failure, only saved by the Reserve Bank's donations. The thesis was also advanced that assistance to Bankorp was provided at a time when a situation of threatening insolvency had developed in what was then the fourth largest banking group in South Africa.

'At that stage', the Reserve Bank's statement continued, 'the banks in the group had more than 90,000 depositors who held more than R25 billion on deposit. In addition, Bankorp had extensive international obligations, a substantial portion of which was affected by the debt standstill arrangements of the South African Government. The potential failure of the group, therefore, did not only pose a threat to the financial stability of the South African banking system as a whole, but also to the banking system's ability to honour internationally agreed commitments.'

'Systemic failure', or an implosion of the whole financial system and the collapse of organised credit, is a nightmare of all central banks, and was being advanced here as the reason for the Reserve Bank's actions. Apart from the fact that the phrase 'threatening insolvency' goes a long way to admitting that Bankorp was actually insolvent, a fact denied only three pages previously, this refers to the assistance given to Bankorp in 1990. The Bankorp lifeboat had been first launched *five years* earlier, at a time when there was no question at all of systemic failure. Bankorp was a modest Sanlam-controlled domestic bank. The deposits totalled not R25,000 million but less than R10,000 million, with capital and reserves of R390 million

The assistance given in 1990, which is that referred to in the Reserve Bank document, was nothing more than an inevitable stage in the rake's progress of Bankorp, which had consistently failed in the previous five years to adhere to any of its undertakings and to hit any of its targets. Equally misleading was the assertion that the aid, admitted as totalling R1,125 million was equivalent to less than 4 per cent of the group's assets. A bank's assets are the sum of its loans, customers' liabilities under acceptances, cash and investments, totalling in that year some R30,000 million. The figure of R1,125 million is quite irrelevant to that sum. It was a capital grant, which should be compared to the issued share capital of R189 million – and was no less than 850 per cent of *that*. If the share premium account and reserves are added to the share capital, then the total shareholders' interests would amount R682 million, something rather less than half the Reserve Bank's assistance. The Reserve Bank had actually presented to Bankorp shareholders – who were for the greatest part Sanlam, one of the richest institutions in South Africa – a grant equal and not far short of *double* their money.

A neat parallel could have been drawn a few months later. In September 1998 the Long Term Capital Management Fund, an American 'hedge fund', was teetering on the brink of collapse, having lost almost all its $US 300 million equity. Had the company been forced into bankruptcy its assets, estimated at some $US 200,000 million, would have had to be liquidated, which would, according to the *Economist* of 3 October, have 'driven the market frantic', and led to investors, mainly banks, losing over $US 14,000 million. As it was, the Federal Reserve Bank, by twisting the arms of international bankers, raised $US 3,650 million to keep the bank alive, literally overnight. (Alan Greenspan, the Federal Reserve Bank's chairman, is said to have kept the bankers immured in his office until they finally agreed, at three in the morning.)

This classic lifeboat, which cost the taxpayer nothing, was accompanied by much pain on the part of the banks and led to the resignations of many senior executives – a very different picture to that of the South African Reserve Bank's unstinted generosity with taxpayers' funds, and tender regard for shareholders' interests. There was, however, one similarity. Both rescues replaced the equity capital of the troubled institution, although the Federal Reserve-sponsored aid fell a little short of the Long Term Capital Management Fund's original capital ($3,650 million cf. $4,300 million) while the South African Reserve Bank had to cough up nearly twice the shareholders' capital (R1,125 million compared with R682 million) – and this at the taxpayer's expense, not at that of the other banks! Moreover, the shareholders of the LTCMF were allowed to keep only 10 per cent of their stake, having therefore lost the better part of $4,000 million.

The differences between statements designed to mislead and absolute lies are sometimes difficult to descry, but when the Reserve Bank publicly stated that 'The present owners of Bankorp, namely Absa, only came into the picture when the assistance agreement was already halfway through its tenure. Absa, however, honoured the commitments of the agreement, and the loan was fully repaid to the Reserve Bank on maturity' they were approaching clear falsehood. The R1,125 million was never repaid. Once the agreed sum had accrued as interest to form the present to Absa, the government stocks were simply handed back to the Reserve Bank. The R1,125 million, it has to be repeated, was a straightforward gift to Absa, and an equally straightforward loss to the Reserve Bank.

Since Sir Kit McMahon's name had been mentioned, Dr Stals also sent, on 24 February, a fax to Sir Kit, saying:

> I was surprised to find in this report that you were quoted as one of the authors of a hostile attack on me and the South African Reserve bank for assistance provided by the Bank during the term of office of my predecessor and myself to South African banking institutions in accordance with the function and responsibility of the Bank as lender of last resort. I can only assume that you were very badly misinformed about the situation that prevailed at the time, and must have been grossly misled by your informers, of the true facts that led the Bank to decisions in this regard.

In addition to the misleading statements made in the press release Dr Stals permitted himself one outright falsehood in his letter to Sir Kit: 'You also apparently did not take account of the fact that I was not involved in the initial decisions in April 1985 or in 1986, when the original decision was taken to provide assistance to the Bankorp Group. I only became involved in 1990, when a desperate situation of threatening insolvency had developed in what was then one of the four major banks in South Africa.' This is of course absolutely disproved by the letter Dr Stals himself wrote in 1985 (reproduced as Appendix D), in which he authorised the loan to Bankorp.

The Governor's statement that 'other banks, that surely cannot be classified as "Afrikaner" Banks' were also assisted during that difficult period was at least highly questionable. In view of the veil of secrecy kept suspended by the Reserve Bank there may have been exceptions, but all the *known* cases of Reserve Bank support refer to Afrikaner banks and in no instance was any attempt made to summon the rest of the banking community to help. Even Nedbank's lifeboat, supplemented and outweighed as it was by Old Mutual's support, was made necessary because of their improvident loan to Louis Luyt.

The South African press was cautious. The Reserve Bank and Absa were too closely linked with the great power of the Rembrandt Group and of Sanlam to criticise with impunity. Hugh Murray of *Leadership* and *Millennium* was obliged to have his company cease trading in March having become insolvent, a circumstance largely owing to the falling off in advertising, the prime source of income for these publications. *Finance Week* believed the Reserve Bank to be under 'conspiratorial siege', finding it curious that parliamentary criticism

> comes at the same time as a . . . conspiracy has surfaced in a London Sunday newspaper accusing Reserve Bank Governor Chris Stals of procedural irregularities in the provision of a lifeboat years ago for an ailing bank, Bankorp. The newspaper cites a report allegedly criticising Stals which appears now not to exist. There are vested interests involved which makes rational argument difficult. But this matter keeps recurring in circumstances clearly aimed to damage Stals . . . Is a conspiracy surfacing to ensure that when Stals goes the Bank and its new governor will be thoroughly within the ideological grip of the ANC and its trade union allies?

The Afrikaner journal *Die Beeld* headlined its comment 'Mischievous Report tries to show Reserve Bank in a Bad Light' and in common with most others, merely reproduced parts of the Reserve Bank's defence. But the issue refused to disappear, and on 29 March Martin Tomkinson, writing in the London *Independent on Sunday*, reiterated the charges, making it clear that a good deal more than 'procedural irregularities' were alleged.

> Mr Stals' rationale for the central bank's soft loans was that they were necessary to maintain banking stability in South Africa. Such assistance, he adds, required complete secrecy. But this issue is specifically dealt with by the former Bank of England officials and their team, who dismiss this line of defence out of hand. The British experts argue that the actions of Mr Stals and the South African central bank fitted no acceptable international pattern and were in fact illegal. Crucial to this line of argument is the fact that Absa's two

main shareholders, the Rupert Group and Sanlam, were fabulously wealthy in 1992.

As a result of the bogus 'lifeboat' Absa had flourished and directors and executives of the bank have benefited from dividends usually taken by way of extra shares. Other investors were denied knowledge of this secret 'buffer' of £250 million.

Tomkinson went further:

> But an even greater scandal remains a possibility. In the dying days of apartheid, a secretive organisation with the deceptively bland title of Directorate of Covert Collections was established. The DCC set up a network of front companies to facilitate the grisly work of apartheid's death squads around the world. Persistent and growing allegations have circulated in South Africa that such companies were organised with the direct assistance of executives of Absa.
>
> To date, the ground-breaking Truth and Reconciliation Commission has not examined any evidence of who exactly funded the terrorist activities of the DCC. But if and when the commission gets round to this the reputations of a number of highly-respected businessmen may be revised. Such men include a politically well-connected English lawyer who allegedly helped to set up the front companies.

There was much speculation in South Africa as to the source of all these interesting allegations. Dr Stals finished his injured communication to Sir Kit McMahon

> As I find it extremely difficult to understand the attitude attributed to you . . . and also your reasons for tendering an opinion on a matter that is complex and difficult for anybody as far detached from the situation as you must be to understand, I have decided to write this letter to you . . . It may help me to find some explanation if you would be so kind as to let me know who the principals were that commissioned this investigation by you and Mr Watts, and also for what

purpose it was done. All enquiries I made with the South African Government failed to produce answers to these questions.

Sir Kit's short answer revealed nothing, but relying on the persuasive abilities of its security chief Absa attempted to obtain a copy of the report. This task was entrusted to Slang van Zyl, who began by offering R50,000 to anyone who might be able to produce one – a reward that had later to be increased to R250,000 (over £25,000), indicating a degree of desperation on the bank's part.

The *Financial Mail* had no hesitation in pointing the finger at 'Mr Askin, we presume'. Peter Bruce, the editor (20 March), sniffed that 'it was astounding McMahon should have allowed himself to be used in this way' and that 'there was little doubt that the report and the revelation of its contents to the *Sunday Times* was the work of the former Tollgate Holdings chairman.' Bruce was dismissive about the 'investigations'. 'It appears that Askin has simply lurched from one journalist to another in his bid to nail Stals and the others. The *Financial Mail* doubts that he will hold Jamieson's [of the *Sunday Telegraph*] interest for long without coming up with some hard evidence.'

Hard evidence was indeed to come, and from a powerful source. At the beginning of April Deputy President Thabo Mbeki announced that the Minister of Justice would ask Judge Heath to investigate the whole business of lifeboats and possible fraud connected thereto. The Afrikaans magazine *Rapport* spoke darkly of 'political motives' behind the possible enquiry, and indeed the communist ANC parliamentarian, Ben Turok, was beginning to ask awkward questions. But the Truth and Reconciliation Commission had also been taking an interest. During a hearing, at which Dr Stals attended, Ebrahim Kharsamy, president of the Islamic Chamber of Commerce, accused the Reserve Bank of helping white financial institutions while refusing assistance to black companies. But it was nearly a month after his deputy's announcement that the Presidential decree came through, on 8 May 1998.

This was the Proclamation no. R 44, 1998, gazetted on 1 May, signed by Thabo Mbeki and Dullah Omar. It required Judge Heath's commission to investigate, and to refer to the Special Tribunal, any:

a. serious maladministration in connection with the affairs of any such State institution;

b. improper or unlawful conduct by employees of any such State institution;

c. unlawful appropriation or expenditure of public money or property;

d. unlawful, irregular or inapproved acquisitive act, transaction, measure or practice having a bearing upon State property;

e. intentional or negligent loss of public money or damage to public property;

f. corruption in connection with the affairs of any such State institution; or

g. unlawful or improper conduct by any person which has caused or may cause serious harm to interests of the public or any category thereof, which has taken place between 1 January 1990 and the date of publication of this proclamation.

Jeremy Gordin, well-informed as ever, commented on the terms of reference given to Judge Heath:

> The central focus of the investigation will be to determine whether the Reserve Bank, the bank of the government and people of South Africa, behaved illegally in secretly giving the lifeline to a private institution.
>
> The investigation will also try to ascertain whether the lifeline was aimed at protecting depositors or at benefiting Bankorp/Absa's major shareholder, Sanlam; whether the package was repaid and whether tax was paid on it.
>
> This means in effect that the Heath Special Investigating Unit will be looking into the conduct of Reserve Bank governor Chris Stals who admitted in 1996 that he had given permission for the aid package.
>
> The unit will also have to consider the conduct of senior Absa officials as well as senior office bearers of Bankorp, Absa and Sanlam. The existence of the lifeline was denied by the

Reserve Bank and Absa until 1995 and it has never been shown in the accounts of Bankorp, Absa or Sanlam.

Gordin apparently had seen the now famous report and quoted from it: 'The so-called loan to Bankorp/Absa is demonstrably a sham ... the transaction falls outside the Reserve Bank's competence and contains every element of common-law fraud.' which is nothing more nor less than the description by Judge Nel of the package as a donation at the expense of the public.

The delay in issuing the proclamation was probably due to President Mandela, who had been greatly annoyed by the adverse criticism appearing in the foreign press, personally intervening. He was further said to be irritated by the off-hand reception he received at Absa, where he was apparently given a similar proposal to that which Christo Faul had tentatively put forward the previous year, that Absa repay by putting an appropriate sum of money into approved government projects. Whilst this would have been in accordance with the President's well-known and consistent policy of bridge-building between the old South Africa and the new, it would have swept the whole dispute under the table. The principles that underlay the Truth and Reconciliation movement were difficult to apply to the detailed technicalities of finance. The clear light of detailed investigation that Heath was able to focus would be more effective – and avoid the temptations to large-scale corruption so often associated with projects beloved of any government. Questions of law were also raised. If wrongdoing was admitted – as Absa's offer implied – it was not only the South African government who would seek redress, but other banks, shareholders, depositors and many other potential claimants.

It did not take long for the President to sense the fundamental lack of seriousness and absence of regret behind the Absa proposals. Angered by the critical reports in the international press, and still more by the shooting dead of an African child by an Afrikaner farmer, Mandela agreed that a formal investigation should be initiated.

CHAPTER TWELVE

The End Approaches

Judge Heath takes up the case

Judge Heath was satisfactorily well armed, with powers of subpoena and coercion that he had every intention of exercising. Three specific areas had been defined in the proclamation – the payment frauds and theft of medicaments, the notoriously corrupt Ciskei Defence Force, and (in what must have been very unwelcome company) the South African Reserve Bank's 'scheme in terms of which the South African Reserve Bank granted a loan to Bankorp to save Bankorp from bankruptcy'. Heath intended to make this, the lifeboat controversy, very much a priority.

During the month of April meetings had taken place between the Judge, his chief assistant Steve Barkhuizen and Eberhardt Bertlesman. Concluding that the Reserve Bank's actions contained every element of common law fraud, that the so-called lifeboat was in truth 'a Spanish galleon sent by the Governor of the Reserve Bank to his political friends', Bertlesman's arguments were accepted as logical by Judge Heath. Indeed, the Judge went further at their first detailed discussion (on 12 April) believing that both the non-payment of tax and the insider share-dealing made possible by the secrecy were grave potential issues that should be followed up.

Insider share-dealing, which used to be commonplace, is now in all advanced countries thoroughly illegal and an offence which carries severe penalties. Looking at the Reserve Bank's flotilla of lifeboats, there are two separate areas where this occurred. Certainly Sanlam and the Rupert interests were privy to knowledge of the Reserve Bank's gifts, knowledge which was denied to other shareholders, but stood, it could be argued, in a special relationship to Absa. Their agreement to freeze their shareholdings at 25 per cent each had been adhered to over the years. But there had been much activity, and on a large scale, in the share dealings of bank executives, especially through the share incentive scheme.

In common with many other public quoted companies, Absa had established an arrangement whereby members of its staff were offered options to purchase shares at a future date and at prices which offered considerable attractions. This method of enabling workers with little capital of their own to participate in the fortunes of their company is also used as an incentive to senior executives to increase their earnings. According to the rules of the Absa share incentive scheme 5 per cent of the total shares in issue might be allocated to participants. No details of the scheme have been published – an omission which would be illegal in England – and it is not known how these shares were distributed among those eligible. The shares were allocated by means of options which could be exercised within five years of the expiry date, which itself appears to have been between eight and ten years from the date of the option's issue. Thus any staff member could, after a certain lapse of time, choose when to use his share option. Depending on the fixed rate at which the option was issued and the market price of Absa shares when it was exercised, some very handsome profits could be made. If, for example the holders of those 2,700,000 options which were valid in May 1998 had chosen to exercise them at that date, and immediately sold their shares on the market, they would have received about R55 per share, or R125,000 million in all. The average price at which the options had been issued to their fortunate holders was something under R10, which would have given a net profit of nearly R100 million: even at that time, with a depreciated rand, worth over £10 million. That is, of course, if the shares had been sold at their highest price; an average for the first six months of 1998 would have been nearer R40 per share, which would still have shown a very satisfactory return.

Since only minimal information about the share option scheme is shown in the annual report it is difficult to evaluate with any certainty how much money was in fact made, as distinct from the potential gains, but some examples can be given. Options that expired in March 2000 would have therefore been exercisable at any time after March 1995. It was stated that they had been issued at an average price of R4.62, presumably in 1990–2. When they first became valid the market price fluctuated between R21 and R23.5. Presuming the option holder sold at the lowest level he would nevertheless have made a profit of over R16 a share, or well over 300 per cent. If however the options had been held until the high of 1998, at which time there were still 184,000 remaining to be exercised before the year 2000, a profit of R8,300,00 would have accrued – over 900 per cent.

Clearly, those executives who knew the innermost workings of the bank, and especially such vital matters as the existence of the lifeboats, were in a much better position to exercise their options at the most profitable time. Usually the opportunities to exercise options are limited to short periods after public announcements have been made, but this was not so with the secret lifeboats, the existence of which was not disclosed for over ten years. In this time any executive who knew of the lifeboat would have been in a highly preferred position in any share dealings.

The number of shares involved was large. Many millions of options had been cashed in the period of the secret lifeboats, and millions more issued. In 1994 over ten million options had been granted, an unusually high number. By 1996 there were nearly 20 million options to be converted, issued at an average price of something over R11, and exercisable between 1999 and 2007. What the share price might be then is a matter of conjecture – doubtless quite anxious conjecture on the part of the option-holders – as Absa's share price slumped by half between May and August 1998. Even more worrying must be the prospect that Absa may be called upon to repay the gifts of the Reserve Bank, and that any individuals who may have been privy to the lifeboats' existence, and who then dealt in the company's shares, may also have to pay their profits back, to say nothing of interest, fines, or even prison sentences.

In his submission to Judge Heath, Bertlesman made one additional point that has been well-aired. He suggested that it was instructive to contrast the various statements made by Stals in order to defend the lifeboats. 'The more Stals has explained, the more he has contradicted himself – and that in itself justifies the conclusion that he is in trouble and the transaction is dishonest.'

As soon as the proclamation was issued Judge Heath moved into action, meeting Bertlesman and Hennie Diedericks. He wanted an affidavit from Diedericks, essentially repeating the evidence he had previously given to the Hoberman Commission, and a copy of the CIEX report. His initial concentration would be on the SARB lifeboat, but other enquiries would follow from this. And, quite specifically, the Judge wanted the co-operation of Oatley and the CIEX team.

Another extended interrogation of Hennie Diedericks followed, paralleling the one that he had undergone in Chester Square three years previously, in which he supplied the Heath Commission lawyers with the facts they would need to issue summonses to Absa – and these, by an ironic logic, would include a demand for the documents Hoberman had sought two years previously, which had never been made public following Absa's last-minute move for that Commissioner's dismissal.

The summonses and requests for attendance began to be issued quickly. Miller Gruss were among the first to receive notice that they would be required to give evidence. They were followed by many others, including those sent to all the board members of Absa/Bankorp, the Reserve Bank and Sanlam for the years of 1986, 1990, 1992, and 1994. Diedericks, now working closely with the Heath team, suggested that the sort of questions that should be addressed to the directors: Did they check on the legality of the transactions? Were they in fact consulted? Were they aware of the relevant sections of the Companies Act? What advice did they seek? All of which would elicit answers which, if honest, would be deeply unsatisfactory, and which would extract the admission that the most important decisions were made by executives working on their own.

On 25 May Judge Heath paid a personal visit to Dr Stals at the Reserve Bank, leaving a list of documents required, and to Absa head office. He had little luck there, since both Cronjé and Nallie Bosman claimed to be 'in meetings', and refused to meet the Commissioner. For his part Dr Stals did not appear happy with the list of documents he was asked to produce, and the explanation that these were particularly wanted in reference to the Commission's investigation of the Cape Investment Bank and Bankorp lifeboats left him distinctly rattled, complaining that he would have preferred a quite different sort of enquiry. Dr Stals assured the Commission that 'nothing untoward' had occurred, and complained that as for the documents required (a) he did not think some of them existed, (b) it would take two weeks to procure them (the Commission wanted them within five days), and (c) he did not see why they wanted them anyway.

But the Governor particularly wanted to know whether Askin was behind the non-existent report, and whether any information had been given to that *bête noire* of the Reserve Bank. He was given non-committal replies.

Moving quickly, the Judge visited Marinus Daling of Sanlam the day following the meeting with Stals. Daling was described as 'aggressive, arrogant and uncooperative', insisting that it was a matter only for the Reserve Bank. When reminded that it was his signature that appeared on the 1990 agreement Daling became 'defensive and sullen'. This attitude could be, and indeed was, taken as confirmation that there was much to hide. Sanlam and Rembrandt were the driving forces behind the appeals for help that led to the ultimate merger of Bankorp and Volkskas, a measure which must have been been confirmed, if not decided, at the highest level of the Broederbond, a subject with which Judge Heath, even as an outsider, was well acquainted.

When such powerful interests were threatened some offensive action would be expected, and it was clear whence this would come. The South African CIEX team member Pavarotti had caught a man following him, who, after some encouragement (Pavarotti is a formidable person), had admitted to being employed by Absa. Pavarotti telephoned Julian Askin on 29 May to say that his telephone and fax were both tapped, and he was convinced that the 'enemy' were becoming very 'uptight and anxious' and that they would become increasingly dangerous. The Askins must be vigilant.

It took very little time for Pavarotti's warning to be substantiated. On 1 June, a few days after the Judge's meetings with Stals and Daling, Askin received a threatening telephone call. In a thick Afrikaans accent, a voice rendered more frightening by its obvious lack of verbal skill made it clear that unless Askin laid off, his life expectation would be short. 'They' knew where he lived, and would have no difficulty in reaching him there (a few months later photographs of Julian and Susie, taken in the street outside their house, at about the same time, were discovered in the possession of Absa's security team, making it clear that even in London the Askins were under surveillance). The anonymous caller made a specific threat against the Askin's daughter Charlotte, who was living in Cape Town. As if to underline the menace, a few moments before the telephone call to London, all the lights in Steenhuis went out. This not uncommon occurrence had previously been associated with telephone tapping, and had been preceded by an unusual noise from the telephones.

Julian Askin decided not to tell Susie or Charlotte of the telephone call, but arranged for Charlotte and her home to be protected.

The threats were by now clearly identified as coming from the security department of Absa, under the direction of a named senior executive to whom Slang van Zyl reported. Given the close relationships that existed between the (now-former) Broeders it can be taken for granted that the Reserve Bank would be kept informed of developments. But it was not only these two institutions which were likely to be affected by any potential investigation. As equal-controlling shareholders Sanlam and the Rembrandt Group were in the firing line, should it be found that they had benefited at the expense of other shareholders.

Once again, Jeremy Gordin was among the first to point this out in his article of 10 May announcing the Heath proclamation.

> The Heath unit is empowered to question people under oath and, if the unit finds any proof of 'unlawful appropriation or expenditure of public money' or 'intentional or negligent loss of public money', it is entitled to institute the equivalent of civil proceedings before a special tribunal consisting of a High Court judge. Especially significant is that it is part of the unit's mandate to claim back money on behalf of the government or the public.
>
> It is therefore possible that Absa or Sanlam could ultimately be ordered to repay the fruits of the lifeboat. This could amount to at least R1,125 billion.
>
> Were this to happen, it could affect Sanlam's bid for a stock exchange listing later this year as part of its demutualisation.

Slavering over free cash

This last point was to become significant. From its origins as part of the Afrikaner self-help movement Sanlam had been a non-profit distributing mutual society, ploughing back the net income from its investments to underwrite the insurance policies it had issued. Mutual insurance societies are part of the early nineteenth-century British working-class movement which comprehended the co-operative and building societies, all dedicated to promoting savings and equally shared benefits. With the foundation of the Old Mutual in 1839 these had been transplanted to the Cape, where their usually high-minded and industrious tone had won much support.

Traditionally, and sensibly, mutual societies' investments ought to be a mixture of liquid resources and solid blue-chip holdings, protecting the hard-win savings of their policy holders. By diverting a large proportion of their resources into high-risk Bankorp shares Sanlam had exposed themselves to criticism. In addition to the drain on resources imposed by their ownership of Bankorp, Sanlam had suffered from its ideologically inspired investment in Federale Volksbeleggings and Tradegro, both demanding and unprofitable. Now, thanks to the Reserve Bank's generosity, Absa was a reasonably prosperous bank, and, if all held good, could feature with some credibility as a sound portfolio investment.

Sanlam needed credibility, since its recent performance had been far from satisfactory. The key indicator, that of value added to policy holders' funds, had steadily declined from R19,2000 million in 1994 to R8,500 million in 1997. As a result the capital ratios were beginning to look weak. With just over R10,000 million of capital and resources, Sanlam had to support policy liabilities of R120,000 million; by contrast its chief competitor, Old Mutual, had R30,000 million of capital and liabilities of R154,000 million – a ratio of 19 per cent compared to Sanlam's less than 9 per cent. Only a year previously the suggestion of Sanlam's demutualisation had been vigorously denied, but there had since been a change of course. The Managing Director, Desmond Smith, had been replaced by Marinus Daling, who took over the duties of chief executive, in addition to those of Chairman. Demutualisation was beginning to look like the only way forward, and one to which Daling had committed his own personal credibility.

The status of mutuality had disadvantages, especially to boards anxious to expand their range of opportunities. Beginning in Britain in the 1980s many mutual organisations, chiefly building societies, had obtained authority to convert themselves into limited companies, usually publicly quoted. Policy holders, borrowers or depositors stood to gain a single reasonably substantial payment, and directors were given wide powers to diversify their businesses. It was a proposal of this sort that Sanlam had decided upon, on 27 January 1998, to be carried through in November 1998.

The announcement in which this intention was first stated, the annual review for 1997, noted the benefits that demutualisation would bring to the policy holders. '1. eligible policy holders will benefit from the substantial release of value through the allocation of free shares; 2. existing and future policy benefits will not be affected by the demutualisation process; 3. the interests of owners and clients will be separated.'

A not unduly cynical gloss is: 1. an immediate one-off payment to policy holders who will be no worse off: but future profits will go to the shareholders; 2. the directors will be free to make a very great deal of money – and in this context it will be noted that Sanlam accounts are reticent on payments to directors, or directors' interests in subsidiary or associated companies.

David Gleason took an acerbic view: 'Is it right for Sanlam even to contemplate a listing on the JSE? Many policy holders are slavering over the free cash they think will come their way. So are merchant bankers and a horde of stockbrokers. But their need – greed? – is not the main issue.' The Absa connection, he went on to say, was.

More respectable reasons for Sanlam's projected action did exist. It would also, once demutualised, be possible to increase the proportion of assets held overseas. 1997 had already seen a sharp increase in Sanlam's overseas investments, up nearly 300 per cent in a single year (from R2,413 million in 1996 to R7,111 million, both figures excluding some R1,000 million of investments in Namibia, which had remained almost static). With a quoted share-base, and the status of a limited liability company, international trading would become much more practicable.

Even in its weakened state, Sanlam was a large institution. Old Mutual might have taken over as market leader, well ahead and more strongly established than Sanlam, and Liberty Life was coming along fast, but Sanlam, as a publicly quoted company, could be expected to be capitalised at something like R40,000 million. The conversion of so substantial an institution, and its introduction to the market, would produce very substantial fees for accountants, lawyers, banks and brokers, multiplying the number of people and institutions with a financial interest in the process: and Marinus Daling's personal position and reputation would be consolidated. With so many people 'slavering', anything that might imperil the demutualisation of Sanlam would produce a sharp and hostile reaction.

By June 1998 Sanlam's prospects were looking less rosy than they had when the decision to demutualise was made. The rand was beginning a precipitous slide, in which it lost 23 per cent of its value in a few weeks; overseas investment from a South African base would therefore be more difficult. Inflation was increasing, as was the deficit in trade; the Reserve Bank's remedial action, increasing overdraft prime rate from 18.25 per cent to 25 per cent, made the returns on equities less attractive, and economic growth had slowed almost to a halt. Under such circumstances it would not take too much to cause the demutualisation project to be postponed; and chief among these circumstances was the growing anxiety over Absa.

More than half of Sanlam's assets consisted of quoted shares, and of these the second largest was the holding in Absa, which they had undertaken to keep in the region of 25 per cent. In the 1997 accounts this was shown at R4,116 million, up from R3,394 million the previous year, representing 23 per cent of the company's capital. Absa's shares also formed a substantial part of Sanlam's capital – over 5 per cent of all its equity holdings, which in total represented 54 per cent of all Sanlam's assets. Some progress had been made in disposing of the biggest of Sanlam's equity holdings, their stake in the mining company, Gencor, which it converted into the new London company, Billiton. In January 1998 Sanlam held shares in Billiton, amounting to some 16 per cent, valued at R4,591 million. This holding was reduced in May 1998 by the sale of 101 million shares, which brought in £160 million, reducing Sanlam's share to just under 11 per cent of Billiton, and making Absa now by far the biggest investment held by Sanlam; an investment in which, by their agreement with the Reserve Bank and the Rupert interests, they were firmly embedded.

David Gleason, as usual, put it forthrightly:

> Sanlam's albatross remains its primary involvement in Absa. It may be tempting to shrug off the past, but it won't go away that easily. It is indisputable that Bankorp, the commercial banking unit put together in Sanlam's stable, was managed by Sanlam edict into a first-rate mess.
>
> Sanlam's Fred du Plessis demanded a hugely expanding loans book – achieved finally by abandoning the cardinal rules of banking probity and conservatism.
>
> The result was a bank that needed either to fold or to be rescued. It was rescued by a Reserve Bank desperate to maintain banking stability. But it was rescued not once but repeatedly and, on the last occasion, the size of the accommodation expanded exponentially – even after it had been absorbed by Absa.
>
> This adds new meaning to the word 'rescue' and it raises, first, the key issue of undue enrichment. An article of commercial faith is that ordinary shareholders must all be treated similarly.
>
> In the case of Bankorp, however, its major shareholder, Sanlam, was privy to the Reserve Bank's rescue packages. But it remains indisputable that, as Sanlam's listing approaches, Absa's annual financial statements fail to reveal the lifeboat, how this had been treated and what tax liabilities it may have generated.
>
> No one has yet justified why a commercial bank that was rescued by taxpayers should be made a present of the huge sums involved.
>
> Second is the matter of Absa's auditors, the distinguished firms of international accountants, KPMG and Ernst & Young. They can hardly fail to have been aware of the Bank's 'loan' and they must still explain why statements that clearly did not reveal the true nature of its financial position were signed off by them.

Third is Sanlam's own failure to tell its policy holders – they own the money – what it was up to. It screwed up Bankorp and then agreed to a secret deal to 'lend' Absa R50m/year for 10 years.

This money will never be repaid – just as, I might add, the taxpayers' R1.25bn given away by the Reserve Bank to Absa was 'deemed' by Governor Chris Stals to have been repaid.

Fourth is the extent to which Sanlam has benefited from the Reserve Bank's charity. The commercial bank it so nearly destroyed was parlayed into a bigger group on the basis of the value not of its usual business but of the now famous 'lifeboat' and Sanlam's stake in the new entity has grown extraordinarily. This was achieved courtesy of the unwitting generosity of SA's taxpayers.

Fifth is the role of Absa's board of directors. They must have known of the existence of the 'loan' from its inception – if they didn't, that raises more questions. Knowledge of the lifeboat must carry with it unusual dangers. I hope none of them – its executive directors particularly – bought or sold Absa stock.

As to whether or not directors exercised properly their fiduciary responsibilities is a matter which, sixth, must be addressed by Judge Willem Heath when his commission delivers its assessment soon.

What the Heath Commission has to say on this subject (if, that is, it is allowed to) now assumes great importance. Until it pronounces – and perhaps even after – the plans to list the assurance giant need to be put on hold.

These were not imaginary dangers. If it was found – and it was extremely likely that this would be so – that Sanlam had conspired with the Reserve Bank to provide illegal help to Bankorp, then Sanlam and its directors would have laid themselves open to legal action. This would come not only from the Heath Commission, but also through the normal court procedures as class actions by discontented shareholders and others were brought forward.

Under normal circumstances many potential legal actions could be discounted, brushed aside in the documentation needed for a stock exchange transaction, as Absa had discounted so many in their own public share issue the preceding year (although that was, by May 1998, looking an unhappy precedent). Merely listing the cases pending, with an anodyne comment, would be enough. The law's delays, reinforced by what Judge Nel had called the 'lack of staff, incompetence and general lassitude' of the Attorneys-General, would ensure that a long period of possibly many years could elapse before those particular birds came home to roost, and in the meantime the business would be done and the money safely gathered in: only if things go very wrong do out-of-date brokers' circulars have a wide readership.

But the Heath Commission was a much more immediate danger. The judge clearly had the bit between his teeth, and as soon as he was satisfied that the evidence was in order, could bring the case immediately, without further ado, to his Special Tribunal. From their decision there was the right of appeal to the Supreme Court, but it is one thing to have a case pending in the courts and quite another to have an adverse judgement going to appeal. Under those circumstances demutualisation and an introduction to the market would be impossible.

Bill Jamieson, in London, caught the uncertainty in a *Sunday Telegraph* article of 5 July:

> Sanlam, the South African mutual life assurance group, may be forced to delay its demutualisation and stock market flotation because of the slump in the rand.
>
> Speculation swept through Johannesburg last Friday that plans for the R20 billion (£2 billion) flotation before December could be pulled.
>
> Currency turmoil has put a question over international support for the share issue. And there are worries that the group's 2.3 million policy-holders, who include the ANC pension fund, would sell their free shares back into the local market, forcing a slump in the price.
>
> More immediately, uncertainties over legislative clearance by the South African government means Sanlam is unable to commit itself to a specific date.

Said a spokesman for Sanlam in London: 'Sanlam was established by an act of parliament and demutualisation requires primary legislation. The bill has yet to be put before the house.'

Three days later the Absa camp received another blow. Askin's action, begun in 1995 to bring Absa before a London court, had repeatedly stalled. On the morning of 8 July his latest appeal was heard. This was to ask for the case to be adjourned to enable further evidence to be produced as to why the case must be heard in England, and not transferred to South Africa. If this application was dismissed there would be no possibility of a successful action. Given the warnings of attempted assassination Askin could not possibly go in person to South Africa to prosecute such a case: and there was no possibility, in spite of all the rodomontade of South African journalists and Attorneys-General, of an application for Askin's extradition even being made, much less succeeding. And, a matter of no little importance, if Askin's appeal were to be dismissed he would be liable for all the legal costs, which could well amount to over two million pounds.

While at previous appearances in court Askin's case depended upon a general appreciation of the South African situation and the unsatisfactory state of justice in that country, on the occasion of this hearing Askin had some compelling evidence. Pavarotti had obtained the sworn statement of the plot to kidnap (and in all probability, kill,) Askin before the attempt to extradite him from Italy had begun. Askin's counsel, David Railton, proposed to show this affidavit to the Bench, but asked that its contents should not be revealed to any of the defendants, but only to their counsel, Trevor Phillipson. The reason was, of course that if the identity of the deponent became known to Absa, then Slang van Zyl's security team would doubtless, and very quickly, dispose of him.

The court needed little convincing, being quite able to understand Absa's reasons for objecting to an adjournment. The real reasons, of course, could not be stated by their embarrassed, and extremely angry, barrister. Absa knew full well that the truth relating both to violent threats against Askin, and quite possibly, violent or illegal action against others, was about to come out. Pavarotti's affidavit (which remained unseen by the court) was only a harbinger of trouble ahead. The case was therefore adjourned to allow Askin to produce more evidence, which had to be handed in by 30 October.

All action was now converging on a single point in time. If the Sanlam demutualisation was to go ahead, then the documentation must also be available by the end of October; if Askin was to win in the matter of jurisdiction he must submit sworn evidence by 30 October, and the penalty for losing his case could be over £2 million. It also appeared that by that date that Judge Heath would have reached, and might have published, his conclusions.

Judge Heath's team were proceeding satisfactorily with their interviews. These were being kept reasonably informal, relying on the witnesses to come when asked politely; no subpoenas were being issued. They began nevertheless to reveal some interesting new facts. Kobus Roetz, formerly managing director of Trust Bank in the 1980s, produced some significant evidence of the way in which the Reserve Bank lifeboat was negotiated, and its probable effect on the Tollgate liquidations. Roetz told the commission:

> When the 1990 lifeboat was being negotiated with the Reserve Bank every relevant person in Trust Bank had been asked to list their bad and doubtful debts. After they had done this they were asked to make the list much larger by Piet Lieben-berg and Hennie van der Merwe, so that they 'could clean up the loan book'. In other words make over-estimates so that the bank could liquidate many clients who were not otherwise either candidates for liquidation or even particu-larly uncreditworthy. Liebenberg said, 'We're going to clean up our book.' The result was that the list submitted to the SARB was a multiple of *five times* that submitted by all the bank and credit managers throughout the group! This meant that the Bank went after clients who would never in normal circumstances have ever been pressed.

During Judge Heath's absence in the USA for three weeks in July his unit worked closely with Hennie Diedericks and Eberhard Bertles-man. Heath had been so impressed by Bertlesman's summaries of the evidence that he wanted formally to appoint him to the Commission, which would need the approval of the Deputy Prime Minister and the Minister of Justice. This was judged to be inappropriate, and Bertlesman's contributions, together with those of Hennie Diedericks and Martin Welz, continued to be informal, although they were working closely with the unit's second in command, Steve Barkhuizen.

Naturally enough, Judge Heath had found that the authorities in the United States supported the view of lifeboats expressed by Kit McMahon. The Federal Reserve Bank expressed themselves amazed at the South African version of what constituted a central bank's proper duties: they had never seen anything like these arrangements, and agreed that restitution of the gifts to Absa should certainly be made. Perhaps even more serious was the possibility that Absa's directors benefited personally from knowledge of the lifeboat, which was completely unacceptable.

Following his visit to the USA, Judge Heath believed that it would be useful to visit London, to talk with the Bank of England, and to meet Julian Askin. As he had foreseen at the beginning of his investigation the lifeboat story would lead to the question of the legality of Tollgate's liquidation. How, for example, could Absa choose to liquidate Tollgate, yet support Russells, a furniture manufacturer and distributor, which owed considerably more to the bank, and whose reconstruction entailed placing Absa executives on the Russell board, for which they were well remunerated?

Judge Heath was planning to be in Cambridge for a seminar on 19 September, which would provide a convenient opportunity to arrange other meetings. In the meantime the Commission continued informal interviews with the leading players. In his interview on 17 August with the Heath Commission, Marinus Daling made the startling admission that the Trust Bank had been insolvent at the time of the 1990 lifeboat. Not, perhaps, a startling admission in view of the weighty evidence to that effect, but very satisfactory confirmation that the Reserve Bank had, once again, been deceiving everyone when they claimed that this was not so, and the bank was merely illiquid. Daling was equally ready to contradict his own previous statements. To the Commission he claimed that he was at that time little more than an investment manager, keeping an eye on Sanlam's many and diverse holdings. To *Finance Week* (3–14 August 1991) Mr Daling argued that many Sanlam investments were 'not merely marketable securities in Sanlam's portfolio . . . with big investments like these, the job is quite different from running a normal portfolio. With a strategic investment, disinvestment is often not an option.'

From the heart of the Beast

The critical October date was approaching and Askin's opponents in South Africa knew only too well what line the Heath investigation was taking (two Absa representatives were present at the questioning of Kobus Roetz). Inevitably, they prepared an offensive action. There was too much at stake, and time was running out. Since there was no legal way of stopping the processes, the opposition resorted to violence and politics.

In August the Askins were taking a short holiday, their first together for two years, in the Algarve. They were celebrating, although with some sadness, the sale of Steenhuis, which Julian had last seen in March 1993. On Sunday 9 August an urgent telephone call came through from an unusually agitated Bertlesman. Susie and Julian were to return to London immediately, taking every precaution, and letting no one know of their intention. It was almost a replay of that Sunday morning on the Steenhuis stoep, when an Afrikaner warned Askin to leave South Africa immediately. A warning had come, as Bertlesman put it, 'from the heart of the Beast'.

For some time Bertlesman had know that van Zyl's agents were attempting to intercept his post and to monitor telephone calls. He had accordingly approached an acquaintance of his, a former senior officer in army intelligence, who had formed a rather more reputable security organisation of his own. This contact had discovered that van Zyl and Maree had been instructed by Absa to monitor all Askin's movements, and those of his associates known to be active in the lifeboat investigations. There existed, he said, 'a very real, immediate and direct threat against the life of Mr Julian Askin'. Both Julian and Susie's movements had been closely watched over the previous twelve months, photographs of them and their car (a somewhat grubby Jeep rather than the Bentley of newspaper stories) had been circulated. The reason for this was unequivocally stated; it was 'because he is suspected of being the driving force behind the present investigation against Absa'.

The informant had, over the seven years Bertlesman had known him, 'proved himself to be not only one of the best intelligence officers he knew, but also a man who is loyal, honest, and absolutely trustworthy.' He had 'absolutely no shadow of doubt about the fact that the information, which he has given me, is correct.' Van Zyl and Maree, he remarked bitterly, 'were the men who killed my friend Anton Lubowski' and they were being let off the leash once more.

The Askins went straight back to London and appraised the situation. It was one the British police well appreciated. The deputy head of C13, the anti-terrorist unit, was well-informed. His men were even then charged with the task of attempting to bring Craig Williamson to England, where Ambassador Babb's agent was wanted for the 1982 bombing of the ANC offices.

Fortunately Chester Square, home to Lady Thatcher and a number of diplomats, was under permanent police surveillance, which would make it easier to keep an informal eye on the Askins. As a safety measure a sophisticated anti-interference device was fitted to the Askins' car, and as an added precaution the fitting was made out of sight in the garage of the Belgravia police station. But the essential protection remained the monitoring carried out in South Africa on those most likely to be involved in any violence.

Other than violence, the remaining tactic of the by now considerably rattled opposition was to attempt to stimulate political reaction to the Heath Commission. In the May budget debate some National Party MPs had attempted to question the appointment of Heath and to defend Absa. Some of the heat was taken out of the situation when, on 4 July, the announcement of Dr Stals' successor was made. This was to be the current Labour Minister, 39-year-old Tito Mboweni, who had been trained at the University of East Anglia as a development economist. He was well regarded politically, but had no banking experience. He was however to be given a year's apprenticeship, since Stals would not resign until August 1999. The *Financial Times* quoted Dave Mohrs, an economist, as saying, 'Now it will be politically very different attacking the Reserve Bank. There will be no more attacks on white

Afrikaner males at the Bank as though the institution was at fault. That's a good thing.'

Which was somewhat missing the point. The serious criticism of the Reserve Bank was not politically motivated, but that it had acted illegally, and defended its illegality by dissimulation and lies.

'My mind is made up. Don't confuse me with the facts'

A lighter note was struck by the final release, after the passage of five years, of the Hoberman-Browde Commission report on 2 September. Under the industrious Hoberman the Commission had, since its establishment on 12 March 1993, interviewed 85 witnesses and sat on 115 days. The transcript of evidence given ran to 8,264 pages, together with 53 volumes of exhibits and appendices amounting to another 10,000 pages.

Mr Justice Browde was more cavalier. He began his report by stating that he had decided to ignore most of Hoberman's work – indeed not even to read all the evidence. He would confine his report 'as far as possible to evidence which I heard personally and some to which my attention was specifically directed.' The persons doing the directing were the two barristers, Gavin Woodland and Jeremy Gauntlett, who had been instructed by the solicitors meant to be acting for the liquidators – Miller Gruss, the firm who had originally instructed Hoberman to apply for Tollgate's liquidation. 'I have been greatly assisted,' Browde acknowledged, 'by memoranda prepared by them' – memoranda which presumably covered those previous hearings which Browde had decided to ignore. Just to make sure that nothing had been missed – or, more probably, indiscreetly included – the barristers' memoranda had been checked by Absa's solicitors, Werksmans. 'As a result,' Mr Browde gratefully concluded, 'I received useful comments from Absa and in what follows I have attempted to have regard to these comments . . .'

With Absa having found a compliant Commissioner, and their lawyers filtering the information, the most troublesome items on the agenda were shelved. Mr Justice Browde would not bother with the question of Absa's security for their loans. He could not do this because, among other things, nobody had said anything to him; (hardly surprising, with Absa in charge!) The uncomfortable fact that Absa were being sued by the liquidators was dismissed as being *sub judice*, and the position of the barristers, who were meant to be representing the views of the liquidators who were suing their client Absa, decently skated over.

Buried, too, was the whole saga of the lifeboat. 'There were certain allegations made before my predecessor regarding the alleged assistance given to ABSA Bank Limited by the Reserve Bank. It was suggested that the Reserve Bank made "soft loans" available to Absa' wrote Browde, suggesting that the admitted facts were little better than speculation. But had not brothers van Zyl and Conradie dismissed these as 'wholly unsubstantiated, irrelevant and devoid of merit'? And the liquidators had themselves (Mr Browde was doubtless assured by Messrs Gauntlett and Woodland) heard all the evidence relating to the 'Lifeboat' and had investigated the matter fully. As far as they were concerned there was no need for any evidence to be led before me regarding the 'Lifeboat' since in their view it was quite irrelevant to the interest of the creditors in the Tollgate group of companies.

On those aspects of the case with which Browde did decide to deal, the usual suspects were arraigned, but not heard. Diedericks, described as 'a former director of Tollgate', with no mention made of his more significant experience in Volkskas and Absa, had asked to be called. 'I declined his request because I was of the opinion that his evidence could not be of benefit to creditors.' Absa had, once again, succeeded in stopping Diedericks being heard in public before an official tribunal. Askin's offer to give evidence was also declined, and for some very unconvincing reasons. Browde was 'not sure' that he legally could take evidence in England, and Askin could in 'no way' be compelled to give evidence and answer questions as he would have been had he given evidence in South Africa; a somewhat sinister reflection.

Instead of making an effort to find out the facts Browde contented himself with repeating the comments made by Judge Berman, on equally flimsy grounds, five years previously, adding some picturesque phrases of his own. 'Persons who are involved in what can fairly be referred to as blatant contraventions of the law with the motive of satisfying their greed for money and in order to enable them to maintain a high standard of living at the cost of others . . .' Whatever truth that might have had in referring to Key and Mackintosh it is undeniable that Askin left South Africa a much poorer man than he had been on his arrival. Nevertheless, Browde insisted, the unseen Askin should be sued for a R32 million 'theft', the details of which made 'sordid reading'. It was the mythical grouse shoot and the helicopter all over again.

Quite how a case could be made out, after five years in which the Attorney-General had not been able to do so, the Commissioner did not condescend to explain. Almost unbelievably, Browde wrote that, 'It seems that the Attorney-General of the Western Cape had it in mind to extradite Askin during 1994 but that proved impossible at the time and since then he had found the difficulties in extraditing Askin from the United Kingdom difficult to overcome. However, I have personally interviewed the Deputy Attorney-General who informed me that the matter of Askin's extradition is still receiving serious attention.' In the face of the indisputable facts that the 1994 application through the Italian courts was thrice judged illegal, and acknowledged by Attorney-General Kahn to be so, and that *no attempt at all has ever been made to procure Askin's extradition from England*, this is an extraordinary finding in an official enquiry. Nor did the fact that Key and Mackintosh had been tried and seen the case against them collapse deter Judge Browde. A civil case could be brought against them, too.

There were also furious reactions from Key, David McCay and Mackintosh who all threatened to sue Judge Browde, and glee in the anti-Askin press. But it cannot have brought much relief to Absa, faced with the prospect of the Heath enquiry's inexorable progress.

At the international symposium on Economic Crime held at Jesus College, Cambridge, on 19 September Judge Nel and Judge Heath both read papers describing their work. One notable absentee was Attorney-General Frank Kahn, due to speak on 'Advancing the cause of victims of Economic Crime'. His absence was not explained but was perhaps tactful, since otherwise he would have had to sit through Judge Nel's denunciation of the 'incompetence' and 'lassitude' of the Attorney-General's office.

From Cambridge Judge Heath continued to seek the opinion of other central bankers on the propriety of the South African Reserve Bank's action. The Bank of England explained their views, confirmed by the

German Bundesbank. They did not accept the propriety of the South Africa Reserve Bank's action. The security said to be taken was no security, but part of the loan itself. There should have been proper security from distinct assets, and above all they could not understand how Absa had managed to escape repayment.

Back in South Africa there was some further work for the Heath Commission. Absa were asked to provide a list of depositors as in 1990, which would, it was thought, show how many of these were Sanlam-related. Were this so, then the lifeboat would be seen as protecting the interests of Sanlam not only as shareholders, but also as depositors. Absa responded by claiming that a. The computer was not working; b. The files were missing; c. or, if they were not actually missing, were hand-written and indecipherable; d. or, alternatively, had been stored for safety in a big black box which, unhappily, could not be found.

But Barkhuisen was able to tell the press that all that remained was to question one or two senior Absa people. He went on to say that 'We have not yet formulated any summonses and if there is any action for recovery of money it will be only next year.' Writing in the *Star* Greta Steyn reported that an official of the Heath Commission had said recently: 'A presentation on the lifeboat has been made to the justice department and it was up to the President to issue a proclamation authorising the unit to continue investigating.'

This seemed to indicate that some interference was running, a suspicion reinforced when on the same day an announcement was made that the Justice Minister, Dullah Omar, was casting doubts on the very existence of the unit.

In a statement to Parliament, Omar asked whether it was appropriate or desirable to appoint a judge in a full-time capacity to head the unit and whether the unit was necessary.

Omar raised the possibility of rationalising the functions of the unit and the public protector.

'Is it appropriate to give the unit a blueprint to investigate any kind of irregularity within its mandate, even of a trivial nature, while such a matter can just as well, and even in a less expensive way, be investigated and disposed of?'

He said the possible rationalisation of the functions of the unit and the public protector would be examined during a summit against crime next month. There was a proposal that government establish one anti-corruption centre and that a cabinet committee be set up to deal with that. 'These are all matters which the cabinet is looking at.'

Omar said the appointment of a judge to the full-time position as head of the unit raised the question: 'What happens to the independence of the judiciary?' Given the political principle and the judicial independence associated with the office of a judge: it should also be asked whether a judge should be doing that type of work.

Omar's announcement was made on 6 October: on the 9th Jakes Gerwel, director-general of the President's office, wrote a stiff letter to Judge Heath. Replying to reports that the Commission had frequently complained of delays in the receipt of their specific authorisation to begin investigations, Gerwel angrily put the blame on the Commission staff. He claimed that requests received, 'priority treatment even over pressing matters of state, and are usually processed within 24 or 48 hours if the president is available.' Any delays which had occurred had 'been at the Justice Department which is required to check your referrals for factual and legal correctness. It is apparently common knowledge that "raw" referrals remitted through your unit have frequently reflected factual and legal flaws: wrong dates, wrong bodies, wrong departments, matters already subject to criminal investigation, insufficient information etc ... Our office has had to assist in dealing with litigation or threatened litigation which arose therefrom or from alleged failure of your unit to operate within its legal limits.'

Justice Minister Omar had spoken in Parliament in response to questions raised by an Inkatha Freedom Party member, Ruth Rabinowitz, who was criticising the restrictions placed on the Commission by the requirement that only corruption involving state assets could be investigated, and that only after specific authorisation. Judge Heath responded instantly, pointing out that the suggestion of reporting directly to a cabinet committee would 'raise the question of whether or not such a body was apolitical' – a polite way of saying that everybody would be convinced that the so-called independent commission would become an obedient servant to the government. To his credit, Omar backed off, claiming that the Heath Commission had done 'outstanding work and is one of the big success stories of the present government. I regard it as an institution that we will need as long as there is corruption in our country.'

Some indication of the likely benefits that Sanlam policy holders might expect were revealed by Daling on 29 October. A free allocation of at least 300 shares would be made, which, at an expected issue price of R6 would constitute a gift of R1800 – very much less than that which had been offered to shareholders in British building societies' conversion, but a welcome present to poorer policy holders. In addition all policy holders would be entitled to a discount of 10 per cent on the issue price, which would enable those with capital to make quite important profits. Anyone 'stagging' (buying, perhaps on borrowed money, with the intention of making a quick sale) the issue to the extent of, say, a million rand, could expect a quick profit of R100,000. Moreover, if the issue was attractively priced, a premium might be expected, which could further increase the profits. It was not envisaged that there would be an 'anchor investor' – a large and solid financial institution which would provide some protection against takeover bids. Sanlam's continuing shareholding would be limited to its asset management company subscribing for up to 150 million of the some 800 million shares which would be on offer. The board had experienced enough trouble as 'anchor shareholders' in Absa to discourage a repetition.

An 'anchor investor' would have been, in any event, difficult to arrange, with the issue limited to the Johannesburg Stock Exchange. Earlier in the year Sanlam had hoped that a London quotation might have been achieved, as had been done with Billiton. Given the very much greater opportunities that would be been offered by having a share quoted on the London Stock Exchange one or two major international financial institutions might have been prepared to take strategic stakes. But a London issue would have required much higher standards of transparency and documentation, which Robert Fleming, acting as Sanlam's advisers, might well have found difficult to provide. Sanlam were therefore obliged to make do with a bathetic second best, a quotation of the Windhoek Stock Exchange, an institution of unparalleled insignificance. 'There were,' a Sanlam spokesman apologised, 'expectations that the shares would be listed in London, but never a firm commitment. The reason for Namibia is that it is a dynamic capital market and that 68,000 policy holders live there.' It should be added that there were some 2.2 million Sanlam policy holders.

At the time of the announcement, Chairman Daling made a guarded forecast that Sanlam's 1998 expected headline earnings would be broadly in line with those of the previous year if conditions did not deteriorate. However, Gensec's high level of profits in the first half-year was unlikely to be repeated in the second half, with the profit from its equity activities having been adversely affected.

One cause of the 'adverse effects' were the rumours reported by David Gleason in the *Financial Mail* on the same day as Daling's announcement. These were fuelled by the fact that Gensec's senior equities dealer, Gawie Botha, who had been suspended by his employer, had applied for the seizure of tape recordings of conversations made between Gensec dealers and Johannesburg stockbrokers. The suggestion was that the quarterly results of Gensec, and hence Sanlam, had been 'cooked'. Gleason queried:

> Is it true, for example, that as close-out approaches, some asset managers invade dealing rooms to consult with their traders? Do they subsequently issue instructions the effect of which is to trade certain selected stocks so as to manipulate their prices? Is the net result of this exercise to guarantee an ability to demonstrate to a largely uncritical public acceptable levels of growth in the funds they administer? The practice is commonly referred to in the trade as 'window dressing', the implication being that those who know a lot about unit trusts won't give the quarterly results a *gravitas* they don't deserve.
>
> As you'd expect in a matter of this kind the market is both alight with rumour and wrong more than half the time. In this case, share price manipulation could well be confused with elements of insider trading and front-running. Botha, it is being said, was a front-runner on a large scale. Fiddling with share prices, however, implies access to price-sensitive information, a difficult area of law. What constitutes price-sensitive information for one thing? And when is information

price-sensitive for another? And why is it always assumed the dirty dogs in this business are brokers? Why not also the directors and senior officials of the companies about which the price-sensitive information is circulating? Of course, if some asset management companies do permit (encourage?) window dressing, then not only do they transgress the law, they also invite attack by those who might claim they were misled by manipulated results.

Gleason concluded his article by writing: 'As for Gawie Botha, well, he has an opportunity to establish himself as a man who didn't stand in the way of the truth. And no, I am not being ingenuous. He tells me he is genuinely anxious to get this resolved. As for the regulatory authorities, I'm not at all certain what they are doing. Perhaps he should consider asking Judges Heath and Nel to investigate the matter too . . . Well then, let the games begin . . . preferably in public.'

One door closes

By 30 October, the day when Askin's case had to be submitted to the British courts, a thunderbolt arrived. Eberhard Bertlesman had telephoned the previous evening to say that he had made some last-minute alterations to his affidavit, which would be transmitted by fax to Askin's lawyers the following morning. The affidavit would be a comprehensive statement of the deadly risks that Askin would be taking if he was to come to South Africa. Based as it was on the hardest evidence and the best authority, from the senior officer persuaded by Bertlesman to tell all he knew, the affidavit was likely to be the decisive factor in ensuring that the case would be heard in London. At 10.30 a.m. on Friday 30 October Bertlesman telephoned Amhurst Brown to say that he would not be allowed to submit his affidavit. It was a massive blow to the Askin team.

As a matter of legal protocol, Bertlesman, as chairman of the Pretoria Bar Association, had sought the permission of the Bar Council, it not being at all a usual matter for a barrister to submit evidence in another case. He had discussed this matter with his colleagues some weeks previously and had secured, as he thought, their approval. Then, at the very last minute, the Bar Council's vice chairman telephoned Bertlesman to say that the Council had decided to withdraw their approval and would not permit the affidavit to go forward. Absa's minions had clearly been at work.

Askin and the layers went into near-permanent session, discussing possible methods of retrieving the situation. As an immediate measure an urgent application was made to the court to allow an extension of 14 days for the submission of evidence. Presuming that this were to be granted, possible actions seemed to be: a. for Bertlesman to obtain permission, once more, to put in his affidavit – which he was anxious to do, sticking firmly to his guns. If this were not forthcoming, b. put in the draft affidavit, which would have to be done without Bertlesman's permission, or, c. to persuade the unnamed source of Bertlesman's information to swear the affidavit himself. This he had absolutely declined to do, being far too well aware of the likely consequences to himself and his family.

Bertlesman himself was deeply distressed by this ambush, and anxious to find some solution. One possibility was for him to be subpoenaed to give evidence at the hearing, which was scheduled for 27 January 1999. This he would be permitted – indeed obliged – to do, and was very willing to follow this course. But this would not help the immediate problem, which was that documents to be submitted in evidence had to be received by 30 October. Unless this were done a future subpoena might well prove irrelevant, as it was quite possible that the Judge would refuse to admit such last-minute evidence. It seemed that the most promising course was for Eberhard Bertlesman to persuade his colleagues at the Pretoria bar to change their minds – again.

At six o'clock in the morning of 6 November Bertlesman telephoned to say that he had succeeded. The vice president of the Pretoria Bar had agreed that Bertlesman's affidavit could be submitted, but anonymously. There was much relief at this, and an amended version of the affidavit was prepared, blacking out references where necessary, to show exactly what had been omitted. All was once more, on course.

But only for a matter of hours. Before midday an unhappy Bertlesman telephoned Amhurst Brown to say that the Bar Council had second (third or fourth?) thoughts and once again turned down his application. And once again 'persuasion' had been at work.

It was decision time. It was not possible to approach Bertlesman's source except through Bertlesman, and this would take time. The only solution was for Stephen Morris, the responsible Amhurst Brown partner, to submit Bertlesman's affidavit himself. This would be accompanied by explanations that this was done by Morris without Bertlesman's approval and consent or that of the Pretoria Bar Council, and was not sworn to. It would however, be warranted as the affidavit which Bertlesman would have sworn had he been allowed to do so. Bertlesman, naturally enough, found this suggestion worrying, although he realised that there was probably little alternative. It was another impossible situation. The barristers comprising the Pretoria Bar Council, officers of the court, sworn to uphold the law, were suppressing evidence – a fact which appalled the London lawyers.

Askin telephoned Bertlesman on Saturday 7 November to tell him of their decision, apologising for placing Bertlesman in a difficult situation, realising that this would mean the end of their productive co-operation. Bertlesman was calm, expecting the news, and saying that he would need time to think through the implications: but in fact these were clear. He could either defy the Bar Council, which would mean professional ruin, or cease to act for Askin; and he inevitably, on Monday 9th, was forced to choose the latter. Morris took the precaution to telephone the source of Bertlesman's information, the military intelligence officer who had to remain anonymous. This officer had been given a copy of the affidavit by Bertlesman, and was able to assure Morris that the facts were as stated, but that he was not prepared to be identified as the informant. The critical statement was therefore duly submitted to the High Court.

But as one door closes, another opens, and this was a very unexpected portal. Askin had told Martin Welz of Bertlesman's dilemma, and Welz, after some thought, made an unexpected suggestion. There was no one who knew more about Absa's tactics and history than their old favourite-turned-bugbear, Bertrand Hoberman. Now in retirement, free from professional restraints, still aggrieved by his treatment, Hoberman might be willing to provide his story. It would not have the force of Bertlesman's despatch from 'the heart of the Beast', but would provide solid evidence of how Asba could deploy its great influence to secure the bank's own ends – and in any event Bertlesman's story would reach the court through Stephen Morris. On the evening of 5 November therefore, Welz called on Hoberman at his home in Greyton.

The old Commissioner was not immediately enthusiastic. He needed this 'like a hole in the head', but realised full well that Askin had no chance whatsoever of obtaining a fair hearing in South Africa, and that, if justice was to be done, it could only be through an English court. His suspicions of Absa's double-dealing that had been aroused during the hearings had never been allayed, and the banal report of his successor had contributed absolutely nothing to the argument.

Welz reported that Hoberman had said he knew how difficult it would be for anyone with no direct experience of South Africa to appreciate how much pressure Absa could exert: he had experienced this in a way that 'cannot be imagined' during his period as Commissioner, and knew the same pressure was brought to bear upon the two judges, van Zyl and Conradie, who had fired him. When he was appointed Commissioner of the Tollgate enquiry he was aware that he was meant to be no more than a figurehead. The enquiry was to be run by the two barristers, Gauntlett and Woodland; Hoberman was there to rubber-stamp events and allow them to get on with it. After a while this had troubled him and he had become appalled by what he was seeing. He eventually became so embarrassed that he decided to take a role and 'intervene' in the proceedings. It was at this moment Absa stepped in and had him removed.

Hoberman added that when he started the Tollgate enquiry he expected it to be merely a small hill to climb. Eventually it became an Everest. He was in the end relieved to be taken away from it.

Under the circumstances, at some personal inconvenience, and with the knowledge that by so doing he would alienate many of his former colleagues in a profession he had followed for thirty-five years, Bertrand Hoberman agreed that he would come to England to provide evidence for Julian Askin's case against Absa. When he heard this from Welz, Stephen Morris immediately telephoned Hoberman to arrange the trip. There was, it was agreed, an essential need for secrecy. Askin's opponents had managed to discover Bertlesman's intentions, and to thwart them. Hoberman could also, if need be, be blocked. Insisting that no one else in South Africa should be told of his intention, Hoberman suggested that, just as Askin had done in 1993, he should not fly direct to London, but take the Air France flight to Paris.

After a few days to sort through his papers, Hoberman arrived in London on Friday, 13 November and settled down to prepare his affidavit. His original indignation over his dismissal, the abrupt and discourteous way Absa had sought this, and the underhand conduct of Gauntlett in obtaining false testimony from Judge Friedland, had been exacerbated by Judge Browde's superficial and summary report.

He was naturally surprised that Browde had not seen fit to read the evidence, without which it would have been impossible for him to report accurately: and there were a number of significant omissions, of which the most interesting was that concerning Christo Wiese.

Of the original Stellenbosch coterie, Wiese had been by far the most successful, chairman of Pepkor, Boland Bank, on the board of the Reserve Bank, reputed one of the richest men in South Africa. When Hoberman had signalled his intention to demand Wiese's appearance before his Commission there had been some consternation. Hoberman recorded:

> The first matter to which I wish to refer in this regard involves Mr Christo Wiese.
>
> Mr Morris of Amhurst Brown Colombotti informs me and I verily believe that in 1992, Mr Wiese was a main Board Director of the SARB and a former director of Duros. It is my understanding that Mr Wiese was and is a very successful businessman and banker.
>
> In the course of my investigation in the Section 417 Enquiry, I decided that it would be appropriate to subpoena Mr Wiese to testify. Mr Woodland was in full agreement with my proposed course of action. The subpoena was not issued because matters were overtaken by the application for my recusal.
>
> Following the application for my recusal as Commissioner, I received a telephone call from Mr Adam Harris of Miller Gruss Katz and Traub in early August 1996. He wanted to have a meeting with me and Mr Woodland concerning a

proposal which he had received from Mr Wiese. There appeared to be some urgency about the matter and Mr Harris was anxious that I attend the meeting. I live in Greyton which is approximately one and a half hours drive from Cape Town. Mr Harris told me that I could charge for my travelling time in order to attend the meeting with him and Mr Woodland. I had previously on numerous occasions travelled to Cape Town from Greyton for the purposes of the Commission but had never before been told that I should charge for travelling time.

I travelled to Cape Town and met on a Sunday at Mr Woodland's Chambers with both Mr Woodland and Mr Harris. Essentially, the proposal of Mr Wiese was that he was seeking to do a deal whereby he would make a payment of a substantial amount to the liquidators in return for the receipt of an immunity, meaning that I would agree not to subpoena him to give evidence before the Section 417 Enquiry. I indicated to Messrs Woodland and Harris that I was not prepared to entertain the proposal about which I had serious misgivings, which I might or might not have expressed, as I did not believe it was appropriate for me to do so in the light of the pending application for my recusal.

Indeed, Christo Wiese was never called upon to give evidence and it is reported that the sum of R2 million was paid to the liquidators. What evidence was thereby suppressed, with the assistance of Messrs Woodland and Harris, remains unheard.

Nothing whatever concerning this appeared in Browde's report. It remains unknown whether Wiese was indeed subpoenaed, whether the deal was done or not, or even whether Browde even read the evidence which had caused Hoberman to want Wiese to appear for questioning.

Nor was anything said about Lewis, whose testimony to Hoberman had revealed that some incriminatory evidence had been destroyed, a circumstance which Hoberman viewed 'in a serious light'. The whole question of Lewis's guilt or innocence was ignored, as was also the evidence of Bill McAdam, another of Hoberman's concerns. No mention was made either of the share gifts made to employees of Trust Bank.

But Hoberman's most important condemnation of Browde's report lay in the fact that so much of it appeared to have been prepared by Absa's barrister friends, Gauntlett and Woodland. They had earlier attempted to persuade Hoberman to accept their version of the enquiry, but he had found so many alterations to be necessary that he had rejected their draft. On reading Browde's report, it was apparent to Hoberman that it bore a 'marked resemblance' to the memorandum the barristers had previously prepared for him. Furthermore, Browde had submitted the draft to Absa's solicitors, Werksmans, for their approval. 'Useful comments' had been received from Absa, and Browde admitted that he had 'attempted to have regard to these comments and to rely as far as possible on what appears to be common cause in relation to the evidence that was led before the Commission before I took up my appointment'. In other words, Browde had relied for the major part of his report on a memorandum prepared by barristers close to Absa, and vetted by Absa's solicitors, rather than making any effort to discover the truth. Neither had any attempt been made to check the memorandum with others, despite the fact that many of the liquidators were locked in legal battles with the bank, and would have had decided views to express. It was therefore hardly odd that no findings adverse to Absa were to be found in Browde's report.

Bertrand Hoberman's revelation (and, he told Askin, he would have much more to say if he could be assured of an indemnity) of the extent to which Judge Browde's findings had been manipulated by Absa was not known to Dr Cronjé when he prepared his own oddly-worded affidavit, his third in the Askin case, on 3 December 1998. 'The suggestion,' Cronjé wrote, 'that Absa would engage in illegal and criminal activities of the type contemplated by Askin, including apparently physical assault and murder, is simply ridiculous.' Apart from the strange suggestion that Askin himself was 'contemplating' such violent actions, the qualification of the sort of illegal activities in which Absa might be tempted to engage silently acknowledges the fact that Absa had already been proved to be guilty of telephoning tapping and other associated misdemeanours. The rest of Conjé's statement was equally carefully hedged. Askin 'allegedly' received telephone calls: if so they were nothing to do with Absa. 'As far as I am aware' the suggestion was 'absurd' – but Cronjé had personally been concerned in the de Villiers episode:

why was it therefore absurd to believe that Absa had not changed its methods? Nor was he prepared to admit that the Armscor document described on p.110 was genuine: he knew nothing of Mr Nel, and did not believe that he was the Cronjé referred to in that memorandum.

When it came to the Eberhard Bertlesman affidavit, Cronjé was ready to dismiss much as 'irrelevant', and denied – again 'so far as I am aware' – that Absa had employed 'any persons by the name of Slang van Zyl or Chappie(s) Maree' to act on their behalf against Bertlesman or Askin – at least 'to the best of my knowledge and belief'. As far as the rest of the Absa group's 36,000 employees were concerned, Dr Cronjé had entrusted the investigation to that faithful servant of the bank, Christo Faul, who had supervised the Tollgate affair since 1992.

Having previously been caught out in numerous equivocations and untruths, Faul could be relied upon to produce the answer required by the board. Sure enough, he discovered that Absa was entirely innocent of any harassment of Bertlesman. Indeed, the bank was quite unaware that Bertlesman had any involvement in the lifeboat investigation, and this was confirmed by Koos Wepener, acting head of the Absa legal department.

Here Faul had gone too far, for Bertlesman, shown Cronjé's affidavit, characterised this statement as a 'straight lie'. At least a month before he prepared his own affidavit, in October, Bertlesman had been confronted in a courtroom by lawyers acting for Absa who had told him 'straight out' that they knew Bertlesman was involved in the lifeboat enquiry. And it can surely be no coincidence that within days of his affidavit being disclosed to the opposition, intimidatory telephone calls began being received at Bertlesman's home number at times when he was away. The intention was clearly to harass Mrs Bertlesman – silences, heavy breathing etc. And on 13 December, a Sunday, when Bertlesman had, untypically, gone in the morning to his chambers, his wife received a call during which a man said to her words to the effect of, 'Well, we know he's not at home, is he? And we know where he is and what he's doing, and he's having a fine time, I can tell you.' The implication being that Bertlesman was engaged in an affair. It was an exact and not very imaginative repetition of the tactics that Absa had previously used.

Bertlesman was certain that all this resulted from his involvement in the Julian Askin case and in the production of the affidavit, and believed van Zyl to be responsible for the calls. In a further incident, on 14 December, the keys to his front door and outer gate were stolen, while the door and gate had been left open for the delivery and recovery of large quantities of documents in connection with another case. Bertlesman was certain that he was under constant surveillance, and a few days later a telephone tap was indeed discovered on an adjoining relay box. Absa were up to their old tricks.

A grudging admission of this was made in Cronjé's statement. In view of the accumulated evidence of a link between Absa and van Zyl, some admission was essential, and the least harmful version was disclosed. It was not Absa itself, but an associated company, who employed Snake.

> Absolute underwriting managers wholly owned by its managing director, Mr R. Faux, in whose board sat two executive directors of Absa insurance, C. de Jager and S. Swanepoel, which had employed Van Zyl and of course not to do anything disreputable; and as it turned out, their services were unsatisfactory.

In attempting to disentangle the web of claim and counter-claim it is worthwhile reflecting that companies engaging in doubtful activities (by no means an uncommon practice anywhere) do not record their instructions in formal language. Some middle manager picks up signals from higher up, and translates them into action which can be deniable by his superiors. If anything goes wrong, then a suitable scapegoat can be found (it may be assumed that Messrs de Jager and Swanepoel have had to undergo a few uncomfortable moments).

The last part of Dr Cronjé's affidavit must have been composed with tongue in cheek. Askin wanted his case heard in London, since it would not be safe for him to return to South Africa. What nonsense!, asserted Cronjé:

> South Africa is a democratic and open society, whose written constitution guarantees every person equal protection and benefit of the law, the right to freedom and security and other essential human rights, including the right to a fair trial, the right to bail (if the interests of justice permit) and

the right of every detained person to humane conditions of detention. I understand from Absa's South African legal advisers that the administration of prisons in South Africa is the responsibility of the Department for Correctional Services, which is fully accountable to the Minister for Correctional Services. The Department is headed by a Commissioner, currently Dr Khulekani Sitole, who is appointed by the government. He is assisted by Deputy Commissioners and other staff.

Coming from one who had been at the centre of the apartheid regime, a director of Volkskas, treasurer of the Broederbond and cashier to the murder squads, a pillar of the white supremacist regime, that statement has to be read as open cynicism.

Finally, Dr Cronjé drew attention to the Browde Commission's criticisms of Askin; he was not to know how thoroughly these had been demolished by Hoberman.

CHAPTER THIRTEEN

Winners and Losers

The Hoberman affidavit demonstrated, on the best possible authority, that Absa had from start to finish controlled the whole 'independent' enquiry, acted decisively to remove the Commissioner when he showed signs of an inconvenient curiosity, and substituted a report drafted by their own lawyers. The investigation into the affairs of Tollgate, which had dragged on for over five years, had finally identified Absa as the villain, and put paid, it might be thought, to any South African case against Askin. Mackintosh and Key had already been acquitted in the face of much more weighty evidence, and McCay, Key's old partner in Tollgate and Kyalami, was preparing to refute Browde's version of affairs, which rebuttal – all 414 pages of it – was duly lodged on 23 December.

But Hoberman's evidence was only marginally helpful to Askin in his London court case. Questions as to the conduct of Lewis, McAdam and Wiese had indeed been raised by Hoberman, but these were incidental to Askin's charges against Absa. More significantly, the revelations of Christo Wiese's transactions with the Hoberman-Browde Commission were stimulating nervous anxiety. During a visit to South Africa early in January 1999, Crispian Hotson, an old friend of Askin's, was approached by both McCay and Key. In conversation with McCay, Hotson said that he had seen documents (notably the Hoberman affidavit) which 'would blow several people out of the water,' including Wiese. Hotson related that McCay 'blanched' and became 'increasingly nervous', saying that Wiese was in Mexico, but that he would immediately speak to him on the telephone. Was there, he asked, any way to stop Askin? 'Yes,' Hotson replied bluntly. 'Money.'

Before leaving, McCay told Hotson that 'Old man Rupert only goes into his office in Stellenbosch every day to worry about one thing, the Absa problem. He's over 80 now, and this is getting to him.'

On the following day (11 January) Hotson met Mervyn Key, who had spoken with McCay and Wiese. After assuring himself that the evidence against Wiese was solid, Key said that a solution had to be found, and that he was willing to act as a go-between. All those allegations against Askin that had been so picturesquely reiterated for so long had been dropped as baseless. Except one, Key reported: the Kyalami question. And that, he asserted, could speedily be dealt with by evidence that he could provide.

Mervyn Key gave his view of Absa. The biggest problem there was that 'certain management officials' who wanted the affair cleared up were willing – indeed, would be happy – to see Cronjé fired. They were opposed by some senior men, and only two people could settle the matter: the representatives of the controlling shareholders, Marinus Daling and Johan Rupert. Key had schedules of all dealings in Absa shares, which gave information on many illegal transactions, and which would be 'explosive', leading to prosecutions and class actions brought by aggrieved shareholders against individual directors.

It was generally accepted that Absa would be obliged to return the lifeboat funds to the government, and Cronjé had found a distinguished berth (and one highly appropriate in view of his long connection with the apartheid regime) as President of the Potchefstroom University for Christian National Education. Surely it was not necessary to have a 'bloodbath' of scandal released in the London courts? Key would be happy to come immediately to London, meet Askin and discuss a possible settlement before the next court hearing, due in fourteen days' time.

At that time it was still unclear when Judge Heath might be able to complete his report. His recovery was proceeding slowly, and when early in December he had come to work for an hour his concerned staff had to ask him to go home. Heath was at least able to give his first press interview since being taken ill, to the South African *Sunday Independent* on 27 December. In it he indicated that he intended to extend his investigation to cover at least another four lifeboats launched by the SARB, and interestingly enough, that this move had been suggested to him by Deputy President Thabo Mbeki himself. Several extra auditors had already been recruited, and the Heath Commission would start the new year with 25 new staff members, among them two senior advocates. Two judges would be permanently attached to the Commission, previously overseen by temporary acting judges.

As for Absa, Heath's assistant Guy Rich said the investigation was on the verge of being wound up, with only one more witness to be interviewed – the recalcitrant Piet Badenhorst. Rich expected that the report would be ready by the end of January. It was looking decidedly likely that his findings would be published too late for Askin's case.

More pressure had arisen from an unexpected quarter. Susie Askin's melanoma had developed, and in August 1997 she had undergone an operation at the Lister Hospital to remove a bowel tumour. Although she seemed to have made a complete recovery, a year later the cancer was found to have spread, and in November 1998 she had another operation to remove some tumours in her liver, a very serious intervention. In spite of Susie's remarkable recuperative powers – she was up and about with much of her usual vigour within two weeks – during the critical months of December and January her health was a matter of grave concern for Julian, overshadowing the events in South Africa.

On 18 January, Key, Hotson, Oatley and Askin met for lunch, at first a cautious affair. Mervyn, Key and Askin had not spoken for over six years, during which time Askin had observed much evidence of Key's capacity for self-preservation, often at the expense of the truth. Key was his usual charming self, very friendly, clearly concerned about the effect of Hoberman's revelations on Wiese's position – and, by implication, his own. Wiese, he said, was the only person involved in all sides of the matter, as a director of Tollgate, the Reserve Bank and Sanlam, and immediate action should be taken to reach an agreement with him.

But Wiese would want 'air cover'. If he 'went public' to ensure that the Reserve Bank and Absa made proper amends, he would need some government guarantee of his own position. This was highly unlikely, since the whole purpose of the Heath Commission was to have an independent investigation, and no interference in its conclusions would be countenanced. But whatever the outcome, Key said, David McCay was going to pursue Absa directors on criminal charges, and would be backed by shareholders who could prove losses due to the undisclosed lifeboat.

Askin was left unconvinced that any action was likely. The defining moment was to be the Heath report; and his hope was that the judge's conclusions would be published before his case was due to be heard in London – and that in only eight days' time.

Endgame

Inasmuch as clearing Askin's name was the main point of his mounting the case against Absa, it could be argued that this was no longer of such importance.

Key's confirmation that all the allegations except one had been abandoned, and that he could provide evidence to prove Askin's innocence on that, only reinforced what had become obvious by the Cape Attorney-General's inaction – that there were no criminal offences alleged against Askin that could be made to stick. But such a negative clearance was not what Askin wanted: he still insisted on proving that he had been a victim of conspiracy; and this could only be done by his bringing an action.

The judgement which was given on 29 January was a disappointment. The three Law Lords found that the evidence that Askin would be in serious danger if he was to go to South Africa was not sufficiently convincing. It was perhaps remarkable that the judges did not appreciate the force of Michael Oatley's testimony. He had spent more time on African issues than any other member of MI6, was one of the half-dozen or so most senior officers concerned with understanding and activating intelligence penetration of the apartheid regime, and held the rank of Under Secretary of State. He had confirmed that Cronjé had been, according to trustworthy evidence, 'the most senior person responsible for the financial and banking arrangements supporting the activities of the apartheid regime's secret services, who knew him familiarly as "Slim Danie".' Oatley did not have any doubt that Askin would be putting his life in immediate danger if he went to South Africa. His affidavit concluded by stating:

On 16 December 1998 I discussed Mr Askin's situation at length with a senior police officer, appointed by the new government whose responsibilities involve him in monitoring the activities of former members of the security and intelligence services in connection with right-wing Afrikaner political groups. He is not prepared to be identified. He told me that he understood very clearly why Askin was regarded as a serious threat to the interests of leading members of the Afrikaner business community, and that he had no doubt that these people, or others working for them, had the means and the motivation for having Askin killed if he were to come to South Africa. If Askin were to be arrested and imprisoned in South Africa, he said, he would certainly not survive.

The judges' decision was the more surprising since Lord Justice Tuckey, who wrote the judgement, had himself been brought up in Zimbabwe, a country whose head of state, Robert Mugabe, is notorious even in Africa for his personal corruption, and where the rule of law is decidedly shaky, in spite of a shiny constitution which promises the maintenance of human rights. Even as Askin's case was being heard in London, Zimbabwean judges were being overruled by military action, with the connivance of Mugabe. Yet Lord Tuckey expressed his confidence that in South Africa 'the 1996 Constitution contains a Bill of Rights which entitles everyone arrested to bail if the interests of justice permit and everyone accused to be presumed innocent'. The lack of presumption of innocence in South Africa had been proved time after time, and the sanctity of life in that most violent of societies, with a daily average of thirty dead by gunshot, and where such proven assassins as Maree and van Zyl were still free, armed and well-funded, was minimal.

There were other indications that the Law Lords had not perfectly acquainted themselves with the facts of the matter. Diedericks (with his name consistently misspelt) was again dismissed as 'a former managing director of Tollgate who was also an ex-Absa manager', neglecting to mention his previous experience in both Volkskas and Trust Bank, essential to a proper understanding of the weight of his evidence, or to defining his high status both there, as managing director, and within South African society, as chairman of the Post Office. Lord Tuckey went on to say, 'there is nothing sinister or unusual about a lifeboat under which a reserve bank may provide support to a bank under its aegis to avoid loss of confidence in the banking system and damage to the national economy. Lifeboats are by their nature discretionary and for obvious reasons their existence is not publicised.'

Such an opinion, in view of the explosive nature of the recent Long Term Capital Management lifeboat, which made headlines in every newspaper, betrays a breathtaking judicial ignorance.

Ironically, it took only three days for the hollowness of the judge's views to be revealed. On 2 February the South African newspapers headlined the fact that Judge Heath had said that Stals and Liebenberg, among others, would be summonsed to stand trial before the tribunal for 'alleged malpractice relating to the central bank's R1.5 million lifeboat to Bankorp'. On the following day, 3 February, the London *Financial Times* carried a prominent headline: 'South African Bank Governor Faces Tribunal Over Bail-Out':

Chris Stals, governor of the South African Reserve Bank, and senior private sector executives may be summoned to appear before an anti-corruption tribunal that will try to recover R1.12 billion (£113 million) used to bail out the Afrikaner-controlled Bankorp in the late 1980s and early 1990s.

The Heath Commission, an anti-corruption unit, headed by Judge Willem Heath, has concluded that the Reserve Bank, Absa (a bank which bought Bankorp in 1990) and Sanlam (the life assurance company that controlled Bankorp and has a holding in Absa) have a case to answer about the rescue.

Investigators said yesterday they should be able to recover the money if they can prove that the transactions involved were unlawful and not in line with normal central bank practice to stabilise a commercial banking system.

'The major shareholder, Sanlam, got off scot-free', said one. 'Basically they flogged the bank at the last minute and walked away smiling.' Some South Africans suspect the bail-out was a case of members of the Afrikaner elite helping each other as apartheid crumbled.

Thabo Mbeki, Deputy President, sought to dispel the

uncertainty surrounding Mr Stals' future by telling the Heath Commission in May last year to investigate the lifeboat and report back to the government 'within the next few weeks.'

Eight months later the Commission has finished its investigations and decided to try to recover the money, although it says it will wait a few weeks while an outside solicitor analyses the transactions before taking the next step.

'The unit has taken a decision to act on the lifeboat case, pending a report from the auditors', Guy Rich, for the Commission, said yesterday. Asked who would be summoned to the tribunal, he said, 'We cannot indicate at this stage who the parties are going to be.'

However, those investigating the bank rescue say Mr Stals, who retired as central bank governor in August, and Piet Liebenberg, former Absa chairman, will be among those called.

Although the results of the Heath Commission's investigations were delayed pending an auditor's report, the thrust of their findings was indicated by Steve Barkhuizen. The emphasis of the investigation and its future action had been concentrated on Absa and Sanlam and their directors, the beneficiaries, corporate and personal, of the Reserve Bank's substantial presents. The role of that body as accomplice and conduit for the flow of money was vital, but had not benefited (as far as could be seen) the Reserve Bank – in fact, quite the opposite. But the investigation had concluded that the lifeboats were illegal, indefensible and fraudulent – a very different conclusion from that of Lord Tuckey, that there was 'nothing sinister or unusual' about them. Furthermore, the money had not all been used for the original purposes, but significant sums were misappropriated and diverted. There would, in all likelihood, be a number of individual prosecutions.

More than five years after the conversation in September 1993 between Johan Rupert and Julian Askin in which the subject had first been raised, the full extent of the conspiracy between that band of brothers, the South African Reserve Bank, Sanlam, and 'the guys at the Afrikaner bank', was officially acknowledged. The London courts may have decided to dismiss any idea that the South African Reserve Bank was in any way to blame, but the truth was out. Restitution and punishment were looming.

But Askin's reputation was still at risk. In one, probably final, outburst of inaccuracy and vulgarity, Nigel Dempster published an article (*Daily Mail* 17 February 1999) with the headline 'Failed Askin Faced his Toughest Battle'.

A fugitive from South Africa following the £80 million collapse of his mini conglomerate Tollgate in 1992, British entrepreneur Julian Askin has received further bad news; his heiress wife Susie has a terminal illness and may not survive this year.

The couple are planning to move from her £1 million Belgravia house in Chester Square to the English countryside after selling their Constantia, Cape Town, mansion Steenhuis for just over £1.1 million – they were estimated to have spent nearly double that on the property in the shadow of Table Mountain.

Askin, 52, and educated at King's School, Bruton, the Somerset public school, is wanted in South Africa on eight charges of fraud involving £6 million.

Among his creditors are the family of leading racehorse owner-breeder Robert Sangster, who tell me they lent an Askin company £3 million – and have received back only £1 million.

Just last month his defence case that he was misled by Absa, South Africa's leading bank, was dented when chairman Danie Cronjé denied under oath charges by Askin of improper conduct or links to so-called covert forces. Askin has been trying to sue Absa in Britain for £10 million over Tollgate.

The court dismissed Askin's appeal against the order staying his proceedings in London against Absa and further refused Askin leave to appeal to the House of Lords.

The stricken Tollgate included the Kyalami Grand Prix race circuit near Jo'burg, Greyhound buses and Budget rent-a-car.

Thrice-married millionairess Susie, who has a Cape Town-based daughter, Charlotte Wilson, by her late second husband

Max, owns the Chester Square house and sold Steenhuis
(Afrikaans for Stone-house) to a European after buying it
back from the sequestrators.

Susie's mother had been given only a controlled account of her daughter's condition, and the offensive article proved a severe shock. Apart from the brutal dismissal of Susie's illness as 'terminal', and Dempster's prognosis that 'she may not survive this year', the article was replete with inaccuracies. Tollgate's liquidation had been for very much less than £80 million. Askin was not facing eight 'charges', but one (in fact no charges have ever been brought against Julian Askin; only allegations have been made – an important difference). Susie's wealth was not inherited (her husband Max Wilson had died shortly after being reinstated from bankruptcy, with few if any assets), but came from her own property-development activities. The Sangster family – a conveniently anonymous source – is quoted as having lent Askin £2 million which has not been returned. It may be recalled that a previous Sangster claim had been that the money was a personal debt: the tune had changed. But whether personal or corporate, the question thrusts itself forward: why had no effort been made to reclaim such a large sum from Askin? Nor had the Sangsters attempted to recover their losses on Tollgate shares by sueing Absa. Askin, it appears, once finished with Absa, intends to investigate the precise role played by the Sangsters themselves in the events that resulted in the Tollgate shareholders losing their investment.

Most significantly, the Dempster piece appeared nearly two weeks after the *Financial Times* had carried the story of the Heath Commission's projected action against Absa and the Reserve Bank; action which, with Stals, Liebenberg and other 'senior private executives' to be summonsed before an anti-corruption tribunal, immeasurably strengthened Askin's case; and Dempster must surely have been aware of so prominent an article in so authoritative a publication. Opinion in South Africa, which was outraged by the article (a letter of complaint bearing some sixty signatures was sent to the editor of the *Daily Mail*), conjectured that Dempster's piece, which appeared shortly after the journalist had visited South Africa, had been motivated by his annoyance at finding how near Askin was to vindication and victory.

What the tabloid journalist could not have known was that the single 'charge' against Askin was about to be withdrawn. In view of the incompetence (to put it at the least damaging) of the provincial Attorneys-General, the South African government had decided to appoint a national officer. On 2 February the new Super Attorney-General Nckuga finally succeeded in extracting the Askin file from Frank Kahn. Not without a struggle, and after many demands: the documents were sent only *after* the London court case had been safely – from Absa's point of view – concluded.

The conclusions of Judge Heath's enquiry were precise, clear, and well-documented. But one vital question remained: would they be published? Delays had abounded, beginning with the judge's illness in November 1998. Uncertainty grew when, at the beginning of March 1999, after Steve Barkhuizen had described the Commission's findings, these still had not been made public.

Powerful interests were involved, and not only in the case against the Reserve Bank. Judge Heath's expressed intention to investigate the government's own performance, as evidenced by the Health Ministry's suspicious expenditure on an AIDS-awareness musical, provoked perhaps well-founded anxiety within official circles. An election was looming, scheduled for June 1999, and scandals within the ANC ranks would be especially troublesome. Some plausible fudge might be welcomed.

Much depends upon the outcome. Will the new government, almost certainly under Thabo Mbeki, take office having demonstrated its determination to weed out corruption? If so, it will win international respect and justifed support; if not, there will be great regret that so vital an opportunity has been missed. At the time of writing the jury of world opinion is considering its verdict.

CHRONOLOGY

1934		Volkskas founded
1954		Trust Bank founded
1977		Sanlam rescues Trust Bank–Bankorp
1978		President P.W. Botha; Total Strategy; official terror squads
1985		'Rubicon' speech; foreign banks withdraw. Nedbank in trouble: first recorded secret lifeboat (Bankorp)
1986		Second secret Bankorp lifeboat
1988		Thomson T. Line sale
1989		Harms Commission Armscor pension fund finances Cardoen arms deal
	May	Daling joins Bankorp board
	June	Askins buy Steenhuis site
	December	Askin's discussion with Claasen/Key
1990	**11 February**	Nelson Mandela released
	4 March	Diedericks sacked from Tollgate
	15 March	Askin signs heads of agreement
	28 March	Tollgate overdraft secretly increased
	June	Absa agrees to support Claasen; Liebenberg joins Bankorp; Diedericks moves to Volkskas; Volkskas buys United Bank
	3 August	Bankorp lifeboat
	December	Absa withdraws Claasen funding; Cape Investment Bank lifeboat

1991	January	Volkskas reveals 1989 'put' option
		Goldstone Commission
1992	February	Stals (SARB) denies participation in Absa formation
	March	Askin complains to Absa
	May–November	Negotiations between Tollgate and Absa. Steyn Commission
	December	Tollgate in liquidation; Absa instruct liquidators, meet with OSEO
1993	January	Diedericks joins Post Office
	February	OSEO search Steenhuis; Askin leaves South Africa
	March	Cape Investment Bank collapse
	June	Hoberman 417 enquiry
	July	OSEO searches Askins' Chester Square house; Susie confronts Guy Sangster
	September	Askin meets Johan Rupert; Berman issues charges
1994	April	First free South African elections: new government
	June	Diedericks accused of frauds
	July	Absa's first attack on Hoberman
	11 October	Askin arrested in Italy; CIEX recruited; civil settlement
	25 November	Absa attempts to effect Askin's return
	24 December	Askin's release to house arrest
1995	17 January	Italian Supreme Court rules in Askin's favour
	18 January	Ambassador Babb claims ruling can be disregarded: attempt to rearrest Askin
	24 January	Florence court attempts second hearing
	28 January	Hearing adjourned to 28 February
	25 February	Askin heart attack
	28 February	Another attempt to arrest Askin; case adjourned
	28 April	Supreme Court's second decision; Askin leaves Italy
	July	Florence court attempts third hearing; Diedericks comes to London
	October	Aldworth comes to London
	December	Attempt to pre-empt Supreme Court hearing

1996	January	Diedericks appears at Hoberman enquiry
	February	McCay trial begins; liquidators insist enquiry investigates Absa
	23 February	Absa attempts to suspend hearing
	26 February	Dr Stals gives evidence
	March	Hoberman seeks Absa documents
	12 March	Askin's London action begins
	21 March	Cronjé gives evidence
	3 May	Hoberman visits Pretoria
	8 May	Diedericks due to give evidence; Absa seeks recusal
	10 October	Supreme Court's third judgement
	18 December	Hoberman dismissed; Browde appointed
1997	21 January	Absa begins attack on Claasen
	March	Heath tribunal instituted
	June	Absa share offering
	November	Nel report on Masterbond
	December	Key acquitted
1998	January	CIEX South African team forms
	February	Diedericks brings action against Absa; Absa settles with Aldworth; Stals denies involvement in 1985 lifeboat
	8 May	Heath directive to investigate SARB lifeboat
	28 May	Heath visits SARB, Absa, Sanlam
	1 June	Telephone threat to Askin
	8 July	Askin given leave to appeal
	9 August	Threat 'from the heart of the Beast'
	2 September	Browde report
	19 September	Cambridge conference
	30 October	Deadline for submission of evidence; Bertlesman silenced
	13 November	Hoberman comes to London
	23 December	McCay sues Browde
1999	10/11 January	Hotson meets Key and McCay
	18 January	Key visits London
	29 January	London court rejects Askin's case
	2 February	Heath conclusions released: Reserve Bank and Sanlam to be arraigned

349

APPENDICES

APPENDIX A

Documents indicating Absa's control over Motorvia's liquidators (see p.93). The final paragraph (17) is clearly in a different typeface from the rest.

MOTORVIA (PTY) LIMITED.
(IN LIQUIDATION)

MASTER'S REFERENCE NUMBER C. 1092/92

RESOLUTIONS

TO BE SUBMITTED AT THE GENERAL MEETINGS OF CREDITORS AND MEMBERS TO BE HELD BEFORE THE MASTER OF THE SUPREME COURT, CAPE TOWN ON TUESDAY 7TH SEPTEMBER, 1993 at 9.00 am.

IT IS HEREBY RESOLVED

1   That the report of the liquidator(s) and his/their actions as referred to therein be and are hereby approved, ratified and confirmed

2   That the actions of the provisional liquidator(s) and liquidator(s) in engaging the services of attorneys and/or counsel on such matters as he/ they found necessary in the administration of the company in liquidation to date, are hereby approved, ratified and confirmed and that the costs thereof be paid out of the funds of the company in liquidation as part of the costs of administration

3   That the liquidator(s) be and is/are hereby authorised to engage whatever further legal assistance he/they may require in the interests of the company in liquidation and that the costs thereof be paid out of the funds of the company in liquidation as part of the costs of administration

4   That the liquidator(s) be and is/are hereby authorised to institute or defend legal actions in order to collect debts owing to the company or in respect of any other matter affecting the company in liquidation including the holding of enquiries or examinations in terms of the Companies Act, 1973, as amended, or as read with the Insolvency Act, 1936, as amended, as he/they may deem fit, and for such purposes to employ the services of attorneys and/or counsel of his/their choice and to pay the costs out of the funds of the company in liquidation as part of the costs of administration

5   That the liquidator(s) be and is/are hereby authorised to settle or compromise any legal proceedings whether instituted or to be instituted by or against the company, on such terms and conditions and for such amount as he/they in his/their discretion may deem fit

6   That the liquidator(s) be and is/are hereby authorised to sell any movable or immovable property of the company in liquidation of whatsoever description and including outstanding debts by public auction, public tender or private treaty in such manner, upon such terms and conditions and for such amounts as he/they may deem fit

7   That the liquidator(s) be and is/are hereby authorised to consent to the cancellation of any bond passed in favour of the company

8   That the liquidator(s) be and is/are hereby authorised to agree to any reasonable offer of composition made to the company by any debtor, to accept payment of any part of any debt due to the company in settlement thereof, to grant an extension of time for the payment of any debt and to

353

abandon such amounts due to the company as he/they has/have been unable to recover or dispose of as he/they may deem fit

9   That the liquidator(s) be and is/are hereby authorised to engage the services of auctioneers or agents to sell the assets of the company in liquidation and to determine the conditions of sale and manner of advertising in his/their discretion

10   That the liquidator(s) be and is/are hereby authorised and empowered in his/their discretion to compromise or admit any claim against the company, whether liquidated or unliquidated, arising from any guarantee or any other cause whatsoever, as a liquidated claim in terms of Section 78(3) of the Insolvency Act, as amended, at such amount as may be agreed upon between the creditor(s) concerned and the liquidator(s) provided that proof thereof has been tendered at a meeting of creditors

11   That the liquidator(s) be and is/are hereby authorised to transfer to the purchaser thereof any immovable property sold by the company prior to its liquidation or to agree to the cancellation of any such sale and to re-sell such property or to agree to the substitution of a new purchaser under any existing Deed of Sale

12   That the liquidator(s) be and is/are hereby authorised to abandon any asset or assets of the company where no purchaser for the asset(s) can be found

13   That the liquidator(s) be and is/are hereby authorised to terminate leases in respect of premises or of any other object entered into by the company in liquidation

14   That the liquidator(s) be and is/are hereby authorised to, if necessary, borrow moneys with or without providing security therefor and that the interest payable on such loans shall be paid as costs of administration of the company in liquidation

15   That the liquidator(s) be and is/are hereby authorised to engage the services of bookkeepers, accountants, auditors or any other person for any purpose in and about the affairs of the company which he/they may require and the costs so incurred to be paid as costs of administration of the company in liquidation

16   That the future administration of the company be left in the hands of and to the discretion of the liquidator(s).

17   That, in respect to resolutions 4,5,6,9,10, 14 and 16 all of same are subject to the proviso that the liquidators shall first obtain the written approval of creditors representing not less than 50% in value of all creditors before finalising the exercise of any such powers granted to the liquidators.

qq CREDITORS   PRESIDING OFFICER

APPENDIX B

Correspondence between Armscor and Banco Banesto (see p.110), revealing the misuse of Armscor pension fund assets.

TELEX PRETORIA (SOUTH AFRICA) (012) 32-0217 FAX (012) 478 5635 PRIVATE BAG X337 PRETORIA 0001

FAX COVER NOTE/MESSAGE

No. of pages inclusive: (1)

To: 0934 (1) 5352810	From: (0) 12 442435
M Conde	C Hendricks
Banesto	Armscor
Madrid	Pension Fund
Spain	Pretoria
	RSA

14/07/87

Dear Mr Conde

Further to your enquiry discussion between Gen. Malan and Mr Botha has taken place at which it was agreed in principal to retain BANESTO as a prime facility for dealings between ourselves and CARDOEN INDUSTRIES.

Further, that our bankers are, in principal, to agree payment of commission(s) by way of KANEKO.

Gen. Malan will discuss/finalise the above arrangements in detail with yourself and Mr Cardoen on 18/08/87.

Yours Sincerely

C Hendricks

TELEX PRETORIA (SOUTH AFRICA) (012) 32-0217 FAX (012) 428-5635 PRIVATE BAG 4337 PRETORIA 0001

FAX COVER NOTE/MESSAGE

No. of pages inclusive: (1)

To: 0934 (1) 5352810 M Conde Banesto Madrid Spain	From: (0) 12 442435 C Hendricks Armscor Pension Fund Pretoria RSA

16/06/89

Dear Mario

Herewith please find copy of document requested.

Yours

C Hendricks

774391001
27
BKRB   16/06/89

To: CARDOEN INDUSTRIES
FROM: BKRB

DEAR SIRS WE ARE INSTRUCTED BY OUR CLIENTS TO OPEN
IRREVOCABLE CREDIT FOR USD 200 000 000 AVALIABLE
LATER THROUGH BANKSTO SUBJECT TO CONTRACT SUBJECT
TO 90 DAYS NOT LATER THAN 17/9/89 STOP

FULL COPY CONDITIONS OF CONTRACT TO BE SUBMITTED
21/6/89 END STOP

REGARDS
RESERVE BANK PRETORIA

APPENDIX C

Telegram from Gianni de Gennaro in Rome to Judge Luigi Vigna in Florence, confirming Askin's arrest on the same day, 11 October 1994 (see p.131).

Moa 36/4 PSC

Ministero dell' Interno

DIPARTIMENTO DELLA PUBBLICA SICUREZZA

DIREZIONE CENTRALE DELLA POLIZIA CRIMINALE

SERVIZIO INTERPOL

DISPACCIO TELEGRAFICO

Precedenza Assoluta

ROMA 11.10.1994

SIG.PRESIDENTE CORTE APPELLO FIRENZE

MINISTERO GRAZIA ET GIUSTIZIA D.G.A.P. UFF.II° ROMA

et conoscenza

MINISTERO AFFARI ESTERI D.G.E.A.S. UFF.IX°REP.II° ROMA

AMBASCIATA REPUBBLICA SUDAFRICANA ROMA

- Cortese attenzione del Sig.TERRY GOVENDER -

PROCURA GENERALE PRESSO CORTE APPELLO FIRENZE

QUESTURA -Uff.Stranieri, Squadra Espulsioni -FIRENZE

> CORTE D'APPELLO
> FIRENZE
>
> 11.OTT.1994
>
> PROT. N°

123/C/3/SZ.1/785609/2=2/AP INTERPOL PUNTO COMUNICASI CHE PRIME ORE MATTINATA ODIERNA 11.10.1994, AT SEGUITO RISERVATE ET LABORIOSE INDAGINI, PERSONALE DIPENDENTE QUESTURA UFFICIO STRANIERI SQUADRA ESPULSIONI FIRENZE HABET TRATTO IN ARRESTO EX. ART.716 CPP IL CITTADINO BRITANNICO ASKIN (cognome) JULIAN MICHEL CUMMING (nomi) NATO IPSWICH/GRAN BRETAGNA 22.6.48. TITOLARE PASSAPORTO BRITANNICO NR.B 379960 RILASCIATO LONDRA CON VALIDITA SINO 9.2.99 PUNTO IL PREDETTO FACEVA OGGETTO RICHIESTA ARRESTO PROVVISORIO FINI ESTRADIZIONALI FORMULATA AT QUESTO SERVIZIO DA PARTE COLLATERALE UFFICIO INTERPOL PRETORIA (SUDAFRICA) SICCOME COLPITO DAL MANDATO DI CATTURA SENZA NUMERO EMESSO IN DATA 13.7.1993 DALL'AUTORITA' GIUDIZIARIA DI CAPE TOWN/SUDAFRICA PER TRUFFE E FURTI COMMESSE PERIODO MAGGIO 1991 - APRILE 1992 NELLA' AREA DI CAPO DI BUONA SPERANZA (SUDAFRICA) PER IL QUALE

Mod 36/4 PSC

Ministero dell' Interno
DIPARTIMENTO DELLA PUBBLICA SICUREZZA

DIREZIONE CENTRALE DELLA POLIZIA CRIMINALE

NELLA DOCUMENTAZIONE ESTRADIZIONALE APPRESTATA DA AUTORITA'
SUDAFRICANE PUNTO AT TAL PROPOSITO RAPPRESENTASI CHE DETTA
DOCUMENTAZIONE ESTRADIZIONALI EST GIA' STATA RICEVUTA DA AMBASCIATA
SUDAFRICANA IN ROMA CHE HABET GIA' PROVVEDUTO AT INVIARLA AT DICASTERO
ESTERI ITALIANO PER SUO SUCCESSIVO INOLTRO AT DICASTERO GIUSTIZIA ITALIANO
PUNTO IL CORRISPONDENTE UFFICIO INTERPOL DI PRETORIA (SUDAFRICA) ET STATO
INFORMATO AVVENUTO ARRESTO AL PARI DI QUEL DICASTE. GIUSTIZIA UFFICIO
REATI ECONOMICI GRAVI (OFFICE FOR SERIOUS ECONOMIC OFFENCES) IL QUALE
HABET MANIFESTATO GRANDE IMPORTANZA ANNESSA AT CATTURA ASKIN DALLE
AUTORITA' DI QUELLO STATO STANTE AMMONTARE SOMME TRUFFATE ET STANTE
AMPIO RISALTO DATO AT CASO DA ORGANI INFORMAZIONI SUDAFRICANI IN PASSA
ET ATTUALMENTE PUNTO PEI DICASTERI GIUSTIZIA ET ESTERI (PER CUI RICHIAMA I
TELESCRITTO DICASTERO GIUSTIZIA EP/672/94/SD DEL 21.9.94) ET AMBASCIATA FIRMA
PEL MINISTRO MASONE PER ALTRI INDIRIZZI FIRMA DIRETTORE CENTRALE POLIZIA
CRIMINALE DE GENNARO

AP/

APPENDIX D

Letter from Dr Chris Stals, deputy governor of the South African Reserve Bank, to G.C. Erasmus, dated 30 May 1985, agreeing an advance of R200 milion to Bankorp (see p.200).

SUID-AFRIKAANSE RESERWEBANK

PRETORIA
0001

POSBUS 427

012

VERTROULIK   30 Mei 1985.

Mnr. C.G. Erasmus,
Besturende Direkteur,
Bankorp,
Posbus 1559,
JOHANNESBURG
2000

Geagte mnr. Erasmus,

Ek verwys na u brief van 10 April 1985 insake finansiële probleme wat deur Mercabank Beperk ondervind word en die versoek dat spesiale hulp aan dié instelling verleen word.

Ek bevestig hiermee dat die Bank bereid is om, met die goedkeuring van die Minister van Finansies, finansiële hulp aan Mercabank Beperk te verleen. Die voorwaardes van sodanige hulp sal as volg wees:

1. Die maksimum bedrag van die spesiale hulp aan Mercabank sal R200 000 000 beloop.

2. Vir spesiale redes sal hierdie voorskot nie aan Mercabank self gemaak word nie, maar aan die maatskappy BANBOL (EDMS.) BPK. van Posbus 4790, Randburg, wat die fondse op sy beurt by Mercabank sal plaas.

3. Die fondse sal op 30 Mei 1985 na rekening nr. 01/03932/148/0 van BANBOL (EDMS.) BPK. by die Sanlamsentrum-takkantoor van Trust Bank in Johannesburg oorgeplaas word.

4. As dekking vir die lening sal Suid-Afrikaanse Regeringseffekte deur Sanlam aan die Reserwebank gesedeer word deur die effekte met behoorlikondertekende blanko oordragvorms by die Kaapstadtak van die Reserwebank in te dien.

5. Rente op die lening sal bereken word teen 3 persent per jaar en sal maandeliks op die laaste werksdag van elke maand betaalbaar wees (bereken teen werklike aantal dae per 365 dae jaar).

6. Terugbetaling sal so gou as moontlik gedoen word, en die lening sal voor 31 Mei 1990 ten volle terugbetaal word.

2.   013

7.   Ten slotte moet alle moontlike inligting wat die
       Reserwebank ookal mag benodig oor die aktiwiteite
       van BANBOL (EDMS.) BPK. en van die betrokke
       portefeulje beleggings wat met hierdie fondse ge-
       finansier sal word, aan die Vise-president van
       die Reserwebank (Dr. A.S. Jacobs) beskikbaar
       gestel word en verslag gereeld aan hom gedoen
       word oor die realisering van die betrokke
       bate-portefeulje.

       Dit sal waardeer word indien u sal bevestig dat u
instem met die voorwaardes van die spesiale lening aan
BANBOL (EDMS.) BPK. soos in hierdie brief uiteengesit is
deur die aangehegte afskrif van hierdie brief te onder-
teken en aan my terug te besorg.

                              Die uwe,

                              Senior Vise-president.

Die leningsvoorwaardes soos hierbo uiteengesit word hier-

mee aanvaar.

Datum: Pretoria 30/6/1985   Namens BANBOL (EDMS.) BPK.

APPENDIX E

Letter from Stals to Sir Kit McMahon, 24 February 1998 (see p.200). The third paragraph states '... I was not involved in the initial discussions in April 1985 or in 1986, when the original decision was taken to provide assistance to the Bankorp Group. I only became involved in 1990'.

SOUTH AFRICAN RESERVE BANK

FROM THE OFFICE OF
THE GOVERNOR

Facsimile Message

TO   Sir Kit McMahon
                     The Old House
                     Burleigh
                     Stroud
                     Gloucestershire GL5 2PQ
                     United Kingdom

FAX NUMBER   0944=171=581-1759

FROM   Dr C.L. Stals
                 Governor

DATE   24 February 1998

NUMBER OF PAGES Four

MESSAGE:

Dear Sir Kit,

I enclose a photostat of an article that appeared in *The Star's Business Report* (a South African newspaper) on 23 February 1998.

I was surprised to find in this report that you were quoted as one of the authors of a hostile attack on me and the South African Reserve Bank for assistance provided by the Bank during the term of office of my predecessor and myself to South African banking institutions in accordance with the function and responsibility of the Bank as lender of last resort. I can only assume that you were very badly misinformed about the situation that prevailed at the time, and must have been grossly misled by your informers, of the true facts that led the Bank to decisions in this regard.

You and your collaborators elected to concentrate your attack on one case of assistance only, ignoring the fact that other banks, that can surely not be classified as "Afrikaner" organisations, were also assisted during the difficult period of sanctions, boycotts and debt-standstill arrangements. You also apparently did not take account of the fact that I was

-2-

not involved in the initial decisions in April 1985 or in
1986, when the original decision was taken to provide
assistance to the Bankorp Group. I only became involved in
1990, when a desperate situation of threatening insolvency
had developed in what was then one of the four major banks in
South Africa. At that stage, the Bank had more than 90 000
depositors, holding more than R25 billion on deposit with
Bankorp. Bankorp also had extensive international relations,
both within and outside of the international debt standstill
agreements of the South African Government. It is sheer
nonsense to allege that the situation of Bankorp did not
provide a major threat to the financial stability of the
South African banking system, or even to the country's
international financial relations.

You are obviously also not aware of the details of the
package that was put together to provide assistance to the
Bankorp Group at that stage. Protracted negotiations took
place, punitive conditions were attached to the loans, all
agreements were drafted and approved by a firm of external
legal advisers to the Bank, with strict directives that all
the arrangements must comply with the conditions of the South
African Reserve Bank Act, and all the details were discussed
with, and approved by, the then South African Minister of
Finance. To assert that the assistance was illegal is, to say
the least, maledictory.

It may interest you to know that the loans were eventually
fully repaid, and the assistance to the Bankorp Group, which
was strictly monitored, to be applied exclusively for
protection of depositors, consisted of the difference between
a low interest rate charged on the loans by the Bank, and the
interest that Bankorp could earn on its investment in
Government Bonds. The unrecoverable debts in the books of
Bankorp were defined and agreed to in 1990, and no other
write-offs could be made against this income.

The present owners of Bankorp, that is Absa, only came into
the picture in April 1992 when the assistance agreement was
a *fait accompli*, and already half-way through its tenure.
Absa, however, honoured the commitments of the agreement and
the loans were fully repaid to the Reserve Bank in October
1995. The total accumulated losses that Absa and shareholders
of the old Bankorp Group had to absorb, turned out to be more
than double the amount of the benefits derived from the
Reserve Bank assistance package.

-3-

To claim, at this stage, that the Government should be able
to recover more than R6 billion (about five times the amount
of the assistance) from Absa and its shareholders in respect
of the assistance that was provided for the protection of the
depositors of Bankorp, is absurd. It is obvious that Absa
would not have taken over the ailing bank without the prior
provision for accumulated bad loans.

You should perhaps also take note of the fact that the South
African Reserve Bank is a privately-owned central bank.
Government does not hold any shares in the Reserve Bank,
which makes it even more difficult to understand some of the
accusations made by you against what, I will suggest, will be
universally approved actions for a central bank in a similar
situation.

As I find it extremely difficult to understand the attitude
attributed to you in the attached newspaper report, and also
your reasons for tendering an opinion on a matter that is
complex and difficult for anybody as far detached from the
situation as you must be to understand, I have decided to
write this letter to you in light of my past acquaintance
with you when you were still in the Bank of England.

It may help me to find some explanation if you would be so
kind as to let me know who the principals were that
commissioned this investigation by you and Mr Watts, and
also for what purpose it was done. All enquiries I made with
the South African Government failed to produce answers to
these questions.

Yours sincerely,

C.L. Stals

Governor

INDEX

Aaron, Sam 208–9

Abrahamsen, Rob 44

Absa Bank (Amalgamated Banks of South
Africa) xii, 41, 77, 84–6, 87, 105–6; and
Aldworth 97–8, 187–8, 256, 258;
Bankorp merger 244; board 108, 174–5,
281, 313, 317; business methods 260;
and Claasen 186, 255, 263; and covert
operations 264, 299; Diederick's
accusations 217–21, 225–8, 253;
formation of 239, 244; and Heath
Commission 301, 306, 323, 338–46; and
Hoberman Commission 103–5, 172–4,
227–8, 245–7, 250–4, 256–7, 260, 261,
262–3, 320–1, 330–1; illegalities 100,
106–7, 123, 171, 174, 186, 213, 256,
269, 285; legal actions against 254, 261,
264, 270, 272, 274–5, 284–5, 314,
315–16; and OSEO 101–3; persecution
of Askin 121–2, 129, 132–3, 134–6,
138, 227; and Reserve Bank lifeboat
171, 189, 213, 222–3, 232–3, 235, 242,
270–2, 279–80, 294, 296–7, 299, 302,
308, 313, 321, 323, 342–3; security
department 264, 290, 307–8, 315, 318;
share option scheme 304–5; share issue
268–72, 293, 314; and Tollgate
liquidation 88–96, 135–6, 157, 177, 186,
217–19, 221–3, 225–7, 238, 241–3,
245–7, 250–1, 253, 254, 260, 317

Absolute 335

Acheson, Donald 290

Adult Education Consultants 264

African Bank 45, 196, 223, 231

African National Congress 12, 30, 34, 37;
and Absa 249; and communism 46–7,
266; in government 122, 196; and
Heath inquiry 268, 338, 342–3, 346;
London headquarters 100; relations
with Afrikaners 191, 265

Afrikaans 13–14, 31

Afrikaner Bond 13, 15, 282

Afrikaner Broederbond xi–xii, 77, 87, 88,
98, 265, 336; business interests 22,
24–5, 29; Diedericks and 61, 175;
financial institutions 16, 19–22, 29, 56,
83, 134–5, 190, 194, 197–8, 204, 231,
255, 281, 307; formation 15, 16, 17;
growth of 19; membership 29; and
Nazism 23; political influence 17–18,
24, 32–3, 190–1; relaxation in 282; in
Reserve Bank 44–5, 191, 196, 213

Aitken Deloitte 178

Alant, Nico 192

Aldworth, Bob: Absa accusations against
97, 133, 187–8, 255; as Absa director
85, 86; on Absa illegalities 106–7; and
Askin 86, 87, 186–7; book by 253, 256;
on Brink 108; career 85; and CIB 208;
damages claim against Absa 249, 285;
flees country 98, 186–7; and Hoberman
inquiry 224, 257; ill-health 97–8, 187;
and Tollgate liquidation 86, 87–8, 90,
91, 247; trial of 188, 258, 285

Aldworth, Mari 98, 186

Alford, Roger 293

Allied Bank 84, 85, 105

Amaprop 160, 161

Amerosso, Brigadiere 152–4

Amhurst, Anthony 118, 119, 129, 133,
138, 142, 181–2

Amhurst Brown Colombotti 118, 327,
328–9

Anglo-American Corporation 30, 43, 52

Anglo-Boer War 9–12, 14

Anglovaal 52

Angola 38, 42, 45

Armscor 28, 86, 108, 109–10, 333

Army, see South African Defence Force

Arnold, Peter 106

Arrowgate 161
Arwa Corp. 54–5, 58–61, 69, 70, 72, 183–6, 239, 244, 255
Askin, Charlotte 308
Askin, Julian: Absa negotiations 87–92; Absa's hatred of 96–9, 101, 110–11, 121–2, 136, 145, 164–70, 227, 307; and Absa share issue 272; and Aldworth 186–7; arrest 1–5, 111–14, 121, 129, 136, 157; background 47–8; career 48–53; civil suit 2–3, 104–5, 125, 129, 134, 157, 164, 167, 223; court appearances 115–16, 130; criminal charges against 104–5, 134, 157–62, 259; diary 126, 181–2; death threats 121, 307–8, 315, 318–19, 327, 340–1; and Diedericks 86, 180–2; flees Italy 155–7; flees South Africa 99; health problems 117, 119, 125, 137–8, 146, 147, 150–1; and Hoberman Commission 104–5, 321–2, 333–9; house arrest 139–55; imprisonment 5–8, 114–17, 119, 125–9, 137–40, 142; and Key 286–8; legal action against Absa 254, 261, 272–3, 274–5, 315–16, 327–8; in London 163; on Mandela's release 46; novels 48, 164; Tollgate acquisition 2, 42, 65–70, 286; Tollgate liquidation 89–91, 241–2; and Tollgate misdeeds 75–6, 79–82, 86–8, 133, 263; Tollgate restructuring 71–4, 79–80, 87–8, 89, 157; Tollgate salary 158
Askin, Susie xii: background 49; in Cape Town 263; danger to 120–1, 145; flees Italy 155; flees South Africa 166; in Florence 1–6, 113–17, 119, 125–6, 146, 149, 152; illness 339, 344–5; and Keys 71; in London 110, 117–18, 120–1; and Steenhuis 51, 164, 166–7, 169
Assault on Private Enterprise (Wassenaar) 30

Babb, Glenn 131, 143, 265, 275, 319
Badenhorst, Frikkie 106
Badenhorst, Piet 339: Absa chief executive 86; attitude to Askin 86–7, 89, 227; feigns death 260; retirement 108, 175, 245; telephone tapping 105–7, 231; and Tollgate liquidation 217, 218, 247; at United Bank 84, 85
Baker Mackenzie 113, 117, 118, 129

Banco Banesto 41, 109, 230
Bank of England 214–15, 225–6, 233, 237, 317, 322
Bank for International Settlements 43
Bank-Bol 199
Bankorp (Bank Holding Corporation of South Africa) 79; Absa merger 84, 91, 194, 240, 244; Askin sues 254; bad debts 91; board 238–9; Liebenberg at 76, 77; Reserve Bank lifeboat 197–204, 210–15, 222, 228, 231–7, 239–40, 244, 252, 257, 272, 279, 294–8, 302–3, 306, 312, 342; and Sanlam 57–8; Volkskas merger 198, 207, 233, 235, 238, 307
Bankovs (Bank of the Orange Free State) 83, 86
Banks Act (1990) 206
Bantustans 27–8, 37
Barclays Bank 19, 20, 42–3, 85, 275
Barings Bank 214, 215
Barkhuizen, Steve 303, 317, 323, 343, 346
Barnard, Freddie 289
Barnard, Gerrie 183–4
Barnes, Maureen 133, 275
Basson, Deon 236–7, 278
Basson, Brig. Dr Wouter 36, 37–40, 120, 266
Beaufre, Gen. André 33
Beck, Graham 48
Bedussi, Wilma 142
Beeld, Die 298
Behrman, Tony 91, 132
Belgian Defence Force 37
Bell, Paul 180, 217, 245, 275
Berlusconi, Silvio 124
Berman, Judge Harold 104–5, 134, 157, 210, 221, 321
Bertlesman, Eberhard 283–4, 303, 305–6, 316–19, 327–9, 334
Beyers, Gen. 13
Biermann, Hugo 48–50, 68, 70
Billiton 311, 325
'Black, Major' 130, 142–4, 146, 152, 156
Boland Bank 54, 194, 199, 201
Bonuskor 22, 56, 83
Borman, Mr 172
Bosman, J.J. 19
Bosman, Nallie 306
BOSS, see Bureau of State Security
Botha, Calla 289–90

Botha, Gawie 326–7
Botha, Brig. J.J. 36
Botha, Louis 10, 11, 12, 16
Botha, P.W. xii, 33–4, 42, 45, 109, 177, 195, 198, 281–2
Botha, R.F. (Pik) 131
Boustred, W.G. 247
Bredenkamp, Hennie 247–8, 257, 280
Bremer, L. Paul 34fn
Brink, David C.: Absa chairman 108, 245, 251, 268; and Aldworth 187–8; on Askin 222; and Diedericks 179, 221; and Hoberman inquiry 247; resignation 280–1; on Tollgate acquisition 260; on Tollgate liquidation 91, 93, 221
Brits, Danie 88–9, 96, 106, 217–18, 227, 228, 242, 250–1
Broederbond, see Afrikaner Broederbond
Broederbond, The (Wilkins and Strydom) 194
Brooke, Peter 114, 118
Browde, Judge, see Hoberman-Browde Commission
Brown, Jean Jacques 98, 269
Browne, G.W.G. 191
Bruce, Peter 300
Bruwer, Major Gen. Gerhard 35
Buffham, Major Roger 39
'Bullet head' 121
Bureau of State Security (BOSS) 31–2, 122, 283
Burger, Col. Staal 289–90
Burger, De 16, 31
Business Day 236
Businessmen for South Africa 35
Buthelezi, Chief Mangosuto 34, 46

Calvi, Roberto 132
Cape Bar Council 172–3
Cape Investment Bank (CIB): audits 208; insolvency 205, 207; and Masterbond 276; Rabie inquiry 207, 210; RCC and 206–7, 209–10, 231; Reserve Bank lifeboat 204, 205–6, 209–10, 213, 229, 234, 257, 279, 306
Cape Supreme Court 136
Cape Times 169–70, 176, 220
Cape Town Board of Executors 82, 87
Cardoen Industries 41, 109–10
Carter, Jimmy 29

Casey, Bill 34
Cede 81
Central Merchant Bank, see Senbank
Chase Manhattan Bank 42, 198
Chemical and Biological Defence Establishment 37
Chiusano, Prof. Vittorio 129, 138, 141, 143, 144, 146, 151–3
Churchill, Winston 11, 23
CIA 34
CIEX xii, 120, 123, 130, 133, 145, 164, 182, 263, 282, 283, 291, 306, 307
Ciskei Defence Force 303
Citicorp of America 43
Citizen 31
Civil Co-operation Bureau 132; Region 6 289
Claasen, Johan 159; and Absa 255, 263, 272; and Askin 67, 69; and Arwa 54, 55, 60, 61, 70, 72, 183–6, 244; background 53–4; and Bill of Exchange 77–8; dubious activities 82, 133, 176; at Tollgate 51, 55–6, 59, 61, 65–6, 263; and Trust Bank 56, 58, 62, 64, 76, 81, 242
Cleaver, Judge R. 276
Coetzee, Capt. Dirk 35, 283
Coetzee, Johan 100, 131
Coetzer, Dr W.B. 56
Cohen, Hank 45
Collier, H.D. 276
Companies Office 276
Conde, Mario 109–10
Confederation of Employers of South Africa (COFESA) 35
Conradie, Judge 256, 321, 330
Cooke, Gerald 113–15, 122, 125
Corbank 204
Crabtree, Alan 99, 133
Craxi, Bettino 124
Crédit Lyonnais 230
Cronjé, Dr Daniel C. 77, 87, 175, 281, 338, 340; at Absa 86, 108, 135; and Aldworth 97; and Askin 227, 254, 256; background 86, 108; and covert operations 108–10, 264, 270, 344; and Diedericks 176–9, 220; and Heath inquiry 306; and Hoberman inquiry 224, 228, 247, 250–1, 252, 333–6; illegalities 107, 109, 171, 231, 269, 271;

Cronjé, Dr Daniel C. – *contd.*
and Moch 260; and Tollgate liquidation
9, 135, 217–18, 242, 250–1; at Volkskas
41, 61, 177–9
Cronjé, Dr F. 30

Daily Mail 165, 344–5
Daily Telegraph 133
Daling, Marinus 108, 203m 338; Bankorp
director 202, 238; as Broeder 77, 194;
and Heath inquiry 307, 317–18; and
Mbeke 196; and Sanlam
demutualisation 309–10, 311, 325–6;
on Tollgate 63
Darner, Billy 259
D'Avirro, Antonio 114, 116, 125, 129, 138,
146
Dawson, Guy 269, 270
de Blanche, Mike 107
de Bruyn, Peter 120
Defence Special Procurement Fund 36
de Gennaro, Gianni 131, 141, 145
de Jager, C. 335
de Klerk, F.W. xi, 37, 47, 100, 195, 196,
207, 276, 281
de Kock, Dr 197–201, 216
de Kok, Col. Eugene 35, 264
de Lange, Pieter 191, 265
de la Rey, Koos 10, 13
Dempster, Nigel 165–6, 167, 344–5
Department of Civil Cooperation (DCC)
109
de Swardt, C.J. 191
Deutsche Morgan Grenfell 268–9
Devenport, Bishop Eric 119, 125
de Villiers, Kevin 105–7, 170, 174–5, 333
de Villiers, Wim 194
de Waal, M.T. 191
de Wet, Christian 10, 13
Diederichs, Dr Nicolaas 22
Diedericks, Alta 176
Diedericks, Hennie: at Absa 244; Absa
persecution of 175–6, 180, 263;
accusations against Absa 217–21, 247,
253; and Aldworth 187; and Askin
180–2; background 61; as Broeder 61;
and Claasen 77–8; and Heath
Commission 306, 316–17; and
Hoberman inquiry 224–8, 238, 245–6,
257, 306, 321; legal action against Absa

255, 272, 284–5; letter to Dawson
269–71; and Moch 260; at Post Office
89; and Reserve Bank 281; sacked 67,
70; suicide attempt 176; Tollgate
executive 61–7, 76, 82, 86–7, 133, 134;
on Tollgate liquidation 88–9, 239, 254;
and Trust Bank 61, 62–6, 67, 76–7,
341; and Volkskas 61, 83, 85, 108,
177–9, 341
Directorate of Covert Collections (DCC)
36, 37, 109, 121, 132, 270, 299
Divett, Miles 90
Downing, Billy 288
Drivetech 55, 59, 248
Dugard, Prof. John 122
du Plessis, Attie 202, 203, 238
du Plessis, Barend 43, 178
du Plessis, D.H.C. 14
du Plessis, Dr Fred 57, 202, 236, 312
du Plessis, L.J. 21, 23
du Plessis, Wentzel 56
du Preez, Max 283
Duros 53–5, 60, 69, 70, 72, 78–9, 81, 82,
160, 182
Duros/Tollgate 55, 59, 62–4, 66, 68–9,
78–9
du Toit, Etienne 242, 243
du Toit, Pierre 283

Ecclestone, Bernie 111, 159, 286–8
Emin, Abu 125–7, 140
Ensor, Linda 259
Entercor 58, 61, 69, 74, 79, 160–1
Erasmus, G.C. 197–202
Ernst & Young 312

F&T Weekly 236
Fairweather, Patrick 118
Fascism 19, 22
Faul, Christo 136, 280, 302, 334; and
Hoberman Commission 246–8, 251;
and OSEO 101–3; and Tollgate
liquidation 89, 92–3, 94, 186, 221, 250,
253
Federal Reserve Bank (US) 296, 317
Federale Mynbou 56
Federale Volksbelegging (FVB) 21, 56, 309
Federation of Afrikaans Cultural
Associations (FAK) 19, 21
Ferreira, Dr Charles 199, 200

Fetlar Foods 103
Finance Week 48, 60, 65, 78, 108, 257,
    293, 298, 317
Financial Mail 102–3, 133, 170, 222–3,
    249, 252, 256, 278, 300, 326
Financial Times 319, 342–3, 345
Finanzbank 65, 67
First, Ruth 35, 47, 131
First National Bank of South Africa (FNB)
    43, 55, 81, 160–1, 219, 224, 233, 243
Fleming, Robert 325
Florence 2, 5–6, 114–17, 119, 125; Court
    of Appeal 130, 143–4, 146, 163
Ford, Gerald 32
Foreign Office 117
Formula One Constructors' Association
    (FOCA) 111–12, 159, 161, 286, 288
Fourie, Brig. 40, 164
Fourie, J.J. 191
Freemasonry 190
Friedman, Judge Gerald 104, 173, 331
FSI Group 185
Fuller, Simon 47

Gant, David 59
Gants 58–9, 69, 72, 78, 86, 95, 182
Gauntlett, Jeremy 172, 224, 227, 263,
    320–1, 330–1, 333
Gensec 326
George, Eddie 237, 291
Gerwel, Prof. Jakes 293, 324
Getz, Keith 99, 117
Gilbey's Distillers 272
Giovene, Laurence 118, 125, 129, 152
Glaum, Francis 92–3, 102, 254
Glaum and Wallace, Messrs 92, 93, 186,
    256
Gleason, David 84, 235–6, 249, 252,
    256–8, 260, 279, 310, 312, 326–7
Global Capital Investments 35
Gold Connection, The (Askin) 48
Goldberg, Laurie 48
Goldfields of South Africa 43
Goldstone Commission 36–7
Goosen, Daan 39
Gordin, Jeremy 256, 278, 284, 301–2, 308
Gordon, 'Peaches' 290
Govender, Terry 131
Graev, Dr 147, 152
Grant, James 68

Grayson, Patrick 120, 123, 125, 128, 138
Greenblo, Alan 65, 132
Greenspan, Alan 296
Greyhound Cityliner 74
Greyling, Alan 246–7
Grieser, Bert 285
Griggs, Judith 111, 161
Groenewald, Barend Petrus 203
Groenewald, Gen. Tienie 193

Hani, Chris 47
Harms Commission 36, 192, 289, 290
Harper, Henry 45
Harris, Adam 101, 180, 331–2
Hartley, Mariette 264
Hartzenburg, Mr Justice 105
Heath, Judge Willem 266, 283, 316–17,
    322, 338
Heath Commission 266–8, 270, 272,
    290–2, 294, 300–3, 305–8, 313–14,
    316–19, 323–5, 338–40, 342, 343, 346
Hefer, Herc 93, 108, 174
Helpmekaar movement 16
Hendricks, Mr 110
Hertzog, Dr Albert 20, 21, 31
Hertzog, Dirk 24–5
Hertzog, James Barry Munnik 11, 13,
    17–18, 20, 33
Hirsch, David 269
Hoberman, Bertrand: Absa's intimidation
    of 172–3, 245; as Absa's barrister 90–1,
    103, 134, 223; condemnation of Browde
    report 331–3; and Diedericks 225;
    dismissal 252, 256–8, 261, 262, 330–1;
    provides Askin affadavit 329–31
Hoberman-Browde Commission: Absa
    and 103–5, 172–4, 227–8, 245–7,
    250–3; under Browde 257, 260, 262–3,
    290, 320–2, 331, 332–7; Diedericks's
    evidence 175, 225–8, 238, 245–6, 248;
    Faul's evidence 248; Marais' evidence
    102; McCay's evidence 161, 248–9;
    public sessions 224; report 320, 331;
    Stals' evidence 210, 229–33, 235–6,
    249; Susie's subpoena 166
Hobhouse, Emily 10
Hofmeyr, Jan 13, 15
Hogg, Alec 293–4
Holmes, Michael 114–15, 117–19, 125,
    139, 151, 153, 154

Holomisa, Bantu 281
Home, George 57
Horwood, Prof. Owen 32, 249
Hosken Consolidated Investments 55, 66, 72, 80, 242
Hotson, Crispian 337–8, 339
HSBC Investment Bank 268–9

Independent on Sunday 298
Industrial Development Corporation 198
Infernal Tower, The (Aldworth) 256
ING Barings 251, 268–9
Inglis, Jamie 48
Inkatha Freedom Party 34, 47, 324
International Freedom Front 132
Interpol 259
Intertechnic 49
Investors Chronicle 53, 94
Invicta Panama 249
IRA 123
Ireton, Cherilyn 163, 168
Irish, Martin 55, 64, 65, 70, 94

J.P. Morgan 268–9
Jameson Raid 10, 16
Jamieson, Bill 291–3, 300, 314
Jaton 68, 73, 74, 93–4, 95, 241
Johannesburg Stock Exchange 52
Johnson Matthey Bank 214–15
Jooste, Tony 136, 160

K&M Civils 247
Kahn, Frank 129–30, 258, 259, 277, 288–9, 322, 346
Kaiser, Bernard 94
Kemble, Christopher 251
Kenny, Pat 99
Kessel Feinstein 172
Key, Mervyn 49, 137, 322, 337–9, 340; Absa's pursuit of 104, 133; and Arwa 54, 58; and Askin negotiations 65–7, 69–70, 80; background 53, 54; business interests 54; and Entercor 61; foreign exchange deals 82; and Kyalami 55, 111–12, 159–62; restraint of trade agreement 81; share dealings 81, 263; Tollgate director 51, 70, 79, 97, 176, 184, 248; trial 101, 285–8; winery 54, 104

Key, Mrs 71, 137
Keys, Derek 239
Kharsamy, Ebrahim 300
King, Mervyn 228, 252
King's School, Bruton 47, 344
Kissinger, Henry 29
Kitchener, Lord 10
Klopper, Henning 14, 15
Konar, Deenadayalen 196
Korsten, Laurie 204
KPMG 93, 103, 108, 312
Kroll Associates 120
Kruger, President Paul 9, 10
Kuschke, Leo 82
Kyalami 54, 55, 58, 92, 111, 136, 158–61, 247, 285–6, 288, 337, 338, 344

Labour Party (South Africa) 16–17
la Cava, Judge Vittorio 131, 142, 143, 144, 146, 147, 153
Ladbrokes 50–1, 95
Lamont Market Research 35
Leadership 298
League of Nations 13, 24
Le Grange, Louis 100
Lemmer, Krisjan 293–4
Lennox-Boyd, Mark 114
le Roux, Egbert 243
Leutwiler, Fritz 41, 43
Levenberg, Max 246
Levi, Carlo 124
Levy, Ivan 228
Lewis, Michael 55, 64–6, 71, 72, 77–9, 80–1, 332
Liberty Life 43, 48, 52, 311
Liebenberg, Gen. Kat 37
Liebenberg, Dr Piet 98, 245; banking Ombudsman 87, 220; Bankorp chairman 76–7, 83, 212, 239; Director of Revenue Services 194; and Reserve Bank lifeboat 194, 202–3, 238, 240, 316, 342–3, 345
Lieberman, Jeff 185–6, 244
Lifegro Insurance 178
Lobengula 27
Lombard, Ivanhoe Makepeace 15, 21, 25
Lombard, Johannes Antonie 203
London School of Economics 48
London Stock Exchange 51–2, 55, 73, 79, 325

Long Term Capital Management Fund 296, 341
Longdon 286–7
Longreach 264
Louw, Martinus 21
Lubowski, Anton 35, 283, 290, 319
Lutuli, Albert 30
Luyt, Louis 32, 44, 204, 297

'M-Net' 170
McAdam, W.J. 82, 332
McCay, David 53, 54–5, 136, 159–61, 248–9, 322, 337–8
Mackintosh, Laurie 65, 104, 137, 322, 337; arrest warrant 111; background 54; and Diedericks 82; extradition 288; and Kyalami 55, 136, 160; and Motorvia 61; restraint of trade agreement 81; Tollgate director 53, 61, 67, 71
McMahon, Sir Kit 282, 292, 294, 297, 299–300, 317
Machel, Graca 282
Mail and Guardian 192, 256, 293
Malan, Dr A.I. 33
Malan, Dr Daniel Francois xi, 15, 16, 17, 22; government of 23, 24, 26
Malan, Gen. Magnus 33, 34, 109–10
Mancer, Peter 105–6
Mandela, Nelson xii, xiii, 30, 35, 36, 46, 122, 164, 265, 268, 274, 282, 291, 302
Mandela, Winnie 282
Manuel, Trevor 122, 196, 265
Marais, Dr Jan C. 56, 265
Marais, Petrus 101, 102–3
Marcus, Richard 227
Maree, Chappies 289–90, 318–19, 334, 341
Martin, Peter 120
Massi, Dr 119
Masterbond Group 209, 210, 276–7, 292
Mbeki, Govan 265, 266
Mbeki, Thabo 196, 265, 282, 292, 293, 300, 338, 342–3, 346
Mboweni, Tito 319
Meakin, Henry and Vicky 115–16
Meiring, Lt. Gen. Georg 37
Mercabank 197–202, 204, 294
Merrill Lynch 268–72, 293
Merriman, J.X. 15
Metropolitan Police 40, 110
Meyer, H.G. 184

Meyer, Piet 21, 23, 194
Meyer, Roelof 191, 281
Mfecane 27
MI6 xii, 123
Millennium 97, 170, 180, 217, 219, 222, 245, 260, 262, 275, 298
Miller, Dave 106
Miller, Lawrence 53
Miller Gruss 172, 180, 186, 256, 306, 320, 331
Mills, Peter 118
Milner, Lord 10, 12
Mitchell, Bill 56–7
Moch, Lee-Ann 260
Mohrs, Dave 319
Monkor Trust Investment Corporation 199
Moore, Robin 48
Morkel, Dr P.R. 83, 86
Morland, Koos 58, 64, 67, 75–6, 78, 87, 183, 254–5
Morris, Stephen 181, 329–30, 331
Moshoeshoe, Chief 27
Mosley, Max 159, 162, 286–8
Motech 59
Motor Racing Enterprises 58, 111, 159–61
Motorvia 59, 61, 74, 92, 186, 254, 263
Motsueyane, Sam 196
Mugabe, Robert 341
Mulder, Dr Connie 31, 32, 35
Multimech 59
Murray, Hugh 170, 180, 217, 245, 261–2, 275–6, 298
Murray and Roberts 108
Mzilikazi 27

Naidoo, Charmain 170
Namibia 42, 45, 326
Nasionale Pers 15–16, 30
Natal 9, 11, 26, 274
National Party 13–17, 23–4, 26–31, 40, 195, 207, 281; covert violence 99–100, 108, 120, 193; Purified Nationalists 17, 22; Re-united Nationalists 22, 23
Naude, Charl 38
Naudé, Dr 15
Nazism 22–3
Nedbank (Nederlandsche Bank voor Zuid Afrika) 19, 25, 30, 43–4, 77, 173, 204, 234, 280, 297

Nel, Col. A. 36
Nel, Judge Hendrick 205, 209–11, 276–7, 314, 322
Nel Commission 276–7, 278–80, 292, 294, 302
Nel, W. 110
Nevill, Glenda 168
New Africa Investments Limited (NAIL) 196
New Order 22
Nicol, Dominus William 14
Noëth, Alwyn 107, 231, 269, 271
Norman, Ronnie and Georgia 114
Norths 69, 79
Norton Villiers 108
Noseweek 133–5, 170, 182, 190, 269, 275
Ntuli, Victor 265
Nxumalo, O.E.H.M. 196

Oatley, Michael 120, 123, 125, 138, 157, 263–5, 282, 306, 340–1
Observer 38
Oelkers, Felix 237
Oerlikon Buhrle 49
Office for Serious Economic Offences (OSEO) 39, 93–4, 97, 100–3, 110–11, 168–9, 175, 259
Old Mutual 16, 43, 44, 52, 85, 234, 280, 297, 309, 310
Omar, Dullah 283, 290, 300, 323–5
Oosthuizen, Carel 237
Operation Marion 265
Oppenheimer, Harry 30
Orange Free State Merchant Bank 86
O'Shea, G.B. 95–6
Ossewa Brandwag (OB) 22–3

Pan African Congress (PAC) 34, 47
Parks, Tim 124
Pasques, Dr 264
Pauw, Jaques 289
'Pavarotti' 283, 307, 315
Pazienza, Francesco 132
Pearson, Major 110, 136
Pelzer, Prof. A.N. 15
Pepkor 54
Phelps, Leslie Stephen 208–9
Phillipson, Trevor 315
Pickard family 204, 205
Pieri, Dr 146, 147, 151

Pim Goldby 249
Pinucci, Neri 114, 125, 129, 138, 151, 153
Pinz, Cmdr E. 35
Pirow, Oswald 22, 274
Postmus, Mr 66
Premier Group 272
Pretoria Bank 204, 276
Pretoria Bar Council 328–9
Price Waterhouse 63
Prima Bank 207, 211, 279
Prins, Tommy 110, 168
Private Eye 163
Progressive Federal Party 30
Project Coast 38–9, 40
Propaganda 2 131, 132
Protectorates 26

Quinn, Jackie 35

Rabie, Judge 207, 210, 232, 234, 237, 257, 279
Rabinowitz, Ruth 324
Rail Commuter Corporation (RCC) 206–7, 209, 210, 231
Railton, David 315
Ramaphosa, Cyril 191, 281
Ramsay, James 187
Rand Merchant Bank 54, 249
Rapport 300
Reagan, Ronald 34
Reeves, Christopher 271
Relly, Gavin 265
Rembrandt Group 24–5, 43, 52, 84, 106, 171, 178, 298–9, 303, 307, 308
Reserve Bank, see South African Reserve Bank
Rhebokskloof 54, 67
Rhodes, Cecil 16, 27
Rhoodie, Dr Eschel 31–2, 35–6, 44
Ricci, Mario 132
Rich, Guy 339, 343
Richemont 25, 124
Ridley, Simon 250, 252
Robinson, Philip 49
Roetz, Kobus 62, 239, 280, 316, 318
Rome Supreme Court of Cassation 132, 138, 141, 143, 146, 152, 153, 155–6, 163, 259
Ronan, Mrs 107
Ronan, Patrick 106–8

Rondalia Bank 204
Roodeplaats Research Laboratories 39
Routledge and Macullum 258
Rowe and Pitman 70, 79
Rubens, Mr 224, 227, 252–3
Ruiterwag 19, 283
Rumpff, Judge 274
Rupert, Anton 22, 24–5, 30, 52, 84, 106, 124, 171, 194, 249, 255, 337–8
Rupert, Johan 25, 54, 84, 108, 171, 189, 249, 262, 338, 343
Russells (Rusfurn) 212, 218, 317

SAF Life Assurance Company 69
Sage Group 84
Sangster, Guy 50, 70, 71, 95, 165–8
Sangster, Robert 50, 165–6
Sangster family 50, 68, 70, 95, 165, 344–5
Sanlam 52, 83, 106; Absa share holding 84, 299, 311–12; as Afrikaner business 15, 16, 19, 24, 30, 194; and Bankorp 58, 76, 77; Bonuskor subsidiary 21–2, 56; demutualisation 308, 309–11, 314–15, 316, 325–7; insider trading 303, 326; and lifeboats 198–202, 204, 213, 216, 226, 231–2, 236, 252, 296, 301, 307–9, 312–13, 323, 342–3; and Mandela government 122, 196; and Tollgate liquidation 63, 238; and Volkskas 57
Sanlam Bank 54, 57, 199, 202, 239
Santam (Suid-Afrikaner Nasionale Trust Maatskappy) 15, 16, 19
Santambank 202, 239
Sasoil 28
Schoon, Katryn and Jeanette 131
Seligson, Mr 229
Senbank 57, 66, 79, 80, 95, 185, 239
SEP Industrial Holdings 94
Seventh Medical Battalion 37, 38, 39
Shar, Sonny 57
Sharpeville massacre 28
Shepherd, Dennis 60
Sherwin, David 87, 89, 90, 94
Shill, Louis 84
Silverman, Richard 271
Simpson, Roy 106, 107–8
Sitole, Dr Khulekani 336
Slovo, Joe 46, 266
Smit, Johan 243
Smit, Dr Robert and Mrs 35–6

Smith, Charles 89–90, 91
Smith, Desmond 309
Smuts, Jan Christiaan 10, 11–13, 16–17, 20, 23–4, 56, 273
Soames, Nicholas 70, 111, 164
Solliciano prison 6–7, 117, 119, 125–9, 139
Sonn, Dr Franklin 196
Sonnenbergs 82, 89, 91
South Africa Party 13, 16–17
South African Communist Party 266
South African Defence Force 36–40, 264
South African Mutual Life Assurance Society, see Old Mutual
South African Police 264
South African Reserve Bank (SARB) xi–xiii: and Broederbond 29, 44, 122, 194–5, 196; directors 191–2, 196, 283; and exchange controls 45, 66, 111, 192–3; and Heath Commission 300–1, 303, 306, 342–3; and Hoberman Commission 229–33; illegalities 110, 193, 207, 214, 226, 237, 249, 282, 292, 293, 298, 320, 322–3; lifeboat facilities 44, 83, 171, 189–90, 194, 197–218, 222–37, 238–40, 242, 244, 248, 250–2, 257, 260, 270, 272, 278–81, 282, 290–303, 316–17; policies of 194–7; press coverage 256, 292, 298–9; reform of 292; Reserve Bank Act (1989) 234, 279; and Tollgate 90, 135
South African Revenue Services 194
South African Rugby Football Association 32
South African Special Forces 270
Southern Life Association 43
Soweto 28, 29, 31
Spaar-en Voorskot Bank (Sasbank) 19
Special Investigating Units and Special Tribunals Act (1996) 266, 270
Spira, John 108
Springbok Atlas 74
Stals, Dr A.J. 21, 22, 25, 191
Stals, Dr Chris 199, 299; as Broeder 191–2; false statements 189, 200, 297, 305; and Heath inquiry 301, 306–7, 342–3, 345; inquiry evidence 224, 228–33, 235–7, 249, 278, 279; and lifeboat 203, 209–11, 214, 240, 244,

Stals, Dr Chris – *contd.*
  313; and Manuel 265; press coverage
  256, 292–3, 298; resignation 319; at
  SARB 191–2, 196–7, 250; at TRC 300
Standard Chartered Bank 19, 20, 43,
  95–6, 219, 224, 227, 228, 233, 242
Star 323
State Security Council (SSC) 34–5, 265
Stavridis, Michael John 101–2
Steenhuis 51, 96, 98, 110, 164–7, 169–70,
  308, 318, 344
Stegmann, J.A. 179
Stellenbosch University 53–4
Stewart, David 55–6, 81, 160
Steyn, Chris 220
Steyn, Greta 323
Steyn, Martinus 13, 273
Steyn, Gen. Pierre 37, 38
Stoffberg, Dirk 110
Stratcom 35
Strategic Supplies Commission 249
Strydom, Gerbie 64, 67, 75–6, 78, 87,
  183–5, 254–5
Strydom, Hans 26
Sunday Independent (South Africa) 338
Sunday Telegraph 96, 111, 291, 300, 314
Sunday Times (South Africa) 163, 168–9,
  175, 189
Sutherland, Judge 269
Swanepoel, Jan Abraham 100–1, 102, 103
Swanepoel, S. 335
SWAPO 35
Swardt, C.J. 202
Swartz, A. 209
Swazican (Swaziland Canning Co) 95, 167
Swiss National Bank 43
Syfrets 92, 166, 173

Table Investments 249
Templeton, Brendan 278
Thompson, James 254–5
Thomson T. Line 50–1, 68, 70, 73, 165
To The Point 31
Tollgate 51–3, 55, 58–65; Askin
  acquisition 65–70; auditors 172; debts
  175; financial misdeeds 75–82, 133,
  249; Hoberman inquiry 103, 134, 173,
  257; liquidation 88–94, 134–5, 157,
  168, 171–4, 186, 217–19, 221–3,
  226–7, 238–51, 316–17; management

158; pension fund 80; restructuring
  71–4, 79–80, 87–9, 157; Sangster family
  and 165–6; TGH Finance 81; Tollgate
  Holdings 79; *see* also Duros/Tollgate
Tomkinson, Martin 298–9
Tonni, Dr 153
Tose, Nigel 70, 71, 95, 167–8
Tradegro 309
Tramway Holdings 59, 73
Transkei 27, 28, 32, 281
Transvaal 9–11, 15, 16, 20
Treurnicht, Dr Andries 31
Triomf Fertilizers 44
Trisk, Benjamin 256
Trust Bank 87, 332; and Absa 84–5, 135,
  239; and Arwa 54, 183–6; and Askin
  xii, 68–9, 71, 75, 79–81, 90, 203, 239;
  and Bankorp 57, 198, 202; and
  Broederbond 56; fraud 99; insolvency
  260, 317; problems 56–7; Reserve Bank
  advance 171; and Tollgate 58–9, 62–71,
  73, 76–82, 161, 174, 263; and Tollgate
  liquidation 92, 218, 238, 241–2
Truth and Reconciliation Commission xi,
  38, 40, 109, 224, 264, 266, 270, 281–2,
  299, 300
Tuckey, Lord Justice 341–2, 343
Turner, Dr Rick 35
Turok, Ben 300
Tutu, Archbishop Desmond 289
Tyfield, Jeremy 104, 105

UBS 268–9
Unionist Party 13, 16
United Bank 84, 85, 179
United Nations 24, 28, 29, 34
United Passenger Transport Investments
  58
Unity Commission 23
Urban Foundation 30
Usury Act 20

van der Bergh, Gen. Hendrik 31, 32, 283
van der Merwe, Hennie 184–6, 203–4,
  212, 242, 244, 255, 316
van der Walt, Chris 238
van der Walt, Hein 35
van der Westhuizen, C.P. 37
van Greuning, Hennie 203, 205–10, 224,
  239, 276

van Herden, Brood 264
van Miert, Karel 124
van Rensburg, Dr Hans 19, 22
van Rooy, Prof. J.C. 18, 19
van Vuuren, J.L.H. 179
van Wyck, Caspar Louw 269
van Wyk, Chris 67, 78, 183, 191, 239
van Zyl, Lt. Abram 'Slang' 289–90, 300,
    308, 315, 318–19, 334–5, 341
van Zyl, Chris 92, 166, 173–4, 246, 248,
    263
van Zyl, Judge 256, 258, 321, 330
Verhoef, Gordon 53
Vernons Pools 50–1, 70
Verster, John 32
Verwoerd, Dr Hendrik 25, 26, 27
Vigna, Judge Luigi 131, 132, 143, 144
Visagie, Gerhard 291
Vitaliano, Esposito 163
Vlakplaas 35, 36, 120, 264, 283, 289–90
Vlok, Danie 94
Volkskas 59, 86, 336; and Absa 41, 84, 85,
    135; and Armscor 108–10; and Askin
    66; Bankorp merger 198, 207, 233, 235,
    238, 307; and Broederbond 19–21, 25,
    30, 41, 85, 194; Diedericks and 61, 77,
    176–9; difficulties 83–4; founded 19;
    illegalities 178, 271; intelligence service
    links 264–5, 270; Reserve Bank
    support 44; and Sanlam 57; and
    Tollgate 78–80, 136, 182; Volkskas
    Centre Pretoria 178; Volkskas
    Industrial Bank 54; Volkskas
    Industrial Financing 177
Voorbrand Tobacco Company 22, 24
Vorster, Balthazar Johannes 27, 30, 32
Vrye Weekblad 283

W&A 185–6, 212, 218
Walker, Julie 175
Wallace, Eugene 186, 263
Walters, Rob 90
Warburg, S.G. 73
Warman, Janice 293
Wassenaar, Andries 30
Watt, Ian 282–3, 292, 294, 299
Webster, David 35, 283, 289
Weekend Argus 170, 220
Weichardt, Louis 19
Welgemoed, Piet 210
Welz, Martin 133–5, 182, 317, 329–30
Wepener, J.N. 136
Wepener, Koos, 334
Werksmans 91, 186, 246, 262, 320,
    333
Whelan, Peter 174
'White, Mr' 130, 142–3, 148, 154, 156
Wiese, Christo H. 53, 54, 160–1, 191, 194,
    261–2, 286, 331–2, 337–8, 339
Williamson, Craig 131–2, 319
Wilmott-Sitwell, Alex 70, 71, 97
Wilson, Max 49, 345
Woodland, Gavin 105, 172, 263, 320–1,
    330–3
Woods, Jeremy 111, 168, 169–70, 259
World War I 12, 13, 14
World War II 20, 23
Worrall, Denis 255
Wragg, Rupert 166
Wright, Peter 131

Young, Alan 45
Young Africa 14–15, 16

Zimbabwe 341